PROTESTANT THOUGHT
IN THE TWENTIETH CENTURY

Whence and Whither?

THE MACMILLAN COMPANY
NEW YORK · BOSTON · CHICAGO
DALLAS · ATLANTA · SAN FRANCISCO

MACMILLAN AND CO., LIMITED
LONDON · BOMBAY · CALCUTTA
MADRAS · MELBOURNE

THE MACMILLAN COMPANY
OF CANADA, LIMITED
TORONTO

Protestant Thought in the Twentieth Century

ཨ WHENCE & WHITHER?

Edited by ARNOLD S. NASH

THE MACMILLAN COMPANY
New York: 1951

27526
Nov. 51

The editor makes acknowledgment to the following publishers
for the use of quoted material: to The Federal Council of the
Churches of Christ in America for Sanford: *Federal Council of
Churches of Christ in America* (Fleming H. Revell, 1949); to the
University of Chicago Press for Nichols: *History in the Theo-
logical Curriculum* (copyright, 1946); to *Christendom* for Van
Dusen: *The Issues of Christian Unity* (Spring, 1946); to
Abingdon-Cokesbury Press, for Van Dusen: *World Christianity
—Yesterday—Today—Tomorrow* (copyright, 1947).

*The dogmas of the quiet past are inadequate to
the stormy present: the occasion is piled high with
difficulty, and we must think anew and act anew.*

ABRAHAM LINCOLN
Annual Message to Congress
December 1, 1862

*All great problems of life must be solved first on
the religious plane and the new synthesis is the
task of Protestantism for the future.*

EDUARD SPRANGER

PREFACE

AMERICA today not only has "come of age," to borrow André Siegfried's phrase, but the American nation as a whole is accepting (the antics of Senator McCarthy and his cohorts notwithstanding) the demands of its political maturity in a fashion that is only credible because it has actually happened. Moreover, the role played by America in current political and economic affairs is one that has its counterpart in the realm of religion. That is true for Roman Catholicism, Eastern Orthodoxy and Protestantism alike. In the counsels of the Vatican no nation figures more largely when decisions are made and thought is implemented than does America; and the Communist jibe against the World Council of Churches to the effect that it is an instrument of American ecclesiastical imperialism in Protestant dress is a recognition of a fact even if it also involves a serious misrepresentation of that fact. Last but by no means least, it is America that provides in Archbishop Athenagoras, if not one of its native-born nationals, yet one of its citizens to become, as Patriarch of Constantinople, the spiritual head of more than a hundred millions of Greek Orthodox Christians.

To point out thus the role of America in the religious life of the world is, of course, to indicate that American life is based upon a unique experiment in cultural pluralism where what binds a nation together is not a particular religion but a certain attitude towards religion. Yet that fact, important though it may be, must not obscure its correlate, namely that the religious roots of American culture lie in Protestantism. A perfect symbol of that fact is that little more than a generation separated the epoch-making event at San Salvador on October 12, 1492, from those at Wittenberg on October 31, 1517.

This book, then, tries to explore what has been happening among Protestant religious thinkers in America over the last fifty years. But the year that sees the publication of this symposium is not only the one that begins the second half of the century in which we live, but that century is one which, it is well nigh universally recognized, sees the end of an age.

A book, therefore, that concerns itself with the question of where Protestant thought in America is going can only do so in the light of some understanding of the cultural crisis as a whole. It is for this reason that the opening chapter of the book considers the "Zeitgeist" of the twentieth century as it has influenced every realm of thought and action and what, consequently, has happened to Protestantism.[1]

In the light of this opening chapter, each of the authors of this symposium was asked to take as his starting point an interpretation of Protestant thought in his particular sphere of scholarship in North America when the century opened and then to proceed to give an analysis of the development of thought in that sphere both in the light of its own development and the impact of events upon it. The further suggestion made to him was that he should conclude by attempting the very difficult task of indicating the problems which in his particular field of study face us now and whose attempted solution, therefore, will dominate, so far as can be seen, the rest of the century.

However, in fairness to each author, I ought to state that these were simply suggestions to serve as guidance rather than a plan to be slavishly followed. In other words, each author was left free to pursue his task along those lines which he would find most conducive to its successful completion, granted the peculiarities of his own field of study and his own personal inclinations. He knew who his fellow authors were and he was left free to consult with them as he saw fit and appropriate, but that was left entirely to his own discretion. The book, then, is a symposium. It does not pre-

---

[1] It is, I think, relevant here to mention that the book had its immediate origin in an article on this very point which I contributed to the *Christian Century*, October 30, 1946. I am indebted to the *Christian Century* for permission to embody substantial parts of this article in the opening chapter of this book.

tend to furnish conclusions about which all the authors agree. They are all too much the children of Protestantism to think that such a hope would be desirable or even possible. Yet, having stated that fact, it gives me not a little satisfaction to have played as editor some part in presenting what is substantially a surprising consensus of opinion as Protestantism faces the future. Surprising, because no deliberate attempt was made to get authors representative of the different Protestant Churches who yet agreed with each other, and pleasing because they exhibit all shades—from Episcopalianism to "Unitarianism"—of the theological spectrum which emerged after the far from "white" light of medieval Catholicism entered the prism of the Reformation.

I should emphasize, too, that by Protestant thought I do not mean self-conscious thought about "Protestantism." Too much thought by Protestants, I know, is precisely that. Moreover, Protestantism is all too often conceived of simply as the opposite of "Catholicism." Rather, the book seeks to present Protestant thought *in action* in all the various realms of theological scholarship.

This book, I would also add, does not seek to give anything in the nature of a Protestant "solution" to the problems of the present age, but it seeks to present the ways in which Protestant thought in America has moved over the last fifty years as it has sought to make its message relevant to the modern era without submerging it under the spirit of that age.

Arnold S. Nash

CONTENTS

AMERICA AT THE END
OF THE PROTESTANT ERA

Arnold S. Nash

ARNOLD S. NASH, now *James A. Gray* Professor of the History of
Religion and Chairman of the Department of Religion at the University of North Carolina, was born in 1906. Educated at the University
of Liverpool, Ripon Hall, Oxford, and the London School of Economics, he holds graduate degrees in chemistry, philosophy and
sociology, the connecting link in his studies being the nature of
scientific method and the part played by science in moulding Western civilization.

In 1939 he came to the United States from England, where he
had been Executive Secretary for the Student Christian Movement
in the University of London to lecture on the relations between
Christian theology, history and the social sciences at various American colleges and universities. He was editor of and contributor to
Education for Christian Marriage, and he is the author of *The
University and the Modern World* and various contributions to
symposia and journals.

I

THE HISTORY of western civilization can be viewed as a great river formed by the confluence of its tributaries from Mesopotamia, Egypt, Palestine, Greece and Rome whereby they produced that mighty stream, *Pax Romana*. But this river of history, like the geographical rivers of the continents of the earth, has not always flowed placidly along. Rivers continually change their speed, their volume and even their course. Sometimes the changes are slow and imperceptible; sometimes they are almost cataclysmic. Then, all these factors just considered are changed simultaneously. Frequently the source of these overwhelming changes is a constituent part of the course of the river itself: such is the Niagara Falls for the Niagara. Often, as in the impact on the Mississippi of its tributary, the Missouri, the origin of these changes comes from a cause external to itself. So, too, the river of western civilization has in its course reached certain turning points after which every aspect of the life of man and his society have been revolutionized. In the history of western civilization during the Christian era there have been, until the last two decades of the twentieth century, two and only two such fundamental revolutions. The first of these occurred when the Roman Empire was destroyed in the early years of the fifth century. Ancient history then ended and medieval history began. The second was reached at the turn of the fifteenth century when medieval history came to a close and modern history was born.[1] Then feudal culture was no more. Manor and serf gave way to the entrepreneur and the wage laborer. Christendom as a theocratic political unity collapsed before the forces of nationalism to give the system of sovereign nation-states. Scholasticism as the

---

[1] As will be seen from what follows, I cannot agree with those who, like the Polish historian, Oscar Halecki, regard these distinctions as simply the product of the imagination of "a second-rate German scholar, Cellarius." See *The Limits and Divisions of European History*, p. 17 (New York, 1950).

pattern of correct thinking gave place to scientific method and historical study of origins as the correct methods for discovering truth.

All these victories were successes of a new social class who demanded, fought for and won a substantial control in the affairs of state. In achieving power they tore down all the fences based on the identification of privilege with the ownership of land as they successfully inserted contract in the place of status as the juridical foundation of society. When they had finished, no longer were the land-owner, the ecclesiastic, and the knight-errant symbols of social prestige. The banker and the merchant, later to be joined by the manufacturer, took their places. The members of this new class soon worked out its equivalent to the code of chivalry and system of canon law that had provided medieval society with its standards of value and its social mores. Whereas the feudal system of mutual dependence based upon personal loyalty harmonized with the medieval system of salvation by sacraments controlled by the ecclesiastical hierarchy, the merchants relied on written documents which, like the Bible, could be understood by all men. Like their medieval ancestors they, too, believed that "Where your treasure is, there shall your heart be also." But their treasure lay in a different place and so they evolved a code of conduct to govern economic affairs which sharply reversed long-established Christian teaching about the danger of money-making. Indeed, their entire ethical system was based upon the conviction that the life of business enterprise was not as spiritually hazardous as the medievalists had taught. Instead, they regarded it as the most appropriate field of operation for the saved soul, and the idea of credit in the bank available for the merchant of sound commercial standing replaced the medieval notion of stored merit in heaven under the control of the ecclesiastical hierarchy on earth. In short, the leaders of the commercial middle classes were Protestants.

However, just as ancient history and medieval history came to an end, so too "modern" history has reached its finale. All the differing realms of human thought and activity, politics, economics, and education are being basically transformed. The recent war simply hastened a process already begun and has thereby thrown into a clearer relief what was already to be seen by those who could recognize the signs of the times. In industry and commerce free enterprise is giving way to an ever-increasing measure of economic planning. We may no longer believe in the just price of the medieval canonists but notwithstanding that fact, we produce, in the idea of a "floor" for prices in time of depression and a "ceiling" for them in time of war, a secularized equivalent to it. In domestic politics virtually all of us, whether Republican or Democrat, now believe in the "welfare state." Only 14 votes could be mustered in the House of Representatives last October *against* the extension of social security, but 313 votes were counted *for* it. In the field of international politics, an awareness of the significance of the atomic bomb has persuaded the stubborn Anglo-Saxon mind, if not the Russian one, to recognize that the issue dominating all others is the need to limit the sovereignty of the nation-state by some appropriate international organization. The war in Korea has vividly underlined this truth to the point that both Democrat and Republican alike are willing to allow the American armed forces to serve in and under the direction of an international authority. That seems a small price to pay if we are to have freedom from the horrors of an atomic war.

The atomic bomb, indeed, furnishes a dramatic illustration of the contention that we have reached the end of our present era. The scientific movement since the days of Galileo has been based on a reversal of the medieval idea that in searching for knowledge the possibilities of evil were as real as those for good. The modern scientist believed until a few years ago that although his discoveries can be used for evil ends, yet ultimately they were a "good thing." Now, however, the scientist's faith in that dogma is severely shaken. Today he is much more acutely aware of the possibilities of immediate use of the atomic bomb for evil than he is of its potentiality for ultimate good. The atomic bomb, more-over, has provided us with a perfect symbol of the intellectual confusion of our times outside as well as inside the scientific movement. Those scientists both in England and America who have been shouting loudest for some years that we should change our present methods of unplanned scientific research and sub-stitute planned team investigation now argue for "free enter-prise" both in the open publication of all results and in unfettered investigation in the laboratory. At the same time the business men who have been loudest in the praise of free enterprise in commerce and trade do not wish to apply their doctrines to the atomic secret: that should remain a closely-guarded federal monopoly.

Thus we see that all the characteristic features of a middle class bourgeois culture—science, politics, economics—are rapidly be-ing replaced by others more capable of meeting the demands of the world now being so painfully borne. Have we any reason to believe that Protestantism carries within itself anything of more permanent worth than the culture, now disappearing, that has, his-torically speaking, been the vehicle through which the insights of the Protestant faith have been made available for the Western world? But before we do, let us examine what has been happening to Protestantism as such. Even that simple fashion of phrasing our task is an index to our confusion. We assume in our conversa-tion and in the organization of our church life in the military forces and out of them that the three religions of America are Judaism, Roman Catholicism and Protestantism. Yet could there be a more egregious error? I am not only thinking of the in-accuracy of such categorizing if we include under Protestantism the various branches of the Orthodox churches or even Episco-palianism. I am thinking of the ease with which we assume that Martin Luther or John Calvin would recognize as Protestants those who today willingly use the term as applicable to themselves. The three typical figures of classical Protestantism, Luther, Cal-vin, and Cranmer, carried over into Protestantism a set of ideas that today in North America we regard as medieval. They believed, for example, that membership of the Christian Church, even if baptism is required, is something, nevertheless, into which a child is born: if he was born in Saxony, then he was a Lutheran, if in the canton of Geneva, a Calvinist, and if in England, an Anglican. On the contrary, most Christians, who today in America would call themselves Protestants, believe that infant baptism is an appealing spectacle and that membership of the Christian Church is the result of a self-conscious act of decision whereby on approaching maturity the Christian elects to join a voluntary and exclusive fellowship. The Reformers believed that religion, in terms of a single type of worship within a particular territory as alone legal and maintained by the authority of the state, should dominate all other forms of cultural life, especially education. Protestantism in America would negate every proposition in such a proposal if it were to be made today on the grounds that it is contrary to the American way of life. The founders of the Reformation believed in the essential corruption of the human will; they believed that witches exist; and they believed that God somewhat arbitrarily interferes with the day-to-day functioning of the physical universe. We reject (whether rightly or wrongly is not the point) all such ideas as contrary to everything that "modern science" teaches.

The explanation of such profound differences between what the Reformers stood for and what the typical American Protestant stood for can easily be given. To use Ernst Troeltsch's classic distinction, the Reformers believed in the "Church" type of Christianity whereas—and to some extent this is true even of Roman Catholicism and Protestant Episcopalianism—we believe, consciously or unconsciously, in Christianity of the "sect" type.[2] It is true that those branches of the Christian Church in North America that stress the importance of episcopal orders have been

[2] This summary, of course, like all historical generalizations, needs severe qualification if we are to do full justice to the sociological complexities of American church life. For some penetrating observations in this direction see "The Ecumenical Issue in the United States" by Reinhold Niebuhr in *Theology Today*, Vol. II, pp. 525 ff.

better able to stand against the impact of a "sect" theology upon their thought and practice than have the other churches. But at many important points they, too, have succumbed. For example, an eminent Roman Catholic educationist recently sought to justify the study of religion at the college level on the quaint ground that religion, like mathematics, is a worthy cultural achievement. To Thomas Aquinas such a remark would have been quite unintelligible. It is a mark of the "sect" type of Christianity to protest against anything that looks hierarchical and so the Episcopal Church shies at the idea of calling its Presiding Bishop an archbishop even when, as now, he has been elected for the rest of his active life. Among Presbyterians the distinction between a presbyterial and a congregational conception of the minister is no longer effective. The modern Presbyterian has strayed so far from his Calvinistic heritage that he is immune against Oliver Cromwell's famous jibe:

"They claim a ministry deriving itself from the Papacy and pretending to that which is so much insisted upon—succession,"

or John Milton's tilt:

"New Presbyter is but old Priest writ large."

As for the Methodists: no branch of Christ's Church has been more insistent on the Protestant insight that the priesthood of all believers means the complete dismissal of the medieval idea that the "religious" life is somehow more pleasing to God than "secular" life. Yet in no church in the whole of Christendom is the minister more expected to be the moral model for the laity. Indeed, one might say that the requirement that a Methodist minister must not smoke while the layman may is a surprising yet exact parallel to the medieval notion that the priest should practise a more lofty ethical code than the laity. But it is not Archbishop Cranmer or John Knox or John Wesley who would exhibit the greatest surprise if he were to come back to earth and gaze with astonishment on his ecclesiastical descendants. That role surely must be reserved for Roger Williams, since no body of Protestants have gone quite so far as the Baptists have in departing from their traditional position. There are many Northern Baptist churches which have not seen a "total immersion" for years and in few is it considered an essential form of admittance to church membership. The Southern Baptist state conventions in many areas are rapidly building up a system of ecclesiastical control that represents a striking departure from the classical Baptist position. Conventions in Oklahoma and Arkansas have refused to seat "messengers" from congregations dubbed "liberal" and from others which permit non-members to participate in Holy Communion or which affiliate with the Federal or World Councils of Churches. As the *Christian Century* decisively pointed out, this policy "violates Baptist principles at three fundamental points. It sets up a creedal basis of fellowship. It runs counter to the Baptist emphasis on religious freedom. It brings into question the Baptist insistence upon the autonomy of the local congregation."

In short, Baptists, like the rest of their Protestant brethren, not only have strayed away from the characteristic doctrines of their forefathers; they have reversed them. The major reason is not far to seek. The Protestant fathers knew where they differed from the teaching of the Renaissance and its characteristic Hellenistic optimism; but we have lost our historical roots and, falling an easy prey to that optimism, we have ended up by making it the basis of our entire ideology. How much of contemporary so-called Protestant life and thought is explained once we recognize that behind them is the conviction that social harmony can be achieved if each person follows what he as an individual wants! [3] This fundamental belief expressed itself in science in the notion that freedom of research would lead to sufficient agreement to give sense to the idea that the word *knowledge* has no plural. It expressed itself in politics in the idea that freedom of discussion would insure sufficient accord for government to be stable and

[3] I would like to express here my indebtedness to Professor Paul Tillich for considerable illumination on this and on many other points. See his prophetic article, "The End of the Protestant Era," in *The Student World,* Vol. XXX, pp. 49 ff. (Geneva, Switzerland, 1937).

for law and order to be preserved. It expressed itself in international politics in the idea that somehow, out of the system of independent national states, universal peace would one day be achieved. It expressed itself in commerce in the idea that freedom of competition in trade for the individual would lead to the greatest economic good of the community. It expressed itself religiously in the notion that only by tolerating freedom of belief to the point of allowing atheism its right of expression can the world be converted to Christ. Today the optimism to which Protestant life and work is culturally and theologically so closely tied, has been so profoundly shaken in every aspect of human life that no Church which links itself to it can hope to survive, except as a vestigial remnant of a culture that has gone.

In short, the "Protestant" era really has ended, and we go forward into an age that many shrewd and informed observers call the post-Christian era. Others feel that that is going too far. In either case the question occurs. Has Protestantism any prophetic word to utter?

The medieval synthesis was born amidst great tribulation when the Christian Church as the residual legatee of the Roman Empire sought to impress law and order upon the wild barbarians from beyond the Rhine. Thanks to the incredible courage, audacity and skill of the missionary monks, the effort was successful and the barbarian hordes became the biological bearers of the spiritual inheritance of Athens, Rome, and Palestine. The result was the idea of Christendom embodied in a culture that for almost a thousand years shone forth brilliantly in art, in literature, in philosophy and all the arts of man. Its claim was to universality. Was there not a universal church, the Catholic Church? And a universal philosophy, Scholasticism? And a universal law, Roman Law? And a universal art in Gothic architecture? And a universal ethic, the code of Christ's commandments? And a universal code of manners, chivalry?

But this civilization was not as Christian in reality as it thought it was. It failed to realize, for example, how much its advocacy of the just price was in fact a subtle defense of the economic self-interest of a land-owning aristocracy of Church and manor. In short it was, to use Reinhold Niebuhr's adaptation, a Tower of Babel. As such it was built on sand and so, when the winds of a legitimate demand for justice and equality began to blow, it collapsed before the onslaught of a class whose religious badge was Protestantism. However, Protestantism, like Roman Catholicism, bears witness to a truth that transcends the historically conditioned movement that gave it birth. Hence for the coming new age the Protestant principle still has relevance; for Protestantism has a witness to make to the world even when the Protestant era has departed. The common conviction of the authors of this book—however divergent might be their individual expressions of it—is that the Protestant witness to this day and age can be expressed in three paradoxes:

(I) Within the context of the ecumenical movement, Protestantism must urge that the Word of God always transcends any form of either literary or ecclesiastical expression of its truth and that, just because that is so, there is always possible a living word to the Church and to individuals. Yet the Church cannot be the instrument of this Word unless she recognizes that in our present mass society that living word can be spoken only if it is in terms of symbols that relate man socially as well as individually to the Living God.

(II) To the world of scholarship and science Protestantism must urge that the source of our present intellectual confusion is not that scientists do not know enough nor is it that thinkers are not sufficiently acute. Instead, it lies in a spiritual self-sufficiency that was the inevitable outcome of an approach to knowledge that began with *cogito ergo sum*. Furthermore, the Protestant witness must gather up within itself all that modern science and humanism have stood for in their insistence that truth is always more than educational organizations or ecclesiastical assemblies can recognize.

(III) The Protestant witness in society must subject the political and economic foundations of contemporary culture to an independent criticism which recognizes that the remedy for the shortcomings of a Protestantism allied with the political right is not to identify it with the political left. Yet in seeking to criticize from a perspective that transcends both capital and labor or the Anglo-Saxon powers and the Soviet block, it must not hesitate to speak and act about concrete issues as they appear on the day-to-day scene.

The task envisaged by such a program is not an easy one. It is indeed one that Luther, Calvin and Cranmer, in terms of their day and generation, all tried to perform. They did not succeed, for it involves nothing less than obedience to Christ's implied commandment to be in the world but not of it. However, against gigantic forces they triumphed sufficiently in their day to furnish us in our day with our opportunity. Like them, judged by the test that they would approve, we too shall fail:

When ye shall have done all those things which are commanded you, say: We are unprofitable servants; we have done that which was our duty to do.

However, that kind of failure is the open door to salvation since we then seek justification not in what we have done but in what God through Christ can do for us and that is the essential timeless Protestant witness.

BIBLIOGRAPHY

Smith, Gerald Birney, ed. *Religious Thought in the Last Quarter Century* (Chicago, 1927)

Cavert, Samuel McCrea, and Van Dusen, Henry Pitney, ed. *The Church Through Half a Century* (New York, 1936)

Tillich, Paul, *The Protestant Era*. Eng. Transl. by James Luther Adams (Chicago, 1948)

Niebuhr, Reinhold, *Beyond Tragedy*, Chapters I, II, and XII. (New York, 1938)

Thomas, George F., ed. *The Vitality of the Christian Tradition* (New York, 1944)

Anderson, William K., ed. *Protestantism* (Nashville, 1944)

Fullerton, Kemper, "Calvinism and Capitalism," *Harvard Theological Review*, Vol. XXI, No. 3, July 1928

Laski, Harold J. *The Rise of Liberalism* (New York, 1936)

Tawney, R. H., *Religion and the Rise of Capitalism* (Penguin Edition, New York, 1947)

Carr, Edward Hallett, *Conditions of Peace*, Part I (New York, 1942)

Commager, Henry Steele, *The American Mind* (New Haven, 1950)

Sperry, Willard L., *Religion in America* (New York, 1946)

Sweet, W. W., *The Story of Religions in America* (New York, 1930)

THE STUDY OF THE
OLD TESTAMENT

George Ernest Wright

GEORGE ERNEST WRIGHT was born in 1909 and graduated from Wooster College, Ohio. He subsequently studied at McCormick Theological Seminary in Chicago, the American School of Oriental Research in Jerusalem, and Johns Hopkins University, where he took his Ph.D. in 1937. Before joining the faculty of McCormick Theological Seminary, where he is now Professor of Old Testament History and Theology, he served as field secretary of the American Schools of Oriental Research. He has been prominently associated with the Bible Study Commission of the World Council of Churches, attending meetings of the commission in Holland in 1948 and in England in 1949. He is the editor of *The Biblical Archeologist*, and he has written several books in that field and in Biblical theology. His *Challenge of Israel's Faith* was published in America in 1944 and in Great Britain in 1946, where it was a Religious Book Club selection. He is co-author with Floyd V. Filson of the well-known *Westminster Historical Atlas to the Bible*.

II

Mｏｄｅｒｎ Biblical scholarship was introduced into this country under the direct influence of German study during the first half of the last century. The two men who were most responsible for this introduction were Moses Stuart of Andover Theological Seminary and Edward Robinson of Union Theological Seminary in New York. Both consciously carried on their work within the framework of a conservative Christian theology and in the service of the Church. Both were primarily professional students of the Old Testament which they approached as Christians completely devoid of any tendency toward Marcionism, that is of conceiving of the God of Israel as somehow very different in character from the God of Jesus Christ. During the second half of the last century, however, a great change occurred, in which the scholarly study of the Old Testament was shaken loose, very largely, from its churchly mooring. Separated from the New Testament, it was carried on as a neutral science closely allied with the fields of oriental research and the history of religions.

The intellectual climate during the second half of the last century has been the subject of frequent treatment and does not call for analysis here. Archaeological work in Bible lands, the decipherment and intensive grammatical and philological study of Accadian and Egyptian, the discovery of the antiquity of man, the theory of evolution, Mesopotamian parallels to the Biblical creation and flood stories, intensive study of comparative religion, Hegelian idealism—these and many other factors, all tied together in the optimism of the Victorian era, contributed heavily to the radical new departure taken by the study of the Old Testament. The oriental language and literature departments, particularly at Harvard, Yale, the University of Pennsylvania and Johns Hopkins University were very active and influential. The last mentioned is particularly important since it was then solely a graduate university, founded on the German model and planned to provide graduate students with a scholarly training equal to that otherwise available only in Germany. In 1883 Paul Haupt, a brilliant young German scholar then only twenty-five years of age, was called to the Hopkins as director of the Oriental Seminary and there continued until his death in 1926. His vivid and forceful personality, his vast learning, his voluminous writings (a list of his publications numbers some 522 titles) had an impact upon American oriental studies, including the Old Testament, exceeded only by his pupil and successor, W. F. Albright.

The American Oriental Society was established in 1842; its *Journal* appeared irregularly until 1896, after which it was published in yearly volumes. Virtually all of the productive Old Testament scholars belonged to the Society, regularly contributing linguistic, philological and comparative religion notes and papers to the proceedings. In 1881 the Society of Biblical Literature and Exegesis was founded. Both Old and New Testament scholars participated, but the two fields of study had become so separated that with occasional exceptions the two groups carried on their work with little reference to one another. A comparison of the contents of both the *JAOS* and the *JBL* in the 1880's and 1890's with that of the 1930's and 1940's reveals little difference in the types of articles printed and in the areas of scholarly interest and concentration. The productive Old Testament scholar had become for the most part an orientalist and a technical philologian; his interest in Israelite faith was largely governed by the current methodologies of comparative religion and by the almost exclusive interest in historical growth and development.

Meanwhile the controversy over the Graf-Kuenen-Wellhausen reconstruction of the history of Israel began. The trial of William Robertson Smith in Scotland between 1877 and 1881 attracted great interest in this country. Various articles on the Wellhausen hypothesis were published; perhaps the most important of them initially were from the pen of Charles A. Briggs, a successor of Edward Robinson at Union Theological Seminary in New York.

He was promptly attacked from several quarters, but the acknowledged leader of the opposition soon became William Henry Green
of Princeton Theological Seminary. Green was a scholar whose
learning was respected; he was, for example, the first and only
chairman of the American committee for the Revised Version of
the Bible. Yet the new views were such a radical departure from
traditional conceptions that the emotions of the conservatives
were aroused as fully as were their intellects. The resulting Presbyterian trials of Briggs and Henry Preserved Smith of Lane
Theological Seminary (now affiliated with McCormick Seminary),
who had come to Briggs' defense, took place between 1892 and
1894 and are the most notorious events of American church history at the end of the last century. Union Seminary in New York
resisted the conservative attack and has remained one of the leading seminaries in the country. Lane Seminary capitulated; the
leader of the opposition to H. P. Smith was made President; and
the institution never recovered from the tragedy. As was the case
in Scotland, the trials did more than anything else could possibly
have done to further the new views in this country, and from that
time on most of the leading scholars of the Church gave willing
heed to the enthusiastic and energetic hunt carried on within the
pages of the Old Testament for J, E, D and P, and for the data
with which the literary, institutional and religious history of Israel
could be rewritten.

II

Such was the atmosphere in which the twentieth century began. The main lines along which the study of the Old Testament
was to proceed were already drawn. The conservative reaction
continued, perhaps culminating in a series of twelve volumes called
The Fundamentals: A Testimony to the Truth, published in
Chicago between 1910 and 1912. These books were composed of
essays by British and American conservatives. They were sent
to "English-speaking Protestant pastors, evangelists, missionaries,
theological professors, theological students, Y.M.C.A. secretaries,

Y.W.C.A. secretaries, Sunday School superintendents, religious lay workers, and editors of religious publications, throughout the earth." The title "fundamentalist," derived from this work, came to be used for the conservative movement. Yet it is to be doubted whether this gigantic project did anything to stem the "modernist" tide. Indeed, one of the chief characteristics of American fundamentalism of the twentieth century has been the steady decline of its scholarly work, and very little of real significance in the field of Old Testament study has been published. The fundamentalist atmosphere of largely negative reaction has evidently not been conducive to the production of brilliant, flexible, highly trained, sensitive and scholarly minds.

Meanwhile, a new enthusiasm and energy had invaded liberal Protestant circles throughout the world. While the Unitarian movement of more than a century before had done much to still an interest in scholarly Biblical study, the newer liberalism accelerated the pace of that study to a degree scarcely attained before or since. Large numbers of able young minds were attracted to the field, and many of the greatest works of Old Testament scholarship were produced. Indeed, the two decades between 1890 and 1910 may perhaps be said to be the golden age of Old Testament study. Certainly no comparable period exists for quantity and quality of work produced.

Let us note, for example, some of the books being reviewed in America during the years 1900 and 1901. The Brown, Driver, and Briggs, *Hebrew and English Lexicon* was appearing in parts; the first edition of the Gesenius-Kautzsch-Cowley, *Hebrew Grammar* was reviewed, together with Mandelkern's *Veteris Testamenti Concordantiae*. These works are still basic tools in continuous use by English-speaking scholars, no matter how antiquated the first two may be. Volumes II and III of James Hastings, *Dictionary of the Bible*, were subjected to detailed examination, as were also the first two volumes of the *Encyclopaedia Biblica* and the conservative *Dictionary of the Bible* by John D. Davis. Among the new commentaries being reviewed and discussed were various volumes in *The Cambridge Bible for Schools and Colleges*, which had been appearing since 1880; in the *International Critical Commentary*, including Henry Preserved Smith's *Samuel* and Crawford H. Toy's *Proverbs*, both works of American scholars; in the *Handkommentar zum Alten Testament*, including the first edition of Gunkel's *Genesis*, one of the greatest works of Old Testament scholarship, Rudolph Kittel's *Die Bücher der Könige* and Kraetzschmar's *Ezekiel*; and in the *Kurzer Handcommentar zum Alten Testament*, including Bertholet's *Deuteronomium*, Duhm's *Die Psalmen* and Marti's *Jesaia*. Among the multitude of other works there may be mentioned especially Carpenter and Harford, *The Hexateuch*, the finest and most detailed analysis in English of the Hexateuchal sources according to orthodox Wellhausenism; R. H. Charles, *A Critical Introduction of the Doctrine of the Future Life;* Karl Budde, *Religion of Israel to the Exile* and *Der Kanon des Alten Testaments;* R. W. Rogers, *A History of Babylonia and Assyria*, the first comprehensive history of those countries in English; and L. W. King, *Babylonian Religion and Mythology*.

The purpose of the above brief sampling is simply to indicate the tremendous importance of the period around 1900, which may perhaps be designated as the first great age of consolidation in which the gains resulting from the new Biblical study were elaborated in comprehensive form. Many of the basic tools, including commentaries, on which we are still dependent were then produced. The scholars of that period are, for the most part, the spiritual fathers of the twentieth century. Through the spectacles which they wore our own eyes have been taught to focus on the light; and, especially since the first World War, their general point of view toward the meaning of the Old Testament has increasingly filtered down through the clergy into the churches. They attacked their work with all the enthusiasm of fresh explorers and their zeal to spread the new truth abroad was akin to that of a young missionary just beginning his work for Christ among the heathen.

The most vivid illustration of the last observation was the phenomenal career of William Rainey Harper. He graduated from Muskingum College at the age of fourteen years; his salutatory oration was given in Hebrew. After receiving his Ph.D. degree from Yale four years later, he spent the next dozen years (1879–1892), most of them at Yale, promoting a wide variety of projects. He was an exceptional teacher, and by means of his inductive method for learning Hebrew he interested people all over the country in the study of the language. As President of the University of Chicago (1892–1906), his Old Testament department became in time one of the leading oriental departments of the country, the greatest of his appointees being the young Egyptologist, James Henry Breasted. In 1882 he began publishing a magazine, *The Hebrew Student*, broadened the following year into *The Old Testament Student*. In 1884 he founded another journal, named *Hebraica*, for more technical aspects of Hebrew linguistics and philology. The fate of these two journals is perhaps illustrative of the fate of Old Testament study during the early twentieth century. In 1889 *The Old Testament Student* properly became *The Old and New Testament Student;* in 1893 it was further broadened into *The Biblical World*. In 1921 this was merged with *The American Journal of Theology* and the result was *The Journal of Religion*. In other words, a journal dealing with the wider aspects of Biblical study was unable to maintain itself. In *The Biblical World* it gradually became so watered that there was nothing to do but to merge it into a general journal of religion. On the other hand, the more technical *Hebraica* was likewise unable to sustain itself on its own merits. In 1895 it became *The American Journal of Semitic Languages and Literatures*, which in 1942 was further broadened to *The Journal of Near Eastern Studies*.

To this writer these journals represent something of the tragedy of Protestant Old Testament study during the past century. As a neutral science, largely separated from any responsible feeling for the on-going life of the churches, its productive work has been attuned and directed toward the general religion field, on the one hand, and toward general oriental research, on the other. Of course, there can be no serious study of the Old Testament without scholarly attention to both these fields. But when the scholars of the Church lose themselves along by-paths, both their subject and the Church is bound to suffer. Most of the professional students of the Old Testament are employees of the churches, either directly or indirectly. Yet the paths which they followed too exclusively so separated them from the work of the churches that in many seminaries during the period between 1920 and 1940 the work of the Old Testament department was looked upon by the students more with amusement than with respect; and the occasional young scholar who majored in the subject was frequently one capable of dealing only with technical details, in all events the butt of considerable derision from his fellows in the practical departments or especially in the departments of philosophy and psychology of religion. Consequently, the first great generation of Biblical scholarship before the first War was actually unable to reproduce itself, and the decline in quality and quantity of worthwhile output since then has been steady and lamentable.

The above remarks, however, should in no way be taken in such a way as to devalue the importance of some of the work done. While America thus far has never produced a large series of Old Testament commentaries of a scholarly nature,[1] we did contribute a majority of the Old Testament volumes in the still incomplete *International Critical Commentary*. Most of the important books were assigned to British scholars, and a number of them have never been finished. Yet the American contributions are by no means inferior products; George Foot Moore's *Judges*

[1] The forthcoming *Interpreter's Bible*, to be published by the Abingdon-Cokesbury Press under the general editorship of George A. Buttrick, will be our first major effort along this line.

(1895) and James A. Montgomery's *Daniel* (1927) rank among the most important in existence on these books.[2] Moore must probably be ranked along with Edward Robinson among the giants of American biblical scholarship. As Professor of Old Testament at Andover from 1883 to 1901 and as Professor of the History of Religions at Harvard from 1902 until his retirement in 1928, he was one of our greatest scholars. His *Judaism in the First Centuries of the Christian Era* (3 vols., 1927–30) is the standard work on the subject, as was also for many years in this country his *History of Religions* (2 vols., 1913–19). He contributed nearly forty articles to the *Encyclopaedia Biblica* (1899–1903), those on "Historical Literature" and "Sacrifice" being considerable treatises. The last mentioned is still one of the best surveys of Israel's sacrificial cultus. His point of view was typical of his time in the circles of left-wing Wellhausenism. Montgomery's best work had a more narrow range, but the intensity of his effort on Daniel, for example, together with his balanced sanity of judgment and appreciation of theological issues, probably isolate this work as among the greatest, if not the greatest, of the critical commentaries produced by Americans. In textual criticism especially he was without peer among Protestants, equaled only by the great Jewish scholar Max L. Margolis.

In the field of Old Testament history America has been singularly weak. No book of outstanding importance, comparable shall we say to Rudolph Kittel's *Geschichte des Volkes Israel*, has ever been published. Some student works have been written: for example, C. F. Kent, *History of the Hebrew People* (2 vols.) and *History of the Jewish People* (2 vols., the second by J. S. Riggs; 1896–1900); H. P. Smith, *Old Testament History* (1903); I. J. Peritz, *Old Testament History* (1915); and E. W. K. Mould, *Essentials of Bible History* (1939). None of these books was ever really adequate, but little else was available except as imported from abroad. Today we are able to use the British work by Oe-

---

[2] The same will be true of Montgomery's forthcoming treatment of *The Book of Kings* in the same series.

sterley and Robinson, *A History of Israel* (2 vols., 1932) and a translation of the French work of A. Lods, *Israel* (1932) and *The Prophets and the Rise of Judaism* (1937). Yet these volumes are unsatisfactory, having been antiquated even before publication.

America has done much better in the field of Old Testament introduction. Among others may be mentioned H. T. Fowler, *A History of the Literature of Ancient Israel* (1912); F. C. Eiselen, *Biblical Introduction Series* (4 vols., 1916–23); C. F. Kent, *The Growth and Contents of the Old Testament* (1925); and J. A. Bewer, *The Literature of the Old Testament* (1922). The last mentioned has been the most popular and widely used. The dominant interest in these works is in literary analysis and dating. They are thus introductions to the Old Testament only in the narrow literary sense; but since the end of the last century, such has been the common conception of what such a work should be. There is little that is fresh or original in these American efforts; by and large they are so orthodox in their following of the Wellhausen position, together with numerous popular modifications of it (e.g., the acceptance of Duhm's "Trito-Isaiah"), that the American student was given the impression that for the most part all major literary problems had been finally solved and was left unaware of the fresh currents of thought on the Continent of Europe. Of especial importance for the American college and theological student during the first part of this century was the work of Charles Foster Kent. This scholar at Yale Divinity School did more perhaps than anyone else in making the results of critical research available in what seemed to be stable, non-technical and fairly final form. His major effort was *The Student's Old Testament*, the first five volumes of which were published between 1904 and 1914; the sixth and last was completed after his death by his student, Millar Burrows, and published in 1927. The standard literary introduction in English used by most scholars until 1941, however, continued to be that of the great British scholar, Samuel R. Driver. His *Introduction to the Literature of the Old Testament* was last revised by the author in 1913, but the demand for it has justly been so great that it has been kept in print.

In 1941 the first truly monumental introduction, from the scholarly point of view, to be produced in America was published by Robert H. Pfeiffer. His *Introduction to the Old Testament* is a work of over 900 pages, and is especially important for its bibliographical survey of the work of other scholars throughout the world. The author's own point of view is by and large fairly traditional Wellhausenism, though with many individual variations (e.g., his separation of an Edomite source, S, from the Yahwist material in the Hexateuch). In importance this book can only be ranked with Otto Eissfeldt's *Einleitung in das Alte Testament* (1934), a literary introduction of comparable range and scope. Yet in the post-war period there is an increasing suspicion, long felt in Europe, that this type of purely literary introduction cannot solve the problems of the historical literature of the Old Testament. The almost exclusive concentration of attention on purely literary dissection leads to an extremely atomized and fragmentary understanding of the literature and to a neglect of other matters. It finds difficulty in comprehending the whole or of understanding either the whole or the part over against the total environment in which the writing was produced. Furthermore, its understanding of religious and theological issues, its ability to deal with matters pertaining to faith, is severely limited and lacking in trained penetration, to say the least.

A different type of approach to these problems may be expected in the future under the inspiration of German form criticism. One of the major difficulties with orthodox Wellhausenism was its assumption that the isolation and dating of the Hexateuchal sources furnished the clue to the reconstruction of the history of Israel. This has been a major reason for the almost exclusive attention to literary analysis in the Old Testament introductions. It was assumed, for example, that the later material in the Deuteronomic and Priestly writings furnishes virtually no dependable information on the institutions of early Israel. The material in a given document must be used for the reconstruction of the period in which the document was composed. This naturally meant the almost complete devaluation of the Mosaic era, with the major emphasis being given the prophetic and priestly periods of dominance after the eighth century B.C. The prophets thus came to be thought of, not primarily as great religious reformers, but as the authors of all that was truly distinctive in Israel, particularly of what was called "ethical monotheism." This position of orthodox liberalism was never completely accepted by all scholars, Rudolph Kittel in Germany and Samuel R. Driver in England being the leading exceptions.

It was the German, Hermann Gunkel, in the introduction to his *Genesis* (1st ed., 1901) who initiated a new method of approach to the historical problems of Israel by means of form criticism and the history of tradition. This new methodology was promptly applied to the Gospels with significant results, but it has been very slow in influencing Old Testament study, so strongly intrenched was the other position. During the past three decades, however, some significant work has been done along this line by German and Scandinavian scholars. In this type of research the Hexateuchal documents are generally accepted without question, though naturally with many individual modifications and variations. But these documents are assumed to be solely the final and crystallized form of traditions which have had a long and complicated history before their final written crystallization. In these last stages we have to do with the work of individual compilers whose greatness lay not so much in their invention of material, not in their ascription of current practices back into Mosaic or other antiquity, but rather in the way they gathered, organized and unified old traditions by various means, chiefly by an overall theme which was the product of intensive theological reflexion. At the heart of the Yahwist's work, for example, is the unifying thread of a confessional recital of God's saving acts (a *Heilsgeschichte*), derived ultimately from old forms of confession used at the Tabernacle (so Gerhard von Rad). Such a point of view involves a closer attention to the nature and peculiarity of

written material as a whole, and particularly to the long history
of the tradition which lies behind the final literary form. It thus
means that the age of a document does not determine the date of
the material employed by it. Each item of tradition has its own
history which must be examined on its own merits. Consequently,
the history of Israel cannot be reconstructed simply by dating
final literary compositions; and the ground is cut from under the
older Wellhausenian assumptions. Thus while there is no reason
for assuming that the documentary hypothesis is set aside (quite
the contrary!), the work of Pfeiffer, important as it is, probably
represents the end of an era in that type of purely literary introduction.[3]

III

We do not have space here to describe the various debates
which have been carried on, some of them by no means ended,
on specific Old Testament problems. The reader is referred to
other surveys for detailed analysis of them.[4] By and large discussion in America has followed issues first raised in Europe.
For example, one of the great concerns today has to do with the
authenticity of the Book of Ezekiel. Before 1920 all was well and
few questions were asked. Since that time, Ezekiel has been
viewed by some as the product of Judaism, rather than the
father of it; and in America all shades of opinion are to be found,
even as in Europe.[5] The same is true with regard to the analysis

[3] Contrast, for example, Artur Weiser, *Einleitung in das Alte Testament*
(2nd ed., 1949), and Aage Bentzen, *Introduction to the Old Testament* (2
vols., 1948), the first a German and the second a Danish work. Cf also for
methodology Gerhard von Rad, *Das erste Buch Mose, Genesis Kapitel 1–12,
9* (1949) and *Deuteronomium-Studien* (1947); Martin Noth, *Überlieferungs-
geschichtliche Studien* I (1943) and *Überlieferungsgeschichte des Pentateuch*
(1948).

[4] See especially Raymond A. Bowman, "Old Testament Research between
the Great Wars," in Harold R. Willoughby, ed., *The Study of the Bible
Today and Tomorrow* (1947), pp. 3–31; and George A. Barton, "The
Present State of Old Testament Studies," in Elihu Grant, ed., *The Haverford
Symposium on Archaeology and the Bible* (1938), pp. 47–78.

[5] One of the most extreme of the American works (besides the book of
Torrey to be mentioned below) is that of W. A. Irwin, *The Problem of
Ezekiel* (1943); more moderate is I. G. Matthews, *Ezekiel* (1939). A scholarly

and date of the Book of Deuteronomy, with the attempt of the German scholars, Volz and Rudolph, to do away with the Elohist document in the Hexateuch,[6] with the Gunkel-Mowinckel view of the cultic origin of the Psalms, including the reconstruction of an elaborate New Year's festival in Israel,[7] with the historical problem of whether Nehemiah preceded Ezra, with the various problems connected with the date of the Exodus and the nature of the Hebrew settlement,[8] etc. One of the greatest of American scholars and at the same time the most controversial has been C. C. Torrey of Yale University. Much of his work has been concentrated on the Exilic and Post-Exilic periods as the titles of three of his works show: *Ezra Studies* (1910), *The Second Isaiah* (1928), and *Pseudo-Ezekiel and the Original Prophecy* (1930). Each work has produced as much study and heated debate as did his subsequent attempt to show that the Gospels were originally written in Aramaic. In each case a majority of scholars, while learning much from him, have rejected most of his central contentions. His book on Second Isaiah is the best American study of the subject, an excellent antidote to the scholarly disintegration of Isa. 40–66; but his attempt to prove that the work

---

defense of the older conservative position from the Albright school, and one that will be difficult to answer except by the critique of marginal matters, is the monograph by Carl Howie, *The Date and Composition of Ezekiel* (1950).

[6] For an independent analysis which arrives at a similar position, see Frederick V. Winnett, *The Mosaic Tradition* (1949).

[7] For an American defense of this viewpoint, see now especially Elmer A. Leslie, *The Psalms* (1949), probably the best American commentary produced on this book, though to the minds of the newer school of Hebrew linguistics and philology it leaves much to be desired. An older and independent study of the liturgical origin of the Psalms was written by the American J. P. Peters, *The Psalms as Liturgies* (1922).

[8] An important study in this area was that of the excellent scholar, L. B. Paton, "Israel's Conquest of Canaan," *Journal of Biblical Literature*, Vol. XXXII (1913), pp. 1–53. Another important American treatment of this and other problems of Hebrew origins is that of T. J. Meek, *Hebrew Origins* (1950). The views of W. F. Albright on the Exodus and the Conquest now dominate the scene. For a brief review with references, see G. Ernest Wright, "The Present State of Biblical Archaeology," in Harold R. Willoughby, ed., *The Study of the Bible Today and Tomorrow* (1947), pp. 83 ff.

was not composed much before 400 B.C. has not been generally
accepted. Equally instructive and much more voluminous are the
publications of the Jewish scholar, Julian Morgenstern. Here
again scholars have read to learn without often accepting all of
the central hypotheses.[9]

IV

While form criticism has dealt a body-blow to the older approach to the Old Testament, it has thus far received little attention either in England or America and it has done little to influence the course of scholarly study in these countries. It is in
the field of Biblical archaeology, on the other hand, that perhaps
America's greatest contribution can be said to have been made.
The pioneer work in this field was done by Edward Robinson
in his *Biblical Researches* (3 vols. 1841). During the second part
of the last century, however, little of any significance emanated
from America in this area. Then came our first major excavation of
a Palestinian site, one of tremendous significance especially for
the scientific methodology of digging. That was the Harvard
Expedition to the site of Samaria, directed by G. A. Reisner and
C. S. Fisher between 1908 and 1910, the results not being published until 1924. It was after the first World War that rapid
progress began to be made. On the one hand, James H. Breasted
succeeded in interesting the Rockefeller Foundation in archaeology, with the result that the Oriental Institute of the University
of Chicago was established, and expeditions were dispatched to
every country of the ancient Near East. The work of Breasted
for the cause of oriental studies and for the contemporary importance of what he called the "new past" can scarcely be over-
estimated.[10] Perhaps because of the humanistic direction of
Breasted's viewpoint, however, the Oriental Institute has done

---

[9] See especially his treatment of the Book of the Covenant, his *Amos
Studies*, his work on the calendar, etc., as published in successive issues of
the *Hebrew Union College Annual*, beginning with the first volume in 1924.

[10] See especially the evaluation of W. F. Albright, "James Henry Breasted,
Humanist," *The American Scholar*, 1936, pp. 287–299.

very little for Biblical archaeology, except in many indirect ways.

On the other hand, the most important work for the Bible has been done by those scholars connected with the American Schools of Oriental Research, an institution carried on as a co-operative effort by a large number of American colleges, universities and theological seminaries. It sent its first Director to Jerusalem, C. C. Torrey, in 1900. Thereafter it sent directors and fellows each year until the first World War suspended activities. The influence of Palestinian study was soon felt in such excellent publications as L. B. Paton's *The Early History of Syria and Palestine* (1901),[11] his *Jerusalem in Bible Times* (and his article "Jerusalem" in the 2nd ed. of *The New Standard Bible Dictionary*, 1926), and C. F. Kent's *Biblical Geography and History* (1911). Paton's *Jerusalem* and Kent's *Geography* never attained the popularity of the larger and more vivid British works on the same subjects by George Adam Smith, but in some respects they were better and more usable. The first edition of George A. Barton's *Archaeology and the Bible* was published in 1916; and the seventh edition (1937), though badly out of date, is still much used since it contains such a convenient collection of material.

It was under the directorship of W. F. Albright, beginning in 1920, however, that the Schools rapidly attained a position of scholarly leadership in the field of Biblical archaeology. Albright came to this work after a careful grounding under Paul Haupt in the whole field of ancient Near Eastern study. Today he has become the leading orientalist of the world, a pioneer in almost every area of study which he has touched. Yet his center of interest has always been the Bible, particularly the Old Testament. Consequently, in the vast range of his archaeological, linguistic, philological and historical work (by 1946 a list of his publications numbered some 613 different entries), he has never lost his way nor failed to see the bearing of the whole upon Bible study. As head of the American School in Jerusalem for

[11] Superceded by the monumental work of A. T. Olmstead, *The History of Palestine and Syria* (1931).

twelve years, he became the acknowledged leader in the field of Palestinian archaeology, and many Biblical students came under his influence, not only through his writings but through his lectures and field work in Palestine. One of his most prominent archaeological pupils, Nelson Glueck, became his successor in Jerusalem. Glueck's archaeological survey of Transjordan is of such importance that he must be ranked among the world's leading archaeological explorers. America's first major Biblical atlas was produced under Albright's direct influence, both the historical text and the topography reflecting his points of view: G. Ernest Wright and Floyd V. Filson, *The Westminster Historical Atlas to the Bible* (1945). And certainly the independent work of Millar Burrows, *What Mean these Stones?* (1941), one of the best surveys of archaeological material bearing upon the Bible, could not have been produced in its present form without Albright's pioneering publications. He has raised the scientific tone of this country's work in Palestine to a higher octave than that prevailing in any other country.

For our purposes here, however, it is Albright's influence on Old Testament study which is of major concern. This is difficult to assess at the moment, since his work is so many-sided. In the importance of Canaanite and Northwest Semitic language and literature for Hebrew linguistics and philology he is an acknowledged leader, and several of the best younger men working in this area are either directly or indirectly his students (e.g., H. L. Ginsberg, Cyrus Gordon and Harry M. Orlinsky among our finest Jewish scholars). More than anyone else, however, he has been attempting to show what a vast difference the archaeological revolution must make in our points of view toward the Old Testament and in our method of approaching it. A vast accumulation of facts from every quarter of the ancient Near East are brought to bear on the understanding of Israel's literature, and to Albright they mean the devastation of the Wellhausenian positions, including a more positive and conservative respect for Israel's historical literature. To the fundamentalists his work has been a source of great encouragement, and a major reason for the return of an increasing number of their younger scholars to serious and technical graduate training in the Old Testament. Liberals have blamed Albright for being misleading and overly reactionary (he has even been labelled "a galloping fundamentalist" himself), but a sympathetic reading of his works would lead one only to a more conservative position and by no means to a fundamentalist one. He believes, for example, that the Pentateuch might be called "substantially Mosaic," but the interpretation he places upon the word "substantially" is certainly not that of a fundamentalist. He believes in the documentary hypothesis, but simply affirms that we must take more seriously the basic reliability of oral tradition. The Old Testament probably contains a maximum of the discrepancies in that tradition; we do not have to do with editors whose major work was the invention of material or the radical revision of it to suit their own interests.

Albright further believes that for an understanding of the Old Testament there must be a more serious attempt to come to grips with the vast array of facts now available from the ancient Near East. Literary criticism cannot solve the historical problems of Israel on the narrow inner-Biblical platform on which it has been standing. The Wellhausen reconstruction was based on Hegelian presuppositions which the facts emphatically do not support today; it was formulated before the archaeological recovery of the ancient world had more than started. Furthermore, the archaeological discoveries mean that the older negativism and skepticism, on which the previous work was largely built, must be discarded.[12] These discoveries do not permit a credulous and uncritical viewpoint; archaeology certainly does not support any theory of verbal inspiration. That it is said to do so is a fundamentalist fiction. Yet a more positive and conservative shift in attitude is certainly called for.

Albright's most elaborate attempts to present these views with

---

[12] For some pungent remarks on the role this liberal skepticism has played in Biblical scholarship and on its ultimate basis in historical relativism, see Paul Schubert, "Urgent Tasks for New Testament Research," in Harold R. Willoughby, ed., *The Study of the Bible Today and Tomorrow* (1947), pp. 212 ff.

a wealth of supporting detail such as almost no other scholar could handle critically are to be found in his two volumes, *From the Stone Age to Christianity* (1940) and *Archaeology and the Religion of Israel* (1942). One of the central contentions in these books is that of Mosaic monotheism, from the traditional Wellhausenian point of view one of the most radical of heresies. So deeply entrenched is the older position that Albright's views are scarcely understood, let alone accepted, save by an increasing number of younger scholars who thus far have not been vocal since they are at the beginning of their scholarly careers. The present writer's *The Old Testament Against its Environment* (1950) adopts Albright's viewpoint on monotheism as the only one consonant with the known facts and attempts to portray in more detail precisely what is involved in the hope of securing wider acceptance of the position. Old Testament monotheism certainly cannot be interpreted as a philosophical monism or in terms suitable to a unitarian position. Yet the farther one is able to push back into the Mosaic era, the simpler the view of the divine world, whereas the later one goes in the literature, the more complex that world becomes.

Since we are at the threshold of a new era of Biblical study, the true impact of Albright's work can only be gauged after another generation. At the moment his school of thought is looked upon in many quarters with some skepticism, even with impatience. A criticism leveled at the historical part of the *Westminster Historical Atlas*, for example, is that sufficient basic work has not been done on literary analysis. This criticism is, of course, based on the assumption that literary work almost by itself can solve historical problems, and it is difficult for those wedded to this assumption to understand that the same literary endeavor does not necessarily lead to the same historical conclusions.[13]

---

[13] E.g., cf. W. F. Albright, "The List of Levitic Cities," *Louis Ginzberg Jubilee Volume* (1945), pp. 49–73; "The Oracles of Balaam," *Journal of Biblical Literature*, Vol. LXIII (1944), pp. 207–233; Frank M. Cross, Jr. and David Noel Freedman, "The Blessing of Moses," *ibid.*, Vol. LXVII (1948), pp. 191–210; G. Ernest Wright, "The Literary and Historical Problem of

V

It is in the realm of Biblical theology, however, that the most widespread dissatisfaction with the state of affairs at the turn of the century is now felt. It is obvious to most of the younger scholars of the Church today that something was radically wrong with a generation whose scholarship could scarcely envisage a theological treatment of Israel's faith except in terms of a history of Israel's religion, based upon the Wellhausenian reconstruction of the history. Considering the presuppositions, the generation of 1900 produced some good works in this area. First and foremost stand J. P. Peters, *Religion of the Hebrews* (1914) and H. P. Smith, *Religion of Israel* (1914); among others there may be mentioned also H. T. Fowler, *Origin and Growth of Hebrew Religion* (1917) and G. A. Barton, *Religion of Israel* (1919). The point of view to which they adhere was given the most lucid and influential treatment in H. E. Fosdick's *Guide to the Understanding of the Bible* (1938), a beautifully written book which did much to fix the older developmental views in the minds of a countless number of non-specialists, in particular those of college students. That this approach to Israel's faith survives in many circles is further illustrated by the important, though extreme, work of I. G. Matthews, *The Religious Pilgrimage of Israel* (1947). Yet if one denies in large measure the historical presuppositions lying behind these works and as well their philosophical basis, he finds it very difficult to use them. It is on these grounds that the Swiss scholar, W. Eichrodt, has called Fosdick's work an obituary of last century's scholarship.

Basic to all of the above-mentioned books is the developmental viewpoint first evolved in Germany during the decades preceding 1900. The most important thing to be said about the Old Testa-

---

Joshua 10 and Judges 1," *Journal of Near Eastern Studies*, Vol. V (1946), pp. 105-114; John Bright, "The Age of King David," *Union Seminary Review* (Richmond), Vol. LIII (1942), pp. 87-109; and Carl Howie, *The Date and Composition of Ezekiel* (1950).

ment in this view is that its religion was evolved through the process of the people's discovery over the centuries from primitive animism and polydemonism, through polytheism and henotheism to the heights of "ethical monotheism." It is difficult if not completely impossible, therefore, to speak of a theology of the Old Testament, because, if the above-assumed growth took place, there were many theologies in the pages of the Old Testament. The only unity existing is the unity of historical process. Environment and growth are used as the almost exclusive clues to historical understanding. If something is "primitive," it must be early; and if something is early, it must be "primitive." Even in "objective" scholarly work one must constantly employ his empirically discovered data within a given evaluational framework. This framework is not derived from the Bible, but from liberal idealism, which in turn attempts to define it vaguely as "the mind of Christ," though in truth it is mostly a compound of conceptions derived from secular idealism. The conception of growth, borrowed from the biological sciences and employed in this framework of an ascending scale of values, has been a useful tool when applied to historical data. The impact which it has had on Biblical studies is so great that never again can we revert to the earlier static views. Yet as a tool to historical understanding it has been used so exclusively that the manifest unities in the Bible have been overlooked. Its one-sided use and the necessity it has imposed upon the scholar continually to evaluate the "primitive" and the "advanced" according to a set of values derived largely from Western secular idealism have done more than anything else to separate the Old Testament from any constructive role in the life of the Church. The study of the faith of Israel has been carried on almost solely in the search for values. Israel has been thought to provide the evolutionary background for the religion of and about Jesus. Its importance is conceived largely in antiquarian terms, of interest for the understanding of the way we have come to the pinnacle on which we stand, but now that we have arrived it is no longer of vital use to us.

It is to this impasse that the confident, optimistic and exceedingly energetic work of our spiritual fathers of the 1900 era has brought us. Yet the course of the times has dealt such severe blows to the idealistic and evaluational framework in which the former views were fixed that the theologians have been taking another look at the Old Testament. The uplifted eyebrows which they have directed toward the Old Testament scholars have so embarrassed them that they too are engaged in a second look and a flurry of uncertain activity. Their scholarly work has been so largely separated from the Church's life that the clergy throughout the present century has looked to the theologians and not to them for enlightenment. Consequently, at the moment they are experiencing severe difficulty in readjusting their perspectives. When they have something of real theological significance to say, they are listened to with a respect which has not been accorded them for fifty years. They thus have before them an unparalleled opportunity, but at the moment there is among them much uncertainty and confusion.

Neither in England nor in America has there ever been produced a careful, scholarly and comprehensive work on Old Testament theology, except for the posthumously edited volume of the Scottish scholar A. B. Davidson, *The Theology of the Old Testament* (1904). This book is still in continuous use, though quite inadequate from many points of view. In America there have been several less comprehensive attempts, among which we should mention the work of A. C. Knudson, *The Religious Teaching of the Old Testament* (1918), a moderate, positive and useful work, though for some reason never widely used; Millar Burrows, *Outline of Biblical Theology* (1946), in which a welcome feature is the attempt to treat the Old and New Testaments together; and Otto J. Baab, *The Theology of the Old Testament* (1949), an earnest and sincere book which attempts to organize the data under the traditional headings of God, man, sin, salvation, etc., an outline which leaves large blocks of material untreated and which raises the question as to whether Biblical theology can actually be comprehended and surveyed through these static categories of dogmatic theology. Badly needed and impatiently awaited in English today is a work of the caliber and comprehensive nature of W. Eichrodt's *Theologie des Alten Testaments* (Vols. I–III, 1933–39), by all odds the greatest work available on the subject and one which is written with exceptional theological penetration.

Our difficulty, however, is that we scarcely know how to proceed. For one thing, we are uncertain as to what the subject is and whether it really exists, as may be seen, for example, in the discussions conducted in the *Journal of Bible and Religion*, particularly the symposia in Vols. XIV, No. 1 (Feb. 1946), XIV, No. 2 (May 1946), and XV, No. 3 (July 1947). A central problem is the relation between the historical and systematic approaches and the balancing of unity and variety. In fact, the whole problem of the unity of the Old Testament is perhaps the central concern of the scholars at the moment in their effort to come to terms with Israel's faith. Furthermore, the World Council of Churches has been focusing the attention of the few Biblical scholars connected with its work on the problem of the relation between the two Testaments, on the interpretative problem of discovering the social and political message of the whole Bible, and on the searching question as to just what Christ means as the goal of the Old Testament for the interpretative work of the Christian scholar. Is it possible for the Church's scholars to be entirely neutral on this last question, or is their assumed "neutrality" a screen for presuppositions of which they have been unaware? [14]

In spite of the difficulties the renewed interest in theology is certainly the dominant characteristic of the Biblical scene at the present time. Liberal scholars of the older tradition are inclined to look upon this new interest with considerable concern. Their

[14] Cf. *From the Bible to the Modern World* (Geneva, World Council of Churches, 1947), and the articles by the present writer in *Interpretation*, Vol. III (1949), pp. 50–61 and 450–456.

reaction is largely negative and born of fear. They are afraid that the new movement may crystallize into a new conservativism which neglects the fruits of the Biblical scholarship of the past in tendentious reaction. This is indeed a real danger because it is so easy to theologize without taking sufficient care to ascertain the data on which one's work must be built. On the other hand, there is an even greater danger in doing nothing. To this writer one of the most serious deficiencies of the new movement is the lack of serious attention to archaeology and to the results of the archaeological revolution. One cannot be a scholar in the Old Testament by training oneself solely in literary criticism on the one hand, and in the work of Barth, Brunner and Niebuhr on the other. One must also become a student of ancient polytheism and of ancient history, and the more he knows about ancient linguistics, particularly of Northwest Semitic, the better he will be equipped to handle the Biblical data in their proper setting.

VI

When we survey the whole course of American Old Testament study, we have no reason to be ashamed of what has been done in many areas. Many excellent scholars have produced important and enduring contributions. Yet some of the criticisms leveled at us by J. A. Montgomery in his Presidential Address to the Society of Biblical Literature in 1918 [15] are still valid. While Germany has been our mistress in scholarship, we have lagged at least a generation behind her. Except for the work of Albright and those influenced by him, "it can hardly be said that we have contributed much to the reconstruction of the Biblical history and life. On the historical side our scholarship has been meager. We have carried on, often parrotwise, our analyses, but when we come to the reconstruction of the original picture, where the criticism should go into the footnotes, we have fallen short." Our serious work in textual criticism has not been large. We have produced no basic and up-to-date Hebrew grammar, though to be

[15] *Journal of Biblical Literature*, Vol. XXXVIII (1919), pp. 1-14.

sure we have done several small ones for introductory students, perhaps the best of which from a scholarly point of view being O. R. Sellers, *Biblical Hebrew for Beginners* (1941). We have done nothing in serious Hebrew lexicography since the publication of the Brown, Driver and Briggs, *Hebrew and English Lexicon* which began to appear in 1891 and was completed in 1906. Yet the advances in our knowledge have been so tremendous that this work is woefully out of date. Furthermore, it was never really adequate. Driver's long articles on the prepositions are excellent, but if one desires to be taught about those things for which the Old Testament exists, he is left to his own devices. The preposition "on, upon" is described in fourteen columns of text, while "righteousness" is given less than four, "justice, judgment" receives two, and "love" one and one-half. It is small wonder that the study of Hebrew by theological students is thought to be a waste of time by the vast majority of the American clergy. Unless Old Testament scholars can do better than they have done in the past in providing basic tools geared both to the subject matter and to the needs of the Church, they can expect nothing but an even greater diminution of interest in serious Biblical study.

Our work in commentaries and Bible dictionaries has also not been strong. We have produced the one-volume *Abingdon Bible Commentary* (edited by F. C. Eiselen and others, 1929) and the Lutheran *Old Testament Commentary* (edited by H. C. Alleman and E. E. Flack, 1948), and as well the several volumes of the *International Critical Commentary* mentioned above. Yet the person who would like a complete set of small commentaries in English on Old Testament books, a work which treats seriously and in a theologically profound manner the faith of which the literature is a witness, such a person is left without help, except as he is enabled to obtain it from secondhand copies of the British *Cambridge Bible for Schools and Colleges* (1880 ff.) and *The New Century Bible* (1904 ff.), all of which are old, badly outmoded, and scarcely adequate in any case. The best thing for him is the annotated *Westminster Study Edition of the Holy*

Bible (1948), a one-volume work which is a model of what a larger and more comprehensive commentary series should be. It is to be hoped that the forthcoming *Interpreter's Bible*, edited by George A. Buttrick and others, may partially fill the need. As for Bible dictionaries, we have published *A New Standard Bible Dictionary* (edited by M. W. Jacobus, E. E. Nourse and A. C. Zenos in the 1st and 2nd eds., 1909 and 1925; in the 3rd ed., 1936, Prof. Nourse was replaced by E. C. Lane) and *The Westminster Dictionary of the Bible* (1944), a completely revised and rewritten edition, by Henry S. Gehman, of the earlier *Dictionary* by John D. Davis (1st ed. 1898). But for larger and more detailed treatments of Biblical subjects we are still dependent upon the major British works inspired by the 1900 era, edited by James Hastings and by T. K. Cheyne and J. S. Black (*Dictionary of the Bible*, 1898–1904; *Encyclopedia of Religion and Ethics*, 1908–1926; *Encyclopaedia Biblica*, 1899–1903).

As for Old Testament theology, our work here can scarcely be said to be more than beginning. It will be difficult for us to do much of lasting significance, except on detailed topics, before basic, up-to-date work in theological lexicography has been done and before serious consideration has been given to the history of Israel in the light of the vast new store of information now available. A new attention also has to be directed toward comparative religion. For the first time, an adequate understanding of the theological structure of polytheism has become possible; in its light the vast difference and the radical reaction of Hebrew faith at nearly every stage of its normative expression is becoming clearer. The metaphor of growth and the comparison of details are no longer sufficient in themselves to explain or to expound it.[16] Furthermore, the revision of our evaluational framework which has been proceeding so rapidly has left us less inclined to view the Old Testament primarily as a sourcebook for values and the evolution of ethical ideals. We are instead in-

---

[16] So the present writer in the monograph, *The Old Testament Against Its Environment.*

creasingly inclined to emphasize its nature as *Heilsgeschichte*, as the record of a proclamation of the great saving acts of God, a proclamation which is primary and which prevents the distortion which has occurred when the Bible has been made into a buttress and support for a religion of ethical idealism. Precisely what this means as an organizing principle for Biblical theology, and what its implications are for Christian theology, have yet to be made clear.

It is thus evident that at the middle of the twentieth century we stand at the beginning of a new era of Biblical study. While we cannot foresee what course world events are to take, it would appear that unless a new era of darkness descends the Protestantism of the second half of this century may undergo as radical a change as it did during the second half of the last century. Old Testament study during the next three decades bears promise of being as productive as it was between 1890 and 1910, this time, however, more seriously concerned with its proper role as a vital part of the Church's life. The manifest tendencies toward increasing conservatism in Biblical criticism and theology among "liberal" Protestants, together with the new movement toward scholarly training among fundamentalists, is already giving promise, not of eradicating the differences completely, but at least of moderating the tension between the two groups. A new and deep theological interest among many younger Jewish rabbis, accelerated by the extreme secularism of modern Zionism, may make possible a closer rapport in Biblical study between Jews and Christians on other grounds than the purely linguistic and historical. Encouraging also is the phenomenal growth of Roman Catholic interest in Biblical study, though it is very problematical whether the Catholic hierarchy will allow this interest to result in greater attempts at mutual understanding and stimulation which Catholic, Protestant and Jewish scholars on their own would be glad to have occur.[17]

[17] For surveys of Jewish and Catholic Biblical study, see the papers by Felix A. Levy and James H. Cobb in Harold R. Willoughby, ed., *The Study of the Bible Today and Tomorrow* (1947), pp. 98–128.

Thus, while on the whole one must say that the study of the Old Testament in this country is in a very uncertain position at the moment and suffering severely from a lack of highly trained personnel with a deep theological interest and a broad cultural background, the future is nevertheless filled with considerable promise. At the beginning of the century the direction of study was determined by what had happened during the Victorian era. It is probable that the events of the last two decades, and the radical shifts in perspective which have occurred, have established the direction of study in the next half century, even though at the moment precise prognosis is impossible.

BIBLIOGRAPHY *

I. General

Eiselen, F. C., and others, eds., *Abingdon Bible Commentary* (New York, 1929)

Davis, John D., *The Westminster Dictionary of the Bible* (revised and rewritten by Henry S. Gehman; Philadelphia, 1944)

II. Introductions

Eiselen, F. C., *Biblical Introduction Series: The Pentateuch* (New York, 1916); *The Prophetic Books* (2 vols., 1923); *The Psalms and Other Sacred Writings* (1918)

Pfeiffer, Robert H., *Introduction to the Old Testament* (New York, 1941)

III. History, Archaeology and Geography

Kent, C. F., *History of the Hebrew People* (2 vols.) and *History of the Jewish People* (2 vols., the second by J. S. Riggs; New York, 1896–1900)

* The bibliography for this chapter is primarily concerned with books dealing with the Old Testament, just as the bibliography for the next chapter is concerned with books on the New Testament. Perhaps the most useful volumes which illustrate, for the Bible as a whole, the transition from "liberalism" to a "neo-critical" point of view are *The Modern Use of the Bible* by H. E. Fosdick (New York, 1924) and *Rediscovering the Bible* by B. W. Anderson (New York, 1951). See also *The Interpretation of the Bible* edited by C. W. Dugmore (London, 1944). A.S.N.

Olmstead, A. T., *History of Palestine and Syria* (New York, 1931)

Albright, W. F., *From the Stone Age to Christianity* (Baltimore, 1940)

Barton, George A., *Archaeology and the Bible* (1st ed., Philadelphia, 1916; 7th ed. 1937)

Wright, G. Ernest, and Filson, Floyd V., *Westminster Historical Atlas to the Bible* (Philadelphia, 1945)

IV. Religion and Theology

Peters, J. P., *Religion of the Hebrews* (Boston, 1914)

Knudson, A. C., *The Religious Teaching of the Old Testament* (New York, 1918)

Burrows, Millar, *Outline of Biblical Theology* (Philadelphia, 1946)

THE STUDY OF THE
NEW TESTAMENT

Floyd V. Filson

FLOYD V. FILSON was born in Missouri in 1896. After taking his undergraduate studies at Park College, Missouri, and his theological studies at McCormick Theological Seminary, he went to the University of Basel, Switzerland, where he took his doctorate in 1930. His entire teaching career has been at his theological *alma mater*, where he has been Professor of New Testament Literature and History since 1930. He has published several books on New Testament criticism and New Testament theology, his best-known volume being *One Lord, One Faith*. With his colleague, G. Ernest Wright, he produced the *Westminster Historical Atlas to the Bible*, and he is also co-editor of the *Westminster Study Bible*. He has played an important role in interpreting European theological thought to the American mind, in particular having translated from the German Oscar Cullmann's *Christ and Time* and being co-translator of Rudolph Otto's *The Kingdom of God and the Son of Man*.

III

Publication of the Revised Standard Version of the New Testament in 1946 underlines one prominent feature of Protestant Biblical scholarship in America. There has been a persistent effort to make the results of research widely available. In 1900, for example, *The Biblical World* had been working for many years to combine accurate scholarship with active teaching in the Church. The modern translations of the New Testament, of which those by James Moffatt and E. J. Goodspeed are the best known but by no means the only ones, have aimed at the same combination of the scholarly and the practical.

Broad Horizons of American Scholarship

Not only in relation to the Church, but also in the area of scholarly study, New Testament students have tried to work with wide horizons. While denominationalism is a peculiar characteristic of the American scene, New Testament scholarship has rarely conceived its work as a partisan denominational activity. This is the more surprising in view of the fact that denominational theological schools train most of the ministers and give the basic training to most of the New Testament scholars.

One factor which fosters broad fellowship is the Society of Biblical Literature and Exegesis. Open to qualified scholars of all faiths and views, it was founded in 1880 and is influential through its *Journal of Biblical Literature*. The National Association of Biblical Instructors, not founded until 1909 and publisher since 1933 of the *Journal of Bible and Religion*, aims primarily to promote effective teaching rather than to foster technical research. But it too illustrates the freedom with which scholars and teachers of various denominations work together.

The broad outlook of New Testament study has been helped by friendly co-operation between Protestant and Jewish scholars.

At times this fellowship has failed to face the crucial issues which divide these two groups, but this is by no means the whole truth. Splendid courtesy and mutual helpfulness have marked the relations between scholars of these two faiths.

Not so close have been the relations between Protestant and Roman Catholic scholars. Many cases of personal friendship and helpfulness occur, but the two groups work quite separately. This does not mean that the Roman Catholic Church has discouraged serious Biblical study. Quite the contrary is true. To be sure, the papal Decree *Lamentabili* in 1907 completely crushed any tendencies to "modernism" in that denomination, and its scholarship must operate within the limits of official pronouncements on certain critical issues. For example, it must reject the current Two-Document Theory of the origin of the Synoptic Gospels, and hold that in some way Paul wrote the Epistle to the Hebrews. Yet papal encyclicals and pronouncements have encouraged thorough study of the Bible.

This prompting has yielded fruit in America in two noteworthy respects. One is the organization of the Catholic Biblical Association, which since 1939 has published the *Catholic Biblical Quarterly*. The other is the publication of books intended to promote study of the Bible by priests and laymen; examples are recent translations of the Vulgate and the Greek New Testament,[1] and Steinmueller's three-volume *Companion to Scripture Studies* (1941–1943), which has had several printings. The latter work shows that Roman Catholic writers know and make some use of Protestant scholarship.

Another notable feature of Protestant New Testament study in America has been its constant reflection of European trends. This has always been true and remains true today. It was feared during the Second World War that Europe would be too exhausted by war to continue to fulfill the prominent role it so

[1] The Confraternity edition (1941) is a translation of the Latin Vulgate New Testament. F. A. Spencer's translation of the Greek New Testament appeared in 1937 under the editorship of C. J. Callan and J. A. McHugh; Spencer died in 1913.

long had held in this field. Such a judgment was hasty. European scholars are still producing the painstaking, thorough research which has put us in their debt in days past.

Acquaintance with such basic work has always been open to readers of learned journals, monographs, and books. Many of these books have been translated into English to give them a wider field of influence. Lecturers from abroad have brought a personal expression of current trends of European study, and some of Britain's great scholars have settled in America to serve as teachers. The names of Kirsopp Lake, James Moffatt, W. Morgan, and E. F. Scott will suffice to make clear how great is American debt to such scholars. Perhaps American Biblical scholarship has at times needed more originality and independence. But it is a partial compensation that the originality, which has not been lacking, has worked against a background of acquaintance with the best scholarship of other countries.

Archaeological Work Continues

Any report of what American New Testament scholarship has done and should do will inevitably reflect to some extent the personal thinking of the reporter. But certain broad lines of development can be discerned.

Characteristic of the last half century has been the earnest determination to do competent historical study. In dealing with an ancient literature and history, this involves alert attention to geography and archaeology.[2] Such study in the New Testament field is not new. Many of the epoch-making discoveries antedate 1900. But steady progress has continued in spite of two world wars. Notable discoveries of papyri have not only provided new manuscripts of New Testament books but also greatly increased

[2] See G. E. Wright and F. V. Filson, *The Westminster Historical Atlas to the Bible* (1945); M. Burrows, *What Mean These Stones?* (1941); C. C. McCown, *The Ladder of Progress in Palestine* (1943); J. Finegan, *Light from the Ancient Past* (1946). Now out of date is C. M. Cobern, *The New Archaeological Discoveries and Their Bearing Upon the New Testament*, published in 1917 and last revised in 1921. G. A. Barton, *Archaeology and the Bible* (1916; seventh ed., 1937), deals mainly with the Old Testament.

the records of the life and culture of the ancient world. Discoveries of ancient synagogues in Palestine and elsewhere, for example, at Dura-Europos on the Euphrates, have thrown light upon the art, architecture, and religious attitudes of Judaism in the early Christian period.[3] In particular, the former theory that the Jews rigidly forbade the artistic portrayal of human beings has been shattered; mosaics and wall paintings depict not only Biblical scenes and characters, but also such pagan features as the signs of the zodiac.

Excavation and exploration has fixed the site of many New Testament cities and towns; Capernaum, for instance, was certainly at Tell Hum. The American Schools of Oriental Research have led the way in exploration of the sites of Palestine, and in particular have mapped all ancient sites in the regions east of the Jordan Valley.[4] The archaeological survey of the city of Jerash, which, like Pompeii, was never fully occupied after ancient times, permits us to see what a city of the Decapolis was like, even if Jerash is mainly a witness to the centuries just after the New Testament period.[5] Various excavations at Athens, Philippi, Ephesus, and other Hellenistic sites have helped to reconstruct the life and history of the days of Paul.[6]

Manuscript Discoveries

Among archaeological finds outstanding importance attaches to discoveries of Biblical manuscripts. Unfortunately, these are usually made by natives who refuse to reveal the place of discovery. At times they even divide a manuscript into parts, in the hope of making a greater profit by selling each part separately.

Fifty years ago little manuscript evidence for the New Testa-

[3] See M. Rostovtzeff, *Dura-Europos and Its Art* (1938).

[4] This exploration has been mainly the work of Nelson Glueck, of the Hebrew Union College. Outstanding in Palestinian archaeology is W. F. Albright. The American Schools publish an *Annual* and a *Bulletin* to provide a permanent record of their work.

[5] The results of the excavations are given in *Gerasa: City of the Decapolis*, edited by C. H. Kraeling (1938).

[6] For non-technical reports, see *The Biblical Archaeologist*, published by the American Schools and edited since its founding in 1938 by G. E. Wright.

ment dated earlier than the fourth century. Further evidence for this later period continues to come to light.[7] American resources and scholarship have brought to publication, among other manuscripts, the notable parchment Washington Manuscript of the Gospels and Acts (W), written in the fourth or fifth century. Perhaps even more significant has been the discovery of papyri from the third and, rarely, from the second century. One such acquisition towers above the rest. The Chester Beatty Biblical Papyri, consisting of eleven manuscripts in all, contains mostly early manuscripts of the Greek Old Testament. But three third-century manuscripts, more nearly complete than any previously discovered New Testament papyri, contain respectively the Gospels and Acts, the letters of Paul, and the Book of Revelation. The manuscript of Paul's letters was sold in three parts, one of which was obtained by the University of Michigan and published by H. A. Sanders (1935).

As a result of these and similar discoveries it has become increasingly clear that no future finds will alter in any essential the text of our Greek New Testament. There are indeed numerous minor variations between manuscripts, and scholars weigh them carefully. But these are relatively unimportant. Even in 1882, as Hort then said, we had a substantially reliable text, and the discoveries of third-century and even second-century evidence makes it doubly certain that we know in all essentials what the first century writers said.

The discovery of thousands of non-Biblical papyri and the more intensive study of Hellenistic writers have thrown much light on New Testament Greek. A century ago, Luke and Paul were compared mainly with the classical authors. Little more than a half century ago, however, Deissmann observed that the Greek of the papyri was much like that of the New Testament.[8] Since

---

[7] For "an account of manuscripts, texts, and versions of the Bible" see I. M. Price, *The Ancestry of our English Bible*. First published in 1907, its thirteenth printing in 1949 was a thorough revision by W. A. Irwin and A. P. Wikgren.

[8] The best popular presentation of Deissmann's work is his *Light from the Ancient East* (revised Eng. Trans., 1927).

then it has been solidly established that the Greek of these early Christian writers was essentially the good current Greek of that time. That is why Goodspeed and others have insisted that a modern translation should likewise be in the current speech of the translator's time.

For a time the papyri may have been overstressed. The center of interest for students of New Testament Greek should be not in the papyri but in the Septuagint. It was the Bible of all New Testament writers; they frequently quote it and even more often reflect it; it is of primary importance for the study of New Testament thought.

The name of A. T. Robertson, and the grammars and other works from his pen, focus attention upon the genuine contribution of Americans to the study of Biblical Greek.[9]

Studies in First Century Background

In keeping with the recent high development of sociological studies, and the resulting great interest in environmental factors of religious life, American Biblical scholars have investigated extensively the background of emerging Christianity.[10]

The result has been a better understanding of ancient Judaism. In this study Jewish scholars have naturally played a major role, but Protestants have made important contributions. Archaeological work has been a joint interest, and so has study of the "intertestamental" period. The two-volume work by George Foot Moore on *Judaism in the First Centuries of the Christian Era: The Age of the Tannaim* (1927) is the classic on this subject.

Noteworthy among the gains of such studies is the better understanding of the positive strength of the Pharisaic position and its commanding place in the history of Judaism. The chief

---

[9] Robertson's chief scholarly contribution was his *Grammar of the Greek New Testament in the Light of Historical Research* (second ed., 1915), a volume of 1367 pages.

[10] See G. H. C. Macgregor and A. C. Purdy, *Jew and Greek: Tutors Unto Christ* (1936); R. H. Pfeiffer, *History of New Testament Times with an Introduction to the Apocrypha* (1949).

question is whether the Judaism of the first century, before the destruction of the Temple, was not really more varied, and less under the "normative" control of the Pharisees, than Moore and others would lead us to think. The recently discovered Dead Sea Scrolls include a "Manual of Discipline," which promises to throw welcome light on a non-Pharisaic Jewish sect of late pre-Christian or very early Christian times.

Because Philo of Alexandria has often been considered one source of New Testament thought, the vigorous recent study of his life and writings deserves mention. It has examined his kinship with Palestinian Judaism, with Hellenistic thought, and with the attitudes of the mystery religions. E. R. Goodenough has even claimed that Philo thought of his Jewish faith in terms of a mystery religion.[11] The argument, even if unconvincing, serves to call attention to the reverent worship and mystical spirit found in Philo; his basic interest was not philosophical but religious.

Philo and Hellenistic Judaism constitute a bridge from the Jewish to the Hellenistic world, which offers an inexhaustible field of study. In this area H. R. Willoughby's capable book on *Pagan Regeneration* (1929) is in two respects characteristic of much American scholarship. It interprets in a winsome way the strength and attraction of the pagan cults of New Testament times; but it fails to give an adequate critique of the weaknesses of those cults.

The attempt some have made to derive important elements of the New Testament message from pagan cults and philosophies has been widely and rightly rejected. Study of the Gentile world throws light on the background and setting and details of the New Testament. But as Cadbury says,[12] there is a noticeable "absence of traceable Gentile religious influence on the New Testament."

---

[11] See his *By Light, Light* (1935). A valuable general study is his *Introduction to Philo Judaeus* (1940).

[12] See p. 90 in his essay on "The Present State of New Testament Studies," in *The Haverford Symposium on Archaeology and the Bible*, edited by E. Grant (1938).

The Study of Gospel Origins

Chief attention should center on the origin and meaning of the New Testament documents themselves. The literary problems continue to deserve attention. At the turn of the century the two-document theory was widely regarded as the solution of the Synoptic problem: the writers of Matthew and Luke used as written sources Mark and a collection of Jesus' sayings (Q). Except for Roman Catholics, who now must reject the theory, it still holds its ground.[13] But it is often expanded. Largely under the influence of B. H. Streeter, special written sources for both Matthew (M) and Luke (L) have been proposed, and some have thought our Luke the result of a complicated development, in which Luke's original compilation of teaching (L) was first combined with Q to form Proto-Luke, and only later was this Proto-Luke combined with Mark to give our present Gospel of Luke.[14] These newer source theories are much disputed. Many are content to stand by the two-document theory, and turn to oral tradition for the further light needed to explain the origins of the Gospels.

Akin to the sociological interest which animated environmental studies is Form Criticism, which emerged as a prominent phase of Gospel study after the First World War and has exercised considerable influence in America.[15] It fastens attention upon the oral tradition, in the early period, and seeks the *Sitz im Leben* or actual life situation in which the gospel tradition was used.

[13] A dissenter is M. S. Enslin, who doubts that Q ever existed and suggests that the author of Luke borrowed from our Gospel of Matthew. See *Christian Beginnings* (1938), p. 433.

[14] On special written sources for Matthew and Luke see E. D. Burton, *Some Principles of Literary Criticism and Their Application to the Synoptic Problem* (1904); B. S. Easton, *The Gospel According to St. Luke* (1926) and *Christ in the Gospels* (1930); B. W. Bacon, *Studies in Matthew* (1930); F. C. Grant, *The Growth of the Gospels* (1933).

[15] See F. C. Grant, *Form Criticism* (1934), a brief introduction and translation of works by Bultmann and Kundsin. An early and incisive study of Form Criticism was made by B. S. Easton in *The Gospel Before the Gospels* (1928). For a later description and critique see E. F. Scott, *The Validity of the Gospel Record* (1938); also my *Origins of the Gospels* (1938), ch. 4.

While it directs initial attention to the form in which the tradition was used and shaped, its real purpose is to reconstruct the development of early Christian life and thought. Ostensibly a purely historical discipline, it often operates with philosophical and theological presuppositions which derive tradition from process rather than a great creative figure. Hence Form Criticism has occasionally led to a practical agnosticism as to what Jesus said and did. To be sure, it is a valuable corrective to the purely literary study which divorced the writing of the Gospels from the life of the Church. It has shown how the tradition was used in the worship, teaching, and controversy of the first Christians. But at times it has almost reduced Jesus to an unknown x.

In our own country, the social-historical school, of which S. J. Case was so prominent a member, made a similar attempt to relate the growth and fixing of the tradition to the social setting of the disciples. The tradition was to be tested to see whether it fitted the Palestinian milieu; only if it did could it be considered as genuine. Case's *Jesus* is typical and classic in this field of study.[16] The problem in all test by environment is how to allow for the originality of the central figure of the story. This problem the social-historical method cannot solve; at best it can rule out obviously extraneous features of a tradition.

C. C. Torrey represents a radical rejection of concentration upon oral tradition.[17] He seeks the setting of the tradition in the earliest Aramaic-speaking Christianity, which almost at once became an Aramaic-writing Christianity. In fact, he inclines to think that even in Jesus' lifetime notes were made of what Jesus said, and perhaps of what he did. Beginning with Mark, in A.D. 40, all four Gospels were written in Aramaic within little more than twenty years. Our Greek Gospels, the first half of Acts (to ch. 15:35), and the Book of Revelation are all translations from Aramaic originals. A. T. Olmstead stoutly championed the theory

[16] See also D. W. Riddle, *The Gospels: Their Origin and Growth* (1939).
[17] *The Four Gospels* (1933); *Our Translated Gospels* (1936); *Documents of the Primitive Church* (1941). I pointed out weaknesses in Torrey's arguments and assumptions in ch. 3 of my *Origins of the Gospels*.

of an Aramaic Gospel back of our present Gospels,[18] but did not develop so complicated a theory as that of Torrey.

These and other men have at least called attention to the strongly Semitic flavor of the New Testament. Even if our Gospels were written in Greek, as I am convinced they were, they nevertheless were in faithful touch with the early Aramaic tradition from which the oral Greek tradition almost immediately derived.

The Debate Over Ephesians

That the origin of the New Testament writings must be sought in the Hellenistic world has been most vigorously asserted by E. J. Goodspeed. He contends, and rightly, that our Gospels were written in Greek. But his chief claim to present recognition is not in this point, nor in his half century of activity in American manuscript study, but in his view of the origin of Ephesians.[19] His theory is that the writing of Acts, about A.D. 90, stimulated an admirer of Paul, who already knew Colossians well, to gather together and master all the letters of Paul he could find. This disciple then wrote "Ephesians" as a summary of Pauline teaching, and published the collection with this summary at its head.

Goodspeed goes on to argue that the presence of groups of letters in the New Testament—the Pastoral Epistles, the three Epistles of John, the collected Catholic Epistles, the seven letters in Revelation—reflects the influence of this publication of the Pauline collection. Therefore, when he writes his *Introduction to the New Testament*, he makes this collection of Paul's letters the key to the entire process. The collector, who also wrote Ephesians, set the pattern of Christian writing for some decades; letters, in groups, became the leading way of presenting the Christian message.[20]

[18] "Could an Aramaic Gospel Be Written?" was his key article, in *Journal of Near Eastern Studies*, 1942, pp. 41–75.

[19] His chief works of this subject are *New Solutions of New Testament Problems* (1927); *The Meaning of Ephesians* (1933); *An Introduction to the New Testament* (1937); *Christianity Goes to Press* (1940).

[20] A. E. Barnett, in *The New Testament: Its Making and Meaning* (1946),

This brilliant theory, by assuming that the collector knew Colossians almost as well as if it were his own writing, does much to silence the objection that the vocabulary of Ephesians is on the whole Pauline. But what if the letters of Paul were collected as a result of Paul's death,[21] or as a gradual process (cf. Col. 4:16)? Goodspeed's theory holds good only if the collection burst upon the world as a new and striking innovation. Publication and not simply writing is for him the clue to the development.

This theory calls to attention the fact that Ephesians is a general letter. Paul can have written it only if he for once decided to set down a general meditation on the Gospel and its meaning for Christian life in the one world Church. To me this latter view answers more questions with fewer unsupported assumptions than does any other possibility.[22]

Is New Testament Eschatology Valid?

As we move from questions of background and literary origin to consider the interpretation of New Testament content, we find eschatology a focal center of interest. For decades, largely through the influence of militant Bible Schools and the wide use of the Scofield *Reference Bible* (1909), of which I am told two million copies have been sold, pre-millenialism has been a prominent factor in American religious life. This school of thought takes the Biblical references to the future quite literally and welds them into a system in which the end of the world is expected in the very near future. It claims that New Testament references to the imminent end of this age refer not to the first century but to the time of the modern speaker or writer.

Quite opposed to this is the "consistent eschatology" which

---

follows Goodspeed's theory. J. Knox, in *Philemon Among the Letters of Paul* (1935), conjectures that Onesimus collected the letters and wrote Ephesians.

[21] This is the suggestion of H. E. Dana in *A Neglected Predicate in New Testament Criticism* (1934), pp. 14–21.

[22] So argues E. F. Scott in his commentary on Ephesians (1930) in the *Moffatt New Testament Commentary* series.

American scholars learned from Johannes Weiss and Albert Schweitzer.[23] On this view, Jesus expected the end of the world at once, but since the expectation was not realized, that entire way of thinking should be abandoned, and the ethical teaching which Jesus and the early Christians based on this expectation should be discounted as an "interim ethic," given for use only in stop-gap living until the imminent crisis should come. Some modern scholars (E. D. Burton [24] is but one of many) absolve Jesus of any share in this apocalyptic view; they hold that the early Church ascribed to him their outlook, which in reality they derived from Jewish apocalyptic. In either case, there results a suspicion of the eschatological features in the Gospels. It is a view sharply at variance with the New Testament's vivid hope.

The Church has moved towards a position in which the urgent eschatological note of the New Testament is generally recognized. It is widely conceded that Jesus and the Apostles expected the end in the not too distant future, although usually it has been realized that the Schweitzer school overstated the extent to which Jesus' thought focused on the imminent future. There is good evidence that Jesus thought of the Kingdom as already beginning in his own ministry and movement; there is also evidence that he anticipated some interval, even if not extensive, between his death and the coming of the end. With his work a new age began. The situation of man henceforth was new. The New Testament sees that the decisive action of all God's work in time was the historical career of Christ, the crucified and risen Lord. In his earthly career was established a new order which will find complete fulfilment in God's perfect final Kingdom. The necessarily pictorial expression and the uncertainty as to the time of the end do not discredit this faith. New Testament eschatology is an essential part of the early Christian message.[25]

[23] See ch. 13 in C. C. McCown's historical survey of *The Search for the Real Jesus* (1940).

[24] *New Testament Word Studies* (1927), pp. 97 f.

[25] See P. E. Davies on "The Relevance of Apocalyptic for Ancient and Modern Situations," in *The Study of the Bible Today and Tomorrow*, H. R. Willoughby, editor (1947), pp. 279–297.

Is the Gospel a Social Program?

To the "consistent eschatologist" the teaching of Jesus is of little direct use today; it was only a temporary way of living for people who were sure that the world was to end almost at once. This is part of a wider question: What is the relevance of the teaching of Jesus? Some sects would say that it is not a social guide by which to remake the society of our time. Jesus did not intend to transform this world; it is doomed. He simply told men how to live until he comes to establish by his divine power a quite new and different order.

In radical opposition to this view is a school of thought which has had tremendous influence in America during the last half century. It found in the social teaching of Jesus the directions by which Christians can remake the world and build the Kingdom of God, the perfect society. This point of view reflected the characteristic American optimism and activism which so often have been condemned by European Christians. It reached back to the prophets of the Old Testament for powerful support, and often looked with unappreciative eye at the high Christology of the Fourth Gospel and the "labored theology" of Paul. In its extreme form it took the heart of the Bible to be the prophets and the social teaching of Jesus.[26]

The Church so often had been quiescent, while its members shared in and frequently profited by the evils of society, that the new emphasis had a partial justification. But it was one-sided. It had no adequate conception of the tenacity of evil, nor of the central New Testament message of the redeeming grace of God

[26] Among the notable advocates of the social relevance of the New Testament were S. Mathews, *The Social Teaching of Jesus* (1897; completely rewritten, with recognition of the eschatological aspect, in *Jesus on Social Institutions*, published in 1928); W. Rauschenbusch, *Christianity and the Social Crisis* (1907) and *A Theology for the Social Gospel* (1917). In S. Dickey, *The Constructive Revolution of Jesus* (1923); C. C. McCown, *The Genesis of the Social Gospel* (1929); and J. C. Bennett, *Social Salvation* (1935), there is a frank facing of the eschatological accent in Jesus' teaching. What is said above applies more to the average advocate of the social gospel than to the scholars cited in this note.

active in the life, death, and living Lordship of the risen Christ. It too often represented a failure to hold fast to the basic Christian message in points of Christology and Atonement.[27] Certain of its champions felt able, with some help, to work out their own salvation, with very little fear and trembling, and without the Apostle Paul's accompanying feeling that "all things are of God, who reconciled us to himself through Christ."

In the first part of the last half century this strong emphasis on the social gospel moved into a place of prominence. Two world wars and an ominous depression changed the theological climate. It is now widely recognized that the social gospel brought a necessary corrective; Christians personally redeemed by Christ are under urgent obligation to give in their social living a positive expression of the mind of Christ. But the strength and permanent truth of the classic Christian message, set forth in the full outline of the Gospels, in the speeches of Acts, and in the letters of Paul, is the real hope of sinful man living in a deeply corrupt society.[28]

Hence in retrospect it is clear that something essential was represented by such militant conservatives as J. G. Machen. He was not infallible in critical questions, he had no proper sense of the social problems of our time, and he was not winsome in theological debate. But his book, *The Origin of Paul's Religion* (1921), and his contention that classic Christian theology is the necessary outcome of faithfulness to the New Testament, were far truer to fact than much shallow theology which often marked the social gospel. Much criticism of such men, as of "Neo-orthodoxy" today, was in reality directed against the common New Testament Gospel. It was only by ignoring the Fourth Gospel, the Acts, the Epistles, the Book of Revelation, and much of the Synoptic Gospels themselves that the Gospel could be repre-

---

[27] See J. W. Bowman, *The Intention of Jesus* (1943), on Jesus' own thought of himself and his work, and Elias Andrews, *The Meaning of Christ for Paul* (1949), for the full scope of Paul's thinking on these themes.

[28] The earnest attempt of Rauschenbusch (see note 26), though it was honest and constructive in spirit, did not issue in a balanced and adequate theology.

sented as a non-Christological social message with no central word
of atonement.

The pendulum may now be swinging too far in the other direction. There may be such a reaction against shallow aspects of the
social gospel that a quiescent Church will fail in its social responsibility. This would be damaging first of all to the Church and its
members; genuine new life in Christ cannot fail to express itself
in social relations.[29]

Is There a New Testament Theology?

The insight that the Gospel is more than the teaching of Jesus
leads to the consideration of New Testament theology.[30] Typical
of the best work in this field a half century ago was G. B. Stevens'
The Theology of the New Testament, first published in 1899.[31]
The rights of literary and historical study were fully conceded,
but the scholarly treatment was accompanied by the solid conviction of the uniqueness, unity, and permanent authority of the
New Testament message. This positive conviction recognized
but confined to a secondary role the diversity of thought the New
Testament contains.

On various grounds this favorable view has been attacked.[32]
The very possibility of a New Testament theology has been de-

[29] Stress on the ethical teaching of the New Testament is found in E. F.
Scott, *The Ethical Teaching of Jesus* (1924); H. Branscomb, *The Teachings
of Jesus* (1931); M. S. Enslin, *The Ethics of Paul* (1930). See also A. N.
Wilder, *Eschatology and Ethics in the Teaching of Jesus* (1934; revised ed.,
1950).

[30] Surveys and analysis of developments on this subject are offered by
C. T. Craig, "Biblical Theology and the Rise of Historicism," in *Journal
of Biblical Literature,* 1943, pp. 281-294, and A. N. Wilder, "New Testament Theology in Transition," in *The Study of the Bible Today and Tomorrow,* pp. 419-436.

[31] Similar in position was A. C. Zenos, *The Plastic Age of the Gospel*
(1927).

[32] R. E. Wolfe, for example, opposes the new interest in Biblical theology.
He stands for objective study based on the history-of-religions approach,
demands the rigid exclusion of the idea of revelation, and would center attention on the prophets and the Synoptic teaching of Jesus. See his article, "The
Terminology of Biblical Theology," in *The Journal of Bible and Religion,*
1947, pp. 143-147.

nied. It has been insisted that the treatment of the New Testament writings as a separate collection is artificial; historical study must ignore the canon, and treat all ancient Christian writings as on the same level.

It has further been asserted that sound historical study outlaws New Testament theology. Such study can only describe the history and religious life of the New Testament movement. No thought of relevance or normative character, no personal faith or thought of divine revelation, can be allowed to influence this purely objective presentation. Sympathy and imagination the scholar must have, but his personal faith and his final evaluation of the results of study must be rigidly excluded from his work. Therefore the word theology should not be used; what we can expect is a treatment of the religion of the New Testament.[33]

Some have heightened this last statement. They deny that there is any basic unity in the New Testament, and so they speak rather of the "religions" of the New Testament.

Further objection to the term, New Testament theology, has come from the claim that the writers of the New Testament books are dependent on non-Christian sources for essentials of their message. The early decades of the twentieth century were marked by diligent study and comparison of the various ancient religions. As the contemporary Jewish and Gentile backgrounds became better known, some scholars were deeply impressed by the parallels between the New Testament and other religious literatures. Perhaps it was natural that at first the similarities drew more attention than the differences. Moreover, chronology was often neglected. Evidence from the second, third, and even much later centuries was freely used to show that the New Testament was dependent upon these other religions, whose data were

---

[33] E. W. Parsons, whose book on *The Religion of the New Testament* (1939) is the best American liberal presentation of New Testament thought in print, insists also that the lack of reflection and system makes the word theology inapplicable. The same point animates E. F. Scott in *Varieties of New Testament Religion* (1943), but Scott sees the deep unity in the New Testament message.

actually too late to warrant such a conclusion. Lack of balance appeared also in the striking readiness to explain as Gentile in origin features of the New Testament message which had a much closer and more natural setting in Judaism, and more specifically in the Old Testament. Furthermore, the stubborn unwillingness to recognize adequately the fresh, creative factor in the emerging Christian movement vitiated much of the earnest study in this field.

Independence, therefore, and not servile dependence, marks the New Testament. The common centering of faith and thought in Jesus Christ, the unvarying interpretation of his career as the redemptive work of God, who has now brought to fulfillment his promises to Israel and through his Spirit is offering the benefit of Christ's work to Jew and Gentile alike—this one basic message, shared by all writers and binding them to the Old Testament, sweeps aside all talk of many competing "religions" in the New Testament. Here is one unique and crucial message which warrants the Church in setting these writings apart in a special group. Diversity there is; the bond with non-canonical writers need not be ignored; living touch with environment certainly exists, particularly with Judaism and the Old Testament; but these writings possess a vital unity, relevance, and originality.[34]

It is not surprising, therefore, that recent publications have recognized the rightful role of New Testament theology. Paul S. Minear's *Eyes of Faith* (1946) brings out the theocentric character and the common mind and outlook of the entire Bible. Millar Burrows' *Outline of Biblical Theology* (1946) moves in the direction of a full Biblical theology. Frederick C. Grant, in *An Introduction to New Testament Thought* (1950), while anxious to stress the diversity of the thought, is nevertheless concerned to do justice to the underlying unity within the New Testament and also between the Testaments.

[34] I have argued for this position in *One Lord, One Faith* (1943). The point leaves full room for dependence upon the Old Testament, kinship with Judaism, and contact with Hellenistic life. Cf. also my argument in *The New Testament Against Its Environment* (1950).

Still disputed is the question whether historical study must be rigidly objective. The necessity to be honest, to avoid wishful thinking and partisan bias, is the essential point in the demand for objective scholarship. But life is not the neutral area which this position assumes; it is impossible to study, correlate, and present truly the origin and classic history of a religious movement without the element of evaluation entering into the process.

This is not all. By the Christian scholar, committed as he is in mind and life to Christ, the demand that he do his historical study without personal response and evaluation must be rejected. Honesty, integrity, fairness, patience, and a sense of his limitations as a man and scholar may be demanded, but neutrality is out of the question. New Testament theology, broadened to become Biblical theology, and frankly combining with its diligent historical research the grasp of the meaning of history in the light of the Gospel, is a Christian necessity as well as a scholarly activity. It is time to be done with the deceptive myth of neutrality.

The Tasks That Lie Ahead

In what directions may we expect New Testament study to move in the next few years? No one can give a complete answer to this question.[35] In textual criticism we may expect solid work but no sensational results, unless unforeseen manuscript discoveries open up new possibilities. An international project to provide a much needed up-to-date textual apparatus of the Greek New Testament is just moving out of the planning stage into the actual detailed work, in which scores of American scholars are participating and the University of Chicago is providing the American center (the other center is at Oxford in England).[36]

[35] The best and most detailed attempt to forecast future trends is *The Study of the Bible Today and Tomorrow* (1947), a symposium of twenty-four essays sponsored by the Chicago Society of Biblical Research and edited by H. R. Willoughby.

[36] The Society of Biblical Literature and Exegesis is sponsoring this project, which the Rockefeller Foundation has aided in its initial stages.

This project concerns church history as well as the New Testament. The essential reliability of the Greek text is now beyond question, and two things remain to be done: we must reconstruct as closely as possible the original text, and write the history—of the text in the various periods of the ancient and mediæval Church.

The study of background will never end, for the material and questions are inexhaustible. Three lines of study should prove important and fruitful. In the Gentile area, the origin and development of Gnosticism will receive increased attention. Extensive new manuscript materials, recently discovered in Egypt, will soon make possible more careful study of this elusive aspect of ancient life.[37] In the Jewish field, further study of Hellenistic Judaism is needed, to determine as clearly as possible the situation in which the Gospel reached out into Gentile lands. More specifically, the Septuagint, which for long was neglected by New Testament scholars because it was the Old Testament and by Old Testament scholars because it was in Greek, calls for even more intensive study; here is the most rewarding single field of study for an understanding of New Testament background.[38]

The study of the canon, which was of considerable interest fifty years ago, has seemed much less important in recent years. But the necessity of a new study of the canon is beginning to be realized. In the last twenty years there has been much objection to the very idea of a canon. I expect to hear less in the next twenty. But the renewed study will not seek merely to determine when and where the New Testament books were first known and

---

Eighteen American scholars are on the Editorial Committee, whose Executive Committee consists of E. C. Colwell, Chairman; M. M. Parvis, Executive Secretary; K. W. Clark; B. M. Metzger; P. Schubert; and A. P. Wikgren.

[37] Thus far I know these discoveries only from a report in the *Theologische Literaturzeitung* for December, 1949, columns 760 f. They are like other evidence for Gnosticism, however, in that they are of post-New Testament date (third and fourth century; in Coptic).

[38] A lexicon of the Greek Old Testament, and a new lexicon of the Greek New Testament, are urgent needs. They should give major attention to the theological usage of the words.

when and how they were declared authoritative; it will center attention rather upon the reasons, including the theological reasons, for the establishment and final definition of the canon.

Since the date and origin of so many New Testament books is still in dispute, there will inevitably be much further study in these areas. Most troublesome is the wide disagreement concerning the Book of Acts [39] and the Gospel of John.[40] Crucial as they are in building a picture of New Testament history, they still offer many unsolved problems. While I hold that Acts is by Luke and gives a basically dependable account of Apostolic Christianity, and that the Gospel of John is built upon eyewitness and blends with that a devout interpretation which is convincing to faith, later datings and less favorable attitudes towards the historical and theological value of these books make urgent their further study.

It may be that the chief cause of difficulty, our immense ignorance of the last third of the first century, can never be overcome. Once the story of Acts ceases, we catch but glimpses of the next few decades. While scholars debate learnedly whether to put a book in the seventies or eighties or nineties, the truth is that we know little about events and developments in the Church during those years. This not only weakens the case for any system of dating of the documents, but also makes it hard to refute conclusively a confident scholar who unhesitatingly dates documents here or there in this ecclesiastical wilderness. It

[39] Basic for thorough study of the Book of Acts are H. J. Cadbury, *The Making of Luke-Acts* (1927), and *The Beginnings of Christianity, Part I, The Acts of the Apostles*, 5 volumes (1920–1933), edited by F. J. Foakes Jackson and K. Lake. No later book has completely superseded A. C. McGiffert, *A History of Christianity in the Apostolic Age* (1897). There is need for an up-to-date one-volume commentary on Acts and for a new comprehensive history of the Apostolic Age.

[40] American scholars have not done much outstanding work on this Gospel. It was a major interest of B. W. Bacon; see *The Fourth Gospel in Research and Debate* (1910) and *The Gospel of the Hellenists* (1933). Among conservative treatments are A. T. Robertson, *Epochs in the Life of the Apostle John* (1925), and H. E. Dana, *The Ephesian Tradition* (1940). Noteworthy critical studies are B. W. Robinson, *The Gospel of John* (1925), and E. C. Colwell, *John Defends the Gospel* (1936).

may not sound either exciting or promising, but there must be continued study to see whether a reasonably strong case can be made for some system of dating the New Testament books.

The central problem of all has to do with the relation between history and theology. Now that the possibility and even the desirability of a strictly neutral and objective presentation of the New Testament message is being denied, and the historian's own interpretative activity is seen to be an integral part of all historical writing, there must be careful study of the proper way to use historical material in Biblical theology as well as in systematic theology.

Biblical theology is essentially an interpreted account of the Biblical history, seen as the advancing work of God Himself. Therefore the real purpose of New Testament study in the days to come must be to get a clear grasp and give a clear statement of the gospel story of the saving work of God in Jesus Christ, the living Lord of the Church. In doing this task it must use every help which geography, archaeology, linguistic and literary study, general historical research, and psychological analysis [41] can give. But it will know that none of these supporting studies yields or controls the Gospel. The climax of all this labor is given by Biblical theology.

Systematic theology, if based on purely philosophical rather than historical foundations, must be asked whether it deserves any longer a place in the life of the Church. The Christian Church gets from the Bible the story of what God has done for men, and its message is that story thus interpreted. It is not the task of theology to surrender that basis of faith and seek a new one. Theology must deal with that Biblical history more directly and seriously than many theologians have done in the last half century.

Future New Testament study will recognize clearly the community-building nature of the New Testament message.[42]

[41] E. M. Ligon, in *The Psychology of Christian Personality* (1935), aims "to interpret the teachings of Jesus in terms of modern psychology" (p. vii).

[42] F. C. Grant stresses this point in his *Introduction to New Testament Thought*, Ch. 11.

Overemphasis on eschatology made the Church look like a lame afterthought. Extreme individualism made it an optional feature of Christian life. A social message bent on political and economic reform often slighted the role of the Church. In the New Testament, however, the Church is essential. Thorough study of the New Testament Church must be an important phase of New Testament history and theology.

BIBLIOGRAPHY

Enslin, Morton Scott, *Christian Beginnings* (New York, 1938). A comprehensive liberal survey of background, history, literary questions, text, and canon.

Filson, Floyd V., *One Lord, One Faith* (Philadelphia, 1943). An evaluation of recent critical theories and an argument for the essential unity of the New Testament message.

Finegan, Jack, *Light from the Ancient Past* (Princeton, 1946). A good popular presentation of "the archeological background of the Hebrew-Christian religion."

Grant, Frederick C., *An Introduction to New Testament Thought* (New York and Nashville, 1950). An excellent up-to-date study in the field of New Testament theology.

McGiffert, Arthur Cushman, *A History of Christianity in the Apostolic Age* (New York, 1897; rev. ed., 1899). An excellent presentation at the turn of the century.

Mathews, Shailer, *Jesus on Social Institutions* (New York, 1928). An outstanding expression of American interest in the social gospel.

Moore, George Foot, *Judaism in the First Centuries of the Christian Era: The Age of the Tannaim* (2 vols. Cambridge, 1927). A third volume, of notes, was issued in 1930. Indispensable.

Parsons, Ernest William, *The Religion of the New Testament* (New York, 1939). An outstanding liberal presentation.

Price, Ira Maurice, *The Ancestry of Our English Bible* (New York, 1907). Thirteenth printing, revised by William A. Irwin and Allen P. Wikgren, 1949. "An account of the manuscripts, texts, and versions of the Bible."

Stevens, George Barker, *The Theology of the New Testament* (New

York, 1899; second ed., 1906). A classic treatment at the turn of the century.

Wilder, Amos Niven, *Eschatology and Ethics in the Teaching of Jesus* (New York, 1939; rev. ed., 1950). The revised edition serves to show what vital problems are under discussion at the present time.

Willoughby, Harold R., Editor, *The Study of the Bible Today and Tomorrow* (Chicago, 1947). Twenty-four essays which survey recent research and discuss the unfinished tasks.

THE PHILOSOPHY OF RELIGION

George F. Thomas

GEORGE F. THOMAS was born in Texas in 1899, and he received his undergraduate training at Southern Methodist University, Dallas. He then spent three years studying theology as Rhodes scholar from Texas at the University of Oxford. On his return to America, he taught at Southern Methodist University, proceeding to Harvard in 1926, where he did graduate work for his doctorate in philosophy. Since 1927 he has taught philosophy at Swarthmore College, at Dartmouth College, and at the University of North Carolina. From 1940 he has been Professor of Religious Thought and since 1946 Chairman of the Department of Religion at Princeton University. He is the author of *Spirit and Its Freedom*, editor of *The Vitality of the Christian Tradition*, and contributor to various symposia. He is an Episcopalian layman, being a member of the Joint Commission of the Episcopal Church on Approaches to Unity, and he is a past president of the American Theological Society.

IV

THE FIRST half of the twentieth century has witnessed a vigorous effort on the part of some of our leading philosophers and philosophical theologians to investigate the nature and validity of religion. This effort has been made, for the most part, by men who have combined a strong personal interest in religion with a firm determination to maintain the independence of their thinking against the claims of every kind of religious authority, whether of Church or Scripture or Creed. Only in the United States, perhaps, could such a combination of religious concern and complete independence have been possible. In the United States the powerful religious impulses set in motion by the Reformation had given rise in the nineteenth century to a number of religious communities, no one of which could dominate the common life as an established church. All of these communities had to make their appeal to the mind and heart of the individual American, without the aid of any external authority. Moreover, the leading universities which were the centers of critical thought had achieved by the end of the century a remarkable degree of academic freedom. Above all, the spirit of American life was very individualistic in the late nineteenth and early twentieth centuries. The frontier had bred a habit of self-reliance and independence. Economic and political life encouraged individual initiative. The liberal spirit favored experimentation and change. As a result, the religious thinking of Americans was almost inevitably individualistic and heterodox, and no one type of religious thought was accepted by all or even most American thinkers. Therefore, it will be necessary to consider several different types as represented by outstanding personal examples. Because of the limitations of space, we shall not be able to deal with all of the various types and combinations of types and we shall have to confine ourselves to one or two personal examples of each type.[1]

Until the first World War, "Absolute Idealism" was the dominant philosophy in America, though for some time it had been challenged vigorously by Empiricism. Josiah Royce had offered a classic defense of Absolute Idealism at the end of the nineteenth century in *The World and the Individual*. In the first decade of this century his thinking underwent a substantial change. *The Philosophy of Loyalty* (published in 1908) and *The Problem of Christianity* (published in 1913) indicated that his thinking differed from that of Hegel in significant ways. It is worth while to examine *The Problem of Christianity* with the question in mind: How far had Royce freed himself from the Hegelian way of thinking about religion?

The essence of Christianity is best discovered, Royce thinks, by a study of St. Paul. Pauline Christianity developed the teaching of Jesus about the Kingdom of God into a doctrine of the Church. The three fundamental ideas of this type of Christianity are: (1) the salvation of the individual man is determined by membership in a religious, indeed, a divine, community in whose life the spirit of Christ attains earthly fulfilment;[2] (2) the individual "is by nature subject to some overwhelming moral burden from which, if unaided, he cannot escape";[3] and (3) the only escape for the individual is provided by an atonement for his sin and guilt which "makes possible the entrance of the individual into a saving union with the divine spiritual community."[4] No one can read Royce's interpretation of these three ideas without being impressed by his insight into certain aspects of the Christian doctrine of sin and atonement. But one cannot read far without discovering not only

---

[1] For example, we have selected E. S. Brightman rather than B. P. Bowne as representative of Personalism, largely because of his influence during the last generation, and we have not considered thinkers as significant as J. B. Pratt, E. Boodin, E. Lyman, and R. L. Calhoun. Paul Tillich also is not included because he is to be dealt with thoroughly in a forthcoming volume.

[2] *The Problem of Christianity*, I, 39.

[3] *Ibid.*, I, 4.   [4] *Ibid.*, I, 43.

that Royce has greatly oversimplified the meaning of Christianity by reducing it to these three assertions but also that he has radically reconstructed Christianity until it has become nothing more than "the most typical, and so far in human history, the most highly developed religion of loyalty." [5]

The most striking example of this is his subordination of Christ to the Church. "Not through imitating nor yet through loving any mere individual human being can we be saved," says he, "but only through loyalty to the 'Beloved Community.'" [6] He concedes that Jesus had taught a doctrine and lived a life that made the Christian community possible, but his doctrine of the Christian life was incomplete and the founding of Christianity was primarily due to "the united spirit of the early Christian community." [7] The name of Christ has always been for Christians simply "the symbol for the Spirit in whom the faithful—that is to say the loyal—always are and have been one." [8] Consequently, Jesus' teaching about love needs to be reinterpreted. Above all, love means loyalty to the "beloved community," one person loving another not merely with "amiable sympathy" but as a potential member of the "beloved community." The eschatological element in early Christianity is dropped and man becomes the builder of the "beloved community" as an earthly Kingdom of God. The "moral burden" or sin of the individual is interpreted as treason to the community rather than rebellion against God. The atonement of Christ becomes a symbol of the "loyal love" of many "suffering servants" for those who have betrayed the "beloved community." It is not so much an act of divine love for sinners as a purely human act of suffering to restore the unity of the community.

In the light of this thoroughly human and social interpretation of Christianity, we are prepared for Royce's virtual identification of the divine with the "beloved community." "Man the

---

[5] *Ibid.*, I, xviii.   [6] *Ibid.*, I, xxv.
[7] *Ibid.*, I, 418.   [8] *Ibid.*, II, 426.

community," he says, "without ceasing to be thoroughly human, may also prove to be divine." [9] That this may be only an extreme expression of the typically Idealistic doctrine of the immanence of God in man is suggested by the later statement that "the divine spirit dwelling in the living Church redeems mankind." [10] But it comes perilously close to a deification of the "beloved community."

It is obvious from all of this that Royce has not really overcome the tendency of Hegelian Idealism to transform an historical religion by distinguishing between its "accidental" historical elements and its "essential" meaning. Following this tendency, he regards Christian doctrines such as the Incarnation and Atonement merely as "myths" which express universal human experiences and needs. This results from his rationalistic approach which does not take seriously the claim of the Christian faith to be a revelation from God and regards as valid only those Christian affirmations that can be demonstrated by an appeal to universal human needs and experiences. In this view, Christianity becomes merely a symbolic expression of the truths of Absolute Idealism, and it will endure not because its basic religious beliefs are true but because "love and loyalty will not lose but grow in human value, as long as man remains alive." [11] Despite his attempt to do justice to Christianity, therefore, Royce does not really see the most distinctive thing about it: that it springs from the conviction that in Christ God has revealed Himself and has reconciled the world to Himself. Without that conviction, the Christian Church as the "beloved community" would never have come into existence and could no longer maintain itself. For the Christian faith is centered in Christ, not in the Church; and it depends for salvation upon God's grace and not upon any human "beloved community."

W. E. Hocking's *The Meaning of God in Human Experience* (published in 1912) is the most important book on religion in

---

[9] *Ibid.*, I, 418.   [10] *Ibid.*, II, 426.   [11] *Ibid.*, I, 422.

general which has been produced by an Absolute Idealist in the last half century. He attacks the subjectivistic view that religion is feeling and that the metaphysical element in it is unimportant. As "anticipated attainment," religion certainly includes feeling. But feeling is unstable and incommunicable; and it cannot be understood except in terms of its cognitive intention, its "destiny" being knowledge of its object. Though we can never comprehend the infinite, it is the object of all our ideas, since knowledge begins with the whole. Moreover, our "whole idea" is the source of our values and their growth.

Hocking's world view as an Idealist is that of monism and absolutism. Monism, which asserts that evil is less real than good, is a necessary condition of optimism. Absolutism is essential because there is a necessary and changeless Reality. However, Hocking seeks to define his monism and absolutism in such a way as to avoid the criticisms of James and others. It is true that monism sometimes averts its eyes from evil instead of combatting it, but the "true use" of the monistic principle of ignoring evil is that "the evil is not merely forgotten, but genuinely disposed of by that to which the attention is turned." In other words, evil is known as "an alterable aspect of a reality which is good." [12] Similarly, Hocking denies that absolutism necessarily swallows up the individual self. "Besides the Absolute," he says, "my Self is necessary to account for my motion." [13] Thus, in his defense of Absolute Idealism Hocking transforms it in the direction of personalism.

Perhaps the highest achievement of Hocking's philosophy of religion is his penetrating study of worship and mysticism. He points out the worth of worship in deepening knowledge of the self and reality, in detaching the self from its immediate environment, and, above all, in renewing its devotion to the Absolute or the Whole as the ultimate Source of all our values. As to mys-

[12] *Ibid.*, 178.   [13] *Ibid.*, 190.

ticism, he describes the "alternation" between work and worship, between the active pursuit of relative values and the enjoyment of the whole which includes them. Only through such an "alternation" can spiritual staleness and fatigue be overcome and the sense of the worth of living be recovered. Moreover, mysticism at its best does not lead to a withdrawal from action on the stage of history. Like Bergson, Hocking insists upon the connection between mysticism and action, going so far as to say that "mystic experience must complete itself in the prophetic consciousness" which seeks to control the forces of history.[14]

Though William James began to write about religion before the end of the nineteenth century, three of his most important books on the subject appeared in the present century: *The Varieties of Religious Experience* (1902), *Pragmatism* (1907), and *A Pluralistic Universe* (1909). Also, he has had his greatest influence in our time, affecting deeply the thinking not only of Pragmatists but also of Realists. Indeed, his Empiricism gave rise to several different types of empirical theology, and during the generation following the first World War it was probably the most powerful force in American religious thought.

James was the sworn foe of scientific, philosophical, and religious dogmatism. He vigorously opposed the Materialism and Agnosticism of scientists, the Absolute Idealism of philosophers, and the rigid orthodoxy of theologians. To all of these ways of thinking James opposed his "empirical theism." He did not claim that he could demonstrate the existence of God by logical argument, but sought to show that belief in Him was more satisfactory than disbelief when all the demands of man's nature are taken into account. Any philosophy must be not only internally consistent and adequate to the facts of nature but also satisfactory to the emotional and volitional side of man's nature. When both of these requirements are taken into account, Theism is more adequate than Materialism or Agnosticism. Moreover, when we are presented with a decision between two hypotheses which is

[14] *Ibid.*, 511.

"forced, living, and momentous," we have the "right to adopt a believing attitude in religious matters, in spite of the fact that our logical intellect may not have been coerced." [15]

But James does not think that belief in God is arbitrary, and in *The Varieties of Religious Experience* he marshals the positive evidence. Feeling is primary, philosophy secondary, in religion, he argues. Natural theology fails to convince by its arguments those who do not already believe; dogmatic theology sets forth "metaphysical attributes" of God such as "simplicity" which make no practical difference to us and "moral attributes" which are important but not proved; and philosophical Idealism is equally unconvincing in its dialectical arguments. James concludes from this that the role of philosophy in religion must be a modest one and that she must "abandon metaphysics and deduction for criticism and induction." [16] When he attempts at the end of his description of religious experiences to draw some general conclusions about the truth of religion, however, the results seem rather meagre, though they are important as far as they go. For example, the religious man is conscious that the "higher part" of him "is conterminous and continuous with a *more* of the same quality, which is operative in the universe outside of him." This "more," James suggests, "is on its *hither* side the subconscious side of our conscious life." Moreover, we are "continuous with a wider self," through our communion with which "work is actually done upon our finite personality, for we are turned into new men." [17] In short, "God is real since he produces real effects." [18]

Thus, religious experience gives us an awareness not only of the divine "presence" but also of the divine "action." It produces "fruits" not only in elevated feeling but also in enthusiasm and incentive for heroic moral effort. One of the most characteristic things about James' Theism is his subordination of contemplation

[15] "The Will to Believe," 1, 2.
[16] *Varieties of Religious Experience*, 445.
[17] *Ibid.*, 505, 6.
[18] *Ibid.*, 507.

and enjoyment of God to active moral effort in co-operation with Him, of security and peace in union with Him to adventurous and ceaseless struggle by His side. This is the key to James' "meliorism." While optimism asserts that the world's salvation is inevitable and pessimism that it is impossible, "meliorism" holds that it is a possibility. Moreover, it is a possibility that depends for its attainment not only upon God but also upon each of us. While the "tender-minded" seek peace and security, the "tough-minded" can find zest and incentive in the knowledge that there is real risk of loss. Moreover, though there is no assurance that evil can be wholly overcome, men do not stand alone in their struggle against it but shoulder to shoulder with their fellows and with God.[19]

The further implications of this "meliorism" were developed in *A Pluralistic Universe*. James attacked traditional Theism as too "dualistic" and "monarchical" in its conception of God as wholly transcendent and remote from man. In contrast, Absolute Idealism restores the intimacy of God with man by virtually identifying them, but its logical argument for an absolute monism is unconvincing and it cannot do justice to the reality of error and evil. In opposition to both, James argues for the pluralistic view of God as a "superhuman consciousness" which has an external environment and consequently is finite. As such, He is not foreign to us, like the God of traditional Theism or "the static timeless perfect Absolute" of Idealism. He is in time and is working out a history like ourselves.[20]

In his anti-intellectualism, moralism, meliorism, and temporalism James is perhaps the best representative of America's moral robustness and optimism in the generation before the Age of Disillusionment dawned.

After James' death, his plea that religion break its alliance with Rationalism and follow the method of Empiricism was heeded beyond his expectations. Absolute Idealism seemed to disintegrate

[19] *Pragmatism*, ch. 8.
[20] *Ibid.*, 318.

after the first World War and by 1925 there were few outstanding Idealists left. Various types of Realism took its place. The new
"Empiricism" affected deeply the philosophy of religion of the
twenties and thirties. However, it took strikingly different forms,
since it was used by advocates of both Theism and Naturalism.
In several seminaries, theology came to be regarded as, in its basis,
an "empirical science"; and in more than one department of philosophy the empirical method was used to defend religious humanism. We shall consider each of these tendencies in turn.

The most outstanding champion of an empirical theology was
D. C. Macintosh of the Yale Divinity School. In 1919 Macintosh
published his *Theology as an Empirical Science* and in 1931 he
edited and contributed a long essay to a volume entitled *Religious
Realism*. The empirical method, he argued, must become "scientific" if it is to be effective. What is to be the nature of this
"theology as an empirical science"?

First, we must start with certain "presuppositions." The most
important of these is that God, the object of this science, exists.
Macintosh insists that this is not a dogmatic procedure, because
"on the basis of knowledge of God through religious experience,
one can scientifically assume *that* God is, although he may have
as yet very little knowledge as to *what* God is." Second, we must
analyze the "empirical data" of theology in order to distinguish
the "divine elements within human experience, the qualities or
events which are to be regarded as more immediate products of
the divine activity" and hence as "revelations" of God to us. Third,
we must seek to discover "theological laws" or "generalizations
as to what the divine Being does on the fulfilment of certain dis-
coverable conditions." [21] The method of attaining these "laws,"
which are based upon the postulate of the "dependableness" of
divine activity, is to start with hypotheses about God and His
activity and then to verify these experimentally by acting upon
them and attaining an "immediate awareness" of the reality of what
was supposed in the hypothesis. To the obvious objection that the

[21] *Theology as an Empirical Science*, 26.

following of certain religious experiences upon certain conditions merely provides the content of psychological laws rather than theological laws, Macintosh replies that according to his realistic theory of knowledge the antecedent cause of the experienced effects can be surely known to be an objective divine Reality.[22]

What is the nature of a "theological law"? It is a law describing the dependable working of God under suitable conditions. The practical importance of "theological laws" is that they give us the power to predict the results of right religious adjustments and thus provide a basis for evangelism and religious education. The religious reader is likely to find little that is new or startling in the examples of "theological laws" offered by Macintosh. For example, one of the "laws of the answer to prayer" is: "On condition of the right religious adjustment with reference to desired truly moral states of the will—God the Holy Spirit produces the specific moral results desired." [23] In view of the nature of these generalizations, one wonders whether they should be called "laws" in the strict scientific sense. Are they formulated exactly enough and can they be verified by every competent observer in such a way as to satisfy the requirements of the scientific method? Are they anything more than simple descriptions of the beginning and development of the Christian life? What assurance is there that, even if the satisfactory results occur, they are caused by "God the Holy Spirit"?

Finally, Macintosh holds that, on the basis of "theological laws" like these, "theological theory" can be developed. On the principle that the Object of religious experience must be such as to account for what It (or He) does, we can infer conclusions about God's attributes and His relation to the world. For example, God is "absolute" in the pragmatic sense of "absolute satisfactoriness as Object of religious dependence, absolute sufficiency for man's religious need." It should be noticed that "theological

[22] In *The Problem of Knowledge*, Macintosh had developed his theory of knowledge, which he termed *Critical Monism*.

[23] *Theology as an Empirical Science*, 48.

theory" consists of rational inferences from religious experiences and theological laws, so that it is not exclusively empirical. As such, it can hardly be regarded as part of "theology as an empirical science," which is thus seen to be very restricted in scope. Moreover, since the basic problems of "theological theory" must be solved by rational argument, the certainty which would end conflicting opinions in theology seems as far away as ever. In view of this, Macintosh's sanguine hope that his empirical method would "separate the gold of genuine religious truth from the dross of untenable dogma" seems unfounded. Actually, his own attempt to apply the scientific method in theology resulted only in a restatement and rationalization of the essentials of evangelical Liberal Protestantism.

The empirical method has also been used to defend the "Personalistic Idealism" which was first developed in America by Borden P. Bowne. Under the influence of Lotze and others, the Personalists broke with Absolute Idealism because it seemed to deny the reality and freedom of finite persons and to conceive of God in impersonal terms. During the last generation Edgar S. Brightman of Boston University has been the most influential advocate of this point of view.

Brightman writes as a philosopher of religion rather than a theologian. Philosophy of religion, he points out, makes use of the conclusions reached by the science of religion, but its own aim is to determine the validity of religious beliefs and to investigate the relation of religion to other aspects of experience. Its method must be empirical rather than rationalistic. This means that it must make a broad survey of religious experiences, develop hypotheses to explain them, and verify these hypotheses by an appeal to experience as a whole. It is at this last point particularly that his empiricism differs from that of Macintosh, for he does not believe that any hypothesis in philosophy can be verified by the experimental method of science. Rather, the test of the truth of any hypothesis is its coherence with all other propositions and with experience as a whole. The claims of religious knowledge that come from every source must, therefore, be arbitrated by reason according to the principle of coherence. Religious experience, intuition, and revelation may all be sources of religious knowledge, but reason is "the supreme source of religious insight." [24] Brightman insists that this appeal to reason and coherence is not a "defection from the empirical method," since "to demand coherence is to demand full attention to all the facts of experience, to neglect none." [25] An important implication of this is that no religious knowledge can be absolutely certain. New experiences will constantly be emerging; and other hypotheses for the interpretation of the facts will always be possible. But, though we must be content with probability rather than certainty, we can accept a "practical absolutism" since our most coherent hypotheses at least enable us to move towards further truth.

Brightman's conception of religion is value-centered. Religion is concern about experiences of value and devotion towards the power that originates, increases, and conserves these values.[26] The primary problem of the philosophy of religion, in view of the precariousness of values, is whether the relation of the universe to man's highest values is indifferent, hostile, or friendly. Brightman's answer to this question is that of Theism: man's values have their origin in the will of God whose purpose is to realize these values and who can be trusted to conserve them. For God is a Person in the sense of a rational will which is creative and purposeful. The evidences for such a personal God include the law and order of nature, the adaptation of means to ends and the presence of a directive force in evolution, the fact that value as a personal experience must have a personal source, and the trend towards monotheism in the history of religion.

The most interesting contribution of Brightman, however, is his argument for a finite God. God, he holds, is "genuinely limited within his own nature by 'Given' experiences eternally present,

[24] *A Philosophy of Religion*, 192.
[25] *Ibid.*, 192.
[26] *Ibid.*, 17.

which his will does not create, but which his will can control, no matter how refractory they may be." [27] He was led to this theory by reflection on the problem of evil. Much, if not all, moral evil can be explained in the traditional way as due to man's freedom of will. But the fact that man was not created so as to avoid moral evil while retaining his freedom cannot be explained that way. Moreover, natural evil is due, not to man, but to God the Creator. Now, the pervasiveness of evil, if it is avoidable, is not consistent with the goodness of God. Since the goodness of God must be maintained by the Theist above all else, we must assert that nature is "the work of a power which aims at ends and achieves them, and also that this power is working under great difficulties." [28]

Brightman shrinks from the theory of Plato that the limiting factor is outside of God, on the ground that this implies a complete dualism. Rather, the limiting factor is inside God; it is "The Given," the passive element, in His nature, which He did not create and which He is ever struggling to control and overcome. This theory, he argues, is not only more in accord with the facts than the traditional one, it is also in harmony with the religious experience of co-operation with God in the struggle against evil. Since it asserts the "perfectibility" rather than the "perfection" of God, it is similar to James' "melioristic" view. But it is dubious whether "The Given" inside God is not open to the same objection of dualism as Plato's "matter" outside Him and whether it does not imply that God is only potentially rather than actually perfect goodness.[29] The appeal of the doctrine, however, is shown by the fact that similar views have been offered in W. P. Montague's *Belief Unbound* and R. A. Tsanoff's *The Nature of Evil.*

The left-wing position in the philosophy of religion is "Naturalistic Humanism," i.e., religious Humanism based upon the philosophy of Naturalism. Religious Humanists, as E. A. Burtt

[27] *The Problem of God*, 10.
[28] *Ibid.*, 331.
[29] W. H. Werkmeister, *A History of Philosophical Ideas in America*, 339-341.

has pointed out,[30] felt that Protestant Modernists had not gone far enough in meeting the demands of modern science. The development of biology, psychology, and anthropology in the nineteenth century made it appear to them that there was no evidence for a cosmic mind and purpose supporting human values and that the universe was an impersonal system ruled by natural laws. The order of nature must be taken to include all reality, since there is no scientific verification of a supernatural or transcendental Reality. Thus, the only philosophy compatible with modern science, they thought, is Naturalism. Some of these philosophers, however, recognized that religion had been a powerful factor in human life, giving meaning to the lives of individuals and directing their energies to the service of social ends. Was it possible, therefore, to reinterpret religion in such a way that it would be compatible with Naturalism and thus enable it to continue serving useful ends? The history of religion suggested the way in which this could be done, by pointing out that religion had always involved a quest for fuller life.[31] Might it not be possible to drop beliefs and rites that rested upon supernaturalism so that religion could serve the same end of fuller life more directly and efficiently?

This way of thinking affected certain theological circles rather strongly in the twenties,[32] but it did not attain an adequate philosophical expression until John Dewey published *A Common Faith* in 1934. Dewey makes a distinction between "a religion," which includes definite beliefs, practices, and institutions, and the "religious attitude," which is simply an aspect of the experience of individuals. In effect, he argues that the latter can and should be separated from the former. The "religious attitude" is devotion to ideal ends that have been constructed by the imagination out of experienced values. Devotion to these ideal ends serves to integrate the self and to direct its energies to worthy social goals.

[30] *Types of Religious Philosophy*, ch. IX.
[31] See A. E. Haydon, *The Quest of the Ages*.
[32] E.g. E. S. Ames, *Religion*.

Unlike most naturalistic Humanists, Dewey makes a place for the term "God," using it to designate "all the natural forces and conditions—including man and human association—that promote the growth of the ideal and that further its realization." [33] This idea of an "active relation between ideal and actual," says Dewey, helps to overcome the lack of "natural piety" in militant atheism. For the religious attitude "needs the sense of a connection of man, in the way of both dependence and support, with the enveloping world that the imagination feels is a universe." [34]

Perhaps it is not unfair to say that Dewey is more interested in harnessing men's religious impulses to the service of ethical and social ideals than he is in religion itself. This is suggested by his insistence that devotion to a transcendental and eternal Reality drains away men's energies from the realization of ideal ends here and now. He believes that Humanism makes it possible to avoid dualism between the "secular" and the "sacred" and to see religious significance in such "secular" activities as science and politics. His chief contribution is not his positive conception of religion, which bears little relation to the facts of religion, but his sharp criticism of otherworldly religion and its reactionary attitude towards social change.

There is no doubt that A. N. Whitehead has been one of the most important philosophers during the last half century. He has probably had a greater influence on philosophy of religion than any other philosopher except William James. Several of his most important works bearing upon religion were published after coming to Harvard from England: *Science and the Modern World* (1925), *Religion in the Making* (1926), and *Process and Reality* (1929). Part of his influence upon the philosophy of religion has been due to his classic study of the implications of modern science in the first of these books, part to his development of a metaphysical system in the grand style in the last of them. His inter-

[33] *A Common Faith*, p. 50.
[34] *Ibid.*, p. 53.

pretation of the nature of religion and of Christianity in the second of these works, though suggestive, is probably less significant.

Perhaps Whitehead's philosophy can be regarded most fruitfully as a modified and modernized form of Platonism. Plato accounts for the actual world by postulating three primary factors: an indeterminate "matter" capable of receiving forms; determinate "forms" which are eternal and universal; and a divine "soul" or "demiurge" who imposes "forms" upon "matter" and thus creates an orderly and good cosmos. Similarly, in *Religion in the Making* Whitehead asserts that the "formative elements" that constitute the character of the actual world are three: "creativity" or pure indeterminate activity; "ideal entities," "forms," or "eternal objects" which are not actual but are exemplified in everything actual; and the actual but nontemporal entity men call "God" which transmutes the indeterminate creativity into "determinate freedom." [35] The similarity to Plato's analysis is obvious, except that a dynamic factor "creativity" has taken the place of "matter." This change radically alters Plato's point of view, emphasizing the creative "process" by which novelty emerges in the actual world.

Why is it necessary to postulate God as well as creativity and ideal forms? In *Science and the Modern World* Whitehead tells us that "every actual occasion is a limitation imposed on possibility" and that "every occasion is a synthesis of all eternal objects" and of "all occasions" in a particular gradation.[36] This is made possible, on the one hand, by an "antecedent selection" of an "actual course of events which might be otherwise so far as concerns eternal possibility," [37] and, on the other hand, by an "antecedent limitation among values." [38] "God" is the name of this "principle of concretion" which determines the particular actual occasions that shall grow together (con-crescere) out of the boundless range of possibilities and the way each of them shall

[35] *Religion in the Making*, 90.
[36] *Ibid.*, 244, 5.
[37] *Ibid.*, 248.
[38] *Ibid.*, 249.

"prehend" or be related to all other actual occasions and ideal forms. It will be noted that this is essentially a form of the cosmological and teleological arguments for God. Though Whitehead does not rule out the possibility of further knowledge about God derived from "the region of particular experiences," i.e., religious experiences,[39] he seems to regard it as definitely secondary.

An interesting distinction is made between the "primordial nature" and the "consequent nature" of God. The "primordial nature" is His nature considered as the primordial limitation upon creativity which is the first condition for the definite character of the actual world. It is described as the "conceptual realization" or "envisagement" of the ideal "eternal objects" which orders or evaluates them. It is not only "evaluation," however, it is also "appetition" and this "involves the becoming of *some* temporal course of events." [40] There is an ambiguity here, since Whitehead speaks of God's "primordial nature" as an "accident" or "creature" of creativity. The distinction between creativity and God seems to be "merely a logical one," both being "complementary sides of the same thing," like the Father and the Logos in early Christian doctrine.[41]

The "consequent nature" of God, on the other hand, is the incoming of the order of "eternal objects" into the temporal course of events; it is God as immanent in the actual world. On Whitehead's view, God and the world need each other. God needs the world because His conceptual feelings become conscious in his "consequent nature"; the world needs God because He "holds the actual entities of the past as objectively immortal in the immediacy of His own nature" [42] and thus conserves the values realized in them. Thus, there is a mutual involvement of God and the world. But his view is not the pantheistic one which identifies God with the world as a whole. For there is evil in the world, and it is not grounded in God but in a lack of conformity of things with

---

[39] *Ibid.*, 250.
[40] Dorothy Emmet, *Whitehead's Philosophy of Organism*, 258.
[41] *Ibid.*, 258.
[42] *Ibid.*, 263.

His creative order. Evil is positive, since actual entities are not consistent but thwart one another. Hence, Whitehead rejects the optimistic view of Hegelian Idealism. At the same time, he holds that evil is unstable and ultimately self-destructive. There is an overcoming of evil through the development of an order that turns even evil facts to good account.

Religion is "world-loyalty." The purpose of the creative order is the attainment of value, especially aesthetic value. The process of becoming is characterized by a "subjective aim" towards satisfaction. The "subjective aim" of each individual seeks satisfaction, but when he realizes his place in the whole scheme of things and his responsibility towards it he seeks satisfaction in harmony with other individuals and the whole. Though in its primitive form religion is social, in its more developed and rational form it is primarily individual.[43] Dogmas are necessary as "clarifying modes of external expression" but "a dogma which fails to evoke any response in immediate apprehension stifles the religious life." [44] They are at best "bits of truth" which are "in effect untrue when carried over beyond the proper scope of their utility." [45]

It is difficult to determine the precise relation of Whitehead's philosophy of religion to Christian beliefs. It is clear, as we have said, that it is based upon the general character of the universe rather than upon an historical revelation. As such, it is silent with respect to Christian doctrines based upon faith in particular historical events, e.g., the Incarnation. The question, then, is whether his metaphysical conception of God and His relation to man is compatible with and can be supplemented by the Christian conception. The answer to this question will be determined partly by one's decision as to whether Whitehead's God is personal. Charles Hartshorne insists that it is. For Whitehead God is both conscious and individual, he says; He is the "personal order" of the universe, which is His body.[46] It would certainly seem that

---

[43] *Religion in the Making,* 47.
[44] *Ibid.,* 137.
[45] *Ibid.,* 145.
[46] P. A. Schilpp (ed.), *The Philosophy of Alfred North Whitehead,* 549.

an eternal actual entity that conceptually envisages and evaluates all possibilities would have to be analogous to human personality. But Whitehead does not say unambiguously that it is personal and his use of terms is so peculiar to himself that it is difficult to decide his full meaning. Certainly, his discussion of the matter in *Religion in the Making* suggests that he rejects the Christian conception of a personal and transcendent God. He argues that "religious experience does not include any direct intuition of a definite person or individual" and that reflective Indian and Chinese religious thought "disclaims the intuition of any ultimate personality substantial to the universe." [47] He adds that the "Semitic concept" of a personal God accepted by Christianity includes His absolute transcendence, whereas any proof of God that starts from the actual world leads to an immanent God.[48] Yet he approves of the stress upon the love of God in the Gospel of John and complains that the Church transformed the Gospel of love into a Gospel of fear. Does not love imply personality? Also, is not the view of God as ordering the world and transmuting its evil more compatible with a personal than an impersonal God? Yet he does not explicitly attribute personal character to God, perhaps because he wrongly assumes that it implies the complete transcendence of God and leads to a dualistic world view.

Whatever may be said about his conception of God, Whitehead's view of religion is inadequate from the Christian point of view. In his view, religion is largely individual and the indispensableness of the religious community is completely neglected. Moreover, it is based upon a conception of the meaning of the world that is more aesthetic than moral. As Kant "saw the necessity for God in the moral order," he says, his own metaphysics "finds the foundations of the world in the aesthetic experience." [49] Though "aesthetic experience" is a far broader term with him than it usually is, it stresses *feeling* rather than purposive *activity* as pri-

[47] *Religion in the Making*, 61, 62.
[48] *Ibid.*, 71.
[49] *Ibid.*, 104, 5.

mary, and religion as moral obedience to the will of a righteous God falls into the background or out of the picture altogether.

The great influence of Whitehead during the last twenty-five years is illustrated by the "Theistic Naturalism" of H. N. Wieman of the University of Chicago Divinity School. Wieman rejected the Naturalistic Humanism of Dewey and others because it minimized or overlooked the dependence of man for his values upon a cosmic principle and not merely upon his own efforts. At the same time, he was convinced that in the interest of truth a more radical reconstruction of traditional Theism was necessary than philosophical Idealists and theological Liberals had been willing to make. Therefore, he attempted to make a synthesis of Theism with the "higher" Naturalism which had been emerging in Whitehead and other thinkers.

In *The Wrestle of Religion with Truth*, published in 1927, he argued that true religion must be based upon a knowledge of and adaptation to reality, upon which man depends for his values. But most religion has been indifferent to truth and has even blinded itself with illusions in order to provide man with "a fairy realm where all is beautiful and happy." [50] Therefore, it is necessary to distinguish between the beliefs and practices of ordinary religion and the basic religious concepts implied in them. The popular *belief* about God in the churches is that He is "someone who will take care of you" i.e., it is an illusion due to wishful thinking. But the *concept* of God is quite different. "God is that character of events to which man must adjust himself in order to attain the highest goods and avoid the greatest evils." [51] Though we do not know fully the nature of this "behavior of the universe," we can discover more about it by living experimentally and observing carefully the results.

In his latest book, *The Source of Human Good*, published in 1946, Wieman develops further his "Theistic Naturalism" and

[50] *The Wrestle of Religion with Truth*, 2.
[51] *Ibid.*, 14.

shows its implications for the theory of value and for Christian doctrine. The "newer naturalism" differs from the older "reductive materialism," he asserts, in holding that "there is nothing in reality accessible to the human mind more basic than events and their qualities and relations." [52] This view is in accord with the Jewish-Christian tradition which "declares that the sovereign good works creatively in history" but it ignores "the transcendental affirmation in the Jewish-Christian tradition of a creative God who not only works in history but resides beyond history." [53] "The only creative God we recognize," says Wieman, "is the creative event itself." [54] As if to emphasize the naturalistic meaning of this assertion he adds that "the form of the creative event itself at our higher levels of existence is determined by the creative process at more elementary levels." [55] Thus, he denies completely every "transcendental reality." Significantly, he now rejects Whitehead's "identification" of God with "an inactive primordial order" and asserts that "the order or structure of the creative event is not imposed upon it but is intrinsic to the very nature of such an event." [56]

Wieman makes a sharp distinction between "created good," which is defined as "qualitative meaning," and "creative good," which is the source of qualitative meaning and which yields the best possible by transforming the mind and the world. God is this "source of human good." Man can do much to provide the conditions that release the full power of the "creative event," giving himself to its service above all "created goods," but he cannot do its work. He is always being tempted to make some "created good" an object of the absolute loyalty that should be given to its source, "creative good," as in modern nationalism or industrialism. "Creative good" is absolute in the sense that its goodness is not relative to human desire, its demands are unlimited, its

[52] *The Source of Human Good*, 6.
[53] *Ibid.*, 7.
[54] *Ibid.*, 7.
[55] *Ibid.*, 7, 8.
[56] *Ibid.*, 193.

worth is incommensurable with created good, and it is entirely trustworthy.[57] The religious life, on this view, consists in yielding to the process of creativity at work in each situation so that one's awareness of meanings is enlarged and unified and one's sense of community with other persons is deepened in a neverending process.

In *The Source of Human Good* Wieman attempts to do justice to Christian doctrines, but he radically transforms them in the process. He attacks as "religious obstructionists" Christian thinkers who hold that God "transcends reason and cannot be observed" and that He transcends time. He rejects the Christian belief in the personal nature of God. He holds that the Christian faith began not with Jesus as such but with the domination of the "creative event" over the lives of his disciples under his influence. Since men need salvation in the sense of emancipation from idolatry of "created good" or human purpose, there is truth in the Christian idea that faith arises from despair of human effort. The "grace of God" is the "creative transformation become dominant in the life of man." [58] It is only in history, not eternity, that man's fulfillment must come. "History is the supreme achievement of the creative event," says Wieman.[59] "Whoever in despair appeals beyond history betrays the holy cause for which we fight, for here in time it must be lost or won." [60]

It seems obvious that, whatever may be said about the "religious availability" of Whitehead's God, Wieman's conception of God as the wholly immanent, impersonal, "creative event" that is the "source of human good" is not, from the Christian point of view, religiously adequate. However, it is greatly superior to the purely humanistic conception of Dewey and other Naturalists, because it springs from an understanding of the fact that man cannot save himself but must be saved by a cosmic creative principle. In addition, there is much insight in *The Source of*

[57] *Ibid.*, 79–81.
[58] *Ibid.*, 49.
[59] *Ibid.*, 307.
[60] *Ibid.*, 309.

Human Good about the spiritual life and the conditions of its growth. However, it is impossible to reconcile Christian Theism with philosophical Naturalism without doing violence to both, and it is significant that his attempt to synthesize them has satisfied comparatively few supporters of either point of view.

Whitehead's influence upon Charles Hartshorne of the Department of Philosophy at the University of Chicago has also been strong. But the results have been quite different. Hartshorne thinks that the new philosophy represented by Whitehead provides a better philosophical framework for theology than the Aristotelianism of St. Thomas Aquinas. In three books, *Beyond Humanism*, published in 1937, *Man's Vision of God*, published in 1941, and *The Divine Relativity*, published in 1948, he seeks to develop a theistic conception of God and His relation to the world which will be adequate to express the fundamental religious insight that God is love. Thus, while he does not appeal to revelation, he regards his conception as in harmony with Christianity and reserves his attacks for what he regards as the Aristotelian perversion of it by Aquinas.

The method he employs differs from the empiricism that has been so popular in recent American thinking about religion. The inductive method alone, he thinks, is not adequate in metaphysics. How, for example, could necessary being be dealt with by observation of and generalization from contingent beings? What is needed is a synthesis of the empirical and the rational or a priori methods. Therefore, much of Hartshorne's work consists of analysis of theological concepts such as "absolute," "perfection," and "power," undertaken in the hope of contributing to the philosophy of religion "logical rigor." On the other hand, he is not a rationalist in the traditional sense, because he holds that we must never deny any fundamental aspect of experience.

One of the main problems dealt with by Hartshorne is that of the perfection of God. In *Man's Vision of God* he points out that Anselm's definition of a "perfect being" as "that than which none greater can be conceived" has usually been taken to imply "absolute perfection in all respects." But there are other possible interpretations, the most important being that which attributes to God "absolute perfection in some respects, relative perfection in others." Hartshorne holds that this is a more adequate interpretation than the traditional one of Anselm. The traditional one regards God as immutable in all respects; but if He cannot change in any respect there can be no time and no possibility of decrease or increase in value for Him in relation to the world. Again, the traditional view implies omniscient or perfect knowledge in all respects; but this is logically hard to reconcile with the contingency of future events such as acts of free will. Further, the traditional view implies that God possesses perfect power or is omnipotent; but "even the greatest possible power (and that by definition is 'perfect' power) over individuals cannot leave them powerless, and hence even perfect power must leave something to others to decide." [61] "In their ultimate individuality," says Hartshorne, "things can only be influenced, they cannot be coerced." [62]

The traditional view of God's perfection as implying immutability, omniscience, and omnipotence is really based upon the Aristotelian conception of Him as transcendent to and unaffected by the world. To this conception Hartshorne opposes Whitehead's view that "all-existence is social" and that God as the highest and all-inclusive being is "social." Far from being "impassible," He feels all the joys and sorrows of all His creatures. In *The Divine Relativity* Hartshorne also attacks the Thomistic doctrine that God's relation to the world is not a "real" relation to Him and that He is "absolute" in the sense of "independent" of His creatures. God says Hartshorne, is "absolute" in one aspect of His being but "relative" in the sense of related to and affected by everything in the world. He is characterized by a "sympathetic dependence" on the world, His sympathy being "exactly colored by every nuance of joy or sorrow anywhere in

[61] *Man's Vision of God*, 14.
[62] *Ibid.*, xvi.

the world." [63] Moreover, God's glory is not so absolute that we cannot contribute to His greatness or value. God is not only the "supreme source" but also the "supreme beneficiary or recipient" of all achievement.

This "social" doctrine of God seems to verge on a pantheistic identification of God with the world, but Hartshorne insists that God is personal and that His essence does not require the actual totality of things. However, since God is relative to all, He has nothing outside Himself. Therefore, Hartshorne asserts the doctrine of "panentheism," "the view that deity is in some real aspect [64] distinguishable from and independent of any and all relative items, and yet, taken as an actual whole, includes all items." [65]

Whatever may be thought of Hartshorne's ideas, they show the fruitfulness of Whitehead's metaphysics when it is used for the purposes of a Theism that is fundamentally Christian.

As one reflects upon these different types of American religious thought, the first thing that strikes him is the tendency to interpret religion as primarily an *individual* rather than a social thing. Lacking a vivid sense of the power of religious institutions to awaken and deepen the religion of individuals and estranged by the rigidity and narrowness of many Protestant churches, many American philosophers have preferred to sit loose to the Church, its corporate worship and its traditional creeds. In his *Varieties of Religious Experience* at the beginning of the century, James admitted his lack of interest in the social forms of religious experience. He was influenced by his interest in extreme rather than ordinary cases of religion but also by his individualistic idea that the religion of average churchgoers is second-hand and conventional. Though Royce stressed the "beloved community," as we saw, it was distinguished by him from all visible, actual churches as an ideal community which was still to be created by the loyalty

---

[63] *The Divine Relativity*, 48.
[64] That is, in its absolute aspect.
[65] *The Divine Relativity*, 90.

of men. Whitehead gave the most striking expression to the
individualistic view of religion when he said that "religion is what
a man does with his solitariness," and Wieman's thought has always
shown more of a negative than a positive relation to the Church.
As a result, many recent American philosophers of religion in
their thinking have seemed remote from and irrelevant to the religious life of the Church and have written mainly for a minority
of intellectuals on the fringe or outside of it. Among the most
outstanding exceptions have been Hocking, Macintosh, Brightman, and Pratt.

In the second place, the philosophy of religion has usually been
conceived during the last half-century as *impartial* between the
conflicting claims of historical faiths, examining religious phenomena provided by the history and psychology of religion in
an objective fashion and maintaining a complete independence of
special revelation. This has enabled the philosophy of religion to
take account of varieties of religious experience and belief little
known to the ordinary churchgoer and in this way to broaden the
popular conception of religion. Several philosophers have made
substantial contributions of their own to the history and psychology of religion, e.g., James, Hocking, and J. B. Pratt.[66] One
of the beneficial effects of this enlargement of the religious horizon
is the growing realization of the virtual universality of religion.
Many have come to see that the most convincing ground for belief in God is the actual experience of Him, though the diversity
of religious beliefs held by men in history may make it more
difficult to reach complete agreement as to the right interpretation of the religious experience.

But this "neutrality" of the philosophy of religion has tended
to weaken its interest in and contact with Christian theology and
philosophy. In the case of many, philosophy of religion has become an enemy rather than an ally of the special revelation and

[66] Pratt's *The Religious Consciousness* is still one of the best books on
psychology of religion and *The Pilgrimage of Buddhism* is perhaps the most
interesting book in English on the development of Buddhism.

doctrines of Christianity. Consequently, it has weakened Christian theology and philosophy by depriving them of the sympathetic but critical thinking of some of the ablest minds of the last generation. It is significant that Royce's *The Problem of Christianity* in 1913 was the last careful attempt of an outstanding philosopher in America to make a philosophical examination of Christianity as a whole. Also, by detaching itself from the Christian revelation and theology, American philosophy has more and more impoverished itself. Attracting the interest of almost all outstanding American philosophers until the first World War, religion has lost its appeal to most philosophers of our generation. Some of the most distinguished philosophers of today, especially Naturalists and Logical Positivists, have paid no attention whatever to it. Moreover, as interest in the problems of religion has declined, concern for the closely related problems of metaphysics has languished and the problems of logic, epistemology, semantics, and social philosophy have taken their place.

In the third place, the philosophy of religion of the last half century has been fundamentally *anthropocentric* rather than theocentric. J. B. Pratt has pointed out in his posthumous book, *Eternal Values in Religion*, that Protestant worship tends to be primarily "subjective" rather than "objective," aiming at beneficial results in the life of the worshipper rather than the glory of God. Similarly, Protestant philosophers of religion have been concerned above all with "the meaning of God in human experience," "religious values," and "the source of human good." Their thinking has been value-centered rather than God-centered. In an essay in the volume *Religious Realism*, Richard Niebuhr pointed out that the religious Realism which had followed the collapse of Idealism, though it stressed the knowledge of God as an objective reality, was itself infected with the spirit of subjectivism and humanism. "Hence it tends," he said, "to define religion in terms of adjustment to divine reality for the sake of gaining power rather than in terms of revelation which subjects the recipient to the criticism of that which is revealed," with the result that "man remains the center of religion and God is his aid rather than his judge and redeemer." [67] Doubtless, this has been due partly to preoccupation with the new philosophy of value but it has also resulted from the complete substitution of general religious experience for the special revelation of historical religion as the source of religious knowledge. It has encouraged the idea that religion is oriented towards God primarily because He is the source and conserver of human good. The Naturalistic Humanism of Dewey simply carried anthropocentric religion to the extreme when it insisted that religion should substitute devotion to ideal human ends for faith in God.

Because of these weaknesses of individualism, neutrality, and anthropocentrism, the theological seminaries have tended to neglect philosophy of religion during the last fifteen years. Absorbed with the theological struggle between Liberalism and Neo-Orthodoxy, the keenest minds in the seminaries have depreciated the philosophical approach to religion. The fact that the indifference of most philosophers to religion has been met by the hostility of many theologians to philosophy is one of the most striking signs of the cleavage between reason and faith in our day.

In this situation two things are needed. One is a recognition by *philosophers* that the neutral, objective approach of *philosophy of religion* to the problems of religion, though useful, is limited in its sphere and function. It can broaden men's knowledge of religion and help them to see its place in experience as a whole, but it cannot take the place of commitment to a definite faith without impoverishing the religious life. Therefore, philosophers who have a strong Christian faith cannot and should not pretend that they are neutral, starting their investigation of religion without presuppositions. They should start with their faith and seek to develop its implications in a *Christian philosophy*. They have every right to do so because God has given them faith to illuminate their reason and reason to understand their faith and to interpret the

[67] *Religious Realism*, D. C. Macintosh (ed.), 425, 6.

world in the light of it. In the process of doing this, they should be ready to use philosophical insights from any source whatever but with a clear realization that any philosophy such as Absolute Idealism or Naturalism whose presuppositions and categories are unchristian must be used only in a very guarded way.

The other thing that is needed is that *theologians* should become more rather than less philosophical in order that they may perform the task of *Christian apologetics* more effectively, especially among philosophers who are contemptuous of religion in general and Christianity in particular. The philosophy of religion of the last fifty years has been living off religious capital accumulated by Christians in the past. As that capital has become exhausted, philosophy of religion has become impoverished and has almost lost its influence. Philosophy of religion will flourish again in America only as a revitalized Christian community produces more Christians and encourages them to become Christian philosophers or Christian philosophical theologians. For deep interest in religion in *general* springs from a religious experience which is *particular*.

BIBLIOGRAPHY

Boodin, J. E., *God* (New York, 1934)

Bowne, Borden P., *Personalism* (Boston, 1908)

Brightman, E. S., *The Problem of God* (New York, 1930)

Dewey, John, *A Common Faith* (New Haven, 1934)

Hartshorne, Charles, *Man's Vision of God* (Chicago, 1941)

Hocking, W. E., *The Meaning of God in Religious Experience* (New Haven, 1912)

James, William, *The Varieties of Religious Experience* (New York, 1902)

Lyman, E. W., *The Meaning and Truth of Religion* (New York, 1933)

Macintosh, D. C. (editor), *Religious Realism* (New York, 1931)

Royce, J., *The Problem of Christianity*, Vols. I, II (New York, 1913)

Whitehead, A. N., *Religion in the Making* (New York, 1926)

Wieman, H. N., *The Source of Human Good* (Chicago, 1947)

SYSTEMATIC THEOLOGY

Walter M. Horton

WALTER MARSHALL HORTON was born in 1895 in Massachusetts. After taking his A.B. at Harvard in 1917 and his theological work at Union Theological Seminary, he studied in Paris, Strasbourg and Marburg, taking his doctorate at Columbia University in 1926. After serving as instructor in Philosophy of Religion and Systematic Theology at Union for three years, he became *Fairchild* Professor of Theology in Oberlin Graduate School of Theology in 1925. He has been actively engaged both in travel and study for the ecumenical movement, serving as consultant at the Oxford, Madras, and Amsterdam World Conferences. He was also attached to the Study Department of the World Council of Churches at its central office in Geneva, Switzerland, during the year 1947. He has traveled extensively in India, China, Japan, Australasia, South America, and Europe, and he is the author of many important books both in systematic theology and the relevance of Christianity to contemporary culture. His latest volume is *Toward a Reborn Church*.

V

SYSTEMATIC Theology in America has gone through three main periods in the last half-century: (1) a period of growing *liberalism*, roughly from 1900 to 1920; (2) a period of sharp controversy and revolutionary realignment, between 1920 and 1935; (3) a period of constructive restatement, since 1935.

1. *Liberalism, 1900–1920*

To understand the American theological situation in the early years of the twentieth century, it is necessary to remember that *Calvinism modified by the influence of revivalism* was the leading tradition in American Protestantism; that the New England Theology, uniting Calvinism and revivalism in a rationally coherent and defensible system, had lingered on in many theological schools until late in the nineteenth century, when it suddenly and completely went to pieces; that the idealistic liberalism of Horace Bushnell and his successors, dating from the middle of the nineteenth century, had proved able to cope with the new problems posed by natural science, Biblical criticism and the new social conscience, as the New England Theology was unable to do; finally, that while conservative Calvinism survived in a pretty vigorous form at Princeton Theological Seminary and elsewhere, it was consciously on the defensive. The prevailing trend in theology continued to get more and more liberal until shortly after the close of the First World War. Conservative theologians felt themselves to be in a state of siege, with insurgent bands of liberals rising up and marching against them from every quarter. Let us examine this situation more in detail.

Of the historic types of Protestantism, there can be no doubt which has done most to shape theological thought in America: *Calvinism.* Anglicanism and Lutheranism have been relatively small minority movements, the one long associated with the

British Crown—hardly a recommendation after the Revolution!—while the other was largely confined to German and Scandinavian immigrant groups, isolated from other Protestants by barriers of language and culture.[1] The American tradition is thus mainly conditioned by the two remaining forms of original Protestantism: the Calvinist and the Anabaptist or sectarian. No other country has been so deeply affected by radical sectarianism; but *Calvinism is the traditional theology of many sectarian bodies*. The *Westminster Confession* was formally accepted by Congregationalists as well as by Presbyterians, while the Calvinistic Baptists have generally outnumbered their theological rivals in that most numerous of all American denominations. Wherever American theology remains conservative, the outlines of the Calvinistic system can clearly be descried. This is true of the two conservative textbooks of systematic theology which were most influential in the opening years of this century, and are still widely used: *Outlines of Theology* by A. A. Hodge of Princeton (Presbyterian) and *Systematic Theology* [2] by A. H. Strong of Rochester (Baptist).

By 1900, the Calvinistic tradition in American theology was already seriously impaired. The New England Theology of Jonathan Edwards and his school had given Calvinism new vigor and new relevance by infusing into it the spirit of the Great Awakening and making it the favorite vehicle of revivalistic preaching. If in the hands of the later Edwardians the position tended to gravitate from Calvinism toward Arminianism, that made possible a friendly alliance between these "New School" Calvinists and the Methodist Arminians who were their principal partners in the evangelization of the western frontier. So long as the winning of the West was Protestantism's main concern, this Calvinist-Arminian alliance held firm. But with the passing of the

[1] *The Resurgence of the Gospel,* by T. A. Kantonen (Philadelphia, 1948), may be taken as evidence that Lutheran thought is now entering the main stream of American theology, and will make important contributions henceforth. The immense influence of Archbishop Temple's theology in recent years is the best proof that the same can now be said of Anglican thought.

[2] Conveniently streamlined in his *Outlines of Systematic Theology*, New York, 1908.

frontier and the rise of grave intellectual problems concerning the authority of the Bible and the implications of Darwinian evolution, it became evident that New England evangelical Calvinism was played out. F. H. Foster remarks that in 1880 the chairs of theology at all the Congregational and some of the Presbyterian seminaries were occupied by adherents of the New England school, and fifteen years later every one had been filled by some one of an entirely different temper. "As it were, in a night," he says, the New England Theology "perished from off the face of the earth" [3]—a most serious break in our one strong link with the Protestant Reformation. If Calvinism survived this break, as it did at Princeton and other conservative schools, it was no longer the aggressive, forward-looking Calvinism of Edwards and Finney, but a defensive, armor-clad system, beset with "fightings and fears, within, without."

What replaced Calvinism in the early twentieth century as the leading American theological tradition was a liberal theology derived from German philosophical idealism—Kant, Schleiermacher, Hegel, Ritschl, Lotze, Troeltsch. In Germany, the idealistic movement was strongly polarized into opposite trends: a mystical, metaphysical trend leaning toward pantheism (Schleiermacher, Hegel, Lotze) and an ethical, social trend leaning toward positivism or humanism (Kant, Ritschl, Troeltsch). In America, as in England, both of these extreme antithetical trends were strongly resisted, by philosophers and theologians alike. At the very beginning of the liberal movement, there were philosophers like Emerson and theologians like Parker, who followed the mystical-metaphysical trend to the verge of pantheism. At the very end, there were philosophers like Dewey and theologians like G. B. Smith and Shailer Mathews who followed the ethical-social trend to the verge of humanism. But far more typical were evangelical liberals such as Bushnell, Bowne, George A. Gordon, Henry Churchill King, William Newton Clarke, William Adams

[3] F. H. Foster, *History of the New England Theology*, p. 543 (Chicago, 1907).

Brown, and Walter Rauschenbusch, who felt the influence of both opposing trends in German thought, and held a fair balance between them. Of all the German idealists, the most generally influential in the early twentieth century were Schleiermacher (his appeal to Christian experience, not his pantheism), Lotze (interpreted as a personal theist by Bowne, King and many others), and Ritschl (whose ethical theism became a principal source of the Social Gospel Movement).

It would be a mistake to suppose that American liberal theology was simply German idealistic philosophy in an American dress. William DeWitt Hyde did, it is true, remark that "metaphysics must be the Alpha, and ethics the Omega, of any theology which is rooted in reason and fruitful in life"; [4] and there was a marked tendency throughout the liberal period for philosophy of religion to get more attention and enjoy more prestige than systematic theology. Yet the two most influential textbooks of liberal theology, Clarke's *Outline* (1898) and Brown's (1906) were Biblical in substance and evangelical in spirit. Clarke went through a long personal struggle to overcome verbal literalism in his use of the Bible, [5] and at length came to the conclusion that systematic theology had a right to seek its sources "anywhere"; [6] but *the Bible centered in Christ* actually remained his principal source, with *evangelical Christian experience* as an almost equally important source. Brown, who at first used Clarke's *Outline* in his teaching, finally decided it needed rewriting because it "included almost no historical material" and "omitted the Church altogether." [7] In Brown's revised version, the Clarke-Brown system contained many of the original definitions slightly modified (as Ritschl often quotes and alters Schleiermacher's definitions) but

---

[4] *Outlines of Social Theology* (New York, 1895), Preface. Examination of the book reveals that all its contents can be deduced from the Hegelian-Lotzean conception of an Absolute Mind or Supreme Person manifested in the world, the self, and the social order.

[5] See his *Sixty Years with the Bible* (New York, 1909); cf. *The Use of the Scriptures in Theology* (1905).

[6] *Outline of Christian Theology*, p. 10.

[7] Brown, *A Teacher and His Times*, p. 109 (New York, 1940).

the whole effect was much more traditional and churchly, expressing Brown's life-long conviction that "underneath all differences of theological expression, there is a common gospel which makes the Church, in fact, one." [8] Brown was a "critical idealist" in philosophy, but his systematic theology was no mere deduction from idealism; it sprang from a conception of the "common Gospel" which had deep historical roots and wide ecumenical sympathies.

Clarke and Brown have had no real successors as systematic liberal theologians. Dr. A. C. Knudson's two volumes on *The Doctrine of God* (1930) and *The Doctrine of Redemption* (1933) together constitute a system, unmistakably liberal, based on Bowne's personalistic philosophy fused with Biblical concepts and evangelical convictions. But these two volumes have never achieved anything like the wide currency of Clarke and Brown; and they came too late, when liberalism was already on the defensive against neo-orthodoxy. During the period of liberal ascendency, theological books were mostly "programmistic" rather than systematic, developing special points of view and proposing specific theological reforms. The most comprehensive of these programs of theological reform was that proposed in Henry Churchill King's *Reconstruction in Theology* (1901). King summarized the new influences shaping theology at the turn of the century in a way that won wide assent: evolutionary natural science, Biblical criticism, and the new ethical-social conscience, with its dual emphasis on the sacredness of the person and his social responsibility. The battle over the first two of these influences had already been fought and won, as is evident from the calmness and maturity of King's treatment of these topics; in the third, he knew he was pioneering. Throughout the first two decades of this century, the new social conscience expressed in the Social Gospel Movement was the most active formative force in liberal theology. Landmarks in this development were King's *Theology and the Social Consciousness* (1902), Gerald Birney

[8] *Ibid.*

Smith's *Social Idealism and the Changing Theology* (Taylor Lectures for 1912) and finally Rauschenbusch's *Theology for the Social Gospel* (1918).

The Social Gospel, with its hope of Christianizing the social order and building the Kingdom of God on earth, was the main positive message of American liberalism at its height, before and during the First World War. In Rauschenbusch himself, and in many others, it was combined with a message of personal redemption [9] derived from evangelical Protestantism; in some of the more radical members of the school, particularly those influenced by Chicago pragmatism, it tended to displace both evangelical religion and idealistic metaphysics, preparing a purely humanistic interpretation of Christianity. Between the continuing Calvinists, the idealistic liberals, and these radical humanitarians, there were deep theological chasms. How matters stood between theological conservatives, liberals and radicals at this period may fairly be judged from a symposium on "The Task and Method of Systematic Theology" in the *American Journal of Theology*, Vol. XIV (1910), in which Warfield of Princeton, Brown of Union and G. B. Smith of Chicago represented the three parties.

Warfield defines the task of systematic theology as the systematic formulation of the results of exegetical theology, which gives us perfect knowledge of God (*i.e.*, God's own verbally documented self-revelation) in its *disjecta membra*, needing only to be logically ordered. Brown distinguishes three main tasks: to define and expound the Christian religion, to establish its supreme value, and to rise through the appreciation of its value to belief and trust in the divine Cause and Source of that value—the third being a task which Ritschl and the pragmatists seek to avoid, but which Brown thinks inescapable. G. B. Smith, in terms reminiscent of Troeltsch, defines theology's task as the confrontation of our historic religious heritage with present religious needs, in such a way as to suggest convictions that are pragmatically efficient

---

[9] See *Theology for the Social Gospel*, Chap. X, "The Social Gospel and Personal Salvation."

and apologetically defensible. Such convictions are frankly relativistic, can claim no divine authority, and are not guaranteed to be
Christian; but if Christianity can continue to meet modern needs
out of its historic traditions, it will survive. It is evident that
Warfield's and Smith's conceptions of theology were poles apart,
and controversy between them was bound to break out; but between Brown's constructive idealism and Smith's relativistic pragmatism there was also deep tension. Liberalism was not inwardly
self-consistent, and might easily become disunited—as in fact it
did, between 1920 and 1935.

II. Controversy and Realignment, 1920–1935

We have set 1920, not 1914, as the end of the supremacy of
idealistic liberalism, and the opening of a new period of theological
controversy and theological realignment. The spirit of idealism, of
liberalism, of social optimism, was very marked in America during the fighting of the First World War. It was afterward, when
the liberal aims for which the war was allegedly fought were
rudely frustrated, that reaction set in, and a series of controversies
began which eventually proved fatal to liberal theology in its
earlier form.

The first of these was the *fundamentalist* controversy (1920–
1925). Fundamentalism as a widespread movement dates back to
1910, when interdenominational conferences began to be held
and booklets on *The Fundamentals* began to be issued. But it was
soon after the First World War that the fundamentalists took
the offensive, and began to challenge "modernists" as wolves in
sheep's clothing, who must not be allowed to get into the Christian
fold. Candidates for ordination in the Presbyterian, Baptist, and
other denominations were certain in those years to be asked
whether they believed in the verbal inerrancy of the Scriptures,
the Virgin Birth and bodily resurrection of Christ, the blood
atonement, and all other distinctly supernatural elements in Christian teaching. Attempts were made to get whole denominations
to subscribe to the new list of Fundamentals, and anti-evolution

bills were passed and enforced in several states. Many candidates were refused ordination, and many liberal preachers (notably Dr. Harry Emerson Fosdick) were made the objects of violent "smear" attacks; but no major denomination accepted the fundamentalist creed, and the Bryan-Darrow debate over evolution at Dayton, Tennessee (1925), tended to discredit fundamentalism and put an end to its aggressive influence.

There were discerning critiques of liberalism in some of the fundamentalist writings, which ought to have been taken to heart by the liberals. Machen in his *Christianity and Liberalism* (1923) vigorously protested against the defective sense of sin and the excessive optimism of most liberal theology. E. Y. Mullins in his *Christianity at the Crossroads* (1924) pointed out the tendency of liberal theology to "reduce" the unique, supernatural elements in Christianity—the divinely revealed Scriptures, the unique and heaven-sent Savior—by including them in a rational scheme with other sacred books and other religious leaders. The *reductio ad absurdum* of this reductive trend would be materialism, which reduces the spiritual to the biological, and the biological to the physico-chemical.[10] To all these warnings, the liberals turned a deaf ear, because these true contentions were mixed with exaggerated charges, plainly untrue, and because the attack upon evolution seemed to prove that the whole fundamentalist movement was "pre-scientific" and "obscurantist" in its outlook. It was only when the humanists attacked the liberals from the opposite quarter, charging them with timidity and half-heartedness in carrying out their own logic, that the liberals were able to feel the force of some objections already made by the fundamentalists.

To understand the *humanist* controversy (1925–1930), consider its economic and social background. Until the Wall Street crash started the depression in 1929, Americans enjoyed a period of unparalleled prosperity and social optimism. It seemed to many

---

[10] It is a question whether Mullins should be called a fundamentalist. His theological system, *The Christian Religion in Its Doctrinal Expression* (New York, 1917), might be described as "modern-positive," like the writings of P. T. Forsyth.

that science, technology and industrialism had at last solved the problem of human welfare, without the aid of any supernatural force whatsoever. If religion was to survive in this new age of ever-expanding prosperity, it was argued that it should drop all supernaturalistic terms, all words like "salvation," redolent of a "pain economy" now happily superseded by a "pleasure economy," and redefine its function positively, humanistically, as "the shared quest of the good life." [11] Instead of trying to reconcile ancient scriptures with modern knowledge in some illogical liberal compromise, religion should boldly and unreservedly put its trust in modern science and modern social idealism, as all-sufficient guides to faith and morals. All this was said with sublime confidence, just when our ephemeral prosperity began to crack beneath our feet, and the abyss of cosmic tragedy began to open up, just two steps ahead! [12] Faced by this startling contradiction between the claims of humanism and the actual course of events, liberals as a group stoutly refused to exchange God for man as their final object of trust, or to abandon the Bible for science as their final source of guidance. In attacking the pretensions of humanism, they recoiled from scientism to the very verge of accepting Biblical revelation; and rejected man-worship so decisively that God's sovereignty loomed up commandingly in their theology. Whatever led toward humanism in their previous thinking, they now heartily repudiated. [13]

In the early years of the great economic depression (1930–1935), many books sharply critical of liberalism and newly appreciative of European neo-orthodoxy began to appear: Walter Lowrie's *Our Concern with the Theology of Crisis* (1932), Edwin

[11] Cf. A. E. Haydon, *The Quest of the Ages* (New York, 1929); cf. C. F. Potter, *Humanism: a New Religion* (New York, 1930).

[12] Cf. Beard's Symposium, *Whither Mankind?* (New York, 1928) with its amazing confidence that our civilization, at last, had found the formula for everlasting expansion.

[13] The reasons for this shift are best stated in Harry Emerson Fosdick's sermon, "Beyond Modernism" (*Christian Century*, 1935). "The watchword will not be, Accommodate yourself to the prevailing culture! but, Stand out from it and challenge it!—we cannot harmonize Christ himself with modern culture."

Lewis's *Christian Manifesto* (1934) and G. W. Richard's *Beyond Fundamentalism and Modernism* (1934). The names of Barth and Brunner, regarded with indifference heretofore, became names to conjure with. Few indeed became their full followers; but their criticisms of liberal theology were widely acknowledged to be sound, and their renewed emphasis upon scriptural revelation and divine sovereignty found favor in many minds. Some preferred the moderate British way of going orthodox (Forsyth, Oman, Temple) to the violent Continental way. Some were influenced by the neo-Thomism of Maritain or the revised Eastern Orthodoxy of Bulgakov and Berdyaev. Piper of Princeton and Tillich of Union, exiled allies and critics of Barth and Brunner, won a considerable following through their continued residence and teaching in this country. But most important of all the influences that turned us about during these five crucial years was no voice from overseas, but a prophetic voice in our midst: that of Reinhold Niebuhr. His *Moral Man and Immoral Society* (New York, 1932) played the same part in America which Barth's *Römerbrief* played on the Continent and Dean Inge's criticism of the idea of Progress played in Britain; it showed that the hope of a Kingdom of God on earth was not immediately realizable by human efforts.

The recoil from humanism did not lead at once to a new constructive effort in theology, but only to a realignment of theological forces, and a general willingness to move in new directions, if a promising lead should be given. By "realignment" we mean the formation of a strong central bloc, opposed to humanism on the left and fundamentalism on the right, in which repentant liberals and moderate conservatives were temporarily united. The slogan under which this variegated host began to rally was *"Realism"*— a broad term covering a multitude of differences, some of them irreconcilable, but still indicating a general orientation. Negatively, the term indicated a sharp decline in the prestige of *idealism*, which had formed the philosophical basis of liberal theology since the time of Bushnell. Personal idealism of the Bowne tradition did retain its vigor, but its ablest representative, E. S. Brightman of

Boston University, took the element of evil in the cosmic process with new seriousness, in his doctrine of "The Given." [14] Evil, matter, "irreducible and stubborn facts" of all kinds, tended to be more emphasized than ideas and ideals. Positively, realism pointed out beyond the self and its subjectivity, beyond humanity and its hopes, beyond the changing processes of nature, to some deep objective Ground of faith and hope, too deep to be shaken by the earthquakes that shatter the dreams of idealists.[15]

How to reach this Ground? By faith in Biblical revelation, said the followers of Barth and Brunner. By mystical intuition, rationally tested, said Rufus Jones and Eugene Lyman. By scientific screening of religious experience, said Macintosh of Yale and Wieman of Chicago, so as to isolate the divine "Dependable Factor" from all subjective and relative factors, and learn the objective conditions upon which human good and human redemption really hang. All these varieties of realism, and more, were included in the Macintosh symposium on *Religious Realism* (1931), the best source-book for the realistic movement in its early phases. It was Professor Macintosh's hope, when the book was published, that these various methods of escape from subjectivism and anthropocentrism might be held together in a sort of three-story theology, beginning on the ground floor with strict scientific theism, such as he had outlined in *Theology as an Empirical Science* (1919), and working up to rational faith and speculative surmise on the upper floors. This hope was frustrated shortly afterward, when Wieman, in a three-cornered debate [16] with Macintosh and Max Otto, a humanist, flatly refused to use any method but scientific empiricism; while those who felt the influence of Barth and

[14] *The Problem of God* (New York, 1930); *The Finding of God* (New York, 1931).

[15] *Cf.* the analysis of the various meanings of "realism" in my *Realistic Theology* (New York, 1934). See also *Christian Realism in Contemporary American Theology*, by George Hammar (Uppsala, 1940). The "provisional realism" of A. N. Whitehead was an immensely important factor in the philosophical revolution which underlay this whole theological realignment; but the influence of political events was still more basic. See also *Man as a Sinner in American Realistic Theology* by Mary Frances Thelen (New York, 1946).

[16] Macintosh, Wieman, Otto, *Is There a God?* (Chicago, 1932).

Brunner presently renounced the empirical method altogether. The realistic united front thus tended to break up as a theological reconstruction began; but the common impulse toward objectivism and theocentrism continued in the ensuing period.

Credit should be given to Macintosh and Wieman for first presenting a persuasive alternative to humanism, in terms which appealed widely to former liberals, and opened the way for them to an objective super-human Ground of trust and faith. At Chicago Divinity School, where the pragmatic theology of G. B. Smith and E. S. Ames was unable to cope with the humanism of Haydon,[17] Wieman's empirical theism really overcame humanism and started a new era. Shailer Mathews adopted the new approach in his *Growth of the Idea of God* (1931) and was hailed by Macintosh as a fellow-realist. While Niebuhr led the negative attack on "utopian idealism," it was Macintosh and Wieman who first gave a positive realistic orientation to American Protestant theology. "Wieman was my Barth," said Charles Clayton Morrison, and others could say the same. If many of Wieman's followers (including Morrison) later turned against him, they ought never to forget that he "kept the bridge" for them at a most critical moment—the bridge they all passed over, from idealistic or pragmatic subjectivism to realistic objectivism.

III. *Constructive Restatement, 1935–1950*

Since the realignment of 1930–1935, American theology has gradually gathered strength for new constructive endeavors. Fifteen years of world chaos, world war, and world leadership have provided plenty of stimulus for such endeavors. A stunned and reeling world has been reaching out desperately for something to cling to, and if an orderly, constructive credo is not available, will clutch blindly at straws. So far, only constructive *trends* have manifested themselves; but a period of constructive *system-building* seems to be at hand.

[17] Cf. the feebly concessive essay in Smith's *Current Christian Thinking*, Chapter IX (Chicago, 1928).

To chart the theological trends of the last fifteen years, we may take our departure from a series of articles published in the *Christian Century* during 1939: "How My Mind Has Changed in the Last Decade." When this series is compared with two other series— its direct sequel in the *Christian Century* ten years later, and a somewhat similar autobiographical collection issued six or seven years earlier [18]—the trend of thought stands out pretty clearly. The first of the three series, though it appeared in the midst of the .revolution of 1930–1935, shows little evidence of what was going on, and reflects the checkered variety of American theology at the end of the liberal era. The contrast between fundamentalism (Machen) and modernism (William Adams Brown) still seemed more important than any other. Henry Nelson Wieman was perfectly clear in his conviction that "we are in the midst of an enormous revolution in all our thinking"; and he announced his intention "to promote a theocentric religion as over against the prevalent anthropocentric"; [19] but only a few of his twenty-two collaborators yet saw the necessity and importance of this realistic shift.[20] By 1939, on the eve of World War II, our most representative religious thinkers had almost all made the shift, but were beginning to be divided into two sharply contrasting schools of realism: neo-naturalism led by Wieman and neo-supernaturalism led by Reinhold Niebuhr, who had suddenly stepped forth in *Beyond Tragedy* (1937) as a great constructive theologian. No such dramatic shift occurred between 1939 and 1949, in spite of the terrific events that crowded those years. The second series on "How My Mind Has Changed" turned out to be far less revolutionary than the first. What did occur during the war years, however, was a resurgence of liberalism in a modified form, dividing the neo-supernaturalists into a neo-orthodox and a neo-liberal wing. Three sorts of realism thus emerged.

[18] *Contemporary Theology: Theological Autobiographies*, edited by Vergilius Ferm. First series (New York, 1932). Second series, 1933.

[19] *Op. cit.*, Vol. I, pp. 344, 346.

[20] Eugene W. Lyman (Vol. II, p. 119) does speak of "the reaction against subjectivism which has been taking place in many fields of thought." Niebuhr does not appear in the symposium; no one then thought of him as a theologian.

The contrast between neo-naturalism and neo-supernaturalism was beginning to appear by 1936, when E. E. Aubrey published his valuable analysis of *Present Theological Tendencies*. Aubrey points out that the new naturalism of Wieman, like that of Lloyd Morgan and Alexander, Smuts and Whitehead, makes room in "nature" for a whole realm of values, meanings and purposes excluded by the old mechanistic naturalism, making it easy to find God in nature; but he also points out that the new naturalism denies all "disjunction between God and nature" and conceives of God as "one aspect of the natural world"—that which supports values and makes for increasing mutuality. Against this identification of God with an aspect of nature, Aubrey sees a "striking reaction" beginning to assert itself, represented in Britain by Oman, Inge, and Temple; in America, by Lyman, Rufus Jones, and Macintosh. If Niebuhr is not named as leader of this trend, it is only because he is somewhat misleadingly classified along with Barth and Brunner, as a dialectic theologian. No one has stressed more than Niebuhr the need of a "dimension of depth," transcending nature, transcending history, if ethical action here and now is to be sustained by a faith that touches absolute bottom. Wieman has steadily refused to admit any such transcendent dimension into his thinking, and remained content with what his former follower, C. C. Morrison, calls a "behavioristic theology." [21] Niebuhr considers that theistic naturalism is a particularly flagrant instance of "absolutizing the relative"—his constant formula for the sin of idolatry. On this issue, American realistic theology remains sharply divided.

For a time, it seemed as though American supernaturalists might reassert divine transcendence as emphatically and one-sidedly as Barth and Kierkegaard. The influence of Continental neo-orthodoxy was visibly increasing on the eve of World War

[21] See the important passage, pp. 33-37, in *The Source of Human Good* (Chicago, 1946), Wieman's definitive work, where the idea of divine transcendence is sharply rejected. If there was doubt hitherto as to whether Wieman was a theologian as well as a philosopher, Chap. 10 in this book removed it.

II. Translations of Aulén and Nygren, plus Ferré's able interpretation of their theology,[22] made a strong impact. The completion of the English translation of Kierkegaard during the War, might have been expected to produce results such as the German translation produced in Germany after World War I. If this did not occur, it was because *the war revealed considerable residual strength in the liberal tradition, both in politics and in theology.* Niebuhr spoke less emphatically during the war about the utopian illusions of liberal democracy, and more about the need of defending its sound core against the perils that beset it.[23] Wieman wrote a political book called *Now We Must Choose* (1941), in which he also called for discriminating support of political liberalism in its time of testing. Since there are historical and logical connections between political and theological liberalism, a similar revival of discriminating liberalism was likely to take place in theology. Dean Sperry of Harvard expressed a common attitude when he said that though liberalism must plead guilty to many of the charges brought against it before the war, *the alternatives to liberalism were generally far worse.* A symposium called *Liberal Theology: An Appraisal* (New York, 1942) marked the first concerted expression of a neo-liberal trend. John Bennett in his contribution to this volume defends human nature and human reason against neo-orthodox pessimism, while acknowledging that earlier liberal optimism needed to be corrected by the tragic insights of Augustine, Luther and Calvin.

In summary, the theological center of American Protestantism now consists of three strong parties, neo-orthodox, neo-liberal, and neo-naturalist, all related to the realistic movement of 1930–1935, but differing between themselves at many points. It is important to note that scarcely any of our neo-orthodox would repudiate the use of reason in theology to the extent that Barth or the Swedish Lundensians do; while, on the other hand, even Wieman and the

[22] *Swedish Contributions to Modern Theology,* by Nels Ferré (New York, 1939).
[23] *Christianity and Power Politics* (New York, 1940); *The Children of Light and The Children of Darkness* (New York, 1944).

naturalists now give more weight to Biblical revelation and its paradoxical symbols than many liberals were disposed to do twenty-five years ago. This being the case, there is measurably less tension between our right and left wings than there was then. Fundamentalists still exist, and they denounce neo-orthodoxy as "The New Modernism"; [24] but many of them would now admit that there are "Bible-believing Christians" in the neo-orthodox and neo-liberal ranks, with whom they can argue as friends instead of parting as foes. Humanists still exist—graduated in thousands each year from our secularized universities; but their faith in man has been greatly chastened by tragic events since 1930. Some of them have found in neo-naturalism a stepping-stone to Christian faith in God.

If American theology is to play the important part in ecumenical conversations to which the course of world events seems to call us, it is highly desirable that our theologians should do more *systematic* and *comprehensive* work than they have in the recent past. It is an amazing fact that the systems of Hodge and Strong, Clarke and Brown (essentially nineteenth-century systems) have had no real peers in the twentieth century as yet. There are signs that we may not have to wait much longer. Christology, the central core of every system of Christian theology, is coming to concern many minds. Biblical theology is becoming more and more productive, and exercising a stimulating effect on systematic theology. Short sketches of the Christian faith, for the laity and clergy, are becoming numerous.[25] Reinhold Niebuhr, in *The Nature and Destiny of Man*, has produced a masterpiece covering half the ground of the Christian faith. Nels Ferré has already begun to issue a series of books presenting a theological system half-way between Swedish neo-orthodoxy and American neo-liberalism. Paul Tillich is issuing the first of two volumes on *Systematic Theology* this year, uniting the philosophic and revela-

---

[24] *The New Modernism*, by Van Til (1946).
[25] *E.g.*, Bennett, *Christian Realism;* Horton, *Our Christian Faith;* Rall, *The Christian Faith and Way;* Harkness, *Understanding the Christian Faith.*

tional approaches at every point: Reason and Revelation, Being and God, Existence and the Christ, Life and the Spirit, History and the Kingdom of God. Closely associated with Reinhold Niebuhr for many years, Tillich shares many of his friend's views; but his mind has a generous comprehensiveness peculiarly his own. May he be the new Aquinas who will find a place within his system for the truth in all our contending theological schools.

BIBLIOGRAPHY

Hodge, A. A., *Outlines of Theology* (New York, 1861; rewritten and enlarged, New York, 1900; Grand Rapids, 1928)

King, H. C., *Reconstruction in Theology* (New York, 1901)

Brown, W. A., *Christian Theology in Outline* (New York, 1906)

Rauschenbusch, Walter, *A Theology for the Social Gospel* (New York, 1918)

Machen, J. G., *Christianity and Liberalism* (New York, 1923)

Macintosh, D. C., *Religious Realism* (New York, 1931)

Ferm, Vergilius, editor, *Contemporary American Theology*, Series I and II (New York, 1932–1933)

Aubrey, E. E., *Present Theological Tendencies* (New York, 1936)

Hammar, George, *Christian Realism in Contemporary American Theology* (Uppsala, 1940)

Roberts, D. E. and Van Dusen, H. P., editors, *Liberal Theology: An Appraisal* (New York, 1942)

Niebuhr, Reinhold, *The Nature and Destiny of Man*, Vols. I and II (New York, 1941–1943)

Tillich, Paul, *Systematic Theology*, Vol. I (Chicago, 1951)

Wieman, H. N. and Meland, Bernard, *American Philosophies of Religion* (Chicago, 1936) *

* This particular book is inserted in the bibliography of this chapter because, as Dr. Horton rightly points out, "philosophy of religion" during the heyday of the liberal period, practically speaking, was identified with "systematic theology." A.S.N.

CHRISTIAN ETHICS

Waldo Beach and John C. Bennett *

* In the writing of this chapter, Waldo Beach was responsible for sections I–V and John Bennett for sections VI–VIII but "the contentions of the whole chapter are shared by both contributors." A.S.N.

WALDO BEACH was born in 1915, and he graduated from Wesleyan University in 1937; subsequently he studied at Yale Divinity School, taking the degree of B.D. in 1940, and the Yale Graduate School, where he took his doctorate in 1944. He then served as College Pastor and Professor of Religion at Antioch College, Ohio, before joining the faculty of Duke University, where he is Associate Professor of Christian Ethics in the Divinity School and the Graduate School of Arts and Sciences. He is a member of the Study Commission on the Church and Economic Life of the Federal Council of Churches.

JOHN COLEMAN BENNETT was born in 1902, and he was educated at Williams College, Oxford University, and Union Theological Seminary. After teaching for eight years at Auburn Theological Seminary, he joined the faculty of the Pacific School of Religion in 1938, leaving there in 1943 to become Professor of Christian Theology and Ethics at Union Theological Seminary, New York. He was Secretary of the Section on the Church and the Economic Order at the Oxford Conference in 1937, and he acted in the same capacity for the Section on the Church and the Social Disorder at the Amsterdam Assembly of the World Council of Churches in 1948. He is the author of several books both on the theory and practice of Christian Ethics. His two latest volumes are *Christian Ethics and Social Policy* and *Christianity and Communism*.

VI

THE HISTORY of the Christian ideal of the "good life" may fairly be treated as variations on the themes sounded in the gospels. Indubitably one main theme of the gospel ethic is the tension between the Christian way and the way of the world, a primal opposition between the requirements of the Kingdom of God and the requirements of the kingdom of the world. The main historical types of Christian ethics can well be understood as attempts to resolve this tension. The monastic version of the Christian way proposed a discipline whereby the Christian could be saved *out* of the world, for the vision of God. Orthodox Protestantism of the sixteenth, seventeenth and eighteenth centuries proclaimed a faith whereby the Christian could be saved *in* the world, for the next life, by living under the Kingship of God. The last part of the nineteenth and the early part of the twentieth century saw the rise and decline of still another attempt to overcome this tension. The "liberal" movement (so-called in this essay for lack of a better name) without being completely "this-worldly" yet construed the Christian life neither as a way whereby one was saved *out* of this world, nor saved *in* this world for the next, but simply as an effort *to save the world*. It proposed that the cause in which the Christian was to lose his life, and thus save it, was in the gradual Christianisation of the social order, to the end of the coming of the Kingdom of God on earth. All of the distinctive features of liberal Protestant ethics are made coherent when viewed in the light of this highest good for man.

The gospel according to liberalism was long in the making. Its theological roots go back to Immanuel Kant, whose philosophy gave impetus to a development in German theology associated with the names of Schleiermacher, Ritschl, Harnack, Hermann, and many others. From nineteenth-century secular thought liberalism also drew heavily: from the environmentalism of the Marxists and English socialists, a realisation of the conditioning impact of social institutions upon human personality; from Utilitarianism, the ideal of social reform to extend the "greatest happiness of the greatest number"; and from Darwin and his followers the evolutionary theory of the unilinear and upward development of the course of human affairs. These ideas permeated the nineteenth-century era of expansion and growth in England and the Continent. When appropriated by the distinctively American temperament of robust optimism, activism, and practicality, the liberal movement penetrated deeply American Protestantism for almost half a century.

There were many preachers and teachers who, at the close of the Civil War period, began speaking the message of a "social" Christianity. Washington Gladden, a leader in its early development, was succeeded by men who led the movement into the 1900's, when the Social Gospel "came of age": Lyman Abbott, George Herron, Samuel Batten, Francis Peabody, G. B. Smith, Shailer Mathews, and above all Walter Rauschenbusch, its major apologist.[1] The more turbulent years following the first World War saw the continuing influence of this gospel in men like Francis J. McConnell, Harry F. Ward, Arthur E. Holt, Harry Emerson Fosdick, G. Bromley Oxnam, and Kirby Page.

There is always a "cultural lag" in religious thought, and the rank-and-file of Protestants in the hinterlands have remained largely untouched by the insights of Protestant liberalism. The virulent reaction against liberalism from the ultra-conservative, Bible-minded Protestants, now on the increase in the mid-century, is one indication that the impact of liberalism on the total Protestant mind was much smaller than its leaders supposed. Nonetheless, the slow percolation of liberal ideas, passing down through semi-

---

[1] The subsequent treatment of liberalism will draw most heavily on Rauschenbusch's thought. His most important books are *Christianity and the Social Crisis* (1907), *Christianizing the Social Order* (1912), and especially *A Theology for the Social Gospel* (1917). The best historical treatment of the Social Gospel is Howard Hopkins: *The Rise of the Social Gospel in American Protestantism, 1865–1915.* See also Henry May: *Protestant Churches and Industrial America.*

nary education and denominational literature, was the most positive
and creative trend in the early years of this century.

II

The task of liberalism was to recall the Protestant church to
the prophetic content of the Hebrew-Christian tradition. During
the latter part of the nineteenth century, Protestant ethics had
fallen, for the most part, into the doldrums of a Victorian, pietistic,
socially myopic, and cushioned-pew program for personal purity.
The common ideal of the Christian life was to avoid the gross
sins of the flesh, to follow the Benjamin Franklin virtues of thrift,
honesty, and respectability, to love one's immediate neighbor in
good deeds of charity, and thus to prepare oneself for the destina-
tion of heaven. The economic structures of life were either regarded as outside the province of ethics or else given a tacit
sanction through the Puritan doctrine of vocation, which had been
transformed into the "gospel of work" and thence into the "gospel
of wealth." The notorious "rugged individualism" of capitalism
was blessed as Christian if mitigated by active philanthropy. The
Protestant church looked at questions of economic ethics through
the eyes of the middle-class bourgeoisie. It passed by on the other
side from the masses of immigrant labor, or else offered them other-
worldly bromides for their spiritual and economic hungers.

Into this complacent atmosphere blew the fresh winds of the
social gospel. Men like Gladden and Rauschenbusch found that
the counsels of pietistic Protestantism were woefully inept in
speaking to the condition of men crushed under the weight of
industrial capitalism. They found it futile for the church to try
to "save souls" one by one when society was destroying them
en masse. For them the task of the church was imperative: to
attack the social order, to remake it after the pattern of the Kingdom of God envisaged by the Hebrew prophets and Jesus, an
earthly kingdom of justice, brotherhood, and democracy.

There was a clear unanimity among liberals in defining the
Kingdom and in asserting its primacy. "By the Kingdom of God

Jesus meant an ideal (though progressively approximated) social order in which the relation of men to God is that of sons, and therefore to each other, that of brothers. . . . This ideal is not beyond human attainment, but is the natural possibility for man's social capacities and powers." [2] "The Kingdom of God is humanity organised according to the will of God. . . . It implies a progressive reign of love in human affairs." [3]

The highest good for the individual is to do battle for this Kingdom. He must contribute to the amelioration of human life by altering the environmental circumstances so as to restore the dignity and worth of persons. Over against orthodox Protestantism, the liberals were environmentalists, in that they discerned both the crippling power and the redemptive possibilities of economic and political institutions. But they avoided the deterministic collectivism of Marxist socialism. They kept the individual and the "personal equation" to the forefront, both in terms of the criteria by which institutions were to be judged and the leverage by which institutions were to be changed.

One of the most radical features of the liberal development was its claim that ethics is prior to theology. Starting with the ethical conviction of the primacy of the Kingdom, the liberal mind judged traditional theology by that faith, and altered it in keeping. The title of Rauschenbusch's most influential book, *A Theology for the Social Gospel* is symbolic. And G. B. Smith's Taylor Lectures of 1912, *Social Idealism and the Changing Theology*, appealed for the transformation of theology to keep pace with the new social consciousness of the church.

The attempted transformation of tradition affected every department of Christian theology. The Christian view of man's nature underwent a considerable revision. The long-established Calvinistic estimate of man as a creature fallen from his original

[2] Shailer Mathews: *The Social Teaching of Jesus* (1902), pp. 54, 77.
[3] Walter Rauschenbusch: *A Theology for the Social Gospel* (1917), p. 142.

nature into a state of sin from which, powerless to free himself, he can only be saved by grace—this view was amended to a more favorable estimate of man's condition. Among liberals, man was taken essentially to be a creature of divine worth and dignity, endowed with intelligence and native goodwill, who sins but who is not congenitally a sinner, and who is capable of moral growth in this life by his own initiative and inspiration from God. It must be remembered that the major thinkers of the Social Gospel took the phenomenon of sin with prophetic seriousness. Rauschenbusch made a penetrating analysis of the pervasiveness and tenacity of sin in "the superpersonal forces of evil," socially transmitted from generation to generation.[4] His was a realism not characteristic of the later ebullient enthusiasts for God's dawning day. But even Rauschenbusch shared the dominant liberal conviction in viewing sin in primarily "horizontal" terms, as selfishness in defiance of neighbor-needs, rather than primarily as the rebellion of the will against the sovereignty of God. Moreover, evil must be regarded "as a variable factor in the life of humanity," he wrote, "which it is our duty to diminish for every young life and for every new generation." [5] Else what is the point of education, or of what use free will? Here he betrays an optimism quite alien to the tone of the Westminster Confession.

Of all the rewritings of the Christian tradition attempted by liberalism, the most thoroughgoing was in the area of philosophy of history. Traditional eschatology looked away from the present "fallen" state of man to a final end brought about by God's intervention and discontinuous with the present and future line of time. This concept proved troublesome if not weird to minds nurtured in evolutionary and romantic nineteenth-century thought. In the stead of the traditional *eschaton* was put the earthly Kingdom of justice and brotherhood, approximated progressively through time by gradual continuity on an upward

---

[4] See *Theology for the Social Gospel*, chs. IV–IX.
[5] *Ibid.*, p. 43.

plane. In short, a Christianised version of the progress philosophy of history, in the name of the Kingdom of God ideal, supplanted orthodox Christian eschatology.

Such a philosophy of history influenced profoundly the ethical temper of liberalism. The bow of moral effort was bent by the tension between the present and the future. What sustained moral energy was the confidence that as the present was superior to the past so the future would realise what was still now unfulfilled. In a real sense, liberalism construed the traditional Protestant dictum of "salvation by faith" in a way quite foreign to the intention of Luther and Calvin. For "faith" came to mean confidence in the future. In effect, then, men are saved by hope, and by works that bring that hope nearer.

The 1910's and 1920's saw the fruition of this new spirit in organisational expression at every level. At the denominational level, various commissions of social service tried to awaken the consciences of their constituency with various "social creeds" and manifestoes. The Federal Council of Churches of Christ in America, established in 1908, provided an agency for the inter-denominational expression of the social convictions of liberalism. Its Social Creed (1912) dealt almost wholly with economic issues. Its support of labor unionisation and of shorter hours and higher wages for labor was viewed (and still is) as "radical socialism" by many of the rank-and-file in the Protestant hinterlands. By 1932 the Federal Council statement of principles extended its scope to include the rural problem, marriage and the home, race relations, and international affairs. Though again the laity remained dubious or inarticulate in their attitude toward war, during the 20's and 30's, Protestant liberalism joined the anti-war crusade with enthusiasm. It was boldly affirmed that "the institutions of religion should never again be used as agencies of warfare." The type of pacifism prevalent in this era among the large denominations was quite different from that of the historic sectarian groups. The Quakers and Mennonites abhorred participation in war for their own adherents as part of their whole perfectionist renunciation of the sinful "world." This new, more positive pacifism sought to convert the nations to the way of Christ by substituting for the way of the sword Christian goodwill and reasonable negotiation among nations to settle their disputes. The "world-renouncing" pacifism and the "world-affirming" pacifism in these decades was a curious compound of sectarian and liberal motifs.

III

It would be difficult to try to discern a date during the last half-century when the reaction against liberalism began to set in. The slow ebb-tide of liberalism came with the devastating and profoundly unnerving events of the 1930's and 40's, which dashed the high hopes of liberalism for the arrival of the Christian century. It found itself with little to speak to the condition of men in conflict, tragedy, and failure. In a dark time, the writings of Barth and Brunner were taken up on the Continent and in England. The school of "Neo-Protestants" (called variously the school of "neo-orthodoxy," "Crisis" or "Dialectical" theology) came to ascendency. In America, the most influential figures in the transition have been Paul Tillich and Richard and Reinhold Niebuhr.[6] The voices of this new school seem to speak much less in chorus than did the liberals. Its themes are more difficult to make out. Moreover, at the point of specific ethical decision, Niebuhr and his followers have joined forces with liberals considerably left of center in matters of economic policy, race relations, and political alignment. With the exception of the issues of pacifism and world government, Niebuhr is found "voting" the same way as the liberals who are his theological opponents. The crucial difference, then, between liberalism and neo-Protestantism is not to be seen

[6] Since Reinhold Niebuhr has been the chief spokesman for neo-Protestantism in America, it is his thought which comes in for consideration in the material which follows in this essay. It is imperative to note, however, that he differs widely from European neo-Protestants at certain crucial points, as too he differs from other neo-Protestants in America.

at the level of the specific measures of social ethics, but at the deeper level of the theological premises, sanctions, and ends which underlie Christian policy in public and private affairs.

The central theological stress of neo-Protestantism is the recovery of the major note of Augustine, Luther, and Calvin: the absolute transcendent sovereignty of God, Whose Will orders the whole universe. God is the continual Creator, Judge, and Redeemer of the world. Neo-Protestantism finds the theology of liberalism lamentably wanting at two crucial points: (1) In construing God as the immanental force for good in society, it loses the sense of the majestic transcendence of God, who is above and beyond any force for good in society. (2) It overlooks the "Fall" of man and the "wrath" of God. In centering thought on God as Creator and Redeemer, making a good order of creation gradually better, it neglects the Judgment of God on man's perpetual corruption of creation.

The transcendence of God is not absolute. In Jesus Christ, the absolute separation of time and eternity is broken through from the side of God. In Christ, He "invades" history from above. The final and unique Word is spoken for man in Him. Neo-Protestantism shares with liberalism a Christo-centric faith. But the Jesus of history who is normative for the liberal is understood more as humanity reaching divinity, while for the neo-Protestant mind the Christ of faith must be understood as the Divine reaching humanity. The "lordship" of Jesus Christ is conceived by liberalism in moral terms; for neo-Protestantism in metaphysical or cosmic terms as well.

These theological affirmations involve important shifts in ethical theory. In the treatment of man's sin and salvation, the transaction is conceived in the "vertical" (man-to-God) dimension, in contrast to its "horizontal" (man-to-society) treatment by liberalism. To be sure, both the condition of sin and the process of salvation have for the neo-Protestant "horizontal" expressions, but these are the fruits of the dislocation and re-creation of man in his primal relation with God.

Neo-Protestantism is well-known for its heavy stress on "original" sin. By its critics this emphasis is dismissed as morbid, pessimistic, and morally enervating. In what sense sin is "original" to man's finite life is not, however, an issue as important in neo-Protestant thought as is its diagnosis of the locus and character of sin itself. Sin is not essentially ignorance, to be exorcised by education and rational enlightenment. Nor does it lie in the body's downward pull upon the upward aspirations of the spirit. Nor again is it to be located in corrupt institutions which defile the naturally innocent intentions of individuals. All these views of sin, more or less current in Protestant circles, are superficial; at the most they are symptoms rather than the causes of man's dilemmas. The real essence of sin is man's wilful (albeit often unconscious) rebellion against the sovereignty of God and the effort to organise his universe of values around himself as the center. It is "pride," presumption, self-will, ego-centrism. "Selfishness" is an appropriate word, if this be defined as self-centeredness in man's encounter with God. In the misdirection of his will toward his own ends in preference to the will of God, man falls perennially into an "eccentric" (off-center) manner of life. His reasoning is corrupted into self-defensive rationalisation, his institutions become the instruments of his will-to-power. He commits all manner of inhumanities to man, often in the name of good. The consequences of this sin are the inner unrest and outer warfares which plague his days—the expressions of God's judgment.[7]

The process of salvation from this sin is somewhat more obscurely and variously described by neo-Protestant theologians. In the main, however, it may be said that salvation is realised by man's appropriation in faith of God's act of forgiveness in Jesus Christ, which effects in the believer the mood of contrition for sin, partial escape from egocentrism, and a predisposition to judge one's own case as severely as another's, as under the judgment of God. Humility and contrition enable one to approach the issues of inter-personal relations with a non-selfdefensive, outgoing

[7] See Niebuhr's *Nature and Destiny of Man*, vol. I, chs. vi–viii.

love, in response to God's love revealed on the Cross. This kind of salvation does not mean "perfection." It will not "solve" the moral problems of our day. But it can mitigate the conflicts of life, secure some reconciliations out of broken community, temper justice with love, and bestow on the believer a sense of being forgiven, even within the grays of sinful existence.

IV

The theological emphases sketched above provide the basis for the neo-Protestant critique of liberalism. In the first place, it finds liberalism's philosophy of history not only inadequate but heretical. The Kingdom of God, says Niebuhr, should not be described in the future perfect tense, but in the present indicative. The phrase means the Kingship of God, the sovereignty of God, a very present reality. It is God's constant activity of creation, judgment, and redemption. Even in sin, men are not outside the Kingdom. The psychological and social maladjustments which follow upon sin are the very signs of God's rule, His "left hand" bringing judgment. It becomes dangerous sentimentalism to claim any assured progressive victory of good over evil within finite time. History gives no sign of being automatically redemptive in itself, for the good achievements of history bring new perils and new corruptions. The realization of this truth leads to despair only if one's faith is grounded in hope for the future. But the true Christian's faith is grounded in a God transcendent of all time and historical achievement.

This difference becomes highly important for ethics. The moral dynamic of much of liberalism was derived, as we have noted, from the disparity between the present possibility and the future hope. This gives a teleological character to liberal morality. The moral dynamic of neo-Protestantism stems rather from the tension between God's transcendent command and the present human situation. It does not first ask: What can we hope for? Its first question is: What does God's sovereignty require of me in this present?

How shall I respond to God's action in faith and integrity? The obedience of the Christian in witnessing to God's command may not be "successful." Indeed, it may fail, when judged by the standards of the world. But the success of the Christian's efforts in terms of the future happiness of man is a quite secondary matter. The first and final sanction of moral action is faithfulness to the will of God.

A second attack of neo-Protestantism is aimed at the liberal view of human nature, in which it finds a curious ambiguity. The social gospel arose as a strenuous prophetic attack against the sinister economic forces of industrial capitalism which were destroying the personality of its subjects. Yet as the social gospel developed in the twentieth century, it was betrayed by its understanding of human nature to what now appears, in hindsight, as a superficial prescription for the "mystery of iniquity." Even Rauschenbusch believed that in America the institutions of the family, education, the church, and political life had become Christianised.[8] It only remained to convert the institutions of capitalism from competition to co-operation. In so far as liberalism located evil externally in institutions, it overlooked the way institutions are sustained from within by corrupted wills. In so far as it regarded some institutions as safely within the fold of the Kingdom, it overlooked the ubiquity of sin to which no institutions are immune.

· There is a third point at which the ethics of liberalism is found wanting by neo-Protestantism. The liberal claims that the solution of our social problems lies in the extension of the personal virtues of the Sermon on the Mount to the relatively impersonal areas of man's collective relationships. But the kind of Christian "love" appropriate to the small circle of the family becomes tortuously difficult, if not impossible, to apply to the relations of economic groups and the affairs of state. One cannot "love" one's far-distant neighbor as one can "love" one's close-at-hand neighbor, given the limiting barriers of the political and economic structures

[8] *Christianising the Social Order* (1912), Pt. III, ch. 2.

through which alone moral motives can be expressed. The situation is worse confounded in that one's self-sacrificial love for one's own neighbor, one's kind, may become the instrument of the collective egoism of patriotism or of ecclesiastical imperialism. "Moral man" thus aggravates the sins of "immoral society." So it becomes too facile to speak of Christianising the social order by the establishment of love and justice in the body politic. Such a high-looking hope trips over the moral ambiguities involved in every finite moral choice.

Another illustration of the ineptness of liberal ethics, according to the charge, is its pathetic innocence in dealing with the problem of power. One of the most important fruits of the social gospel was the pacifist movement between World Wars I and II. This pacifism counterposed the "Christian way" to the "way of power," expressed in the use of military force or economic sanctions. The only alternative for the Christian must be the renunciation of power and might. Reinhold Niebuhr, the most influential critic of this pacifism, has maintained that this alternative is too "simple." Unless the Christian retreat from the world entirely and leave it to be run by burly sinners, he is involved inevitably in power relationships at every level of his corporate life—relationships which are always an admixture of relative good and evil. The real question is not, then, shall the Christian employ coercive power? The real question is how can the necessary use of power be made to secure a relatively more just and a relatively less tyrannical social order? These Niebuhrean strictures against liberal pacifism were in part responsible for a sharp shift among Protestant leaders from pacifism to interventionism during the nervous uncertainties prior to Pearl Harbor. After World War II, the problems of Christian ethics in international affairs have continued to be couched in these terms, rather than in terms of the liberal pacifist's alternatives.[9]

[9] See for example, *The Amsterdam Assembly Series*, Vol. IV: *The Church and the International Disorder* (1948).

EDITOR'S NOTE:—Another important contribution to thinking in this area has been John Bennett's book, *Christian Ethics and Social Policy* (1946).

V

At mid-century, neo-Protestantism is certainly the most influential school of thought at the levels of Protestant theological education, in America hardly less than in England and on the Continent. A closer look at the tenets of this school, particularly in its American variety, discloses that while it has attacked liberalism at some points, it is deeply (and often unconsciously) indebted to liberalism at others. It is not a straight return to the beliefs of orthodox Protestantism as it evolved in the sixteenth, seventeenth, and eighteenth centuries. Something new has been added. And the "new" is derived precisely from the whole liberal development in theology, along with its nineteenth century concomitants in scientific and social thought. In its method, for one thing, it shares with liberalism an empirical temper, receptive to truth from all sources, "secular" or "sacred." In its characteristic themes, the neo-Protestant movement in theology and ethics can best be understood as a transitional synthesis of Protestant orthodoxy with Protestant liberalism. It has drawn its cardinal theses from orthodoxy, but it has also been greatly beholden to certain insights of liberalism which arose in antithesis to orthodoxy.

Niebuhr and others like him have returned to the orthodox belief that sin and salvation must first be understood as taking place in the heart of man, as he stands in vertical transaction with God. To turn from Him is to fall, in misdirected love, toward one or another idolatry. To be turned again to Him by grace is to be restored. The real locus of sin, then, is the inner man. But on the other hand, with liberalism, neo-Protestantism has affirmed that the most destructive expressions of sin are to be seen in the *public* rather than the private life of man. The sins of the prideful heart run rampant in nationalistic imperialism, racial pride, and economic misbalances of power. The neo-Protestant, like the liberal, is quite nonchalant about the kinds of private and fleshly sins that preoccupied the Puritan, and still constitute the scope of "ethics" for many orthodox pietists.

The early Reformers inherited a medieval conservatism which regarded the social structures of the family, the state, and economic life as God-given and fixed orders, *within* which the individual was to work out his salvation. One looks in vain in Luther, Calvin, Baxter, Wesley, Edwards, and all the major figures of three centuries of Protestant writing, for any more than incidental treatment of the problems of the economic, political and legal *structures* of life. The realisation of the fluidity of social structures and the capacity of man to alter his political and economic environment is a nineteenth century insight, which became the inheritance of liberalism and neo-Protestantism as well. The Oxford and Amsterdam Conferences of the World Council of Churches, where neo-Protestant thought was central in influence, were deeply concerned with structures of contemporary Western civilisation. By its serious view of sin, neo-Protestantism is kept from the too-easy confidence of liberalism that the social order can be transformed into the divine. But that does not constrain it the less to judge man's disorder by God's design, and to redeem these disorders in so far as possible. Thus the inward and vertical perspective of orthodoxy is conjoined with the outward and institutional reference of liberalism into a bi-focal perspective of high importance.

VI

The theological development of neo-Protestantism, a development that is so fluid that any label can easily mislead, has changed the assumptions on which Christian ethical thinking now goes forward, but it has meant no abandonment of the essential impulse expressed through the Social Gospel. In this tragic period of history Christians may have to act in quite different ways from those which were assumed to be "Christian" in calmer days. But the requirement of responsible Christian action is made no less urgent by the loss of the optimistic hope of the Social Gospel. What may now be said of some of the major ethical problems which must engage the thought of Christians during the next half century?

The most urgent and, perhaps the most baffling problem is to discover Christian guidance for action in society under conditions which preclude the absolute identification of Christian ethics with any of the decisions that are open to us. Protestant Christianity differs from Roman Catholicism in having no clear Christian law interpreted by an absolute authority for the complexities of economic and political life. The Protestant knows the ultimate standard by which all things are judged. He knows many of the goals that he should seek, but there is a twilight zone of methods and next steps in which Christians have to use their best judgment without benefit of absolute guidance of any kind.

If we ask what a Christian should do to prevent a third world war, we find ourselves forced to make decisions which are highly ambiguous and often repellent. For one thing, the prevention of a third world war is not the only end that we must have in view. Another end which is to many Christians more important is the prevention of worldwide tyranny. If this second end is emphasized, the prevention of a third world war must be sought by methods which will not put one group of nations into the position of having to surrender to the overwhelming power of another group of nations. What these methods are is much debated among Christians who seem to be equally sincere in their loyalty to Christ. Judgment about these methods depends in part on interpretations of fact, in this case on interpretations of the intentions of the rulers of the Soviet Union. There are no Christian answers to those questions of fact and yet every decision about preventing war today which a Christian makes will depend upon his judgment concerning such questions of fact.

Another example of the kind of issue which no Christian ethical precept can settle for us is the attempt to secure stability of employment in our economy. It is obvious that a period of mass unemployment in our society would be ruinous, that Christians are obliged to do what is possible to prevent such a catastrophe from occurring. Here decisions depend upon expert knowledge of economic cause and effect. They depend also upon our scale of values, because the prevention of unemployment is not the only end to be sought. It is also important to find methods which will not lead us to totalitarianism. And yet this fear of totalitarianism must not be used as a bogey to prevent all social experiment in which the state has an important part. What methods will work and how we relate such competing values as freedom and security are questions to which Christians as Christians have no absolutely clear answers.

It will be hard to live without "Christian" programs, without absolute laws, without panaceas of any kind; but there is no other way open to us. Such economic stereotypes as Socialism and Capitalism are no longer helpful for Christian thinking about economic institutions. The formation of a Christian mind concerning these ethical issues is a continuous process in which the special knowledge of experts and the concrete experience of Christian laymen who participate in all phases of economic and political life are essential factors. Two new emphases in modern Protestantism are especially important. One is the emphasis upon the Christian vocation of laymen and the other is the emphasis on the need of co-operative Christian thinking within the fellowship of the Church. The judgment about what ought to be done cannot be prescribed by ministers or theologians for Christians in other occupations. This judgment must take account of the knowledge and intuitive understanding that are found chiefly among laymen who are directly responsible for economic and political activities. It may seem that this approach to the formation of Christian judgments implies complete ethical relativism. But this process must be guided by Christian faith and love at every point. These should control motives, they should determine goals and they should be a basis for criticism of all methods even though they cannot, of themselves, solve all problems of method. The warning against idolatry that is implicit in the Christian faith is the warning against the very attitudes which are most destructive in society, for one form of idolatry is to put in the place of God one social group or cause or value.

In this process of forming Christian judgments on ethical issues there will be developed from time to time a broad consensus that will have considerable authority. Probably no formulation of this consensus will long be satisfactory. There will always be a large body of opinion that is only nominally Christian or at least uninstructed that will reject such a consensus, but it may be an important source of ethical guidance and provide its slow ferment of influence. So far the best statements of consensus that we have are those which come from a succession of national and international conferences such as the Oxford Conference in 1937, the Amsterdam Assembly in 1948 and conferences on world order or economic problems called by the Federal Council of Churches.

VII

A second area of Christian thinking which must go forward is the discovery of the basis for co-operation between Christians and non-Christians in a mixed community. Sometimes the problem involved is the difficulty of deciding how far to go in co-operation with a government that is hostile to Christianity. This is the form of the problem that Christians face in countries that are controlled by Communist governments.

The form of the problem that is most important in America arises out of a widespread acceptance of many common ethical standards by Christians and non-Christians in the American community. Indeed, there are often more serious conflicts between economically progressive and conservative Christians than between Christians and non-Christians with common political views. But even when this co-operation on concrete issues is easy there are problems, often below the surface, about which much more thought is required. One danger is the general dilution of Christian ethics both within and outside the Church. A symptom of this is the tendency of public men to assume that the political and economic policies with which they are concerned are based upon the Sermon on the Mount. Another danger is that Christians will identify themselves too unreservedly with the political and economic problems which, on the whole, they support.

The question of the relation between Christian ethics and ethical ideals which have sources which are independent of the Christian faith is one of the major issues in Christian discussion in Europe. It is one phase of the more general question of the relation between revelation and reason. There is always a danger of a kind of Pharasaism in reverse in Christian ethical thinking. While it seeks to emphasize the uniqueness and authority of Christian ethics it may discount unfairly the moral sensitivity and moral achievements of those who acknowledge no Christian influences upon their thought and life. Whatever of common moral judgment exists in the community which is on the side of honesty, social justice, the rights of minorities, a humane spirit is so precious that Christians should avoid any tendency to isolate themselves from it or to set themselves above it even in theory. To recognize fully this common morality does not mean, however, that we should not see that it is precarious without deeper roots than it often has in our society.

VIII

American Christian ethical thinking will need to enlarge its scope. During the early period of the Social Gospel the emphasis was almost exclusively on economic issues. This was quite necessary at the time, and economic issues are still fundamental. More recently the problem of war has been emphasized. We have been delivered from preoccupation with the pacifism-nonpacifism conflict and much attention has been given by both pacifists and nonpacifists to issues connected with world order. Also, there has developed a Christian form of nonpacifism which involves real gains in Christian sensitivity as compared with conventional attitudes toward war in earlier periods. The issue of race has within the past ten years gained attention in a spectacular way.

None of these issues named can be neglected, but a series of events has forced Christians to give great attention to political issues, to problems of government, to the basis of civil rights. Many of these problems are, of course, interlocked with economic issues. The discussion of the welfare state is inseparably political and economic but it raises a dimension of political problems about which there has been very little careful Christian thinking in this country. The relation of the state to education is a phase of the larger problem of the welfare state but it raises great issues of its own. The problem of Church and State is not far away; that quandry which we thought had been solved by a simple formula of "separation" bristles with open questions. The basis and the limits of the rights of minorities is a most persistent question, for which there are no ready answers. The success of Communism in other parts of the world has forced upon American Christians the responsibility to find alternatives to Communism in countries which are desperately poor and which have had little political experience. Democracy as we know it cannot be universalized but it does stand for values which Christians should seek to preserve in every society. What are those values and how can we define them without appearing to absolutize American institutions and ways of life?

All of these political issues stem from one basic dilemma which we encounter on all sides. It is a dilemma at which political and economic problems meet. How can we preserve freedom for persons and for many non-political institutions in the face of the unity and centralization which are implicit in modern techno-logical developments? The Church, not only in its thinking but also in its very existence, can contribute to the solution of this problem because it is one of those non-political institutions which must preserve large areas of freedom for its own life and work.

BIBLIOGRAPHY

The *Amsterdam Assembly Series: Man's Disorder and God's Design* (New York, 1948)

Bennett, John, *Social Salvation* (New York, 1935)

Bennett, John, *Christian Ethics and Social Policy* (New York, 1946)

Ehrenstrom, Nils, *et al.*, *Christian Faith and the Common Life* (Oxford Conference, vol. IV) (New York, 1938)

Hopkins, C. Howard, *The Rise of the Social Gospel in American Protestantism, 1865–1915* (New Haven, 1940)

May, Henry F., *Protestant Churches and Industrial America* (New York, 1949)

Niebuhr, Reinhold, *Moral Man and Immoral Society* (New York, 1932)

Niebuhr, Reinhold, *An Interpretation of Christian Ethics* (New York, 1935)

Ramsey, Paul, *Basic Christian Ethics* (New York, 1950)

Smith, G. B., *Social Idealism and the Changing Theology* (New York, 1913)

Rauschenbusch, Walter, *Christianity and the Social Crisis* (New York, 1907)

Rauschenbusch, Walter, *A Theology for the Social Gospel* (New York, 1918)

CHURCH HISTORY

George H. Williams

GEORGE HUNTSTON WILLIAMS was born in Ohio in 1914, and after studying as an undergraduate at the University of Munich, he received his B.A. from St. Lawrence University in 1936. Three years later he graduated with the degree of B.D. from the Meadville Theological School and, as Cruft Traveling Fellow, he studied at the Catholic Institute in Paris and the University of Strasbourg. He received the degree of Th.D. from Union Theological Seminary in 1946. He joined the faculty of Harvard Divinity School in 1947, previously having taught Church History at the Starr King School for the Ministry and the Pacific School of Religion in Berkeley, California. His major published contribution to historical scholarship is *Re-thinking the Unitarian Relationship to Protestantism: An Examination of the Thought of Frederic Henry Hedge (1805–1890)*.

VII

In a paper[1] read before a session of the American Historical Association and reported in its *Review* for 1899–1900, a member of the Church history section discussed the then recent effect of the study of Church history on the life of the Church. Noting that in the first third of the nineteenth century the spirit of union and co-operation had prevailed, the writer went on to show how this era of good feeling was followed by a second phase extending through the middle third of the century when the several competing denominations become conscious of their special missions. Strife and division ensued. In an effort to ground their several claims, denominations resorted, among other things, to Church history as an instrument of denominational policy. But the unexpected consequence of their enterprise was the gradual diminution of prejudice and the development of mutual respect and appreciation, "the recent service," as the reader of the paper concluded, "of Church history to the Church."

From our present vantage point we may say that the clergyman's third era had reached a high point by 1888. For by that year interdenominational goodwill had been sufficiently advanced to make possible the organization of the American Society of Church History. Hitherto there had been only denominational historical societies which had drawn off the interest and commitment necessary to undertake the forming of an interdenominational learned society. Thus from 1888, about which year cluster a number of significant events and publications in the field,[2] we may conveniently date the next era of American Church

[1] The Rev. William Given Andrews, "A Recent Service of Church History to the Church," *American Historical Review*, V (1899–1900), p. 427.

[2] Henry Steele Commager, in speaking of "The watershed of the 'nineties," has quite recently underscored the importance of this general date line for marking a new epoch in all fields. *The American Mind: An Interpretation of American Thought and Character Since the 1880's* (New Haven, 1950).

history, an epoch that extends roughly to 1933. To characterize the epoch from 1888 to 1933 in the writing of Church history and to set it off from the era we are at present traversing, it may be said that in the former, Church history emphasized *history*, rejoiced in it as a method, as an objective approach to the solution of those doctrinal and institutional problems which had vexed and held apart Christians in the nineteenth century, while in the current epoch, with its mounting interest in social criticism and ecumenicity, Church history has been increasingly concerned to re-examine and redefine the *Church* and has also become amenable to practical assignments laid upon it by the Church.

And there is another important difference setting off the spirit of the two eras from each other. From 1888 on, Church historians were conspicuously eager to assimilate their field and methodology to that of their secular or academic colleagues, but in the epoch beginning with the advent of Hitler and Roosevelt, Church historians have become increasingly aware of their strategic location for returning some answer to the widespread query of our time as to the meaning of history. And there are some contemporary Church historians who, while steadfastly refusing to abandon anything of the methodology of the older scientific school of objective research, are willing to entertain the possibility that a very important supplementary understanding of Church history is vouchsafed to those standing committedly within the historic community of faith. Of this tendency, more in the second half of our survey.

1. The Teaching and Writing of Church History in the Era from 1888 to 1933 [3]

If the formation of the American Society of Church History in 1888 marked the onset of a new epoch, the publication (1893–1895) under the auspices of this Society of a thirteen-volume set of

---

[3] There are three natural subdivisions within this epoch, 1888–1900, 1900–1918, and 1918–1933, to which I shall occasionally allude as "phases" without allowing this further chronological structuring of the treatment to obtrude.

denominational histories (in which the volume on the Unitarians stands next to that on the Roman Catholics), provided the visible symbol of the recent achievement. Of comparable significance is the proliferation of general Church histories written within the denominational context but informed with the interdenominational spirit and committed to the newer historical methodology. Up to the publication of Schaff's seven-volume *History of the Christian Church* (1882–1894), Americans had depended upon European, particularly German, Church histories, but between 1882 and 1904 substantial American histories and compendia made their appearance.

Philip Schaff (1819–1895) himself belonged actually to an earlier school of ecclesiastical historiography than that of Americans writing Church histories at the time of his revised publication. A pupil of August Neander, Schaff was of the mediatory or Romantic school. It had been in 1851, the year following the death of Neander, that his distinguished Mercersburg pupil first published in German the *History of the Apostolic Church*.[4] Unlike his master Philip Schaff did not feel at all hampered by his Reformation convictions in an understanding and appreciation of the Middle Ages. Indeed, Schaff's conviction that Protestant and Catholic principles or emphases were alike essential to a full Christianity, along with his profound feeling for the liturgical and the institutional (though it called forth a party of opposition to him within his own German Reformed denomination) constituted the basis of his distinctive contribution to the ecclesiastical historiography of the land of the Puritans, as he liked to say; namely, an appreciation and an understanding of the Patristic and Medieval Church. His masterful editing in the English translation of the two series of *Nicene and Post-Nicene Fathers* (1886–1889 and 1890–1900) and of *The Creeds of Christendom* (1890) were the products of his ecumenical and historical convictions.

[4] This was followed by an English translation in 1853–1854. Then under the influence of fresh developments in German historiography, he revised his first study and published his *History of the Christian Church 1—600* in two volumes in 1858 and 1867.

Medieval Church history and, in effect, well-proportioned general Church history could not be adequately taught and written about in American seminaries until the bias against what seemed to be nothing but decline, deviltry, and disaster between the perfection of the Primitive Church and the renewal in this or that sect had been worn away in the numerous academic centers of American Christianity of both Reformed and sectarian antecedents. Within evangelical Christianity Schaff had been a pioneer in the recognition of the achievement of the medieval Church.

Of comparable significance in the academic line was the work of the layman and secular historian, Ephraim Emerton (1851–1935), professor of ecclesiastical history at Harvard Divinity School from 1882 to 1918. Emerton's *Introduction to the Study of the Middle Ages* (1888) was epoch-making in that it aroused widespread interest in medieval history. Emerton thus greatly reinforced a trend suggested by Schaff. One of the founders of the American Historical Association, Emerton was a most articulate spokesman of what may be called "secular" Church history. On several occasions, first in 1883 and subsequently,[5] Emerton insisted that all theological presuppositions must be strenuously eliminated from the study of Church history and rejoiced that for the most part Church historians had indeed acquiesced in the fusion of ecclesiastical and secular history, the former being but a chapter of the whole.

Peers or would-be peers of the academic historians, many American chroniclers of Christianity were, like Emerton, utterly committed to this "scientific" approach to their materials. The decision of the newly formed Society of Church History, to reorganize in 1896,[6] as a section of the American Historical So-

---

[5] "The Study of Church History," *Unitarian Review and Religious Magazine*, XIX (1883), p. 1; "History in Theological Education," *Theological Study Today, Addresses Delivered at the Seventy-Fifth Anniversary of the Meadville Theological School, 1920* (Chicago, 1921), ch. 5; "A Definition of Church History," *Papers of the A.S.C.H.,* 2nd series, VII (1921), p. 55.

[6] In 1906, the Society of Church History was reconstituted and has remained independent of the American Historical Association ever since.

ciety, heartily favored by Emerton, may be taken as an indication of the victory of the proponents of purely objective science, but there was opposition.

An example of the opposition was the reception of Presbyterian-Congregationalist Arthur Cushman McGiffert's *History of Christianity in the Apostolic Age* (1897), launched in the stormy waters of the Briggs controversy. A long and thorough critique, entitled "Dr. McGiffert's Historical Method," in *The Presbyterian and Reformed Review* for 1900 may be taken as representative of the resistance still offered in some well-informed but conservative quarters to the German methodology. McGiffert was charged with being "subjective." Indeed, he may well have opened himself indirectly to the charge when, in his inaugural address in 1893, "The Study of Church History," [7] he endeavored to distinguish a spiritual and *invisible* behind an *empirical* Church history, the latter being the primary concern of the scientific historian. Yet McGiffert, Harnack's first American pupil, was destined to give the tone and direction to the writing and teaching of Church history in the era spanned by his academic career.[8]

A good representative of the mediatory group between, on the one hand, the "scientific" Church historians like Emerton and McGiffert unqualifiedly committed to the new methodology and distrustful of theology and, on the other, the intransigent conservatives, was the Southern Baptist, Albert Henry Newman. Indeed, the publication in 1900 of the first volume of his *Manual of Church History* provides us with a quite convenient date and production with which to characterize the passage from the nineteenth to the twentieth century. In his Introduction,[9] Newman gives six reasons for studying Church history, pointing out not only that it is a vast commentary on Scripture which shows us

---

[7] *Bibliotheca Sacra*, L (1893), p. 150.

[8] Harnack, regnant in Germany during the same period, died in 1930.

[9] "Preliminary Observations on the Study of Church History." Newman was head of the Church History Department of the New Schaff-Herzog Encyclopedia, successively professor at Rochester Theological Seminary, McMaster University in Toronto, Baylor University, professor and dean Southwestern Baptist Theological Seminary, and Mercer University.

how the slightest departure from New Testament principles has resulted in error—here the older sectarian concern is operative— but also that the study of Church history nevertheless increases charity and mutual understanding, thus promoting Church unity— here the newer interdenominational interest is to the fore. New- man's references to the sources and to foreign and secondary literature are uncommonly rich.[10] In keeping with its denomina- tional origin and sponsorship, the *Manual* gives prominence—still one of its merits—to the dissenting tradition down through the centuries, a survival of an older denominational objective within the framework of German ecclesiastical historiography.

From the date line 1900, marked in American Church historiog- raphy by Newman's *Manual*, we may glance backwards and for- wards to take note of other representative mediatory publications in the field. In the extensive Introduction of the two-volume *History of the Christian Church* (1897–1900) [11] by the Methodist John Fletcher Hurst (1834–1903), we are particularly fortunate in having the whole perspective of the history of Church history opened before us as seen by one standing at the threshold of the twentieth century. Student at Halle and Heidelberg, administrator of mission institutes in Bremen and then Frankfort, professor and then president of Drew Theological Seminary, bishop and historian of rationalism and Methodism,[12] Hurst represented the new his- toriography, situated within the denominational context but keenly conscious of the universal Church and thoroughly com- mitted to, and informed by, the newer German methodology. He thus spoke with authority when, after surveying the comparative poverty of American ecclesiastical historiography thus far and its dependence until recently upon Europe, he declared:

[10] To be regretted, however, are Newman's adherence to a largely political periodization.

[11] "The Science and Literature of Church History," I, 15–57. Hurst also published a *Short History of the Christian Church* in 1893, which had the merit of being translated into Spanish and German.

[12] *History of Rationalism* (New York, 1901); *History of Methodism*, 7 vols. (New York, 1902–1904).

The conditions which have limited our development . . . in the past are rapidly disappearing. The American Church has been compelled to address itself to grave social and evangelistic questions, and has confronted them with courage and vigor. At its distance from the great fields of persecution and protracted controversy it will in time acquire that needful equipoise of mind for inquiring carefully and pronouncing judiciously concerning the great matters of the general life of the Church. Concerning that past we can well expect the American Church will be a wise inquirer and an apt disciple at its feet.

It will be seen that Hurst could write quite easily of *the* Church, in the history of which "we observe the constant presence of the divine and human factors."

Methodist Henry Clay Sheldon (1845–1928) of Boston University wrote his *History of the Christian Church* in 1894 for both students and laymen as a contribution to general culture, reducing the doctrinal portion of his narrative, since he had elsewhere written on the history of theology (1886). Significantly, Sheldon devoted three of his five volumes to the modern Church, feeling that within such proportions he could best explain Methodists and American Christians generally to themselves.

Another representative of the mediatory school was the Congregationalist, George Park Fisher (1837–1909) who in 1901 ended his career as professor of ecclesiastical history at Yale. By disposition and achievement more a theologian than a historian in the new objective sense, Fisher in his *History of the Christian Church* (1887) betrays, or shall we say, preserves something of the older denomination-based theological and apologetic interest in the subject.

Williston Walker (1860–1922) succeeded Fisher at Yale in 1901, affording us thus a convenient basis for comparison and a final opportunity for characterizing the earlier phases of the epoch in terms of representative historians. Fisher had written from within the Church: he had been sustained by its ministrations and he had been committed to its theology, an adaptation of the New England theology in the tradition of Nathaniel Taylor. Walker, a Leipzig Ph.D. and, in his first post, a successor to Woodrow Wil-

son at Bryn Mawr,[13] was more interested in the biographical than
the theological dimension in Church history and never felt
prompted, by way of theological and historiographical prolegomena, to define the Church and delimit the scope of Church
history. He had a disciplined historian's grasp of the development
of his own denomination and that of the larger Calvinist tradition.
Yet one detects in his works and particularly in his *History of the
Christian Church* (1918) the absence of any sense of his writing
from the interior of the Church. In effect, by 1918 the denominational vantage point from which Fisher, Hurst, and Newman once
wrote their general Church histories had been pretty much eroded.
To say that the universal Church histories of these older men had
been disguised expansions of denominational histories reaching for
larger perspectives would be inexact, but the anchorage of their
authors had been the denominational fellowship more than the
academic community. Walker, in contrast, was like Emerton a
thoroughly academic historian. The University and the nation
were for him the primary communities. Thus in his textbook on
Church history, published just as the dominance of Germany in
all fields was being brought to a close, Walker curiously repro-
duces, more than any of the historians mentioned, the perspectives
and proportions of the German compendia.[14] It is as if he were
seeing Church history from the standpoint of his Leipzig days.
England, America, and the sects are assigned the limited space
more appropriate in the manual of a German state-churchman
than of an American free-churchman. By the time Walker completed his textbook the old denominational basis was no longer
adequate for writing a warm, committed history with some sense
of "I was there" and "This concerns us." The World War had
temporarily shattered the international Christian community. And
a consciousness of the Christian whole, in the world but not entirely of it, from the interior of which a vital reconception of

---

[13] Afterwards he went to Hartford Theological Seminary (1892–1901)
as Church historian.
[14] Though for the most part up to date on the monographic literature and
skillful in summation, Walker's textbook is chronologically maddening.

universal Church history might have been undertaken,[15] had in
effect passed when Walker tried his hand at it in 1918, a belated
production.

Yet, despite the inadequacy of their definition of the Church
or often indeed their want of any such definition of the primary
object of their researches, Church historians from 1900 to 1918
seem to have forced a general acceptance of their own evaluation
of the importance of their field. For example, that genre of essay
or address, defending and clarifying the function of Church history in the seminary curriculum—common just before and at the
beginning of our epoch around 1888 and destined to flourish once
again around 1933 and thereafter—falls off markedly in the period
of consolidation from 1900 to 1918. Confident of themselves as
the peers of their counterparts in college and university and, like
these, thoroughly committed now to the monographic approach
and the other principles and skills of scientific historiography,
the early twentieth-century Church historians are keenly conscious of their advantage over their colleagues in systematic
theology. Often in that posture which suggests overbearing de-
ference and sometimes with supercilious expressions of esteem for
the theological approach, which they nevertheless eschew, they
insist upon their right to explore the same body of tradition by
the historical approach. Something of the confident, indeed magis-
terial, pride which possessed the Church historians (and their
allies in biblical studies) of their regnant period in the divinity
school curriculum comes out, for example, in the presidential address of Williston Walker before the newly reconstituted American Society of Church History in 1907 and in that of the Unitarian
Francis Christie in 1909.[16] Both presidents proudly survey the
field like generals from a hilltop, noting the deployment of the

---

[15] But significantly, Walker took part in 1919 in a commission looking
toward Congregational and Episcopal unity. He published in that year *Approaches Toward Christian Unity.*

[16] "The Current Outlook in Church History," *Papers of the A.S.C.H.*,
2nd series, I (1907), p. 17; "The Year 1909 in Church History," *ibid.*, II (1910),
p. 53.

army of Church historians the world over in the struggle against ignorance and bigotry. As reports of victories on the various national fronts are communicated from the presidential vantage point, and the announcement of achievements of American Church historians follow dispatches from afar, one no longer detects anything of that earlier American uneasiness in the face of foreign scholarship. To be sure, Walker notes the want of any long-range, systematic, and collective historical projects such as Europe knew, but this is intended as exhortation to further effort and not as depreciation of American achievement to date.

These monographic studies, be it noted, could be undertaken quite successfully without reference to general concepts of, and convictions about, Church history as a whole.[17] Significantly, no important *general* Church histories were written during this period and, as we have already noted, a comprehensive American Church history remained for the future, when a new national and churchly self-consciousness would provide the needed motivation and perspective. But some sense of having passed into a distinctly new season of American culture informs all these writers as they look back. Thus far we have considered their view of Church history as a whole. We turn to their understanding of the historic role of American Christianity.

The twentieth century had opened with the Church historians absorbed and reconstituted (1896) as a section of the American Historical Association, conscious of certain general obligations in respect to American civilization at large and the history thereof. Shortly before the absorption, Henry Mitchell MacCracken of New York University had expressed the conviction that the study of Church history in colleges would strengthen and encourage the study of history in general.[18] After an extensive survey of the place of biblical and ecclesiastical history (subsumed for him together under Church history) in American colleges, Continental

[17] Cf. the characterization of H. S. Commager for the two generations after 1890: "from seeming order to ostentatious disorder." *Op. cit.*, p. 407.

[18] *Papers of the A.S.C.H.*, 1st series, III (1891), p. 217. Newman in the Preface of his *Manual* saw in Church history a similar value.

gymnasien, and English public schools, MacCracken with a certain eloquence and with the exhilaration of one sustained by a sense of mission, outlined a program of "Church history" for each of the four college years.[19] In support of his program, the then president of the Society of Church History declared that Church history unifies the study of history and philosophy generally and that Church history is indispensable to a proper understanding of America. It is MacCracken's recognition of the importance of religion as a factor in the rise of American civilization as a whole that we may emphasize, a point of view freshly appreciated by his colleagues as Church historians of the early twentieth century looked back upon the century traversed.

Revivalism had been a characteristic and controversial feature of the surging vitality of Christian expansion in the century gone by. But as early as 1902 sufficient perspective and objectivity had been gained for William James to write his *Varieties of Religious Experience* and therewith to lay the foundation of a new and distinctively American contribution to the understanding of religion and its history. Frederick Morgan Davenport presented the *Primitive Traits in Religious Revival* in 1905, Frank G. Beardsley having recounted *A History of American Revivals* in 1904. Henry M. MacCracken had pushed beyond Jonathan Edwards, the fiery preacher and careful observer of the Revival, to Edwards the American philosophical Idealist in *Jonathan Edwards Idealismus* (Halle, 1899), while Frank Hugh Foster of Finney's Oberlin changed his theological convictions in the course of writing *A Genetic History of New England Theology* (1907).

Three other major elements in the shaping of nineteenth-century American Christianity, conflict between science and religion, the problem of slavery, and the impact of successive waves of Continental immigration, had been so farreaching and complicated that a comprehensive chronicling and evaluation thereof was

[19] Old Testament in the freshman, New Testament in the sophomore, ecclesiastical history proper to the Reformation in the junior, and its continuation to the present in the senior year.

not yet generally essayed, although mention may be made of Rationalist Andrew D. White's spirited *History of the Warfare of Science with Theology* in 1896 and W. E. Burghart Du Bois' report of a social study made under the direction of Atlanta University in 1903, *The Negro Church*.

Tremendous missionary activity had characterized the foregoing century. Delavan L. Leonard traced *A Hundred Years of Missions* (1895), William E. Strong told *The Story of the American Board: An Account of the First Hundred Years* (1910). In the person of missionary and prophet-reformer Josiah Strong, the mission of the Church was radically reconceived by the end of the nineteenth century. His epoch-making *Our Country* (1885) and climactic *Expansion under New World Conditions* (1900) gave expression to two new emphases in the Church's missionary outreach; namely, internally social betterment and externally the spread of American democratic righteousness.

With the same dynamism and much the same concern but with greater resources and with more disposition for self-criticism, the Church historian of Rochester Theological Seminary, Walter Rauschenbusch, published *Christianity and the Social Crisis* in 1907. Scarcely remembered as a professor of Church history, though that he was from 1902 until his death in 1918,[20] Rauschenbusch gives a very good idea of his conception of and indebtedness to Church history in the very year of his epoch-making book in an article, "The Influence of Historical Studies on Theology." [21] With his assertions that "Sectarianism is part of original sin" and that "History broadens the sympathies and counteracts sectarian narrowness" we may make the connection between the more academic Church historians thus far considered and the proclaimer of the Social Gospel who, in reinterpreting the divine mandate of the Church, himself made history, and in

[20] Previously he was professor of New Testament in the German department of the Seminary (1897–1902), succeeding therein his father.

[21] *The American Journal of Theology*, XI (1907), p. 111.

thus enlarging the social outreach of the Church, incidentally, called attention to that social dimension destined to become so prominent in subsequent American Church historiography. "History and prophecy are organically related," he declares, and prophetic churchmen must study history and learn "to prolong the curve of the past," for "prophecy is an essential function of the Christian Church."

Rauschenbusch begins his article on the role of Church history by taking note of the recent overturn in the seminary curriculum to the advantage of "historical theology" (Church history) and at the expense of "systematic theology" so long the ranking discipline. He compares this with the curricular revolution of the sixteenth century occasioned by the Reformation elevation of "exegetical theology" (biblical study) over systematic theology, which had long reigned supreme in the Middle Ages and which recovered the throne only after Protestantism had itself entered a scholastic or credal period, now belatedly, as he remarks, drawing to a close in America.

Rauschenbusch, the prophet-historian, insists on a scientifically realistic examination of history, holding it to be the first duty of the professor to rob students and they in their turn their parishioners of all the facile history they know, in order to clear the way for "Church history to furnish the mind with illustrations of immense force, . . . to proclaim in tones of thunder that sin will wreck both men and nations; that light is sown to the righteous, but that when men or churches say to the Lord 'Depart from us,' not even the Almighty can do anything for them." After enlarging on two examples of realistic historiography (giving a primarily social explanation for the Reformation and revising the story of the Roman persecution to the moral advantage of the Roman Empire over the later Roman Church during the Inquisition and over both Protestant and Catholic states during the Wars of Religion), Rauschenbusch concludes in reference to such "illustrations of immense force" that "No sermon could speak to me with such abiding and compulsory power, bidding me to be up and doing before our country [likewise] is beyond the point of recovery."

Rauschenbusch was not himself the author of a Church history but as a valid interpreter of signs and portents, a maker of it, pointing out also a neglected aspect of Church history that the next generation of Church historians were invited to explore. The whole Chicago school—in whose organ his article had appeared— with its emphasis upon social Christianity and environmental factors exemplifies the later effects of the fresh vitalities released by Rauschenbusch for the study of Church history. The effect of Rauschenbusch specifically on Church historiography in America may be set down as comparable to that of James Harvey Robinson in general history whose several essays and articles brought together in *The New History* (1912) gave definition to an analogous trend in American historiography at large. Just as here Freemanesque history as "past politics" was greatly enlarged by the new emphasis on social and cultural factors, so Church history, alerted by the Social Gospel, became dissatisfied with the role of Church history as past dogmatics.

So much for some of the achievements in the widening and deepening of Christian America's understanding of its own past. The monographic and archival basis had been made for a comprehensive, denomination-crossing history of American Christianity in terms of common trends and factors, but as David Schaff wrote quite simply as late as 1912: "The church history of the United States has yet to be written." [22] To be sure, Friedrich Nippold had published his *Amerikanische Kirchengeschichte* [23] and in the very year of the founding of the Society of Church History, Daniel Dorchester with the intention of distinguishing trends and

[22] "The Movement and Mission of American Christianity," *The American Journal of Theology* XVI (1912), p. 51. Schaff's six characterizations of American Christianity and his four directives to American Christianity are still helpful pointers.

[23] As Vol. IV of his *Handbuch der neuesten Kirchengeschichte* (1880–1906).

cutting across denominational lines, published his richly factual *Christianity in the United States* (1888). But a more inclusive churchly self-consciousness and a profounder national self-consciousness were alike prerequisites for a more comprehensive history. These, the War and the new conditions and temper that followed it supplied. As it fell out, the national-democratic-social emphasis preceded the churchly-theological stress, the latter being the motif of our second epoch (beginning about 1933).

It was the national-social emphasis that sustained the heightened interest in American Christian history characteristic of the last phase (1918–1933) of our first epoch, a quite natural consequence of the new American self-consciousness resulting from involvement in the War. But it is also related to the general decline of interest in the Old World during the 'twenties. As such it is the church historical analogue of isolationism! Peter Mode, for example, despite his Canadian background, in assembling his massive *Source Book and Bibliographical Guide for American Church History* (1921) neglected to mention foreign works on American Christianity and failed incidentally to provide any new categories or a fresh periodization and principle of organization. Subsequently, however, Mode, following the lead of Frederick J. Turner, introduced in *The Frontier Spirit in American Christianity* (1923) a new category into the interpretation of American Church history. Another production in the field suggested by the times was that of E. F. Humphrey who in *Nationalism and Religion in America* (1924) discovered the potency of religion during the Revolution not unlike that of the churches during the War for democracy. One of the features of post-war American historiography was the way in which secular (academic) and ecclesiastical historians turned to the same materials, the former rejoicing in the freshly discovered resources and dimension of their field,[24] the lat-

[24] As representative of the academic historians who have greatly strengthened our grasp on American Church history we may mention Arthur Schlesinger, Vernon Louis Parrington, Ralph Gabriel, Herbert Schneider, and more recently Henry Steele Commager, Perry Miller, and Arthur

ter greatly stimulated by the new directions, skills, and categories suggested by the cultural historians.

A good example of the direct impact of academic history on American Church history is the career of William Warren Sweet, himself an academic historian before he came to the Divinity School of the University of Chicago in 1927 to occupy the first chair of American Church history in the United States.[25] After filling a widely felt need in preparing a general *Story of Religions in America* (1930), Sweet energetically expanded his field introducing from secular history the new skills, among them co-operative research. A series of massive volumes on the accommodation of the several denominations to the frontier issued from his hands and those of his students. The exhilaration of the fresh approach had still not spent itself as the theme was applied to ever smaller groups and local situations. All these studies have been rich in sources but perhaps more scanty in theological and interpretive elements than even the poverty of such in the period and area considered would have warranted.

II. The Teaching and Writing of Church History in the Current Epoch, 1933–

Symptomatic of the oncoming interest in the compulsion of ideas, theological and otherwise, and the mounting quest of a regnant principle in the shaping of American Church history was the attempt of Thomas C. Hall (who left Union Theological Seminary to become professor of philosophy at Göttingen) to identify Wycliffite dissent as a dominant though socially obscured factor in America in *The Religious Background of American Culture* (1930). Of much greater significance was the bold pre-empting of the theological and ideational interpretation of New England culture—too long neglected on the part of Church

---

Schlesinger, Jr., whose contributions to the field fall largely in the period following 1933.

[25] It was Roman Catholicism that first became institutionally conscious of American Church history in instituting in 1922 the Catholic University Studies in American Church History.

historians—by Perry Miller in his brilliant *Orthodoxy in Massachusetts* (1933).

Likewise marking the shift of interest and therewith the onset of a new epoch are two contrasting books by H. Richard Niebuhr. His *Social Sources of Denominationalism* (1929) was a valuable analysis of the history of American Christianity in terms of the social and economic factors to which Rauschenbusch and the whole Chicago school of religious history influenced by him had drawn attention. *The Kingdom of God in America* (1937), written, as Niebuhr says, to correct and supplement the socio-economic interpretation of his earlier work, happily embodies or suggests five of the most distinctive characteristics of the Church historiography of the current epoch: (1) a concern for the ultimate meaning of history, (2) a recovery of interest in doctrines as successive transcripts of divine realities traced for the community of faith out of faith and as such charged with a potency of their own in shaping events, (3) a fresh appreciation of the Church as a divine community, reflecting and pointing to the ultimate Kingdom or Rule of God, and in this connection (4) a renewed interest in the historical dynamic and the achievement of community among the voluntarist "sects" as distinguished from the "churches," and (5) a vigorous re-examination of the historic relation between the Church, democracy, and the state.

For this reconception of the scope and office of Church history as indeed of so many other fields, the advent of Hitler and Roosevelt more clearly mark the beginning of a new epoch than did the termination of the War in 1918. The widespread disavowal of the more than half-secular faith in the inevitability of progress (which had managed to survive the World War in America though shattered in Europe) as the specter of Hitler darkened, could not fail to have profound effects upon American conceptions of history and consequently the task of tracing it. The conjunction of Roosevelt and Hitler pointed to a cosmic opposition of good and evil in history, while at the same time the rapid deterioration of German universities brought emphatically to a close a long epoch of American dependence upon German historical scholarship, and this coincided with the intensification of debate as to the proper role of the American people in world history.

The importance of 1933 specifically for Church historiography is confirmed by the clustering of significant events around this date. The year before saw the publication, for instance, of the first volume of *Church History*, the new organ of the reorganized and revitalized American Society of Church History. This Society had heard a stimulating address by John R. Mott in 1931 and in response to his suggestion organized a Church History Deputation to the Orient to ascertain (1) what had been done and what could be done about preserving the original sources for the history of the younger churches and (2) what place Church history then occupied and should occupy in the training of leaders for these churches.[26] In the same year the Church historians of or affiliated with the University of Chicago, published *A Bibliographical Guide to the History of Christianity*, which, with its nine co-ordinate divisions, including (VII) History of Eastern Christianity [27] and (IX) Christianity in Newer Fields, marked the consolidation of the new ground gained in the course of the foregoing period, from which to view, as from a vantage point at once American and ecumenical, the unfolding of Christian history as a whole.

Kenneth Scott Latourette's multi-volume history of Christianity in terms of expansion is written from this new vantage point.[28] Of significance also is the publication in 1933 of the Augustana

[26] See Shirley Jackson Case, "The Church History Deputation to the Orient," *Church History* I (1932), p. 107.

[27] Matthew Spinka, first of Chicago Theological Seminary and then of Hartford, had already appraised the available Western works on the subject and called attention to the general neglect of Slavic Church history in America in "The Present Status of Slavic Studies in Church History" (1925), *Papers of the A.S.C.H.*, 2nd series, VIII (1928). Since then he himself has, along with Slavic and Byzantine academic historians, greatly enriched the field.

[28] *A History of the Expansion of Christianity*, 7 Vols. (1937–1945); restated in *Anno Domini: Jesus, History and God* (1940).

Lutheran Lars P. Qualbens' *A History of the Christian Church,*
one of the first [29] general Church histories to come from among
the foreign language churches, a compendium which significantly
assigns almost a third of its space to North and Latin American
Christianity.[30] In such a textbook, which corresponds in type to
the histories produced by the older denominations at the end of
the nineteenth century, denominational interest determines selection and emphasis. But also beginning about this time, a new type
of interpretive Church history or textbook makes its appearance
from the pens of historians standing within the older denominations or at least formed by them. Immediately after the First
World War, the few new Church histories had been prepared
for young people, an effect of the new religious education
emphasis. Then in 1931 the textbook of Henry Kalloch Rowe of
Andover-Newton appeared with its fresh periodization and its
new conception of the Church as implied in the title, *A History
of the Christian People,* an example of what might be called
Christian cultural history with a new interest in the full dimension
of history and in the compulsion of ideas. This development
represents in part the penetration and fructification of American
Church historiography by impulses stemming from James Harvey Robinson's *The New History.* Another development, making
1933 stand out in American Church historiography is the collecting and editing of fresh ecclesiastical sources under the Work
Projects Administration. And of an entirely different order is the
death also in 1933 of Arthur Cushman McGiffert, whose two
volume *History of Christian Thought* (1932–1933) constitute a
particularly fitting legacy from an epoch of "historical theology"
to the new epoch of "theological history."

Such are some of the events which make 1933 the dividing

[29] Save for Schaff's that of Lutheran C. M. Jacobs appears to have been
the first such, *The Story of the Church* (1925).

[30] The medieval Church is given less than a tenth of the space. The primitive Church is presented in harmony with a conservative Lutheran view
of the New Testament.

line between two eras. By way of corroboration one may remark that 1933 marks also a nodal point in the development of secular historical thinking in America. I refer to the controversial presidential address of Charles A. Beard before the American Historical Association in 1933 "Written History as an Act of Faith" and Theodore Clarke Smith's despairing retort the following year.[31] Significantly it was a German *Church* historian Karl Heussi (*Die Krisis des Historismus*, 1930) along with Benedetto Croce who fortified Beard in his onslaught upon historism (the whole system of supposed objectivity in research and in the delineation of actual history) within the American Historical Association. It should be observed in this connection that academic and ecclesiastical historians in the United States have been in general much more responsive to stimuli from foreign historians, secular or churchly, than either to impulses from their colleagues on the other side of the local "wall of separation." Such has been one of the consequences of scholarly isolation in the land where Church and State, Seminary and Academy are separated on principle.

Since the new epoch in American ecclesiastical historiography, with its renewed interest in the theology of history, is characterized also by its being fully abreast of trends in Europe, phases here being now almost completely synchronized with phases there, and the old cultural lag having been made up, it is appropriate to mention a parallel in Europe precisely in the area of the history of Church history. Walter Nigg, *Die Kirchengeschichtsschreibung* (1934), after distinguishing seven types of Church historiography down through the centuries, looks forward to a new historiography which, while abandoning nothing of scientific methodology so hard fought for in the theological field generally, will reappraise the place of theology in Church history and will be particu-

---

[31] For Beard, *American Historical Review*, XXXIV (1933-1934); p. 219 and the further attack on presumed objectivity in "That Noble Dream," *ibid.*, XLI (1935-1936), p. 74, and for Smith prepared to go down in the controversy with the flags of studied objectivity flying, "The Writing of American History, 1884-1934," *ibid.*, XL (1934-1935), p. 439.

larly concerned to define the Church and to recover the divine dimension thereof. Walter Köhler had already drawn attention to the problem of historiography in the face of the anti-historical or rather the meta-historical implications represented by Barth.[32] But it has been precisely the American analogue of Barthianism which has insisted upon the importance of history and has in consequence commanded attention for a realistic, Christian, and prophetic analysis of our historical situation. Thanks to Reinhold Niebuhr,[33] Paul Tillich and Wilhelm Pauck among others, the radical reconception of orthodox theology based upon a fresh examination of Reformation and hence Augustinian theology, American Protestants are paradoxically (quite appropriately!) more history-conscious now than during the ascendancy of the historical method.

Perhaps nowhere does the impact on Church historiography of this fresh emphasis become so palpable as in the utterances of Church historians in that special type of literature, already several times alluded to, the essay or address or textbook prolegomena entitled "What Is Church History?" Probably no theological discipline has been more self-conscious, at least in America, than Church history. Again and again, Church historians have felt called upon to defend or define their field. Obviously, behind all these efforts to explain the nature and function of their discipline one can overhear the stresses and strains within the American seminary curriculum, adapting itself to ever new community needs and adjusting itself to all the philosophical and theological blows and counterblows. To catch the full significance of the contemporary articulation of the nature and office of Church history we return

[32] *Historie und Metahistorie in der Kirchengeschichte* (1930).

[33] The Reformation "doctrine of 'justification by faith' contains implications for an adequate interpretation of history which have never been fully appropriated or exploited, probably because most Protestant theologies which are interested in the historical problem, have drawn their inspiration from the Renaissance rather than the Reformation." *Nature and Destiny of Man* (1943), II, p. 155. Cf. his *Faith and History: A Comparison of Christian and Modern Views of History* (1949).

for a moment to the era traversed to take note of a representative few of the earlier defenses of Church history.[34]

Within the traditional American seminary "quadrivium," [35] each of the four fields has successively tried to "imperialize" over the others in its regnant period. For the most part in the period between 1900 and 1918, Church history did not have to justify itself; it was taken for granted as worthy of all esteem. It was rather in the immediately preceding phase, as we saw, that the newly developing discipline had to establish its claim over against (depending on the seminary) the previously dominant "exegetical" or, more commonly, "systematic" theology. Then in the phase following the First World War, Church history had again to defend itself, this time over against practical theology. In the spirit of the new functionalism, religious education, social service, and pastoral care were bulking large in the seminary curriculum,

[34] In the nineteenth century before 1888 there were, for example:

E. A. Park, tr., "Theological Encyclopaedia and Methodology: From the Unpublished Lecture of Prof. Tholuck," Sections 27–30 on Church history, *Bibliotheca Sacra*, I (1844), pp. 569–575.

Philip Schaff, *What is Church History?: A Vindication of the Idea of Historical Development* (Philadelphia, 1846).

Henry B. Smith, "The Nature and Worth of the Science of Church History," *Bibliotheca Sacra*, VIII (1851), p. 412.

William G. T. Shedd, "The Nature and Definition of Church History," *Lectures upon the Philosophy of History* (Andover, 1856), Lecture III.

Egbert Cotton Smyth, *Value of the Study of Church History in Ministerial Education* (Andover, 1874).

Joseph Henry Allen, *On the Study of Christian History* (Cambridge, 1878).

Ephraim Emerton (1883), above, n. 5.

John De Witt, *Church History as a Science, as a Theological Discipline, and as a Mode of the Gospel* (Cincinnati, 1883); reprinted in *Bibliotheca Sacra*, XLI (1884), p. 95.

For the epoch beginning with 1888 up to 1918 there are, for example:
Philip Schaff, *The Reunion of Christendom* (New York, 1893).
Arthur Cushman McGiffert (1893), above, n. 7.
John Fletcher Hurst (1897), above, n. 11.
Albert Henry Newman (1900), above, n. 9.
Walter Rauschenbusch (1907), above, n. 21.

[35] This is W. Barnett Blakemore's helpful re-employment and definition, "The Nature and Structure of the Practical Field," *Journal of Religion* XXIX (1949), p. 248. His introductory observations are particularly instructive.

while history was widely scorned. The comparatively large number of Church histories in the twenties, and thereafter, adapted to church schools and adult classes are evidence of the tribute paid by Church history to the new contender for hegemony in the seminary curriculum. Writings on the nature and function of Church history now appealed to the practical. We may instance Robert Hastings Nichols, "Aims and Methods of Teaching Church History" (1920),[36] John Alfred Faulkner, *On the Value of Church History* (1920), Ephraim Emerton, "History in Theological Education" (1920),[37] Roland Bainton, "Church History and Progress" (1922),[38] and Conrad Moehlman (who even from the early 'twenties was very much interested in schemes of popularizing history and who has continued to be especially interested in education), "Is the History of Christianity Practical?" (1926).[39]

Then, with the advent of the current epoch, efforts to redefine Church history become once again numerous, symptomatic of the readjustment and enforced re-evaluation of the discipline in the face of the world situation and the return of theology to her throne within the seminary curriculum. In this change of dynasty, "historical theology"—to perpetuate the older term for Church history for the moment—finds itself either a fierce foe of the new "systematic theology" or its enthusiastic ally while still carrying out a rearguard action against practical theology.

As representative of the lingering concern that Church history as a seminary discipline renew its credentials from time to time as a useful subject, we may take the inaugural address, "What is

[36] *Papers of the A.S.C.H.*, 2nd series, VII (1921), p. 39.

[37] See above, n. 5.

[38] *Education for Christian Service* by Members of the faculty of the Divinity School of Yale University (New Haven, 1922), p. 243.

[39] *The Rochester Theological Seminary Bulletin*, LXXVI (1925/26), p. 204.

We may mention here as belonging to the genre but not illustrative one way or the other of the trend, William Walker Rockwell, "Rival Presuppositions in the Writing of Church History," *Papers of the A.S.C.H.*, 2nd series, IX. It is largely concerned with Catholic bias in ecclesiastical historiography.

the Value of Church History for the Minister?" [40] by John T.
McNeill of Union Theological Seminary,[41] who in so many of
his writings exemplifies that responsiveness, characteristic of many
contemporary Church historians, to appropriate assignments suggested by the ongoing life and changing concerns of the Church.[42]
"The Task of the Church Historian" [43] (1940) by Sidney E. Mead,
Sweet's successor at Chicago, combines this high-level practical
concern with the newer convictions about the special vocation of
the Church historian in the academic community: to both tradition-
bound and secularized students, he says, "in the final analysis the
church historian is an evangelist." Mead significantly combines the
older sociological emphasis of the Chicago school with the newer
interest in the theological dimension of Church history. Utterly
loyal to scientific methodology, he is pleased to observe that
" 'Objectivity' is not indifference to the outcome for the historian
any more than for the detective." And while pointing to the important function of history in the emancipatory process of developing personal and communal "self-consciousness," he puts one
on guard against any fundamentalism or catholicizing, which would
obtrude a creed or an institution into the relationship between
man and God in the present attempt to check secularism.

Mead's colleague at Chicago, James Hastings Nichols, is prepared to go further. Nichols' emphasis on the Church and his
ascription of almost epistemological importance to committed

[40] *Anglican Theological Review*, XXVII (1945), p. 41.

[41] Formerly of Chicago (1927–44) and before that of Knox College,
Toronto.

[42] To mention only some of his books, around which could be clustered a
very much larger number of related books and articles: *Unitive Protestantism*
(1930) pointed up the survival of conciliar catholicity among sixteenth century Protestants, to which the ecumenical movement could appeal for historic support; *Christian Hope for World Society* (1937) provided historical
perspective and inspiration for Christian social action and indirectly threw
considerable light on contemporary debate on Church-State relations; his
editing of *Medieval Handbooks of Penance* (1938), while it grew out of
his earlier doctoral interest in Celtic Church history, provided historical
specimens of their art for those concerned with pastoral care.

[43] *The Chronicle: A Baptist Quarterly*, XII (1949), p. 127. The introduction is given over to a helpful identification of four meanings of "history."

membership therein for a completed understanding of its history are all the more significant for the reason that this Church historian, son of a distinguished Church historian, served for a while in teaching and in writing on general cultural history.[44] His conception of Church history has found expression in two essays, "Church History and Secular History" (1944)[45] and "History in the Theological Curriculum" (1946).[46]

In the former article he shows the dependence of secular historiography on Church history not alone in the chronological sense but also in the profounder sense of its basic concerns, noting that it was precisely Augustine, the first to write an extended interpretation of all history, who also wrote the first real biography. "Christianity revealed a new *man* quite literally, as well as a new type of human *community* for such men, and modern secular history is inconceivable without these presuppositions." Then, noting how nineteenth-century historians advanced beyond the rationalist historians of the Enlightenment in their appreciation of what might be called the sacramental aspect of history (culture) he observes that *Kultur* itself "becomes the holy church of modern secular man, and the historian becomes his priest." Nichols notes the way general cultural history was progressively nationalized[47] and Christian categories of history were secularized. But Nichols goes on to deplore the further particularization of history with the consequent loss of universal perspectives leading to the present crisis in history and concludes:

Surely there is a particular vocation for church history, especially modern church history, in this crisis, a church history broadened beyond ecclesiastical and doctrinal considerations to include the whole moral and spiritual life of those called to Christian loyalties, even at

[44] His first teaching position was at Macalester College. Some of his ideas on history are expressed in his Introduction to Jacob Burckhardt's *Weltgeschichtliche Betrachtungen,* tr. as *Force and Freedom: Reflections on History* (New York, 1943).

[45] *Church History,* XXXI (1944), p. 87.

[46] *The Journal of Religion,* XXVI (1946), p. 183.

[47] "Ranke was practically the last of the great historians who could comprehend the variety and intransigence of the new secular national states from the catholic perspective of a humanist church historian."

second hand. With the rapid decrease of the number of humanist historians of good will (of Judeo-Christian derivation), secular society is losing interpreters with insight for the values of universal humanity, universal moral standards, individual moral responsibility and a humble sense of the imperfection of all earthly institutions. Even secular society then may be served by historians based, not on a demonstrated theodicy, but on a wager and prayer to the Revealer of these truths that the destiny of mankind be indeed hidden in Christ and the God of Abraham, Isaac and Jacob.

Turning from the office of Church history for culture to its function for the Church, Nichols becomes more explicit about taking a stand avowedly from within the community of faith. He breaks explicitly from the school of Church history that in concentrating on environmental factors had "put second things first." Deploring the impoverishment of the sense of history in America, a legacy of the eighteenth-century rationalism and individualism which has shaped the contours of the American mind more than that of any other major people, Nichols rejoices in the ecumenical movement which has at length obliged us to think genetically about our denominational differences and has thus indirectly helped American Christians recover a sense of history, "not so much in the sense of knowing, as *belonging*." He points out, moreover, that Christianity properly "insists on its historical origins . . . because the initiation of the Christian faith was, itself, not a communication of a theology or ethics but a dramatic intrusion of God in Christ"; and thus in the profoundest sense "the Christian communion with God is not possible without a minimum of historical knowledge. . . ." And since history like autobiography ("history is the autobiography of a community") is usually written "from the vantage point of some decisive turn in life," Nichols expects that some of the best Church history will be composed in our time.

With convictions allied to those of Nichols, the Episcopalian Cyril Richardson of Union Theological Seminary declares in "Church History Past and Present" (1949) [48] that history has a

---

[48] *Union Seminary Quarterly Review*, V (1949), p. 3. The larger part of the inaugural address is given over to an attractive account of the history of Church history at Union.

prophetic function, alluding here to the inclusion of the historical books among the Prophets, and that the Church historian "cannot, if he tries to write sacred history in its fullest sense, be content to confine himself to that bare record of events which we know as *scientific* history [italics mine] . . . he has to tell the story against the background of ultimate meanings. He has to recognize that he stands on the boundary between symbol and fact, between myth and history, because the events with which he deals are transfigured by the holy." And like several other historians mentioned, Richardson holds that "Church history is inevitably the fountain from which reformation springs," instancing, for example, the many reformations which have appealed to some freshly rediscovered aspect of Augustine.

It is clear from this sampling of what might be called the self-conscious reflections of strategically located contemporary Church historians that Church history, where it is in league with the new theology, is conscious of a fresh sense of vocation after the aimlessness or self-apology in the presence of the practical field common during the history-debunking 'twenties. Moreover, as "theological history" it has fully recovered both the self-esteem and the outward respect within the seminary curriculum which as "historical theology" it had formerly enjoyed during the period from 1900 to 1918, when it had been, as we can see in retrospect, somewhat over-confident in the redemptive role of scientific method.

But this theologizing has not gone on unchallenged. As an opponent of what he pillories as "the revival of historical dualism" we may mention Shirley Jackson Case, sometime head of the Chicago school of religious history, who expressed his alarm at the new trend in *The Christian Philosophy of History* (1943). And in an essay [49] in the same year, the sometime Catholic priest George La Piana, Church historian at Harvard Divinity School (1917–1947), quite properly distinguished between the philosophy

[49] "Theology of History," *The Interpretation of History*, edited by Joseph R. Strayer (Princeton, 1943), p. 149. Cf. also his sensitive and at points almost vicariously "autobiographical" address "Ernesto Buonaiuti," *Harvard Divinity School Bulletin*, XLIV (1947), p. 47.

and the theology of history, isolating the four pillar myths of the latter, whether it be the Augustinian, the Democratic, or the Fascist "theology of history." He takes no notice of the currents astir in Protestant thinking. More obviously irritated than alarmed by the orthodox trend, is the New Testament scholar Chester C. McCown of the Pacific School of Religion, expressing thereto hostility in his article "In History or Beyond History" (1945).[50] These random outbursts are probably representative of a much larger, as yet inarticulate or perhaps as yet unaffected body of Church historians, than these few writings would indicate. But it is clear that there is among Protestant Church historians nothing comparable to the debate raised in academic history circles, for example, by Carl Becker's rarification of supposedly hard historical facts (1926)[51] and particularly by Charles A. Beard's address, "Written History an Act of Faith" (1933).[52]

Turning now from the contemporary expressions concerning the nature and function of Church history, we may, in conclusion, take note of the topics and issues of greatest current interest and of the prospects for achievement in the field.

American Church historians are increasingly concerned with collecting and editing New World source materials. Old World sources are being translated apace. Of interest here is Campbell Bonner's important addition to Patristic sources in his editing from the fourth-century Michigan-Beatty codex, Melito's *Homily on the Passion* (1940), and A. J. F. Ziegelschmit's editing of *The Greater Chronicle of the Hutterian Brethren* (1943), a capital source long believed to be lost, which came to light in an American settlement. In 1949 the American Society for Reformation Research assumed joint responsibility with its revived German counterpart for the ongoing publication of the old *Archiv* as an international series under the title *Archivum Reformationis Historicum*.

[50] *The Harvard Theological Review*, XXXIII (1945), p. 41.
[51] "What are Historical Facts?" Presidential Address before the American Historical Association in Rochester, N.Y.
[52] See above, n. 31.

The exploration of the left wing of the Reformation, already greatly stimulated by the work of Roland Bainton of Yale Divinity School, will be further extended with the mounting scholarly interest in their own sources among the numerous representatives of the Old World sects, notably the Mennonites. New classifications and fresh categories of interpretation, suggested by sociology, economics, and psychology, have already clarified the field.

We may expect also extensive exploration in the historic concepts of the Church of which Cyril Richardson's *The Church Through the Centuries* (1938) is undoubtedly a harbinger. Nor is it ecumenicity alone that will promote such studies. A full-length history of ecclesiology has never been written; it is only as institutions are gravely imperiled that we seek to define and defend them. Liturgical history and liturgy as a source will become increasingly prominent.

We may expect fresh research into the role of the foreign language churches in the process of acculturation and especially into the tensions both within the individual immigrant and between the first and second generations—tensions in which, by a reversal of socio-psychological roles all too frequently overlooked, it is the melting-pot democracy which becomes the community of *rebirth*, venturesome commitment and hope while the foreign language church serves in effect as the community of *birth*, protective cohesion, and memory. The half articulated feeling for America as at once a gathered Church and the Kingdom of God in process of fulfilment invites continued exploration into the relationship of Christianity and democracy with special attention in the future to the relationship of the Church to labor. Henry F. May's *Protestant Churches and Industrial America* (1949) and before it C. H. Hopkins' *The Rise of the Social Gospel in American Protestantism* (1940) belong in this line. Studies of the religious sources of democracy like those of Parrington and Gabriel will be succeeded by studies critical of the often too easy conflation of Christianity and nationalism recently probed by Koppel Pinson, *Pietism as a Factor in the Rise of German Nationalism* (1934), and Salo Baron, *Religion and the Rise of Nationalism* (1947). One may observe, incidentally, in connection with these writers, that the cultural ethos of America is such that American Jewish scholars feel utterly free to carry their researches into the Christian field with no religious self-consciousness and often, indeed, with extraordinary perception of the subtleties of Christian theology: witness e.g., the foregoing writers and Harry A. Wolfson of Harvard on the ongoing influence of Philo in the Fathers.

The present year has seen the publication of a three-volume climax to a mounting series of monographic and general studies on a theme of ever increasing interest and concern, *Church and State in the United States* by Anson Philips Stokes. Magnificent achievement that it is, we may expect numerous other studies freshly examining the more ancient sources and exploring also the bearing of changing Christologies and ecclesiologies on the historic relations between Church and State with a view to ascertaining the viability of the present doctrine of strict separation. Paul Tillich in his distinction between "autonomy" (in this context, secularism) and "heteronomy" (in this context, ecclesiasticism) and his clear definition of the middle position so difficult to perpetuate, "theonomy," has introduced a new set of theological categories that will prove especially valuable in guiding American research into the history of Church and State.[53]

As contemporary concern with Church-State relations invites or rather compels historical inquiry, so it is possible that the newer practical disciplines which are currently undergoing redefinition (religious education, church management, pastoral care, the interest in healing) and the older but undermined disciplines (preaching, for example) will press for historical exploration, documentation, and inspiration—as examples R. C. Petry's edition of medieval sermons, *No Uncertain Sound* (1948) and Carl J. Scherzer's *The Church and Healing* (1950).

[53] Paul Blanshard's *American Freedom and Catholic Power* (1949) is a splendid example of the strength and the limitations of the attack upon "heteronomy" from the vantage point of "autonomy." A "theonomous" inquiry remains a desideratum.

As far as geographical areas go, given the stimulation of Latourette's magnificent history and the general American interest
in the Pacific, we may reasonably expect substantial local and
national histories of the younger churches of the Orient to make
their appearance soon. If written by Americans in the cultural-
historical mood, these histories will undoubtedly give prominence
to problems of cultural interpenetration, ethical compromise and
syncretism and, incidentally, will throw further light on the expansion of Christianity in the Greco-Roman and the Barbarian
worlds.

As to epochs or periods of Church history, it is quite probable,
given the fateful contraction of German scholarship and academic
means, that New World scholars will feel emboldened to explore
Germany in the Reformation century, the more so for at least
three reasons: the extended Occupation, the maturation of the immigrant churches on the American scene pressing forward to
wider academic interests, and finally the renewal of interest in the
Reformation induced by the new theological emphasis. Roland
Bainton's clear and discerning *Here I Stand* (1950) and E. G.
Schwiebert's massive *Luther and his Times* (1950) are the rich
first fruits in the line of Preserved Smith. Another period for
which revisions are in store is Christian antiquity. Robert M. Grant
in his recent survey entitled "The Future of the Ante-Nicene
Fathers" [54] describes the recent gains and declares that the Golden
Age in this area lies just ahead. The maturation of American
biblical scholarship and the skills and achievements of American
archeology will make up for the decline in classical studies and
in conjunction with the extensive textual preparation underscored
by Grant, insure great advances in the history of the Ancient
Church. The monumental *Christianity and Classical Culture*
(1944) by the Canadian C. N. Cochrane is an example of the kind
of bold revisions we may expect in this field.

And finally, if we follow James Hastings Nichols' suggestion
as to the relationship of crisis, catastrophe, and momentous decision

[54] *Journal of Religion*, XXX (1950), p. 109.

to the writing of autobiography and history, perhaps we may expect some comprehensive (I should like to say, momentous) historical interpretation of the nature and destiny of American Christianity. It is quite possible that it will be written by an American Negro historian of the Church, reaching back for basic categories of interpretation to the Judaeo-Christian experience of redemptive suffering and to the concept of God's Covenant with His ongoing Israel of history.

BIBLIOGRAPHY

Mode, Peter, *The Frontier Spirit in American Christianity* (New York, 1923)

Niebuhr, H. Richard, *The Kingdom of God in America* (New York, 1937)

Schaff, Philip and David, *History of the Christian Church* (New York, 1882–1910)

Walker, Williston, *A History of the Christian Church* (New York, 1944)

Latourette, Kenneth Scott, *A History of the Expansion of Christianity* (New York, 1937–1945)

McNeill, John T., *Christian Hope for World Society* (New York, 1937)

Hardy, E. R., Jr., *Militant in Earth* (New York, 1940)

Hurst, John Fletcher, "The Science and Literature of Church History," *History of the Christian Church* (1897/1900), I, pp. 15–57.

MacCracken, Henry Mitchell, "The Place of Church History in the College Course of Study," *Papers of the American Society of Church History*, III (1891), p. 217.

Rauschenbusch, Walter, "The Influence of Historical Studies on Theology," *The American Journal of Theology*, XI (1907), p. 111.

Schaff, David, "The Movement and Mission of American Christianity," *The American Journal of Theology*, XVI (1912), p. 51.

Nichols, James Hastings, "Church History and Seculary History," *Church History*, XXXI (1944), p. 87; "History in the Theological Curriculum," *The Journal of Religion*, XXVI (1946), p. 183.

PASTORAL THEOLOGY
AND PSYCHOLOGY

Seward Hiltner

SEWARD HILTNER was born in Pennsylvania in 1909, and he was educated at Lafayette College and the Divinity School of the University of Chicago. Prior to taking up his present position as Associate Professor of Pastoral Theology in the Federated Theological Faculty of the University of Chicago, he was for twelve years Executive Secretary of the Department of Pastoral Services of the Federal Council of the Churches of Christ in America. In this capacity he organized many research groups and spoke at numerous conferences in almost every state in the union. He is the author of several well-known books and numerous articles and pamphlets on counseling, the relations between psychology and religion, co-operation between doctors and ministers, etc. His best-known books are *Pastoral Counseling* and *Religion and Health,* and he edited *Clinical Pastoral Training.* He also serves as consultant for *Pastoral Psychology* magazine.

VIII

THE TITLE of this chapter is a kind of recent history in minia-
ture. If we referred only to "pastoral theology," we should be
attempting to link the pre-scientific formalism of the nineteenth
century with current dynamic thinking, and largely ignoring the
intervening stages of development. If our term were only "pastoral
psychology," we should be emphasizing a basic period of development, but implying that it had no antecedents or no future as an
inherent part of the Protestant Christian enterprise. Both terms,
and their relationship, are needed if an accurate assessment of this
field is to be made.

In 1900

By the end of the nineteenth century, pastoral theology in the
United States was a combination of formalism, dedicated intentions, and assiduity. The formalism was little in evidence in the
great evangelical churches like the Methodist and Baptist, but
was important in the liturgical or doctrinal churches like the Episcopal, Lutheran or Presbyterian. The former groups, although
settling down in a more settled country, were still basking in the
afterglow of the frontier movements with their revivals, their feeling of prophetic expansiveness, and their general itch to be up
and moving. They had little time for or interest in the laborious
and formal analyses of pastoral, moral and ascetical theology which
had been developed in Great Britain and Germany. Their theme
was evangelism, not edification. The "interviews" that accompanied revival meetings were not sufficiently individualized to
lead toward a pastoral theology.

Pastoral theology in the formal sense had been developed as a
study by an established priesthood or ministry. When the line
between minister and layman became hard to draw, educationally

as well as sacramentally, it was natural that there should be little interest in formal studies developed in a different context. Besides, these churches simply counted on the group itself to perform the edifying or sanctifying function. Growth in the Christian life was to come about through association with one's brother pilgrims. Since no priestly intermediaries were necessary, the practical conclusion often drawn was that no professional assistance was likely to be helpful. In short, these churches were not only uninterested in pastoral theology; they were even disinclined to ask the questions out of which a pastoral theology might have emerged.

The more liturgical and doctrinal churches were in a different position. Their closer emotional relation to the more settled churches of Britain and Germany was reflected in their tendency to stick closer to the eastern seaboard or, if they moved west as did the great German migrations of the nineteenth century, to become settled societies as rapidly as possible. We now see a fairly obvious connection between their urge to establish social stability and their interest in liturgical or doctrinal correctness, a marked need for order being the requisite in both instances for feeling at home. This was in contrast to the more ebullient churches which captured the frontier, where vitality was more important than order, and expansiveness than stability.

The orderly churches continued to insist on an educated ministry. The patterns of theological education reflected little of Emerson's American scholar, and were largely taken over from those of the respective mother countries. Study was liberal arts, stressing languages and literature, plus a continuation of the same patterns into theological education itself. Indeed, the most striking fact about the theological seminaries at the turn of the century was that they conceived their task to be chiefly an extension into a particular content of the procedures of liberal arts education.[1] The notion that professional education ought to analyze operations as well as content, the people as well as the gospel, was not firmly

[1] See "The Nature and Structure of the Practical Field," by W. B. Blakemore, *Journal of Religion*, Vol. 29, No. 4 (October, 1949).

grasped. The very business of having a seminary and insisting on formal theological education seemed against it.

There were in the seminaries some courses on practical or pastoral theology. Those in the Reformed tradition were almost entirely about methods of preaching. Those with Anglican ties studied moral and ascetical theology, which were in their turn descendants at long range of the penitentials and at briefer range of clear-headed British casuistry. The English penchant for common-sense moral thinking was clear. They did not, however, have a "case-work" point of view as we would think of that today. Moral theology, so far as it dealt with individuals, dealt with their offenses. Ascetical theology was procedural, but on the basis of a generalized Christian man.

The seminaries in the Lutheran tradition had, thanks to the German pastoral theologians of the early nineteenth century, a more comprehensive theory and framework than did the others. They recognized the unity of the ministry, and attempted to analyze pastoral operations so as to stress that unity while approving the obvious diversity of activities. But they were, from our contemporary point of view, lacking in content. They had the form and structure and order of a pastoral theology, but little to say within it.

In general, therefore, the pastoral theology of 1900 was formalistic where it existed at all. It was also compounded of dedicated intentions and persevering "art." The books of this period which were not purely formal in character tended to exhortations, to the pastor or theological student, to love people, spend time with them, call upon them. We would have a parallel if the clinical textbooks of medicine should consist mainly of urging that the physician value clinical practice, make home visits, not rely on people coming to his office, and be devoted to serving his patients. In either event, such books have a valuable place. But in medicine they were not at that time confused with clinical texts.

Thus, most of the writing on pastoral theology in that period was either formalistic or anecdotal or both. Once a formal framework had been established, the assumption was that a pastor proceeded by art and assiduity. It was and is clear that there is always a personal element transcending not only mechanical procedures but also attempts at formal definition. But the emphasis on exploiting one's charm, and doing his duty by pastoral work, betrayed the assumptions that there was no body of knowledge on which to build and that pastoral work was a price one paid for the privileges of preaching or conducting worship. This meant that there was no intellectual challenge in pastoral theology except at the point of the purely formal and theoretical.

This analysis is not meant to suggest that no good pastoral work was being done. We cannot doubt that here, as throughout the history of the church, the thoughtful and sympathetic interest of pastor and congregation were immensely helpful to multitudes of people. Besides, the decline of group discipline over the individual church member during the nineteenth century tended to extend the range of human problems on which pastor and congregation felt an impulse to help and not merely to correct.[2] This humanizing trend undoubtedly extended the number of persons who were helped by the practice of pastoral theology.

But even when they did well, they knew not what they did. And they were certainly ignorant, when they failed, of the reasons for failure. In our current perspective, they were not wrong to be interested in the formal and theoretical at one end, and humanitarian anecdotalism at the other. They were wrong in not realizing that the area in between was being neglected, and that in it lay the hope of a new pastoral theology. This middle area we could characterize variously as psychological content, as the study of interpersonal and intrapsychic processes, or as the application of scientific method, broadly conceived, to understanding what is actually occurring in people as the pastor goes about his work with them.

Psychology gave no help on this during the previous century.

[2] See the forthcoming *A History of the Cure of Souls,* by John T. McNeill.

Until the time of Wundt, in Germany, after the American Civil War, psychology was pre-scientific, introspective, and a handmaid to any particular philosophy. It was structural in character, based on the faculties in terms of content. The first advance came with the creation of Wundt's psychological laboratory, with the consequent movement for attempting to understand psychological processes by observing them systematically. At first such methods, naturally enough, were applied to apparently simpler phenomena, which mean that they were relatively divorced from the totality of man's complex experience as man. Neither faculty psychology, which lingered on, nor experimental psychology, which was rapidly growing, could at that stage help put meat on the pastoral theological bones.[3]

In our modern sense, there was no pastoral psychology at the beginning of this century. Experimental psychology had not got far enough to become a general dynamic psychology, and hence offered no adequate background. Faculty psychology was being exploded at specific points by experimental work. Not until there should be dynamic trends in psychology, which nevertheless moved closer to man and not just some function of man, could there be a base upon which a pastoral psychology could be erected.

In this analysis of where we were, no mention has been made of the fact that William James, John Dewey, Sigmund Freud and George A. Coe began their work before 1900. Each of them, in his own way, was to be, however unintentionally, a stage designer for the new drama of pastoral theology and psychology which the present century would produce. But their influence, while beginning earlier, did not have such an effect until after 1900.

Psychology of Religion

There were four broad movements or currents of thought which seem to be chiefly responsible in the first part of the century for the developments which have led to pastoral theology and

[3] See *Historical Introduction to Modern Psychology*, by Gardner Murphy.

psychology as we now understand them. These are the study of the psychology of religion, progressive education and religious education, psychoanalysis and the development of the several psychotherapeutic professions, and the successive theological movements, to use the common labels, of the social gospel and neo-orthodoxy. We shall consider them in turn.

In America the psychology of religion was begun not by pastors or professional churchmen but by university scholars who sensed, in the broadly empirical method which psychology had begun to use, opportunities for understanding certain religious phenomena for which no previous process explanations had been offered.[4] By those who tended to be sympathetic to religion and the church, the analysis stressed religious phenomena of the more extreme type, not practiced by the respectable. In those with an antipathy toward religion, notably J. H. Leuba, the tendency was to debunk even the religious theory and practice of the respectable.

The great American classicists of the psychology of religion were Edwin D. Starbuck, J. H. Leuba, G. Stanley Hall, Irving King, E. S. Ames, George A. Coe and, pre-eminently, William James.[5] Hall, Leuba and Starbuck began with adolescence and the relation of that developmental age to sudden religious conversions. This set a pattern for many followers, so that the most frequently discussed subjects under the rubric of psychology of religion came to be conversion and mysticism.

King and Coe made the first attempts to link the incipient process knowledge of religious phenomena with the normal course of religious development in the individual, Coe's far-reaching contribution being second only to that of James in the whole field.[6] Ames attempted to link patterns of social understanding with psychological knowledge. The greatest work was of course by James. Perhaps most important among his many contributions

[4] For a general survey, see my "The Psychological Understanding of Religion," *Crozer Quarterly*, V. 24, No. 1 (January 1947).

[5] *Varieties of Religious Experience*.

[6] *The Religion of a Mature Mind* (Revell, 1902), and *The Psychology of Religion*.

was at that time his demonstration that religious phenomena could be understood through analysis of their development, and that such understanding did not necessarily detract from their validity. Pastors and theologians were wary of James's pluralism; but his positive emotional tone toward religion was often more convincing than his pluralistic ideas.

Except through his writings, however, James did not teach pastors or theological students. George A. Coe did. In the tens and twenties, one citadel after another of heretofore psychologically unstudied religious phenomena was examined by him, his students, and others. The way religion operates—any religion, in any kind of person—was susceptible to examination. Nearly all the theological schools introduced at least one basic course in the psychology of religion. If its purpose was in many instances chiefly apologetic, to prepare students against this new source of theological attack, it could not remain wholly at that level, but became also positive.

During the twenties there appeared many new texts on the psychology of religion, most of them simply building on the work of the classicists without any new orientation. During the thirties and forties there was very little writing which called itself the psychology of religion, and but one significant new general text in the field.[7] The single genuinely original contribution was by Anton T. Boisen in the mid-thirties, who successfully challenged the contention, made even by James, that a fairly clear line could be drawn between understanding normal and pathological religious processes.[8] It has not been until 1950 that a new general avenue of progress for the psychology of religion has found its way into print, based on James but taking all of the intervening developments in dynamic psychology and psychotherapy into account.[9]

The fact is that the psychology of religion has won the point

[7] *Psychology of Religion*, by Paul E. Johnson.
[8] *The Exploration of the Inner World*, by Anton T. Boisen.
[9] *The Individual and His Religion*, by Gordon W. Allport.

which brought it into being. Religious phenomena are capable of being understood like any others. If the methods are complex, if analysis is sometimes made the cloak for reductionism, if our knowledge is mightily incomplete, still it is valuable even for religionists to learn what can be learned about the processes of religious development.

It is possible that the trend represented by Allport may result in the recrudescence of a study known as the psychology of religion, especially since psychology in general has become less scientistic in its philosophy and less attached to a laboratory point of view which would exclude reflection on meaning. Certainly there will be more work and studies. Pastoral theologians and psychologists of religion have now a basis and temper for work together which has not previously existed.

The significance of these developments in the psychology of religion for pastoral theology and psychology is plain. There could be no far-reaching pastoral theology unless there were a content in pastoral psychology. And there could be no such pastoral psychology if the processes of religious development in the individual were unexaminable. If they were to be examined for purposes other than general debunking, there had to be a conviction that whatever was found would in the long run strengthen the religion which ought to be strengthened. This is the permanent contribution of the psychology of religion to pastoral theology.

Religious Education

The second evocative movement was progressive education and religious education. The prophet and leader in secular education was John Dewey. Although Dewey remains incomprehensible to Europeans, and his permanent contribution is hidden under the bushel of turgid prose and metaphysical positivism, his fundamental influence upon education and religious education will remain as constructive. Dewey's basic point was that people learn in proportion as they recognize their interests to be touched.

If their interests are recognized to have some inherent worth, and they develop as contact is made with these, then there emerges a theory of education which refutes any authoritarian approach in education.

Because Dewey's philosophy and psychology were evolved around education, they did not partake of the fragmentation with which early twentieth century psychology was afflicted. Hence Dewey was close to a theory and practice of total personality years before the psychologists caught up.[10] It was his totalism and developmentalism which caught the eye of religious educators. They were trying to teach religion. But they became suspicious of Bible verses and homilies on love. They wanted not just to communicate knowledge about religion, but to bring about an inward appropriation of religion. It occurred to them that there was a difference between the intention of the educator and the performance of the pupil. This led to consideration of methods, and direct to Dewey. If they wanted children, and adults, to appropriate and assimilate meaningfully, voluntarily, and from within, they would do well to begin by touching existing interests or felt needs. If they were not imposing something external, they had better prove it.

It is difficult for us now to realize how radical this philosophy of religious education sounded forty years ago. For meanwhile the basic point has been won, to such an extent that we can not envision what it fought to conquer. It is true that Horace Bushnell had adumbrated such a notion as Schleiermacher had done still earlier for a psychology of religion. But Bushnell's point had been that children did not have to have life direction completely re-directed if it were rightly routed in the first place. The new point went further. Possibly children's needs, as made known in one way or another by children themselves, might say something about where they should go. It is true that reactionaries in religion and education have tried to make a mockery of the

[10] See article on Dewey's psychology by G. W. Allport, and Dewey's reply, in *The Philosophy of John Dewey*, edited by A. Schilp.

Dewey views. Yet the essential point in those views has won over every form of reaction. Education, secular and religious, is the beneficiary of the fight which Dewey and the religious educators waged against education in terms of the intention of the educator apart from the relationships involved in the educative process.

The immediate result of the Dewey trends in religious education was to create an educational group within the church but not of it, a group of educational leaders paralleling the ecclesiastical leaders but with a philosophy of development instead of a philosophy of transmission. The details of this development do not belong in this chapter. But the influence of the trend upon pastoral psychology's development does have a place here.

As soon as the religious educators took seriously the developmental idea, they found themselves with a point of view which plainly had as much significance for work with individuals as for work with groups, for pastoral work as for religious education. Along with this, in theological seminaries' departments of religious education, came a vital sense that here was the new against which the old could not stand, that here was a point of view which was relevant not alone to religious education in the narrow sense but to the work of the church as a whole. Consequently courses began to appear on religious education and worship, religious education and counseling, religious education and something else. Unintentionally, a powerful movement had been set in motion for breaking down the artificial lines of division in the operations of the pastor and the church. The fact that this was done imperialistically, as if religious education were the creditor and everything else the debtor, was inevitable but unfortunate.

The religious education movement became like the hospital chaplain who has seen the patient through a serious illness. The chaplain is remembered gratefully, even revered, so long as the ravages of illness persist. But so soon as his basic work has been done and the patient is again on his own feet, the last thing the chaplain can expect is gratitude. The fact that, in this case, the metaphorical chaplain insisted that he alone could help every patient did not add to his chances of receiving the gratitude due.

The fact is that the developmental point of view, which is the cornerstone of pastoral theology and psychology, was brought into theological education and church practice by the religious educators. Their concern was to study the processes of development, to find the norms from the study of process. Although this may at times have been placed in a naive philosophical framework, its permanent though partial value is beyond price.

Psychoanalysis

The third, and perhaps ultimately the most significant, trend which has evoked pastoral psychology has been psychoanalysis and psychotherapy. Freud, trained in the thought processes and assumptions of nineteenth-century medicine and therefore the positivistic philosophy of physical science of that age, nevertheless broke through this in discovering the meaning of what he called "unconscious" psychic processes and therefore of the powerful reality of dynamic and conflicting psychic forces.[11] We cannot question today the great positive significance of his essential discovery. It was he who found the key, in a systematic way, which has unlocked the dynamic meaning of the life sciences, that is, which sees man's psychic life in terms of forces, energies, pressures and values which affect and conflict and liberate him though his head be ignorant of the process.

Freud's findings in themselves tended to controvert all rationalistic or purely conscious psychologies. As has often been noted, they were, in the psychological realm, as threatening to idealism as were Marx's ideas in politics and economics. Whatever their detailed errors, both insisted on something more than intentions, and asked instead: What are the real forces operating here?

No doubt this fact would have produced religious reaction to Freud in any case. But when Freud attached to his findings a reductionist and positivistic philosophy of nearly everything including religion, the reaction became certain. So it was that the

[11] *The Basic Writings of Sigmund Freud.*

first response of churchmen to Freud was negative, and that his philosophy prevented them from proper assessment of his findings. Even the religious educators, whose views we now see should have made them congenial to Freud's findings, were very slow to take them into account. Indeed, it was not until the late twenties that a good beginning was made at disentangling the Freudian findings from the philosophy which had become attached.

It may be true, as some believe, that Freud would never have got a religious hearing if it had not been for Jung.[12] Joining himself with Freud in the first decade, Jung found himself after some years increasingly at odds with Freud's therapeutic rigidity, sexual theory, opposition to religion *per se*, and other things. Dissociating himself to found a new school, Jung seemed to many thoughtful religionists to be forming a dynamic psychology which permitted more positive affinity with religion. There are controversial issues here. While welcoming Jung's acceptance of religion as a fact of psychic life, often as a positive fact, some of us have considered that Jung's mystical tendencies, his creation of a new mythology of the psyche, and his resort to a collective unconscious make him an unsafe guide along theoretical lines. With others of more tender-minded spirit, as for example, the Guild of Pastoral Psychology in England, he has become the patron saint.

In any event, Freud's central principle of psychic dynamics has become so widely accepted that even those who criticize him fail to realize that they are indebted to him for it. The "unconscious" may be an unsatisfactory term; yet the notion that there are forces in the psyche which influence behavior and thought, but which are nevertheless unwitting in their operation, is widely accepted. It is indispensable to a comprehension of inner psychic forces and interpersonal relationships.

So far-reaching has been the influence of this key concept that, for a time, it tempted even pastoral psychology to neglect conscious or "Ego" factors. Such a pendulum swing was probably necessary to achieve an eventually truer perspective.

[12] See especially *Psychology and Religion* by Carl G. Jung.

Psychoanalysis and the associated trends in psychiatry, medicine, social work and elsewhere, have influenced both the theory and practice of pastoral psychology in a large way. We have already indicated that the heart of the theoretical contribution was in what the unconscious implied. The practical contribution has been at the point of understanding a particular parishioner, and then suggesting broad leads whereby ways of helping him could be found.

With a few unfortunate exceptions, pastoral psychology has not attempted to take over the distinctive therapeutic methods of psychoanalysis.[13] But it has greatly profited from learning how to understand the parishioner, how to assess the relationship between pastor and parishioner, and how to see whether the attitude and approach of the pastor is leading in a therapeutic direction in performance as well as intention.

Theology

The fourth set of evocative forces which led to modern pastoral theology and psychology was theological, first the social gospel movement and more recently what is usually known as neo-orthodoxy. The most obvious initial effect of the social gospel movement on pastoral psychology was negative. If the church made its influence felt and its ideals were more nearly actualized in social practice, less attention would have to be paid to the individual. There probably was an undue note of social optimism which tended to produce impatience about the relatively slow processes required to change individuals.

But in later perspective, it seems likely that the net effect of the social gospel on pastoral psychology has been positive. Before there could be deep and serious study of psychic processes, the naive individualism embodied in movements like revivalism had to be transcended. Once the churches committed themselves unmistakably to attempts to "Christianize the social order," they had made a decisive step toward understanding all the kinds of

[13] See my *Pastoral Counseling.*

forces, psychic as well as social, which can impede or help such a movement. If they had to reach some new disillusionment about the limitations of what was possible, recognition of social limitations was bound eventually to compel new consideration of psychic limitations. This did occur.

In so far as neo-orthodoxy has been a deepening movement in theology, an attempt to find the meaning of the Christian gospel through a deeper social and psychological realism, it should have had a positive and wholesome influence upon the development of pastoral theology and psychology. Since much neo-orthodox thinking has been more than that, especially in the wholly-other European brands, it has often appeared opposed to any kind of pastoral theology which conceives itself to be analytical in character and to get some of its data from empirical observation. Continental theology has not only not produced a pastoral psychology in the American sense, but seems still so preoccupied with the apologetic problem that it actively prevents the development of such a study by ruling it irrelevant.

Current American theological trends, reaching such a brilliant climax in Reinhold Niebuhr, have until recently held back pastoral psychology. They first introduced large scale realism about social, economic and political forces. When they went on to discuss the parallels in individual life, they often read general conclusions, socially derived, into individual experience without adequate study of the distinctive individual factors. Such a tendency helps to create the notion that, with the enunciation of a distinctively Christian theory, the details are of secondary significance. Since pastoral psychology is, in this context, details, it may simply be ruled irrelevant or derivative.

If the trends mentioned above are considered as swings of the pendulum, and what is now emerging is a more centrist view, then the deepening effect of the American neo-orthodox movement may have positive significance for pastoral theology and psychology. That this is beginning to occur is shown in such recent books as David E. Roberts' *Psychotherapy and a Christian View of Man.* Its viewpoint transcends both liberalism and neo-orthodoxy, but would have been impossible without both of them.

Pastoral Psychology and Pastoral Theology

The first practical movement leading toward modern pastoral theology and psychology was, as we have noted, religious education. But it tended to be preoccupied with the normative and the group, at the expense of the therapeutic and the individual. For this reason, it was not responsible in a major way for developing current pastoral psychology, even though it did create indispensable conditions for such development.

The second, and most influential, movement was that for clinical pastoral training.[14] Formally initiated in 1923, this movement attempted to bring clergy and theological students into intimate and daily contact with people, under supervision from the pastoral point of view. The locus of such training has usually been health and welfare institutions, where human problems are thrown into bolder relief than ordinarily. Several thousand clergy and students have now had such training, and its direct influence has been to underscore the importance of a dynamic pastoral psychology as one of the foundations for all the pastoral operations. Its secondary influence, such as effect on the formal theological curricula, or the stimulation of more expert writing and research in the field, has been of at least equal significance. Most of the top American leaders in the field at present are the products, at least in part, of the clinical pastoral training movement.

The shifts of viewpoint within clinical pastoral training have largely paralleled the shifts in development of pastoral psychology itself. In the first days of clinical discovery, during the twenties and early thirties, concentration was on understanding the parishioner, out there, as from a detached point of view. The dynamics of the life history became the focus of study. Then Richard C. Cabot and Russell L. Dicks discussed methodology in ministry to the sick, thus presenting an incipient theory of

[14] *Clinical Pastoral Training,* edited by Seward Hiltner.

relationship between pastor and parishioner.[15] To the life history advocates, however, Dicks' interview analysis did not seem sufficiently dynamic. For a time it seemed there would be two groups—one accused of non-dynamic methodism, and the other of detached dynamism. Fortunately these began to come together in the forties, when it was clearer that relationship as well as parishioner had to be studied, and that both could be examined dynamically. This paralleled a similar trend in psychoanalysis and other forms of psychotherapy, and was especially aided by the psychological work of Carl R. Rogers.[16] The most recent emergent has been a concern to study the attitude and approach of the pastor as he tries to counsel or administer or perform some other operation. This means study of the congruence or discrepancy between his intention and, considering the whole situation and relationship, his performance. This is the third dynamic link in the chain which includes parishioner, relationship and pastor. Study of all is now recognized to be essential to an adequate pastoral psychology.

The new knowledge and insight which has made possible this development has been the result of the sciences of man or the life sciences, whether it be a fact or process turned up by a psychiatrist and taken over by the pastor or something which the pastor, through his own observations and reflections, has found out for himself. Thus it has been natural that the new pioneers have stressed their connection with and indebtedness to psychotherapy, psychology, psychoanalysis, psychiatry, and the other life sciences or technologies. The focus has been, and still is, mainly on pastoral *psychology*.

Of very recent date, however, a new pastoral *theology* has begun to emerge. This is apt to be thought of as having a different or conflicting content from pastoral psychology. Actually, the content is the same. But it has a different frame of reference and

---

[15] *The Art of Ministering to the Sick.*
[16] *Counseling and Psychotherapy.*

sees its content in a different context. It has begun to appear as two points have become clearer. First, we see that the content of pastoral psychology has begun to fill in the gap which has always existed in pastoral theology through the centuries. Second, we realize that any concern and enterprise of the church must have its chief focus as theological in the broad sense, and that adequate study of any such concern is not to be viewed as merely the application of the Christian faith, understood and assimilated elsewhere, but as also an avenue for better understanding and assimilation of the faith itself.

Most pastors still prefer pastoral *psychology*, for it sounds as if it had some content and were not merely formal in character. But as it becomes more widely recognized that the dynamic content of pastoral psychology is also the dynamic content of pastoral *theology*, it seems likely that the latter term will once again come into wide use.

The Future

There is already very widespread interest within the churches in pastoral psychology. If my judgment is correct, this is rapidly expanding into a pastoral theology context as well. An effective new monthly journal entitled *Pastoral Psychology* has brought to four the number of journals dealing significantly with this field.[17] If the general trend of theological thinking becomes more positive toward pastoral psychology, as it may do in the United States, this will help remove some of the barriers to proper development of the field.

There are a few things which it seems possible to say about future development of this field with reasonable certainty. It is clear that we can never return to mere formalism or mere artistry and assiduity, or to them in combination. The new dynamic

---

[17] *Pastoral Psychology*, monthly (Great Neck, N.Y.); *Journal of Pastoral Care*, quarterly (Cambridge, Mass.); *Journal of Clinical Pastoral Work*, quarterly (New York, N.Y.); and *The Pastor*, monthly (Nashville, Tenn.).

knowledge, not alone in detail but in the very fact that there is an explorable body of knowledge, has made any such return impossible.

A second point is that the scientific method, if understood generically, is in the field to stay. At any time the pastor observes his work critically, in the light of his dynamic knowledge, in order to improve his understanding and his practice, he is in some respect a scientist as well as a helper or an educator. This of course dissociates generic scientific method from any necessary connection with unconcerned detachment, lack of interest in outcome, etc.

A third point is that pastoral care and counseling of individuals is here to stay, that the rise of however many therapeutic professions will not succeed in depriving the pastor of some therapeutic obligation to his people. But the rise of these other groups means that his results are judged by standards never before available. Hence, good intentions without study and knowledge become increasingly impossible.

A fourth point is that we are likely to see soon some genuinely advanced work, on both an academic and a clinical level, in pastoral psychology. So far study and research has been on an introductory plane. The chances of merging the interests of the church, the clinic, and the university have never been greater than they are likely to be in the years immediately ahead.

Fifth, pastoral psychology and now pastoral theology have begun to reach a point of maturity when they may be able to make basic contributions to our understanding of the Christian faith itself. Every examined version of Christian faith and expression has had one foot in some kind of psychology; for study of the human psyche is psychology. Not a few of the great theological insights of past ages have emerged out of what is basically psychological examination. With superior psychological knowledge and tools, it would be strange indeed if we could not gain certain new and deeper appreciations of the faith through proper psychological study.

BIBLIOGRAPHY

Allport, Gordon W., *The Individual and His Religion* (New York, 1950)

Boisen, Anton T., *The Exploration of the Inner World* (Chicago, 1936)

Coe, George A., *Psychology of Religion* (Chicago, 1916)

Cabot, Richard C., and Dicks, Russell L., *The Art of Ministering to the Sick* (New York, 1936)

Freud, Sigmund, *The Basic Writings of Sigmund Freud* (New York, 1938)

Hiltner, Seward, *Pastoral Counseling* (New York, 1949)

——, *Religion and Health* (New York, 1943)

James, William, *Varieties of Religious Experience* (New York, 1903)

Jung, Carl G., *Psychology and Religion* (New Haven, 1938)

May, Rollo, *The Meaning of Anxiety* (New York, 1950)

McNeill, John T., *A History of the Cure of Souls* (New York, 1951)

Roberts, David E., *Psychotherapy and a Christian View of Man* (New York, 1950)

Wise, Carroll A., *Religion in Illness and Health* (New York, 1942)

PREACHING

Charles W. Gilkey

CHARLES W. GILKEY was born at Watertown, Massachusetts, in 1882. He graduated from Harvard in 1903 and from Union Theological Seminary, New York, in 1908, where he received a fellowship for two years post-graduate study in Germany and Britain. He served as minister of the Hyde Park Baptist Church in Chicago from 1910 until 1928, when he became Dean of the University of Chicago Chapel and Professor of Preaching in its Divinity School, also teaching some courses in homiletics at the McCormick Theological Seminary and Garrett Biblical Institute. Retiring under the rules of the University of Chicago in 1947, he now lives at South Yarmouth, Massachusetts, and teaches part-time homiletics at Andover Newton Theological School. He has received honorary degrees from eight colleges and universities; he was elected by his fellow-alumni to the Harvard Board of Overseers from 1946 to 1948; and he is a member of the boards of George Williams College in Chicago and of Union Theological Seminary in New York.

IX

THERE are two characteristics of Protestant preaching—its endless variety, and its limited accessibility—which make definite answers to the double question raised in this book—whence and whither—peculiarly difficult in this area of contemporary American Christianity. Most other chapters in this symposium survey and appraise specific fields of Protestant thought, in each of which creative leadership is exercised by a comparatively few scholars and thinkers, who group themselves into diverging schools. The distinctive characteristics of these individuals and schools of thought have been made quickly and definitely accessible by the publication of books which most of them have written and nearly all of them read—in relation to which their respective points of view have been defined and developed.

But every Sunday in the year, in thousands upon thousands of Protestant churches across this American continent, nearly as many ministers preach more than as many sermons—for many of them preach twice. The content and quality of each man's preaching is likely to vary considerably from week to week: only occasionally is he at his own best. Anyone who has had personal contacts, not only with denominational differences, but with sectional and theological traditions and homiletic habits in different parts of the United States—to say nothing of the wide variations in professional training and personal gifts among all these individual preachers—will have gained some sense of how next to impossible it is to generalize about American preaching with any accuracy, or to trace any trends in contemporary preaching that are not subject to endless exceptions and contrary local evidences.

Again, very few of these countless weekly sermons have any accessible permanence other than in the memory of their hearers (which in most of us is short at best for any kind of public speaking, and notoriously so for sermons)—or in the notes or manuscripts (if any) stored away in what before the days of filing cabinets used to be called the preacher's "barrel." Such sermons as get themselves into print, in clerical periodicals like the *Christion Century Pulpit,* or in annual collections like *"Best Sermons of 19 . . . ,"* or even in volumes of sermons by some one minister widely enough known to justify by their sale the mounting costs of their publication—all these represent almost as much the selective invitation of an editor, or the selective favoritism of the preacher himself, as any typical characteristics of contemporary preaching as a whole.

Some arbitrary and partial selection among the available data seems therefore inevitable for any survey of the last fifty years of American Protestant preaching; and the basis of this selection is best stated frankly in advance.

In 1924 *The Christian Century* undertook to "get at the mind of the ministry for the purpose of getting at the mind of the church," by sending out ballots to about 90,000 Protestant ministers in all parts of the country, asking them to co-operate in finding "the twenty-five most influential and representative living preachers of our time." Nearly 25,000 ballots were returned, and on them 1162 different names were voted for. These last were obviously the preachers to whom at that time their fellow-ministers, and through them their churches, looked for light and leading. The twenty-five who led that poll were then asked to submit one characteristic sermon for inclusion in *The American Pulpit*—a collection edited by Dr. Charles Clayton Morrison, at that time editor of *The Christian Century.* Included in this volume are theological points of view and homiletic techniques as different as those of Dean Charles R. Brown and Dr. William P. Merrill, on the one hand, and Dr. Mark A. Matthews and "Billy" Sunday, on the other.

A study of these twenty-five sermons, as a primary source for the earlier period under review, has been supplemented from various volumes of *Best Sermons of 19 . . .* that have appeared in many of the years since 1924, and from volumes of published sermons by such outstanding preachers throughout this period as Dr. Harry Emerson Fosdick and Dr. Henry Sloane Coffin, as well as by younger men like Dr. Harold Bosley. Some of the annual Lyman Beecher Lectures on Preaching, given at Yale, which tend to reflect and clarify contemporary pulpit standards and ideals, have provided background and perspective; and for these later years, the files of the *Christian Century Pulpit* have made accessible a much wider range of selected sermons by younger and less widely known preachers.

Hardly less valuable than these printed sermons have been my own vivid personal memories of outstanding preachers at the turn of the century—Lyman Abbott, Maltbie D. Babcock, Henry van Dyke, George A. Gordon—whom I began to hear as a college undergraduate. And even more valuable was my weekly chance to listen, as Dean of the University of Chicago Chapel from 1928 to 1947, to the best preachers we could invite from all over the country and all the major Protestant bodies, who through those nineteen years did much the larger part of the preaching in that Chapel. Most of these visiting preachers were liberal in their theological outlook and mindful of academic proprieties in their style: but at the same time divergent trends in current theological thinking and in ecclesiastical affiliation were well represented among them; and the men who were most powerfully influencing contemporary student and faculty attitudes toward religion were regular and usually annual guests in our university pulpit.

As one looks back across these fifty years of continuing effort to hear and to read as much as possible of the best contemporary American preaching, one is struck by the constantly close relationship between that preaching and the changing intellectual and spiritual needs, the shifting moods and changing climates within this cataclysmic half-century in human history; and conversely, with the difficulty of estimating at its true contemporary value the preaching of another period than that from which one now looks back. The "age of confidence" before 1914 (as Henry Seidel Canby called it), found it easy to follow and respond to Lyman

Abbott when he used to preach on the reign of law on all levels of human experience, or to expound in a college pulpit "the theology of an evolutionist." But that optimistic and complacent time would have little understood the eagerness with which in this present "age of anxiety" (as W. H. Auden calls it), students and faculty on any and every campus in either America or Europe listen to Reinhold Niebuhr on the inability of human nature to save itself except by the grace of God. Whether they fully understand Niebuhr or not, he "speaks to their condition."

Conversely, men of to-day who are deeply concerned and often almost hysterically anxious about the future of civilization, find it hard to believe that one of the most famous preachers of that "age of confidence" should have said early in this century in a university baccalaureate sermon—before Hitler and Mussolini and the Kremlin, and the atom bomb in our own American hands, had given their terrifying evidence to the contrary:

> The forces of civilization were then, as always, beyond the reach of violence. In ordained tranquillity, they moved majestically forward to shine on Athens as they had never shone on Babylon; to shine in deathless splendor on New York as they had never shone on Rome. And it was because of the war which their light made on all darkness that the woe of Rome's expiring Paganism was a long-drawn agony, which, please God! may we never know again. . . .
> The despotisms which hitherto harassed men are gone forever.[1]

The difficulties involved in any fair appraisal of the strengths and weaknesses of the preaching of other days than our own, and the changing canons of judgment from one generation to the next, are familiar in the realms of literature. Stevenson and Kipling are quoted as far below par in the contemporary literary marketplace, as in our youth they were both quoted above it—up where Melville and Kierkegaard for instance are quoted to-day. As RLS himself shrewdly put it: "Times change, and opinions vary to their opposite"—and this holds for preaching also.

And yet it also remains true that the greatest preaching, like

[1] *Great Sermons by Great Preachers*, pp. 589, 597 (John C. Winston Co., 1927).

the greatest writing and music, has something timeless about it that speaks convincingly to men of every age at the deepest levels of their common human capacity and need; and for Christian faith this is especially true of preaching which can catch and re-echo the authentic notes of the Christian gospel. Phillips Brooks' sermons "live" for us, as we read them to-day, only less than for our fathers as they heard them. Almost sixty years after his death, thirty of Brooks' best sermons, selected and edited by Bishop William Scarlett with the assistance of Dr. Harry Emerson Fosdick, have been republished by Macmillan in 1950, for the benefit of our own contemporaries.

In a discerning chapter on "Religious Life and Thought" in his recent book on *The American Mind* from the 1880's to the present day, Professor H. S. Commager of Columbia remarks that three hundred years of Calvinistic theology and evangelical Christianity, with their common emphasis on the sinfulness of man before God, have had strangely little effect on the characteristic optimism and complacency of the American outlook on life. He notes that American Christianity has on the whole been little concerned with the profounder theological issues, and has tended to be traditional rather than creative in its thinking; and even so, he expresses surprise that Fundamentalism has persisted so long and so late as a major force in American Protestantism. He emphasizes the degree to which both church membership and church attendance have tended during this period to become nominal and conventional, and notes the lessening influence of organized religion on the main currents in American life.

There is one among the symptoms noted in Professor Commager's diagnosis of our American religious case-history, little emphasized in his treatment, which has considerably greater importance for our own purposes in this chapter: namely, the widespread weakening and increasing breakdown during the last half-century of the *social habit* of regular church attendance—only less evident among nominal church members than among the half of our adult population who have no affiliation with organized

religion. Those of us who have lived for successive decades in
the same community, whether in northern industrial and commercial centers, in their more sophisticated suburbs, or in rural
New England, as we have watched this process among our own
neighbors and gathered statistical evidence on it in our own
churches, have become convinced that the optimistic figures showing that church membership more than keeps pace with the growth
of our population, are the less important part of the total religious
picture. This is true except in the South (and also in Canada),
where the northern visitor rubs his incredulous eyes on Sunday
morning—and often again on Sunday evening—to see the high
proportion of the community that still moves churchward. Except in such untypical local situations as that of the Riverside
Church or the Madison Avenue Presbyterian Church in New
York City, or the First Methodist Church in Evanston or Lincoln,
or the First Congregational Church in Los Angeles, church members do not as a rule attend as habitually, or non-members as
frequently, as they did in our own youth at the turn of the century. The preaching is often very much better than it was then:
but the attendance is usually less—and its make-up considerably
less regular.

By and large, even our ablest Protestant preaching speaks to the
ear, and probably to the knowledge, of a smaller proportion of
our population than at any earlier period within living memory.
Brunner's remark was doubtless made first about his own Continental Europe: but it applies increasingly to our own changing
America: "The traditional form of preaching as a part of the
religious cult and the Sunday service in the church has become
strange and remains strange to a great proportion of our contemporaries."

From these sources and against this background, our next concern is to try to locate certain major trends in the preaching of
the last half-century, which—like the Gulf Stream in the Atlantic, and other well-marked ocean currents in all the seven seas—
may help us to discern whither Protestant preaching is tending,

through the influence of its leaders on their brethren; and to ask what influence it is likely to exert on the moral and spiritual climate of the second half of the twentieth century.

The Reinterpretation of Religion

Probably the most evident and certainly the most controversial trend in Protestant preaching at the opening of the century was that which sought to reinterpret and restate the Christian faith in terms consonant with the rapidly growing historical and scientific knowledge of the time. Those of us who received our education and began our ministry in that period, are carried swiftly back to the theological climate and controversies of our youth, when we find side by side among the twenty-five representative preachers in *The American Pulpit* in 1925, the militant Fundamentalist Mark A. Matthews, minister of the largest Presbyterian church in the United States, the First of Seattle, choosing as his theme "The Virgin Birth of Jesus," which he declared in his opening sentence to be "the most important subject that could possibly be discussed"; while in the very next sermon Dr. William P. Merrill, minister of the Brick Presbyterian Church in New York, set forth "Christ, Our Religion" in a warmly religious but theologically undogmatic statement of the centrality of Christ as "the way, the truth, and the life." The difference in tone and temper between those two sermons recalls, across the crowded years between, the sharp theological controversies within American Protestantism during and after World War I, controversies in which Dr. Harry Emerson Fosdick became an embattled figure.

The economic and international cataclysms of the second quarter of the new century, however, soon carried the attention of both preachers and congregations to more urgent issues than those of theological controversy. The Great Depression after 1928 raised searching questions about our social order, and the high hopes raised by a victorious "war to end war" were darkened by the gathering shadows of World War II. Disillusionment and cynicism about the capacity of human nature to manage its own more and more complicated affairs in a shrunken world, and to escape the inevitable consequences of the pride and the greed for gain and power, not only among its neighbors but within its own heart, displaced the earlier optimisms and complacencies, and deeply affected the tone as well as the content of Christian preaching. A younger generation that had never known anything but a world of uncertainty and danger, and college graduates who took for granted the freedom of faith for which their fathers had had to contend, began to protest against the vagueness and uncertainties of the optimistic liberalism in which they had been reared, and to seek, not only for firmer ground in their thinking, but for more positive and dynamic convictions about the centralities of Christian faith, and for more shared reality in Christian fellowship.

Meanwhile theological students in conservative and liberal seminaries alike were coming under the stimulating influence of new emphases in contemporary theology. Among Biblical scholars, Dodd in England, Dibelius in Germany, Craig at Yale and Drew, and Knox and Muilenburg at Union, were emphasizing the faith and shared life of the early church as prior to all the New Testament sources and writings, and the total historical "event" of Jesus' life, death, and resurrection as the central and fundamental fact on which the Christian gospel builds its faith and hope and love. With all their theological and philosophical differences, the far-reaching influence of Barth and Brunner on the Continent, of the two Baillies in Scotland, and of the two Niebuhrs and Calhoun in America, has struck a much more positive note of Christian assurance about the self-revelation of God in Christ, and the adequacy of the grace of God to redeem and transform even the pride and folly of self-centered and sinful men. There is no mistaking this more confident and dynamic note in the self-dedication of larger numbers of men of high intellectual and spiritual quality to the work of the Christian ministry since the close of World War II, or in the preaching and pastoral work of the younger ministry—no matter under what contemporary theological banner they may march—as in 1950 they face toward the unknown future.

Looking back over the half-century since 1900, we whose entire active ministry has been carried on within that period rejoice in the widening recognition that equally honest and earnest Christians have never used exactly the same forms of thought when they started to reflect on the faith in Christ they share, or exactly the same language when they tried to express it to others—either in our own lifetime, or during the Protestant Reformation, or in the early church, or in the New Testament itself. We rejoice still more that so many Christians the world around, of so many races and names and signs, including many Fundamentalists and more conservatives, are more concerned in these critical times to win new believers to their common faith in Christ than to argue with their fellow-Christians about their theological differences. We see heartening evidences of the presence and power of the Holy Spirit within the Christian Church Universal, wherever brethren not only of different races and names and signs, but of differing theological views, are drawn and held together by the God-given realization that they are "all one in Christ Jesus." We know from the experience of our own generation that our successors will face new problems for thought, and new challenges to action, under changing conditions which we cannot now foresee; and we pray that they may be given the guidance of that same Spirit, and so know how to maintain, on the one hand, "our liberty which we have in Christ Jesus" (Gal. 2:4), and, on the other, "to keep the unity of the Spirit in the bond of peace." (Eph. 4:3)

The Socializing of Christianity

After the two worst wars in human history, it is not easy even for us whose youth was set in the sunny and sheltered years before 1914, to recapture their crusading enthusiasms. We who were then preparing for and entering upon the parish ministry well remember, even across the tragic years and decades between, the impact of Dr. Charles R. Brown's *The Social Message of the Modern Pulpit*, followed by the successive books of Walter Rauschenbusch, and especially his *Prayers of the Social Awakening*, not only upon our own youthful thinking, but upon the leadership of American Protestantism. Our own opening ministry was released thereby from complete preoccupation with theological reinterpretations, into the immediate challenge of urgent social tasks. Our conscience was deeply stirred about social conditions which American complacency and optimism had too long overlooked. Our eyes were opened to the contemporary relevance of the Hebrew prophets, and our daily prayer, "Thy Kingdom come," suddenly came alive at the heart of our personal religious life. The "Social Creed of the Churches," adopted by the Federal Council in 1908, was not only a landmark in the history of American Protestantism: it was a lighted beacon.

This swelling stream of social idealism was by no means limited to the Christian churches. It was the heyday of progressivism in American politics, of Theodore Roosevelt's "Square Deal" and Woodrow Wilson's "New Freedom." Then—like the Niagara River at the brink of the Falls—all this social idealism was precipitated by World War I into a kind of Niagara Gorge of confusion and frustration, at new and deeper levels of relationship and responsibility. The white water of the Rapids below the Falls, and the suddenly emerging back-eddies down the long miles thereafter, inadequately symbolize some aspects of our American experience during the thirty-six years since 1914.

To one who has watched those eddies as they twist and boil up to the smooth green surface of the river miles below the Falls, and then disappear again further downstream as suddenly as they emerged, there is at least some light on the oft-repeated question as to what has happened to the "social gospel" in American Protestantism. It has reappeared in the strong pacifist reaction against both the horrors and the follies of war as "mankind's chief collective sin," and has echoed in the preaching not only of such outstanding leaders as Tittle, Buttrick, Scherer, Luccock, and Bosley, but of scores if not hundreds of other ministers less widely known; and even more compellingly, in the personal decision and conduct of Christian conscientious objectors. It is not less evident in the strong reaction of the Christian conscience, especially among students and the younger generation generally, against the racial discrimination and religious prejudice that are so deeply rooted in American traditions; and likewise in the many religious movements, including in some cities local churches, that are completely inter-racial.

Commager remarks in *The American Mind* that Reinhold Niebuhr is the spiritual heir of Walter Rauschenbusch: better understood he thinks and more influential in Europe than in this country. But though Niebuhr and the younger ministry whom he and others have so deeply influenced, hold a very different "theology for the social gospel" than that which Rauschenbusch proposed in pre-war days, they insist, as Rauschenbusch did, on the social relevance of the Christian gospel, not only as an essential part of their preaching, but as part of their Christian responsibility in the life of their community.

Other seminary teachers like Holt of Chicago, Bennett of Union, and Pope of Yale, have likewise combined a critical realism, in dealing with complex social facts and forces, with a deepened conviction that only the guidance and grace of God can show us the way through the anxious years ahead. Their teaching and example suggest that the next generation of Protestant preachers may be less disposed than were their predecessors to draw blue-prints on Sunday morning for a "Christian social order"—or even for the guidance of their laymen in the complicated situations they confront—much less to sit in judgment on those who may not agree with them on involved social issues as they suddenly arise. But even so, they will agree with those same predecessors that in these areas also (as John Robinson put it more than three hundred years ago), "God hath more light and truth still to break forth from His Holy Word."

The New Emphasis on the Church

The stress laid in present-day thinking on the *social* aspects of all human experience, would doubtless have led in any case to a new appreciation of the fact that Christian faith is given to us all within a shared fellowship—as we are born into a family, and achieve our personality within a society. But this current emphasis on the collective side of the shield, as our fathers had stressed its individual side, has been reinforced by two main currents in the Christian thought and life of our generation.

One of these is the stress laid by our best Biblical scholarship on the historical fact that the early Christian church preceded the New Testament. Before there were any gospels or epistles as we now know them, groups of believers were keeping alive and sharing with each other their memories of Jesus, their experience of his continuing presence in their midst through the Holy Spirit, and their knowledge of the work and writings of Paul. Historically speaking, the church gave us our New Testament and its gospel, and out of its fellowship down the generations our personal religious life has been born and sustained.

The other is the ecumenical hope and faith, which seems to so many of us God's best gift to the church through the dark years in which our ministry has been chiefly set. Out of this very "time of troubles," as a child of the missionary movement, has been born a new sense of unity between Christians of all nations and races and generations, and a new perspective on our differences of creed and ceremony and order, as far less important than the God-given realization that we are "all one in Christ Jesus." The Christian church has proved to be the one fellowship that has kept its inner unity of spirit and loyalty, even through the strains of worldwide war. And this, as Archbishop William Temple pointed out, has not been the result of any human planning or organization. "This is the Lord's doing, and it is marvellous in our eyes."

The impact of these two creative forces can plainly be seen

in the changing attitude of many ministers of our generation toward the church, both local and universal. In our student days many of us were decided individualists in religion, and quick to criticize the church, not only for its theological conservatism and religious formalism, but for its unawareness or time-serving on social issues, and for the timidity of its leadership. We were fond of quoting "More of the divine fire, and less of the ecclesiastical candle-stick," and also the story about the devil, who when his assistant reported that they couldn't make head against the Christian religion, replied, "Then *organize* it." In this we were reflecting the perspectives widespread among our college teachers, many of whom conceded that personal religion might well be an asset in individual cases, but maintained that organized religion had usually proved to be a social liability in human history—or at the very least a drag on progress.

But already in seminary the teaching, and above all the example, of devoted and constructive churchmen like Henry Sloane Coffin, was leading us toward a maturer attitude. When we found ourselves in a parish of our own, we began to repeat the experience of one contemporary who said, as he looked back on a long and distinguished ministry, "I have rediscovered the church." Our pastoral visitation gave us a new sense of the spiritual support given by the church to its members through times of stress and strain—a sense greatly deepened when we ourselves were in hospital. The terrible wars of our time revealed to us the social significance of the church as the defender of individual freedom against totalitarian prejudices and pressures, and as the one worldwide fellowship that was able to maintain its relationships across the gulfs and against the bitternesses of war. Meanwhile the historical relation of the early church to the New Testament, of the Bible to western culture and democracy, and of the missionary movement of the nineteenth century to the ecumenical movement and the inter-racial fellowships of the twentieth—these perspectives opened our eyes to the long-range significance of the Christian church as the carrier and sower of the seeds of a better human future, the harvests of which will be gathered by generations later than our own—under the blessing and guidance of God.

These longer perspectives and deepened convictions have had a profound effect upon our own preaching—turning it more and more toward the building up of the local church. We know, at least as well as their numerous critics, the faults and failures of the contemporary churches—have we not lived with them seven days in the week, and most of the waking hours of each day? Some of our brethren have suffered cruelly at the hand of organized religion, as did the Master long ago, and the prophets before him. But we believe in the church as we believe in our family and in our country, even while we know their faults and seek to correct them; and even more deeply we believe in the church, because she is what Paul called her, "the household of God." She has sins of omisson and commission aplenty to confess; but she has also resources beyond her own wisdom and strength, through her faith in the God Who called her into being through Jesus Christ her Lord.

We believe further that this trend in contemporary preaching will increase and deepen, because to our joy we find this focussing of interest and concern upon the local church to be apparently stronger in our younger colleagues in the ministry than in ourselves, who had to outgrow our earlier individualism—and strongest of all in the post-war theological students we know at firsthand. We are heartened not only by their greater numbers, but by their individual quality: they seem to us on the whole an abler lot intellectually, and a much deeper and warmer lot spiritually, than we were at their age. We are the more impressed to find that many of them hold a far more definite and "higher" doctrine of the church than we ever had, in which there is emphasis on the role of the church, over against the world and modern culture alike, as a worshipping fellowship within a "house of prayer," and also as the custodian of the "Word" from God which gives Christian preaching both its message and its authority.

With such a high conception of the church, it is small wonder that we do not so often find among them the same ambitious eye lifted in the direction of "big pulpits" in city churches, that was more frequent among us. We note among them too a concern for what they like to call "pastoral counselling," and in many cases a deliberate choice of smaller parishes and communities, because they provide closer personal contacts. Some of them seem to recognize instinctively what it took us time to learn by experience the hard way: that, as Hugh Black put it, "we who are critics of the past are also its children." We, their elder brethren in the pastorate, conclude from all this, that this increasing emphasis on the life and work of the local church, and this more understanding and devoted concern for the "cure of souls," which has begun in our own time, will be much more characteristic both of their preaching and of their pastoral ministry in the half-century ahead.

The Democratizing of Preaching

One Sunday morning well before World War II we welcomed as our visiting preacher at the University of Chicago Chapel a famous Scottish minister, whose sermon seemed a masterpiece to those who know and love the best traditions of that home of the homiletic art. It was a rich and colorful tapestry woven of Biblical quotations and allusions, in which Scriptural scenes and characters subtly emerged into a unified and cumulative procession as the well-planned sermon unrolled. But in the middle of the sermon a graduate student in physics got up and went out, sat down on the steps outside, and began to read the *Chicago Tribune*. When a passing fellow-student asked him why he had left the Chapel, he replied, "I will not stay and listen to a man who cannot talk about religion in a language which his contemporaries can understand."

The incident reflects the growing "religious illiteracy" which is so widely characteristic not only of college students, but of Americans generally. A present-day preacher cannot assume on the part of his congregation the knowledge of the Bible or of Christian history, or the sense of their significance, which his predecessors could take for granted. Such ignorance is wide-spread, not only among church members, but even among theological students!

Some of the most obvious trends in recent American preaching are directly related to this situation. Topical sermons advertised on the bulletin board and in the Saturday newspapers, problem-sermons, life-situation sermons, book-review sermons, have grown more frequent as expository and even textual sermons have become fewer. The prominence of illustration, whether in such masters of "picture-thinking" as Fosdick and Merton Rice and Halford Luccock, or in less skilful hands as anecdotes of doubtful relevance but sometimes of deliberate humor, culled from inexpensive collections thereof—this is in part adjustment to a national temperament much more responsive to story-telling than to abstract or logical thinking, and in part a recognition by the preacher that any congregation, religiously illiterate or otherwise, is far more likely to remember his illustrations than his text, his exegesis, or his theology.

When Charles Cuthbert Hall, himself one of the outstanding preachers of the opening century, returned in 1907 from his second series of Barrows Lectures in the university centers of India, he remarked to one of his students that the current religious crisis seemed to him even more acute in America than in the Far East. He felt that most American preaching was then falling between the Scylla of an unintelligible piety, and the Charybdis of an unreligious liberalism. It had too many men who had a gospel, but did not know the language of their time—and so men would not stop to listen; it had also too many men who knew the language of their contemporaries perfectly—but had no gospel for them! If American preaching fifty years later is to escape that same difficult dilemma, it must labor and pray to learn how to combine the solid substance and positive gospel of Edwards and Bushnell and Brooks, with the contemporaneousness and vividness of Beecher and Fosdick, and the "inevitable word" that George Buttrick so often finds.

And yet there may prove to be assets as well as challenges for the preacher, in the anxious years that apparently lie ahead. A generation that buys half a million copies of Rabbi Liebman's *Peace of Mind*, or that realizes how precarious is the prospect of its hitherto boasted civilization, may be more likely not only to come to church, but to listen with open ears and heart to a sermon on either the inner life or the social gospel, than a generation that thanked God it was not as other men, or races, or generations— or that knew not that in the sight of God it was "poor and blind and naked."

The very fact that so many people are getting their religion these days from religious books or magazine articles, or by sermons over the radio, suggests to the watchful preacher the existence of a potential congregation whom he may have to discover and enlist by personal contact and cultivation. And the evident interest and concern of the more thoughtful younger generation in the great issues of human life and destiny with which religion deals, suggests that preaching disciplined to deal with these deeper issues in language that this generation can understand, may not lack for hearing in the days ahead. Along some such lines "evangelism" may find its way forward, under the guidance of God, out of its nineteenth-century traditions that no longer fit our present needs, into the twentieth century where genuine religious revival is so sorely needed both within and outside the church.

The editor of a thoughtful religious column in the *Manchester Guardian Weekly* remarked recently that, with a few outstanding exceptions such as Fosdick, American preaching seemed to him to deal too much with "problems"—and to lack depth. There must be many of us who would admit in our franker moments, to our consciences even if not to our colleagues or our congregations, that both these shafts hit at least the periphery of the target. But we who listened hungrily as students to George A. Gordon, and read him to this day with a satisfaction that is partly intellectual but even more deeply spiritual, know that this has not been true of all American preaching since 1900, as it was not true of Edwards in his time or Bushnell in his. Professor Roger Hazel-ton in his recent book, *Renewing the Mind*, pleads for more serious grappling by the American pulpit with the central issues of human life and destiny, and the central faiths of the Christian gospel.

This is not to say that all the best American preaching, past or future, has been or ever will be alike—or ought to move on parallel lines. The mantle of Beecher and Gunsaulus and Quayle is not the same as the mantle of Edwards and Bushnell and Gordon; and there is besides a long tradition of "popular preaching" that has made its own contribution to American democracy and its own appeal to the American conscience. Ever since the Day of Pentecost, men have said of successive generations of Christian witnesses, "We hear them speaking *in our tongues* the mighty works of God." It is the agelong task of the Christian preacher to bear that witness in his own tongue to his own contemporaries.

Chrysostom and Augustine, Savonarola and Luther, remind us also that Christian preaching has reached some of its greatest heights in difficult times. As the nineteenth century turned into the twentieth, one of the great Scottish church leaders of the earlier era, Marcus Dods, said in his own later years: "I do not envy those who will carry the banner of Christianity in the twentieth century. . . . Yes, perhaps I do: but it will be a stiff fight."

That prediction has been already fulfilled; and it is not less timely to-day.

BIBLIOGRAPHY

Collected Sermons

Morrison, C. C., editor, *The American Pulpit:* by Twenty-five Representative Preachers (New York, 1925)

Coffin, Henry Sloane, *The Creed of Jesus* (New York, 1907)

Newton, Joseph Fort, editor, *Best Sermons, 1924* (New York, 1924)

Fosdick, Harry Emerson, *The Hope of the World* (New York, 1933)

Bosley, Harold A., *On Final Ground* (New York, 1946)

Books About Preaching

Coffin, Henry Sloane, *In a Day of Social Rebuilding* (New Haven, 1918)

Newton, Joseph Fort, *The New Preaching* (New York, 1930)

Buttrick, George A., *Jesus Came Preaching*, Beecher Lectures (New York, 1931)

Atkins, Gaius Glenn, *Preaching and the Mind of To-day* (New York, 1934)

Sperry, Willard L., *We Prophesy in Part* (New York, 1938)

Thompson, Ernest Trice, *Changing Emphases in American Preaching* (New York, 1943)

The Mind of the Twentieth Century

Commager, Henry Steele, *The American Mind:* An Interpretation of American Thought and Character since the 1880's (New Haven, 1950)

CHRISTIAN EDUCATION

H. Shelton Smith

H. SHELTON SMITH was born in 1893 in North Carolina, graduating from Elon College in 1917. He served as a chaplain with the American Expeditionary Force in France during World War I. After receiving the Ph.D. degree from Yale University in 1923, he joined the staff of the International Council of Religious Education. In 1929 he became Associate Professor of Education at Teachers College, Columbia University. He subsequently served on the faculty of Yale Divinity School and then took up his present position as Professor of American Religious Thought and Director of Graduate Studies in Religion in Duke University. He has been actively associated with the ecumenical movement both locally, where he was founder and first president of the North Carolina Council of Churches, and as a member of various committees of the Federal Council of Churches and the International Council of Religious Education. His particular field of scholarship is the history of American religious thought, but he is best known as an author for his book *Faith and Nurture,* which has had a wide and deep influence on Christian thought about education. Dr. Smith is a member of the Congregationalist Church, and for several years he was vice president of the Congregational Home Board.

X

Rᴇʟɪɢɪᴏᴜs education, as qualified by the adjective "progressive," is chiefly a development of the twentieth century. Strictly defined, it has always been a rather small current in the total educational movement of the American churches. Nevertheless, its leading exponents have written books in educational philosophy of rarely equaled competence.

The basic theory of progressives was maturely formulated by the close of the First World War. During the next decade progressive principles achieved considerable experimental application in the better equipped local churches. Since the later thirties, however, the foremost progressives have spent much of their energy in defending their positions against what they call "theological reaction." In the category of reactionists they usually include not only avowed Barthians, but all those who have seen fit to abandon or seriously modify the traditional thought-patterns of left-wing Protestant liberalism.

Some of them have even revealed a marked distaste for all theology, often implying that those who concern themselves with it are at least side-stepping the main issues in religious education. They not infrequently apply the epithet "authoritarian" to those who find any significant value in the new theological trends.

Does this mean, then, that progressive religious educators have no theology of their own? Frankly, no. For any careful analysis of their chief publications in educational theory will show that they operate upon important theological assumptions. Those assumptions, to be sure, are not always made explicit, but they are present nevertheless.

It is the purpose of this essay to demonstrate the truth of this affirmation, and then to indicate the possible future of the progressive educational movement in American Protestantism.

Considered historically, progressive theory of religious education is indebted both to educational philosophy and to Protestant theology.

On the educational side, the movement of thought that has contributed most to the progressive theory of Protestant nurture is that of which John Dewey has been the prime determiner. When the twentieth century opened, he had already won recognition as an educational philosopher of unusual magnitude. His compact little treatise, *My Pedagogic Creed* (1897), ranks as an educational classic. It contains most of the germ elements that have characterized the progressive current in secular educational thought. Some of the more significant ideas found in that *Creed* are these: The aim of education is the continuous reconstruction of experience; the condition of effective learning is purposeful self-expression on the part of the child; the creative and unifying center of the curriculum is the pupil's own social activities; the school is democracy's primary agency of social progress.

Close on the heels of the *Creed* followed two other small books: *School and Society* (1899) and *The Child and the Curriculum* (1902). Both were essentially elaborations of the *Creed*. In *School and Society* Dewey identified his philosophy with what he termed the "New Education."

Of particular importance in the new education is his view of the relation that should exist between the school and society. The ideal, said Dewey, is "to make each one of our schools an embryonic community life, active with types of occupations that reflect the life of the larger society and permeated throughout with the spirit of art, history, and science. When the school introduces and trains each child of society into membership within such a little community, saturating him with the spirit of service, and providing him with the instruments of self-direction, we shall have the deepest and best guaranty of a larger society which is worthy, lovely, and harmonious." [1]

Dewey's definitive educational thought is set forth in his epoch-making work, *Democracy and Education* (1916). Its phil-

[1] *School and Society* (Revised edition, Chicago, 1929), pp. 27-28.

osophical framework is Pragmatism, a doctrine that Dewey did not formally adopt until the early years of the present century. The pragmatic theory of ultimate reality is avowedly naturalistic, and therefore it is definitely inhospitable to a Christian world view. Pragmatists generally prefer to deal with specific values in their immediate natural and social contexts, rather than to concern themselves with the problem of ultimate origins.

While Dewey was in the process of formulating his own pragmatic views, he recognized a positive aid in Darwinian evolution. Thus in a lecture given at Columbia University, in the year 1909, he made the following highly significant observation with respect to Darwin's contribution to the new logic: "In the first place, the new logic outlaws, flanks, dismisses—what you will—one type of problems and substitutes for it another type. Philosophy forswears inquiry after absolute origins and absolute finalities in order to explore specific values and the specific conditions that generate them." [2]

Whether or not Darwin may be considered the prime factor in the rise of the new logic, it is well known that Dewey both firmly defends empirical method and sharply condemns any philosophy that concerns itself with absolutes and finalities. Dewey's attitude at this point is definitely shared by a good many progressive religious educators.

There is another feature of *Democracy and Education* that should be made explicit. Dewey here views both education and democracy from a common perspective of growth. Education, he observes, has no end beyond itself; it is "all one with growing." Democracy, considered as a mode of mutually shared meanings and purposes, also is all one with growing. Both education and democracy thus converge on the concept of growth.

In his emphasis upon progressive growth, Dewey further reflects the decisive impact of Darwin. It was an easy mental step from biological evolution to an evolutionary philosophy of democ-

[2] *The Influence of Darwin on Philosophy and Other Essays in Contemporary Thought* (New York, 1910), p. 13.

racy and of education, and Dewey took that step unhesitatingly. Here, in particular, his influence upon the progressive educational movement in the Protestant churches has been far-reaching.

The second historical source of progressive theory of religious education is a version of Protestant thought which has always been distinctly critical of all forms of theological orthodoxy. Important elements of this new theological trend were active in American culture long before the dawn of the twentieth century. For example, three anti-Calvinist currents had already infiltrated New England Protestantism before the year 1850: Arminianism, Rationalism, and Transcendentalism.

But a liberal movement of far greater influence emerged in response to the Darwinian theory of evolution. During the closing decades of the nineteenth century, this school of thought often characterized itself as "The New Theology." In the year 1883, Dr. Theodore Thornton Munger, an influential New England minister, set forth the major tendencies of the new theology in a very illuminating essay. Among other things, he observes that while the new faith "does not part with the historic faith of the church," it does hold to the idea of a progressive faith. For him, revelation is a process "which is to be evolved in the history of the world." The Bible itself "is a continually unfolding revelation of God; it is a book of eternal laws and facts that are evolving their truth and reality in the process of history." [3]

Munger drew a logical conclusion from this evolutionary idea of revelation: there can be no final formulation of the Christian faith; it must always remain in process of revision in order to keep step with a growing revelation. He writes: "It is a mistake to regard the truths of the Christian faith, even those that are called leading and fundamental, as having a fixed form. Were they revelations *from* God, they might perhaps be so regarded; but being revelations *of* God, they imply a process of unfolding." [4]

In fairness to Munger, however, it must be noted that he was

---

[3] *The Freedom of Faith* (Boston, 1883), pp. 8, 19–21.
[4] *Freedom of Faith*, p. 59. Italics in original.

not quite so radical as that assertion implies. For him, traditional statements of the Christian faith are not altogether obsolete; indeed, they contain at least a "germ or heart" of truth which persists under new forms of expression. Thus all historic Christian doctrine must be approached as representing an "intermingling of permanent and changing qualities." The history of theological thought will therefore reflect both continuity and change.

By the opening of the twentieth century Munger's New Theology had already gained a considerable following. The term "new" was soon superseded by that of "liberal," but the general emphasis remained the same.

The foregoing analysis of late nineteenth-century educational theory and of Protestant theological thought shows that the opening years of the twentieth century were ripe for just such a movement as the new religious education. Significantly, leaders in religion and education alike accepted an evolutionary theory of history. They also agreed that the principle of progress provided the central clue to the reconstruction of both educational theory and Protestant theology. When, therefore, the insights of these two movements were fused, they made possible what could rightly be called "progressive religious education."

The year 1903 is historic in the rise of the progressive educational movement in the churches, for it was in that year that a national conference was convened in Chicago with the expressed purpose of seeking a way to unite the religious and educational forces of America in a great forward movement. Outstanding leaders in both religion and education attended in large numbers. Though Catholics and Jews were present, liberal Protestants really determined the main emphases of the conference.

Doubtless the most decisive achievement of the conference was the launching of the Religious Education Association. It was prophetic that both John Dewey and George Albert Coe were foremost participants in the process that gave birth to the Association, for this organized fellowship did more during the first quarter of the century to integrate the insights of progressive secular education and of progressive Christianity than any other single agency. Free from ecclesiastical and dogmatic restraints, it nurtured freedom of expression both in its official journal, *Religious Education*, and in its annual assemblies. Those who spear-pointed its policies and programs became the major creators of the progressive theory of Protestant nurture.

While many able thinkers took part in this pioneer movement, Professor Coe was unquestionably *primus inter pares*. He entered the gateway of the new century with excellent academic preparation in both philosophy and theology, and he had the added distinction of having taken postgraduate work at the world-renowned University of Berlin. At the time that the Religious Education Association came into being, he was occupying the chair of Moral and Intellectual Philosophy at Northwestern University. From 1909 to 1922, he served as professor of Religious Education in Union Theological Seminary. Thereafter, until his retirement in 1927, he taught at Teachers College, Columbia University. Unlike most retired educators, he published three of his ablest books after leaving the classroom: *The Motives of Men* (1928), *What Is Christian Education?* (1929), and *Educating for Citizenship* (1932).

Professor Coe has had no superior in his creative fusion of just those intellectual tendencies that were most essential to the development of the new theory of religious education. He was among the first to perceive the value of the psychological approach to religion, and from first-hand research he published two pioneering works in this field: *The Spiritual Life* (1900) and *The Psychology of Religion* (1916). Even before the century began, he had fully accepted both Biblical criticism and liberal theological views. In his *The Religion of a Mature Mind* (1902) ideas from these areas are woven together illuminatively. The new social emphasis in Christianity met with his instant approval, and from this viewpoint he wrote one of the most provocative educational works of his generation: *A Social Theory of Religious Education* (1917). How readily he embraced John Dewey's doctrine of the New Education is indicated by the fact that his first

major book in religious nurture, *Education in Religion and Morals*
(1904), quotes him more often than any other educational philosopher.

In light of such multiple intellectual interest and versatility,
no one should be surprised that Professor Coe became the ablest
theorist in progressive religious education that America has produced. Because of his acknowledged preeminence this essay assumes that the most authoritative way to document the basic
theological presuppositions of the progressive doctrine of Protestant nurture is to concentrate upon his own views.

II

Prior to the Chicago conference Professor Coe had published
some notable essays on the new theory of religious education.
The most significant essay is entitled "Salvation by Education." [5]

Professor Coe here clearly indicated, among other things, that
the new teaching movement of the church must bridge the gap
between religion and education. This could be done, he thought,
by fusing the new educational and religious ideals that were then
emerging. He wrote: "If . . . we compare the ideals of the new
education with those of progressive Christianity, we discover no
such gulf as is commonly supposed." Indeed, the two are "tending
toward a higher unity." For, in the first place, both explicitly take
the position that spiritual values are immanent in the total round
of human events; secondly, both are definitely committed to a
philosophy of history based upon evolutionary growth. [6]

In advancing these two basic notions, Professor Coe gave
progressive religious education an orientation that has fundamentally characterized it ever since. What are their theological
assumptions and implications? In answer to this question, let us
begin with the idea of divine immanence, for it is that idea that
is presupposed in Coe's claim that spiritual values are inherent in
every aspect of the common life.

[5] *The Religion of a Mature Mind* (Chicago, 1902), pp. 293–396.
[6] *Ibid.*, pp. 299–302.

1. *An immanent God*

No one at the turn of the century was more alive than Coe to the idea that the new theology as well as the new education must dissolve the dichotomy that split existence into two realms, the natural and the supernatural. On the other hand, he did not, as did Dewey presently, try to solve the problem involved by adopting an unqualified naturalism. Instead, he sought relief in the philosophical principle of the divine immanence. That principle became deeply rooted in liberal Protestant thought in the late nineteenth century by the growth of the idea of evolution. Joseph LeConte's widely publicized idea that evolution takes place "by means of resident forces," was eagerly assimulated by theological Darwinists like Lyman Abbott, John Fiske, and George Harris, and translated into an immanental interpretation of God's creative working in nature. Even the more cautious liberal evangelicals, including William Newton Clarke, Borden Parker Bowne, and Henry Churchill King, made the idea of divine immanence basic in their schemes of religious thought.

As Coe correctly observed, the new theology entered the twentieth century "committed to the doctrine of the immanence of God." He made constant use of the principle of divine immanence in his own religious thought, especially while under the dominance of philosophical idealism. This principle is, indeed, a theological cornerstone of his book, *Education in Religion and Morals*. After pointing out that the idea of an immanent God is the logical deduction from the premise of an evolutionary view of God's creative action, he writes as follows:

This means, among other things, that material atoms are forms of divine activity; that the laws of nature are simply the orderly methods of his rational will, which is in complete control of itself; that evolution does not suffer any break when man, a self-conscious and moral being, appears, because the whole of evolution is, in reality, a process of realizing a moral purpose; that the correlation of mind and brain is just the phenomenal aspect of the real correlation of our mind with the divine power which sustains us; that the development, physiological and mental, that man receives through nature is part of an all-inclusive educational plan, and that, in our work as educators, God is working through our reason and will to carry forward the universal plan.[7]

No one reading that statement can escape the conclusion that Coe believed in God's immanence in the whole of nature, including man. Even when, as in his later writings, he leaned more heavily on a functionalistic psychology and philosophy, he still predicated the immanental activity of God.

One can easily disclose the operation of this postulate of immanence in Coe's theory of Christian nurture. To this end, let us analyze his thought in a two-fold context.

(a) Basic in Coe's educational theory is his claim that the religious growth of the child from birth "takes place entirely within the kingdom of grace." [8] This doctrine underlies his famous formulation of the aim of Christian education: *"Growth of the young toward and into mature and efficient devotion to the democracy of God, and happy self-realization therein."* [9]

We are not now concerned with Coe's Christian democratic criterion of growth, but only with his thesis that the child starts its growth from *within* the kingdom. It is this thesis that makes him repudiate the classical evangelical view that distinguishes sharply between the natural man and the spiritual man, the lost and the saved. Correlatively, it makes him repudiate also the evangelical tendency to view the nurture of the little child as a process that merely anticipates later religious experience, rather than as a process that involves actual religious experience from the outset. Unmodified evangelicalism, he argues, has "no workable conception of a present Christian life" for the young child.[10] Even the ritualistic type of Protestantism, he points out, can provide the basis for a present religious experience of the young child only by employing an artificial mode of infant baptism.

[7] *Education in Religion and Morals* (Chicago, 1904), p. 43.
[8] *Ibid.*, pp. 37–40, 44–49.
[9] *A Social Theory of Religious Education* (New York, 1917), p. 55. Italics in original.
[10] *Ibid.*, p. 326.

As against all such traditional notions, Coe begins on the explicit predicate that infant human nature is not a total moral vacuum. He holds that the infant possesses naturally the very life-germ of divine grace, and that this life-germ is the potentially regenerate seed out of which the spiritual life grows from more to more.[11] Thus there need be no moral break between the old life and the new.

But what about total depravity? The answer is that ever since Coe published his essay, "Salvation by Education," he has always sharply scored that doctrine on both theological and scientific grounds. If its logic were to be completely followed, says Coe, it would paralyze child nurture, since the little child would possess only Satanic impulses and inclinations. But empirical science, he observes, does not support any such dogma; for it discovers in the young child the love-impulse, and this is the very tap-root out of which the Christian life can grow.

A word of caution must be added here, lest one get the idea that Coe believes that the infant descends from above trailing clouds of glory. That, Coe would readily reply, is a sentimental illusion. Indeed, as early as 1904 he issued a note of warning at this point. "In every one of us the good has a struggle against evil; in every one of us the good is so modified by evil that ideal character is never quite attained. Before a child can form a moral judgment he displays tendencies which, if they develop without check, will issue in a bad character." [12]

In that statement Coe shows that he is no uncritical romantic; he perceives that the child manifests tendencies to evil as well as to good. But in spite of this element of realism, there is evidence to indicate that he leans, on the whole, toward an optimistic notion of human nature. For while he admits the existence of evil tendencies in the child, he apparently believes that those tendencies derive, not primarily from the child's own rebellious self, but

[11] "What Does Modern Psychology Permit Us to Believe in Respect to Regeneration?", *The American Journal of Theology*, XII (July, 1908), pp. 356–361.
[12] *Education in Religion and Morals*, p. 49.

from the morally warped mores of society.[13] Thus although the child's conduct manifests both good and evil, the child at the core of his being is really good.

Now this idea that the child is naturally good and is therefore in possession of the germ of divine grace is a logical deduction from the assumption that God is immanent in human existence. Coe's doctrine of human nature thus accords with his theology of divine immanence.

(b) The postulate of divine immanence is no less involved in Professor Coe's idea of the nature of God's relation to human society considered collectively. If, as we have seen, God is the indwelling germ-principle of the individual self, then it is logical to assume that God is also the indwelling germ-principle of the community of selves. The postulate of divine immanence is thus applicable to society as it is to the individual.

Now this postulate is basic to Coe's "social" theory of Christian nurture. As already indicated, his social theory holds that the kingdom of God constitutes the ultimate end of Christian education, and that growth is the process of attaining maturity within that kingdom.

But in order to apprehend the inner nature of the kingdom as Jesus understood it, Coe says that it is necessary to interpret the kingdom in terms of the idea of democracy. Jesus' desire for brotherhood, he observes, "leads on with the inevitableness of fate to the ideal of a democratic organization of society." In Jesus' "fusion of divine with human love," he "presents us with a divine-human democracy as a final social ideal." [14]

In unfolding this social ideal, Coe reveals his faith in an immanental God in various ways. To take only one crucial example, he fuses divine with human love so completely as to teach that there can never be any love to God that does not also include love to men. This is why he distrusts all so-called private relations with God. This is why, also, he makes fellowship with God con-

---

[13] *A Social Theory of Religious Education*, pp. 145, 171.
[14] *Ibid.*, p. 54.

tingent upon prior fellowship with men. Thus he writes: "In and through his growing participation in the creation of an ideal society the pupil will realize his fellowship with the Father." [15] It is upon this premise that Coe sharply protests against those who teach children to "get right with God" first, and then be brotherly.

Considered, then, both in its individual and in its social aspects, Professor Coe's theory of Christian nurture definitely presupposes an immanentist conception of God's relation to human nature.

2. A progress-making God

The idea of evolutionary progress is no less basic in Professor Coe's religious and educational thought than is his conception of divine immanence. For him, the very term "progressive" derives its ultimate significance from a dynamic interpretation of the world-order. Like progressive Christians in general, he conceives the cosmos in terms of *a continuous becoming*, including both structural and functional changes.

Coe accepts as a matter of course the idea that man is integral to organic evolution. But for him the most significant fact is not that man emerges from within, and crowns, the animal series, but that man is himself a self-transcending being. Just as the whole world-order is continuously growing, so is man, as a part of that world-order, continuously growing.

Significantly, the central clue to Professor Coe's theory of religious education is to be found in his conception of the nature, growth, and worth of persons. This inclusive idea he often summarizes in the phrase, "the personality-principle."

An extremely important feature of Coe's doctrine of the personality-principle is his belief in the capacity of persons to remake religion. This belief is vitally connected with his theory of mental dynamics. The human mind, he holds, is not a static and finished entity; on the contrary, if considered from a functional standpoint, the mind is actually undergoing dynamic evolution.

[15] *A Social Theory of Religious Education*, p. 56.

Growth in mental functions reveals itself in the fact that the mind is always achieving new desires or wants. The mind not merely repeats ancient wants; it creates genuinely unprecedented wants. In the human struggle for existence, novel mental functions lead on to a better existence. Now this element of mental variation constitutes mental evolution.[16]

The evolution of religion, says Coe, is intimately connected with this growth of mental functions. For mental evolution manifests the function of a selective or preferential principle at the very center of the personal self. By reason of the operation of this selective principle, the self is not satisfied with old values; it strives for genuinely new values. In this dynamic process of the revaluation of values religion itself undergoes evolution.

This conception of the continuous evolution of religion in and through the valuative growth of persons involves Professor Coe in important theological assumptions.

(a) First of all, Coe perceives profound theistic implications in the fact that persons have emerged within nature. This leads him to contest the straight naturalistic interpretation of reality. The naturalist's trouble, he believes, arises largely from a preoccupation with subhuman elements of the cosmos. Thus he writes: "What is known as naturalism seems to me to draw its conclusions about man, on the whole, from inquiries that do not deal as seriously with the phenomena of personality as with the phenomena of the sub-personal." [17]

As against this tendency to dwell almost exclusively on subhuman structures and functions, Coe himself grapples with the unique functions involved in the growth of human selves, including self-identification, self-valuation, and self-transcendence. From this critical analysis he is led to posit the existence of a Divine Person who is immanently active in those functions which characterize growing persons. Thus he writes: ". . . the phenomenon of human personality taken in the large manifests an

[16] *The Psychology of Religion* (Chicago, 1916), pp. 215–221.
[17] *What Is Christian Education?* (New York, 1929), p. 89.

interfused personality, or God. I know not how else to construe the history of human personality." [18]

This personalistic approach to metaphysics lies at the very heart of Coe's religious thought, and it separates him sharply from the John Dewey school of naturalism. It also distinguishes him from all types of theistic naturalism that de-personalize ultimate reality.

(b) Professor Coe clearly perceives that his theory of the continuous evolution of religion raises the issue as to whether Christianity contains within itself any element or principle of permanent validity. Is the Christian faith a passing phase of evolving religion, or is there in it something that is unchanging and therefore permanently normative for the Christian educator?

Forthrightly Coe faces this basic issue. There is, he admits, something in Christianity that will persist through all change and therefore can serve as a continuing criterion for progressive Christian nurture. But that permanent element is not, he urges, to be found in any sort of theological dogma, nor even in any special person. Where, then, is that permanently normative reality to be found? It is found, replies Coe, in the principle of worth that Jesus ascribed to persons.

But what about Jesus himself? Is he not, in his unique being, the finality of the Christian educator? Coe's unequivocal answer is no. Because Jesus both perceived and demonstrated in his own life the value of persons, he will always remain a permanent source of strength and inspiration to the progressive educator. But even if Jesus had never grasped the personality-principle at all, that principle would still be final for religious faith. Thus Coe writes: "We hold to it [the personality-principle] because of its inherent validity, just as he [Jesus] did; it is not secondary to anything or anybody . . . The loyalty of the Christian, accordingly, is loyalty not to one person, even Jesus, but to persons." [19] This remarkable conclusion represents the logical deduction of Coe's

[18] *What Is Christian Education?* p. 94.
[19] *Ibid.*, pp. 181–182.

evolutionary theory of history and of religion. Reasoning, as he does, from the premise of a continuously growing religion, he has to reject the classical Christian view of the finality of the Christian revelation.

(c) Professor Coe's belief in moral progress is a definite factor in his optimistic interpretation of the human predicament.

As already noted, Coe denied the doctrine of total depravity on the predicate that the newly-born child inherently contains the germ-principle of the Father's kingdom, and thus from birth only needs further growth from within that kingdom.

This view, as Coe himself pointed out, does not mean that the child has nothing to struggle against. For, indeed, on an evolutionary theory of moral growth, the revaluation of moral values always implicates the self in a conflict with traditional values. From this point of view, the struggle with sin is both a reflection of prophetic religious awareness, and is also, in one sense, a pre-condition of the achievement of new values. Nevertheless, Coe's faith in moral progress gives his notion of the human predicament an optimistic tone. In fact, he makes his optimism explicit in these words: "If we look at society in historical perspective, we perceive that it is, on the whole, an evolutionary process in which we are working out the beast, and training ourselves to have regard for what is humane." [20]

On this assumption the progressive religious educator may take courage as he faces the future. For even though sin is rooted in instinct, confirmed by habit, and propagated by social processes, brotherliness will triumph over selfishness. "Love of one another," says Coe, "produces a degree of cooperation, which is the massing of human energy, that is impossible to greed, licentiousness, and the lust of power. Selfishness tends to disorganization and ineffectiveness in the long run." [21]

Now if one adds to this belief in growing brotherliness the further belief in man's essential goodness, one must admit that

[20] *A Social Theory of Religious Education*, p. 167.
[21] *Ibid.*, p. 168.

Coe's view of the human predicament is considerably tinctured with optimism.

III

In light of the foregoing analysis, is it not evident that Professor Coe's progressive theory of religious education is governed by important theological assumptions? Furthermore, is it not equally clear that his assumptions are those usually associated with the more radical forms of Protestant liberalism?

But if there is any lingering uncertainty on this point, Coe's recent critical comments on the newer theological tendencies should dispel all doubt. Ever since the late 1930's he has lost no opportunity to speak out on the dangers of those tendencies. In pointing out their dangers he further clarifies his own theological thought.

Professor Coe holds that Christian education is imperiled not merely by the more extreme Barthian forms of thought, but also by those milder types that characterize much of the recent ecumenical thinking of Protestantism. For example, he says that the Oxford Conference of 1937 "united intense religiousness with theological reaction." He believes that the World Council of Churches, in framing its basis of fellowship in terms of a high Christology, has "reverted to an utterly dogmatic and authoritarian test." [22]

Professor Coe is not satisfied merely to generalize in his criticisms of the current "theological assault upon Liberalism," for he is convinced that "there is a life-and-death issue" at stake in the area of Christian education.

First of all, he observes that there is a basic conflict over what attitude the teacher should take toward historic Christianity. Specifically, is the teacher to regard Christianity as a finished faith, and therefore to use educational method merely as an authoritarian tool with which to force the young to accept it as it

---

[22] "The Assault upon Liberalism," *Religious Education*, XXXIV (April-June, 1939), p. 88.

is, or is the teacher to assume that Christianity is a constantly growing faith, and consequently to employ educational method as a means of reconstructing religion by releasing the creative religious experience of the child? According to Coe, the former assumption dominates the mind of the new theologians. They represent an "anti-scientific reaction" within Protestantism which "involves a reversion to authoritarianism." [23]

Progressive educational theory, on the other hand, challenges this static notion of Christian faith. It sees in the growing experience of the child the growing-point also of the Christian faith; and therefore its primary concern is not to transmit the faith of yesterday, but to create the faith of tomorrow.

At another point Coe is troubled over the educational implications of recent theology. He notes that there is "almost a scramble to get more of God into religious teaching." He does not, of course, object to including God as a part of Christian education, but he does seriously object to beginning the educational process with some a priori idea about God, for he thinks that this approach is not only usually dominated by a transmissive and intellectualistic conception of teaching, but that it short-circuits the very creative point of Christian nurture, which is the present relations of living persons.[24] Thus the educational weakness of the newer theology is that it wants to lug God in at the very beginning of the teaching process and will not let God grow out of an experimental pupil-teacher quest for growing values. In other words, to paraphrase Coe, it is too anxious about God and not anxious enough about men. In contrast, Coe believes that a really vital Christian nurture will lead the pupil to an experience of God in and through a creative process of re-valuing personal-social values.

Coe notes a third point of conflict over the role of theology. The newer theology, he contends, is monopolistic, since it pre-

---

[23] "The Assault upon Liberalism," *Religious Education*, XXXIV (April–June, 1939), pp. 87–89.

[24] See Coe's significant statement as incorporated in Professor Edwin E. Aubrey's article, "A Theology Relevant to Religious Education," *Religious Education*, XXXIV (October–December, 1939), p. 199.

sumes to furnish all the factual data that will be needed in Christian nurture. But, says Coe, religious education is itself an important source of theological data, for it explores the present religious experience of growing persons. Thus formal theology can furnish "only a part of the basic and controlling ideas of religious education." Besides, "a theology that springs wholly from outside religious education, if it undertakes to prescribe either the content or the procedure of religious teaching, becomes thereby a self-deceived interloper." [25]

Finally, Professor Coe observes that there is a crucial issue between educational progressives and the newer theology over the nature of man. In the Oxford Conference, he says, "The dogma of depravity was treated almost as if it were the corner-stone of religious metaphysics." [26] Nothing is more outrageous to Coe than the revival of the idea of human depravity.

This summary of particulars shows beyond question that there is a fundamental clash between the left-wing liberal theology in which Professor Coe's educational theory is rooted and the new current in Protestant thought.

IV

In observing the new theological scene, one may well ask, what about the future of progressive religious education? As I size up the prospect, progressives have three courses of action open to them.

One course is to continue to reaffirm their already established theological convictions. This is apparently the choice of some of the best known American educational progressives, including Professors Coe, William C. Bower, and Harrison S. Elliott.[27]

[25] "A Theology Relevant to Religious Education," p. 199.

[26] "The Assault upon Liberalism," *Religious Education*, XXXIV (April–June, 1939), p. 88. See also Coe, "Religious Education Is in Peril," *The International Journal of Religious Education*, XV (January, 1939), p. 10.

[27] See W. C. Bower, "Points of Tension between Progressive Religious Education and Current Theological Trends," *Religious Education*, XXXIV (July–September, 1939), pp. 164–172; *Christ and Christian Education* (New

This emphasis will continue to serve as a counterweight against such extreme types of Protestant orthodoxy as Barthianism. This form of service, to be sure, is not unimportant, for there are elements in ultra-orthodoxy which do really imperil a constructive and vital doctrine of Christian nurture. On the other hand, if the progressive merely contents himself with criticism of this kind of orthodoxy, his role will necessarily be a negative one.

A second alternative for progressive educators would be to align themselves with metaphysical naturalism and abandon the distinctive Christian tradition altogether. This tendency, as a matter of fact, has been implicit in much of the thought of those left-wing educational liberals who have adopted an extreme functionalistic view of religion.

It is the current distinction of Professor Ernest J. Chave of the University of Chicago to affirm a naturalistic religious philosophy without reservation. In his compact little volume, *A Functional Approach to Religious Education* (1947), he sets forth a theory and a program for "a new day" for genuine progressives. The religious education for the new day, he contends, must be frankly naturalistic in its theory of reality. While it will connect man with "personality-producing forces," it will not identify his origin with a Divine Creator, nor will it ask him to worship "a blurred image." It will frankly recognize that the only forces of redemption "are in the growth processes of normal life," and that religion "is but the discovery, exaltation, and use of these." [28]

This consistent naturalism has at least one merit: it makes possible the fusion of religious education with progressive secular education. The logic of Professor Chave's position should lead him to seek such a fusion. John Dewey and other educational pro-

---

York, 1943); Harrison S. Elliott, *Can Religious Education Be Christian?* (New York, 1940).

[28] For a brief statement of this same position, see Professor Chave's recent article, "Religious Education for Liberal Progressives," *Religious Education,* XLV (March–April, 1950), pp. 67–72. A variety of evaluations, *pro* and *con*, are given on pp. 73–100.

gressives could have no objection to including "religion" in our state schools on this basis. Since, however, precisely this sort of religion is already present in the better public school curricula, it is difficult to see how progressive religious education could make any unique contribution to the splendid ethical and social processes that are now operative in such curricula. Its role, accordingly, would be essentially that of strengthening and extending the values that are already present in secular education. But in following this course, the obvious price that progressive religious education would pay is alienation from the distinctive educational work of the American Protestant churches.

There remains a third possible choice for educational progressives. They could undertake to reconstruct their theological foundations in light of the more realistic insights of current Christian faith. In this direction, as I see it, would lie their greatest constructive opportunity.

Recently a growing number of Christian educators have come to see that left-wing Protestant liberalism has largely lost its power of compulsion. Like Professor Coe, they were at first definitely negative in their attitude toward the newer Protestant theological trends, but today they show a more hospitable spirit toward many of those trends.

This new temper is significantly reflected in a special study that was sponsored by the International Council of Religious Education and released to the churches in the year 1947.[29] One of the eight major parts of that study is a thirty-six page document that deals primarily with the Christian presuppositions that should undergird Protestant nurture in the new era.

The new emphases are striking. First of all, the older optimistic notion of human nature is missing. Instead, man is said to reveal a "dual nature." Man's duality consists in the fact that he "is a

[29] *The Study of Christian Education* (The International Council of Religious Education, Chicago, Illinois, 1947). The material of this study has been interpreted in more popular form by Professor Paul H. Vieth in a book entitled *The Church and Christian Education*, published by Bethany Press, St. Louis.

child of God" and "is also a fallen creature." Continuing, the study says: "Man is alienated from God by the rebellion of his sin; he denies his true nature by his sensuality and his pride; he is prone to make himself the primary object of worship, confusing the copy with the original." Furthermore, "man is not a problem to himself because of the world in which he lives but because of his own nature. The impediment is not outside but inside. . . . Our civilization may increase the basic conflicts, but it is not their ultimate source." [30]

A second major accent is upon the nature and special content of the Christian revelation, including the centrality of Christ and his Church.

This study recognizes that the term "revelation" may be interpreted broadly to include God's manifestation of himself in the works of nature and in the course of general history, past and present, but it uses the term chiefly in its Biblical connotation. As thus understood, revelation refers to that special series of historical Biblical events through which God has savingly revealed himself. The integrative center of that series of revelatory events is Jesus Christ, "who is the embodiment of the gospel, the good news of the saving grace and power of God." "God commended his love toward us in the death of his Son. Here was more than man's utmost devotion to the divine will. Here was the redemptive act of God himself through a human life in history." Faith in the Christian revelation involves faith in a community which centers in Christ. "It began with the group to whom Jesus promised entrance to the kingdom of God. After his resurrection it was the group who looked to him as Lord and upon whom he poured out God's Spirit." It is within the church "that our faith has been formulated and passed on through a living succession of believing witnesses. The church has been the mother of us all, and there is truth in the historic statement, *extra ecclesiam nulla salus.*" [31]

[30] *The Study of Christian Education: II—Theological and Educational Foundations,* pp. 10, 11.
[31] *Ibid.,* pp. 16, 18, 19, 24.

From this brief account, it is evident that the educational leaders in the International Council have already recognized the value of the new currents in Protestant thought. They are not, to be sure, uncritical of those currents; they rightly distinguish between those tendencies that are compatible with a vital theory of Christian nurture and those that are detrimental to it.

As a whole, this study is a good example of the cautious yet favorable attitude that progressive religious educators might well show toward the new theological awakening that is emerging. Were they to abandon their purely negative attitude and participate sympathetically in this new renaissance in Protestant thinking, they could again become a great creative force in American Christian nurture.

BIBLIOGRAPHY

Bower, W. C., *The Curriculum of Religious Education* (New York, 1925)

Case, Adelaide, *Liberal Christianity and Religious Education* (New York, 1924)

Coe, George A., *A Social Theory of Religious Education* (New York, 1917)

————, *What Is Christian Education?* (New York, 1929)

Elliott, Harrison S., *Can Religious Education Be Christian?* (New York, 1940)

Hartshorne, Hugh, *Character in Human Relations* (New York, 1932)

Miller, Randolph Crump, *The Clue to Christian Education* (New York, 1950)

Smith, H. Shelton, *Faith and Nurture* (New York, 1941)

Soares, Theodore G., *Religious Education* (Chicago, 1929)

Vieth, Paul H., *Objectives in Religious Education* (New York, 1930)

Wiegle, L. A., *Jesus and the Educational Method* (New York, 1939)

Williams, J. Paul, *The New Education and Religion* (New York, 1945)

REUNION AND THE ECUMENICAL MOVEMENT

Henry S. Leiper

HENRY SMITH LEIPER was born in 1891, and he is now one of the Associate General Secretaries of the World Council of Churches. For more than two decades he has acted as an ambassador from the American churches to many countries throughout the world. He took his undergraduate studies at Amherst College, and then he studied at Union Theological Seminary and Columbia University. He served in Siberia during World War I, and in 1946 he made a flying trip to India to survey famine conditions, consulting Mahatma Gandhi, Pandit Nehru and M. A. Jinnah, as well as numerous church leaders. Dr. Leiper is the author of several widely read books, and he is, in particular, known as the editor of *Christianity Today*—a unique symposium about the work of the Church throughout the entire world. He is an editor of *Christianity and Crisis*, and he contributes regularly to various journals on both sides of the Atlantic.

XI

THE MOST representative American theological books issued at the dawn of the century assume that progress is inevitable. They reflect little anxiety about the future of Christianity. Representative thinkers confidently hoped that by evolutionary processes the Christian movement was destined to attain universal spiritual ascendancy in a peaceful world. Freedom, it was assumed, would soon be achieved by all mankind and would be lasting. The eschatological note was almost entirely lacking. This complacency was bolstered by theological views minimizing the sinfulness of human nature, seeing religion as chiefly a personal concern, and neglecting the significance of the Church either as a world-wide fellowship or a supra-national institution.

Partly because of this lack of anxiety, little concern for Christian unity appeared except in the trenchant writings of such men as Josiah Strong, Philip Schaff and William Reed Huntington. There was manifested little corresponding to what William Temple calls "St. Paul's horror of Christian divisions." To most of those who were at all concerned with unity, it was thought of as capable of satisfactory expression along functional lines through the co-operation of individuals across denominational frontiers. This was shown in the working policy, if not in what might be called the philosophy, of the Evangelical Alliance, the student Christian movement, the Sunday School movement, the Bible Societies and the foreign mission enterprise. Significantly there was at that time no movement for *Church* as distinguished from *Christian* co-operation or unity.

Indeed, there had not at that time been any union of denominations in America for years and none seems to have been under discussion. Although the so-called "Chicago Quadrilateral" had been in existence since 1886, it was only after it was taken up as a basis of discussion by the Congregationalists in America and the

Lambeth Conference in 1910 that it attracted any general attention.

Even federal unity of a corporate sort, although it had been envisioned in some detail by Dr. Samuel Schmucker, the Lutheran from Gettysburg, Pennsylvania, in 1846, was far from the center of American Christian thought. It was considered at the Chicago meeting of the World Alliance in 1892. And it was defined with singular foresight by Dr. Philip Schaff at an earlier meeting of that same body. In discussing the "Reunion of Christendom" he said: "Federal or corporate union is a voluntary association of different churches in their official capacity, each retaining its freedom and independence in the management of its internal affairs, but all recognizing one another as sisters with equal rights and co-operating in general enterprises such as the spread of the Gospel at home and abroad, the defence of the faith against infidelity, and the elevation of the poor and neglected classes of society, works of philanthropy, charity and moral reform."

Dr. Samuel McCrea Cavert gives it as his opinion that the Evangelical Alliance, just referred to, deserves more credit than is usually assigned to it for contributing the Church emphasis which was lacking among those who at the turn of the century thought of Christian unity in non-denominational terms. Under the influence of men like Dr. Schaff, he—Dr. Cavert—sees the Alliance pioneering for what came to be the Faith and Order Movement more definitely than any other interdenominational body of the years before 1900. It was, however, largely pan-Protestant and its constituency was personal rather than ecclesiastically delegated.

When the followers of Dr. Schaff in 1900 used the term "federal union," they apparently meant what we now mean by federation or federal *unity*. Federal *union* today connotes some such organic merger as would come about if the Stanley Jones proposals were to be accepted, i.e., the formation of a single Church with parts or branches corresponding to the present denominations but with voluntarily limited sovereignty.

Since the Alliance was inclined, apparently, toward what came to be known as the Faith-and-Order (theological and ecclesiastical) emphasis, Dr. Josiah Strong, one of its dynamic leaders, had left it shortly before 1900 to form what was called the "Open and Institutional Church League." Out of a meeting of this body and the influence of the "Federation of Churches and Christian Workers" in New York City, there came a meeting of minds in 1900 at a special conference which called for a national expression of the kind of Christian unity broadly described by Dr. Schaff in the quotation above. Here, perhaps, we find the genesis of what became the Federal Council of Churches.

In this connection, it is important to keep in mind an observation made by Dr. E. B. Sanford, historian of the early days of the Federal Council which, while definitely not a direct approach to church union, marked a notable advance toward unity and differed from most of the earlier attempts in being directly concerned with the churches rather than simply with Christians as individuals. Dr. Sanford's view [1] was that "this movement is towards the unity for which Christ prayed—not a unity necessarily of organization, but a unity of spirit and of purpose in the evangelization of man, and in creating social conditions which shall make men as helpful and blessed as may be in this world." In an early conference of Josiah Strong's "Open Church League," just mentioned, Dr. Sanford dealt with the relationship between common Christian social concerns and church union.—"This League seeks in its fellowship to bring together believers of every name asking: what can be done to make the church of Christ a more efficient instrument in accomplishing His redemptive work in the world? Organic ecclesiastical unity we may hold as a dream of the future or dismiss with the interrogation, is it desirable? But Christian unity as a spiritual reality and as a practical factor bringing the denominations into federative relations through which they can work out the problems of Christian service in city, country, and abroad without the present waste of forces, who that loves the

---

[1] Sanford: *Federal Council of the Churches of Christ in America* (Revell, 1909), p. 148.

Kingdom of our common Lord can but desire and long to see consummated? It is coming and in its coming I believe that the Open and Institutional Church League seeking in its counsels to exalt the work and mission of Christ in the life of the church is destined to play an important part." [2]

In his book, *Christian Unity in the Making*,[3] Dr. Charles S. Macfarland says: "The early leadership was by prophetic individuals and groups induced by practical objectives to meet certain demands of human life. There were no preconceived plans for ultimate organization. . . . This period was characterized by its simplicity of thinking and its practicality in action. There was a growing sense of freedom, an absence of abstract theorizing, much practice in prayer. These men accepted and assumed each other's faith in the fundamental verities of the Gospel and one another's experience of life in Christ." That they avoided theological approaches was due, Dr. Macfarland thinks, to the general "assumption that institutional Christian unity implied an identical confession of theological belief or a uniform mode of worship or a common theory of the church's ministry and ordinances."

Three main purposes were incorporated later in the Constitution of the Federal Council of Churches which was not actually launched until 1908. These were: the manifestation of the essential oneness of the Christian churches of America in Jesus Christ as their divine Lord and Saviour; the promotion of the spirit of fellowship, service and co-operation; and the prosecution of work that could better be done in union than in separation. Only at a later date were the churches of the Council prepared to add to the Constitution recognition of responsibility for promoting "the application of the law of Christ for every relation of human life." Co-operation and not competition would manifest to the world a new oneness in Christ, thus advancing the Kingdom. "Working together the churches will minister to human need as never be-

---

[2] Hutchison: *We Are Not Divided* (Round Table Press), p. 124.
[3] Macfarland: *Christian Unity in the Making* (Federal Council, 1948), p. 25.

fore, and in so doing prove that the Gospel is the supreme remedy for all evils."

It is worthy of remark that at the founding meeting of the Federal Council in Philadelphia, December 1908, a very special emphasis was likewise laid upon the idea that unity would strengthen the world mission of the Church. The report on "Co-operation in Foreign Missions," presented by Dr. James L. Barton, secretary of the American Board, Boston, stressed five things: en-thusiastic support for co-operation abroad; fellowship at home in developing support for the world mission; "the closest possible federation of all Christian Churches in Foreign Mission fields"; union educational institutions wherever practicable in foreign mis-sion areas; and interdenominational efforts to create an adequate Christian literature in the vernacular for the people in all mission fields.

This pragmatic thinking about the objectives of unity in the world mission was going on alongside of united planning for ad-vances in home missions. A fivefold report and appeal to the sup-porters of the home mission cause went out from the Philadelphia meeting. It extended also to the social application in industry and commerce of the Christian Gospel seen as truly independent of denominational differences.

Bishop Hendrix, first President of the Federal Council, in closing this historic and truly creative Philadelphia meeting, said: "The Council fervently appeals to the churches to search out the common ways of united and unselfish ministry, to give sway to the holy passion of saving men, to demonstrate unanswerably, in complete surrender to their Lord, the permanent reality of this profounder sense of unity, by eager loyalty, intense, unswerving, to the mighty purpose of salvation which brought Jesus Christ to Humanity. . . ." [4]

There was, however, so much hesitation to deal directly with unity—meaning then organic union—that a proposal to include

[4] Sanford: *Origin and History of the Federal Council of the Churches of Christ in America* (S. S. Scranton Co., 1916), pages 271–272.

it in the stated objects of the Council was rejected, and even the proposal to favor local union churches was set aside in favor of the idea of federation.

In the thinking of those who led the movement, there was thus a threefold concern—the first for practical forms of unity; the second for evangelization; and the third for social betterment, i.e., the creation of conditions which "will make man as helpful and blessed as may be in this world."

The second of these concerns—evangelization—was likewise the dominant concern of the missionary leaders in 1900 but although they did describe their world conference in New York in that year as "ecumenical" it was not because they were to consider union or even unity, rather their world-wide evangelistic interest led to the selection of that name, particularly because of its connotation "having to do with the whole world-wide household of faith." At the center was emphasis upon evangelization as if it could be achieved with little or no reference to either social transformation or church unity. It must, however, be parenthetically observed that the actions of many of these persons and the organizations with which they were related indicated a consciousness of being members one of another, and this seems to have made inevitable their later expressions of concern for unity as such.

There was yet another current of thinking which even in 1900 was preparing many minds for new advances in unity. It was due chiefly to the World's Student Christian Federation, organized by Dr. Mott in Sweden in 1895, which had trained a considerable body of future leaders of the ecumenical movement. That has often been recognized. What is not so frequently noted is what might be called the prolegomena to modern ecumenical philosophy which was being worked out by many of those responsible for the literature and program of the Federation. Many expressions of their thinking appear in addresses at such student conferences as were conducted by the Student Volunteer Movement.

As Dr. Henry P. Van Dusen points out in his book, *World*

Christianity,[5] the bodies constituent to the Student Christian Movement "have been among the most potent, indeed indispensable, forces in furthering the advance of Christian unity on every front. Their contributions have been principally at three points: a) They have, by daring experiments congenial to youth, prospected the most promising routes toward Christian fellowship and cooperation, and have discovered the circumstances and terms under which progress may hopefully be expected. . . . Especially noteworthy has been their courage in probing the deeper issues which divide Christians, issues of theological conviction which some other ecumenical movements have been hesitant to tackle.

"b) They have raised up the great bulk of the ablest leadership for every branch of the developing Christian unity movement in almost every country. . . . The late William Temple, Archbishop of Canterbury . . . testified that it was in conferences of the British Student Christian Movement and later of the W.S.C.F. that he first experienced the reality of ecumenical Christianity and became converted to its possibility.

"c) These Christian youth movements have in their own life demonstrated the reality of that ideal to which all the various efforts for Christian unity are in principle committed."

Another contribution of lasting importance is stressed by Tissington Tatlow, in his *Story of the Student Christian Movement*.[6] It was the working out of a clear distinction between undenominational and interdenominational (cf. p. 138).[7] The latter is so familiar to this generation that it is hard to realize how definitely new it was and how radical a departure from the view that one left one's church behind when joining in a cooperative Christian enterprise of non-ecclesiastical nature such as the Y.M.C.A. On both sides of the Atlantic, the students and their leaders pioneered this transition so full of significance for the future of the unity movement.

---

[5] Van Dusen: *World Christianity* (Abingdon-Cokesbury, 1947), pages 89-91.
[6] Tissington-Tatlow: *Story of the Student Christian Movement* (S.P.C.K., 1933), Chapters VIII to XVIII.
[7] *Ibid.*, Chapters VIII to XVIII.

As direct confirmation of the views just recorded, we find in Clarence Shedd's *History of the Student Christian Movement During the Last 200 Years:* [8] "The tendency to eliminate all geographical, confessional, and racial barriers to the realization of brotherhood among the students of the world has characterized the student movement from the beginning." L. D. Wishard (a student secretary in the '90's) saw "one world-wide movement of Christ for the students of the world and the students of the world for Christ." [9] In the amazing spread of the movement into the United Kingdom, Scandinavia, Germany, China, Turkestan, Japan, India, Ceylon, Persia, Kurdistan, Syria and elsewhere in the last decade of the nineteenth century, Dr. Roswell Hitchcock remarked that the students' "witness to the essential unity of the Church of Christ is a mitigation of the deplorable effect of our too disintegrated Protestantism." [10]

Yet another important current of Christian thought about unity has already been mentioned. The Chicago Quadrilateral of 1886, later to be known as the Lambeth Quadrilateral, involved an approach radically different from that of the Federal Council, the various functional agencies of a non-denominational character, the missionary movement, and the student Christian movement. It was not concerned with the idea of federal union, or functional unity of a pragmatic type, nor even with the world mission of the church as ordinarily conceived. These, like the modern ecumenical movement, were extroverted. The thinking of the proponents of the Quadrilateral was introverted: it had to do almost exclusively with the specific doctrinal bases of ecclesiastical organic union. These four bases are well known, i.e., the Bible, the Nicene Creed, the two Sacraments, and the historic episcopate.

Yet it took an exceedingly practical missionary statesman in the dynamic atmosphere of the Edinburgh Conference to see how this emphasis needed to be correlated with the others which had

[8] Shedd: *History of the Student Christian Movement During the Last 200 Years*, page 321.
[9] *Ibid.*, page 324.
[10] Wishard: *A New Programme of Missions*, page 85.

emerged in the general advance towards something more rational and more Christlike than an atomized Christianity. The 1910 meeting followed that of 1900, the former being the eighth of a long series marking a rising tide of interest in co-operation functionally for the sake of the world mission of the Church. Before taking up the story of Bishop Brent's contributions, attention must be drawn to other more immediate aspects of the tremendous thing that took place in the Assembly Hall of the Church of Scotland on the famous Royal Mile leading to "the Rock"—Edinburgh's justly famous castle, where was born James VI, patron of the English Bible.

It may seem something apart from the development of American thinking on the matter of unity. It was by no means without its many intimate relationships to that thinking, for in part it owed its character to American leadership and in part it stimulated a series of remarkable advances led by American churchmen of whom Brent was one.

One distinguishing mark of the 1910 meeting in Scotland was the presence of *delegated* representatives of mission boards rather than persons who came of their own initiative and without representative capacity. The significance of this was, of course, that mission boards as related parts of the churches were beginning to think in terms of a corporate responsibility for more co-operation. At that stage, however, even a suspicion of technical involvement in anything pointing toward organic union would have frightened away a considerable number, if not the vast majority.

Next to the growing recognition on many sides that missionary advance called for a united approach, the most immediate practical thinking growing out of Edinburgh had to do with next steps in the technical process of developing functional co-operation. It led, under the guidance of Dr. John R. Mott, who chaired the conference, to the only official decision of the Assembly, i.e., the decision to establish "continuation committees" in all the major areas of foreign missionary activity. Although it could not have been realized by many at the time, this was to lead in due course to the establishment of bodies in most parts of the so-called "non-Christian world," which were in time to become the National Council of Churches (although at first composed of missions *and* churches). Here was the idea destined to produce the International Missionary Council which in 1950 links thirty-one autonomous councils of varying constituencies—churches and missions, Anglican and Protestant—all embodying the idea of federal unity in some form and many, in due course, producing indirectly significant organic unions among constituent bodies.

As has already been intimated, the 1910 Edinburgh meeting saw the beginnings of a transition from the idea of unity as non-denominational co-operation in various functional forms to a real concern for inter-church approaches to working unity. It also was the seed ground for ideas which led not only to "Lausanne 1927" but also to "Stockholm 1925."

Concern for the fulfillment of the "Great Commission" was acute in the heart of Bishop Charles Henry Brent, eminent American Episcopal Bishop of the Philippines. He brought a new idea to focus as he incisively stated the chief reason for his growing conviction that organic church union as such should be intensively studied and fearlessly faced. He wrote: "It is little short of absurd to try to bring into the Church of Christ the great nations of the Far East unless we can present an undivided front. For purely practical reasons we feel the necessity of the Church's realization of unity. It must be either that or failure in our vocation." [11]

To the other ideas current among advocates of unity such as sensitivity to "practical necessity," coupled with tremendous conviction as to the will of Christ for oneness among his followers, Brent set out to add the definite consideration of organic union.

When he came to undertake the launching of a movement, he found a readiness to respond among the leaders of his own communion. What more natural than that they should suggest the relevance of the "Quadrilateral" to the studies the intense mis-

[11] Zabriskie: *Bishop Brent* (Westminster Press), page 92.

sionary Bishop proposed to inaugurate? And as a leader in the Federal Council of Churches, as well as in the Anglican communion, Brent easily found other companions ready to travel the new multi-lane highway toward the much desired goal.

But the central emphasis in Brent's thinking was not technically theological although it had even more profound theological significance than the Chicago Quadrilateral (by that time renamed for Lambeth, as has been noted). The central emphasis in his thinking was on wholeness. He repeatedly points out that *wholeness* is synonymous with *health*—both etymologically and ideologically. To him lack of communion among Christians was a lack of wholeness and hence a diseased condition; and that within the very body set to bring healing—wholeness—to the nations. For him "sectarianism in spirit and form is *par excellence* the cult of the incomplete" so that "there is no graver offense than to use a catholic garment to hide a sectarian heart." Indeed, in another connection, he points out that "Catholicity has nothing to recommend it unless it is the condition in which everything is measured and considered in terms of the whole." With his wide experience in the missionary tasks of the Orient, it was naturally clear to him that world-wide unity was essential because only so could the central message of the Church be incarnated in the life of the visible Church. For him co-operation was first. But it was not enough. The Christian fellowship to be achieved must somehow make available to its members the heritage of all Christians—past and present. And unless individual Christians became united first of all in the will to obey Christ's command "that they be one in love at all costs," they would never be able to end the sin of ecclesiastical disunity.

In the ten years between Edinburgh and the next great step in specific unity consultations at Geneva in 1920, competition developed between (a) devotees of the idea of working together on the social applications of Christianity without discussing the profound differences which all saw in the area of theological convictions; (b) advocates of missionary expansion as practically the sole concern of the churches collectively; (c) proponents of united church approaches to the problems of international understanding; and (d) the faith and order group of which Brent was the natural leader. But it was characteristic of the real catholicity of Brent's thought that he was almost alone in being genuinely interested in all the different lines of approach to the thing he cared about so passionately. Many of those with whom he was closely associated did not have his breadth of vision. Even as late as 1935, it was regarded as a bold move to suggest the holding of two world conferences then in prospect for 1937 in adjacent cities and at a time when it would be convenient for members of the one to attend the other. By that time Charles Henry Brent had gone from the earthly scene: although his spirit made itself felt in those who most closely shared his vision.

But it is necessary in tracing the developing idea of Christian unity to go back to a point only four years after Edinburgh, 1910. In the fateful year of 1914, the approach listed under "c" above had been attempted. It was one which was not aimed at internal unity as such but at increasing the effectiveness of the churches in developing international friendship. Largely through American initiative, supported by the generous gifts of Andrew Carnegie, a meeting had been called at Constance when it was still hoped that war might be averted.

Like other aspects of the total unity movement, this was to have consequences which nobody foresaw. One, not often recognized, had to do with the ancient Orthodox Churches of the East. For the long centuries after 1054 they had held wholly aloof from Western Christendom. What brought about the new contacts between them and the leaders of the Anglican and Protestant communions? It was the result of the pragmatic thinking of the leaders of the World Alliance for International Friendship Through the Churches and the Federal Council, as well as the financial aid of the former. Personal approaches were made after 1918 by officers of both bodies to the Orthodox leaders in the Balkans. The result was the somewhat hesitant acceptance on the part of influential

Orthodox prelates of invitations to consult with the Christians of the West about world peace.

Limitations of space necessitates omitting even brief reference to the many following developments. But it should be noted that in 1920, partly as a result of the approaches just mentioned, the Ecumenical Patriarch in Stamboul issued a precedent-shattering call for the formation of a world consultative council made up of the leaders of the churches. He frankly stated that he felt the time had come for it; and seemed prepared to have it develop into a genuine council of churches.

From that point on, the participation of the Eastern Orthodox Church in all important steps toward greater unity was an increasing factor with important consequences not commonly appreciated by Protestant observers who, unfortunately, tend to write off the nineteen Eastern Churches as if they were without significance in any genuine approach to world-wide Christian community.

Stockholm 1925 and Lausanne 1927 saw the genuine sense of fellowship with these churches growing to the point where it was impossible to conceive of an ecumenical progress which did not take into account the great traditions of the East, however difficult and long might be the process of finding viable solutions to the problems raised by them for the West. Fifteen of the nineteen Eastern Orthodox Churches were represented at the two conferences.

It was not until after the Jerusalem Conference of 1928 that a few Americans, notably John A. Mackay, then a missionary returned from Latin America, began to give the term "ecumenical" a new currency among Protestants and a somewhat new significance. The term has, of course, always been used by the Eastern Church, by Rome, and by many non-Roman Western Churches of continental origin. But its coming into the thinking of Americans was more than an etymological process, more than an accidental circumstance due to broader contacts with the churches of the rest of the world.

At the Oxford World Conference of Church, Community and State in 1937, Dr. Mackay, in his report on "The Church in the World of Nations," distinguished "interdenominational" or "international" from "ecumenical." The former terms were associated with the idea of separate units being assembled for co-operation in some form. The latter assumed an inherent or given unity. It started from the concept of wholeness as earlier stressed by Bishop Brent. His own later definition of "ecumenics" brings out the full meaning. He writes: "Ecumenics is the science of the Church universal conceived of as a world missionary community—its nature, its functions, its relations and its strategy."

The distinctive things only foreshadowed in earlier writings about the theme of Christian unity and the ecumenical movement were the emphasis upon the dynamic missionary character of the Church universal, its inherent God-given oneness, and its character as a community. The latter is the least commonly understood even in 1950! In this concept of fellowship, familyhood and *koinonia* lies the key to an understanding of this element—hitherto unprecedented—in the ecumenical movement as it has developed in the last decade. But it is important to look at the other two concepts with some care. The movement for Christian unity has been in America—as the earlier parts of this chapter amply reveal—accompanied by a recurring stress upon the need of unity in order that the evangelistic task of the Church may be performed. Yet all too often the idea has somehow gotten abroad that enthusiasts for unity had in mind only the merging of existing churches in some technical or organic way. The conception of God-given inherent oneness, on the other hand, is as old as the Church though it has been left too long in the background. Disunity has seemed normal. To desire unity—not to say union—struck many as abnormal. In the greatest crisis of His life, the Lord of the Church prayed for unity. In our inverted scale of values, it gets put off to a more convenient season.

Dr. Van Dusen has listed eight different types of Christian fellowship and co-operation all springing from the urge for more unity.[12] All of these were much in evidence in the two decades prior to the provisional launching of the World Council of Churches of which they were, many of them, anticipatory. These eight are: (1) associations of individuals of different denominations; (2) conferences of individuals of various denominations; (3) nondenominational associations; (4) interdenominational conferences of official representatives; (5) interdenominational organizations; (6) denominational world associations; (7) federations of churches; (8) church unions.

It appears that by emphasizing co-operation in common tasks rather than organic union a tide was set in motion which actually resulted in more organic unions with each passing decade until the number becomes little short of astonishing to the uninformed. On merely empirical evidence, there appears to be a correlation between the advance in various kinds of co-operation and the achievement of the full organic union. Unity in foreign missions lands grew perceptibly between 1927—following Lausanne—and 1936. In that decade, according to a report entitled "Unity in Foreign Missions," (a report of a joint committee of the Federal Council and the Foreign Missions Conference), of the twenty-three significant negotiations looking toward possible unification, thirteen occurred between two or more younger churches." In this period, of the ten unions fully consummated, six concerned younger churches. . . . In seven areas where missions have planted Christian churches—in China, in North India, in South India, in Siam, in the Philippines, in Puerto Rico, in Japan—unification of churches which in parent lands are still separate has been sufficiently extensive to warrant the title 'United Church.' " [13]

The same alert observer tells us that in the past two decades—1937 roughly to the present time—the number of unions of related and those of unrelated churches are exactly equal. With the consummation of the United Church of South India, mergers have now involved Baptist, Congregational, Christian, Evangelical,

---

[12] Van Dusen: *World Christianity*, pages 84–100.
[13] *Ibid.*, page 104.

Methodist, Presbyterian, Reformed, United Brethren, and Anglican bodies. Commenting on what this has meant for the witness of the Church, Dr. Van Dusen adds: "In every area of severest testing (particularly during World War II)—in occupied Europe, in Germany, in China, in Japan, among the youngest churches— fidelity in witness and effectiveness in action have been in direct ratio to the unity of all Christian groups. . . . Nothing less than the *whole* Christian community has proved able to 'withstand, and having done all, to stand.' "

Dr. Van Dusen and Dr. John Bennett see forms of church unity classified as follows:

1. Unofficial organizations and fellowships that have a specific purpose.
2. Mutual recognition involving:
   a. Interchange of membership;
   b. interchange of ministries;
   c. intercommunion;
   d. comity arrangements in missions and church extension.
3. Federation for co-operative witness, teaching and action.
4. Federal union which presupposes mutual recognition and adds to it a federation to which is committed responsibility for missions and other selected activities of the churches.
5. Full corporate union that involves a single church government as well as the forms of unity previously mentioned.

But these representative free churchmen—Presbyterian and Congregational—agree in adding an important observation: "Christian Union which does not imply and make possible whatever degree of church union may be held to be the ultimate desideratum is something less than genuine and true Christian unity." [14] They would insist, as do other free churchmen and a considerable number of Protestant Episcopal leaders, that what Canon Wedel has called *The Coming Great Church* must make "room within itself for the freedom to pioneer and to criticize that characterized the sects at their best." John Bennett, whose words I have just quoted, adds: "If it fails to do this, the radical ferment in the Christian Gospel will break through the carefully wrought,

[14] Van Dusen: "The Issues of Christian Unity," *Christendom*, Spring, 1946.

unified structures of the Church, and a new sectarian protest will have to find its home outside the united Church." [15]

It is now time for some brief summaries. Unlike the thinking of the opening years of the century, contemporary Christian thought in America is burdened with the sense of great reversals of what had seemed established trends. The "ground swell" of the time is against Christianity; and indeed against all that most enlightened men have regarded as progress. Science is for the first time afraid of its own powers of destruction. Instead of complacency, there is general alarm lest the world now so obviously one in a physical, scientific and logistic sense, destroy itself because of its failure to become one in any spiritual sense. The achievement of world community has become a life and death issue. The relevance to it of the only existing world fellowship—that of the Christian Churches—is becoming clearer to many minds.

It is notable, in view of these facts and what they imply that the ecumenical movement has more and more stressed community after the pattern of familyhood as the norm for Christians concerned for world order. The very fact that the movement has been so widely misunderstood, as Kenneth S. Latourette points out, is evidence that it is something new. Old analogies do not fit the new facts.

American as well as European and Asian Christians shared in the formulation of a 1950 statement of the World Council's Central Committee on "The Church, the Churches and the World Council of Churches." In that contradictions are held within larger agreements and centrifugal tendencies are resisted or overcome by stronger centripetal forces.

This document, which reflects much American thinking, makes a very clear distinction between church unity and church union. In contemporary ecumenical theory, the latter is solely the con-

[15] Nolde: *Toward World-Wide Christianity* (Harper & Brothers, 1946), page 74.

cern of the autonomous churches themselves. The former is the concern of all who know the compulsion of the will of the great Head of the Church toward more adequate expression of the community of interest which He has inspired in a growing number of Christians. While the World Council is not a Church and is emphatically not a super-Church, and while there are churches in its membership which do not even recognize other member churches as being "true" churches, there is manifest a bond of fellowship which has grown stronger as the need for unity in a divided world has become more tragically evident.

The statistical method of approach to measuring such a growth in the movement for ecumenical advance is open to objections, but it has some value, nevertheless, and what it shows is revealing. Many Christians on being confronted with the facts are so amazed that they exclaim: "We did not have any idea such things were happening." Well did Will Rogers—who had some insight denied to many theologians—remark on one occasion: "Everybody is ignorant—but on different subjects!"

What does the record show? Since we are considering a world movement, a glance at the world scene seems justified even though our immediate concern is with developments in America. Whereas at the dawn of the nineteenth century there were about 240 denominations in what is now the constituency of the World Council of Churches, at the dawn of the twentieth century the number had been reduced by organic unions to 200—at a rate of not quite one union for each two-year period. At the midpoint of this century, the number has gone down to 160 as a result of an increasing acceleration in the process of uniting organically. The rate was about one per year. From 1800 to 1910 the roster of outstanding events manifesting the growth of unity among Christians totalled 102, less than one per year. But from 1910 to 1940 the number was 215, a six-fold increase. The number of such events in the last ten years was 252. And organic mergers continued to be consummated at the rate of one per year on the average.

It hardly seems true that the thinking of those concerned with this matter has failed to register in outward and visible signs of change in the actual structure of the Church!

As for certain other contrasts between 1900 and 1950 in the matters related to the theme of this chapter, consider the following: In 1900, despite the influence of men like Schaff and Huntington, no churches were formally discussing unity—not to speak of union. In 1920 only 70 in all the world were willing to discuss the subject informally at the call of the American Churches. Today, 158 denominations (30 of them American with a membership of over 30,000,000 in the U.S.A.) are now officially a part of the World Council of Churches and have gone on record with the affirmation: "We intend to stay together." They have affirmed their conviction that God wills unity and have dedicated themselves to try to manifest more fully the unity which he has already given them.

In contrast with what was true in 1900, no one in the ecumenical movement today thinks that progress is inevitable. No one feels that co-operation between individuals undenominationally is full ecumenical co-operation. No one feels that interdenominational co-operation which does not commit the churches as such is ecumenical in any genuine sense although it may be helpful and lead in the right direction.

In contrast with what was true up to 1937, the Life-and-Work emphasis is now inseparable from the Faith-and-Order emphasis. Part of the reason for this is that the leaders of the latter have recognized more clearly the place which non-theological factors have in the experience of the churches and in their relationships. Progress in actual achievement of full organic union, as we have just seen, has been phenomenal. More progress has been made in this respect than in any previous period in a like space of time.

There is less willingness to salve the Christian conscience about the divided state of the Church merely by talking about the "Church Invisible." More and more Christian thinkers deny that there is any authority in the early tradition of the Church for such an idea. The Church, many insist, is a historic community which has certain marks and exercises certain functions. Most agree that its supreme function is to witness to the revelation of the redeeming love of God in Christ who incarnated a new covenant with the community of the faithful.

Again, Christ cannot be the head of each denomination as if he had many bodies. He is head of the whole Church. The objective of the ecumenical movement, as Charles Morrison puts it, is "the restoration of visible and functional unity to the body of Christ which is the community of Christian believers throughout the world."

For such a view, the authentic character of the ministry is always clear if that ministry witnesses to the central fact of Christian history—God's sacrificial self-giving for man in Christ. The true succession is to be found by the application of that test rather than any formula having to do with the form of ordination or the sacerdotal theory of any priest, minister, or bishop.

It is interesting to discover in the work of Charles Morrison, in his Lyman Beecher lectures at Yale, published under the title *What Is Christianity?* a return to very much the same position as that taken by Dr. William Reed Huntington, first in his volume on the Church Idea published in 1869 and later in the second edition of the same work brought out in 1899.[16]

Dr. Huntington saw as marks of the idea of the visibility of the Church evidence of the indwelling spirit of God, unity and capability for perpetual renewal. "Rome exaggerates the idea, Puritanism diminishes the idea, liberalism distorts the idea." The object of those concerned for the health of the Church should be to restore all four of the marks of the Church, and for him it could be done through acceptance of the Quadrilateral (which he has been credited with first giving wide currency in American Church circles). Under such a formula he hoped to incorporate Congregational, Presbyterian and Episcopal ideas or order. His argument for the historic episcopate is not so much on a sacer-

---

[16] "Christian Unity in 19th Century America," Bulletin of Franklin and Marshall College, Vol. 4, No. 3, May, 1950.

dotal as on a pragmatic and practical basis grounded in human experience with the problems of group government. And the Church is to him "a family, a brotherhood, a household, to whose guardian care the archives of the faith have been entrusted."

For Morrison, as for Huntington, although with different overtones, the problem is the restoration of the lost catholicity of the Church. Morrison puts it thus: "This means primarily that the community shall recover to itself the structure which has been stripped away from the body (by being) set up as sectarian structures in the denominational order."

The curious thing about the progress that has been made by churches in uniting structurally is that about as many of unlike types have merged as of types that are closely related theologically. The detailed study of causes of division which has gone on intensively since 1927 has revealed two areas: in the doctrine of the Church and in the nature of the ministry.

Although it took place in India, the merger of the Anglican with the Reformed Churches to form the United Church of South India was the concern of many Americans and has affected the thinking of many. Here for the first time the typical Catholic and the typical Protestant traditions—one seeking continuity in the historic episcopate and the other seeking it in the body of witnessing Christians, were blended despite many difficulties.

In general, however, the antinomy is marked and the clarification of the issues awaits further study and spiritual growth. It may well be that the Anglo-Catholic opposition to the South India Union, which has delayed inter-communion between that great new Church and the mother Church of Anglicanism, may undergo some considerable change as a result of the apparently deliberate recent action of the Vatican in widening the gap between Rome and all other parts of Christendom.

Although not definitely in the area of Faith and Order, the consummation in the closing weeks of 1950 of the merger of eight co-operative Christian bodies of an interdenominational character to form the new National Council of the Churches of Christ in

America has very great relevance for those interested in the progress of Christian unity. It is not in any strict sense ecumenical because it is without direct relationship to the rest of the church world. (Unless one thinks of the relationship between the Council and the International Missionary Council whose United States link—the Foreign Missions Conference—now becomes an integral part of this new body.) But the indirect effects of this action, taken officially by so significant a cross section of the Protestant and Orthodox Churches, will be very great. It is too soon to make any prediction as to just what these effects will be, although it seems safe to anticipate that they will further the cause both of national unity and of ecumenical co-operation on every stage.

The fact is that in areas of practical co-operation even the more aloof of the denominations find a way of participating. The Southern Baptists and the Missouri Synod Lutheran have taken part in the work of Church World Service, a body set up by the Foreign Missions Conference, the Federal Council and the former American Committee of the World Council (now the Conference of U.S.A. Member Churches). As this relief agency becomes a part of the new National Council the way seems open not only for the continuance of co-operation in this one area but for the development in due course of more co-operation and consequent closer relationships of a general character.

"History is stronger than logic," and the history of Christian co-operation, as we have noted, turns out to be in many instances the history not only of unity but of union. No one is wise enough to predict just what the Spirit will say to the Churches of the second half of the twentieth century. But they can ill afford to be lukewarm to the promptings of sensitized consciences with respect to their duty to take ever more seriously the desire of their common Lord for oneness among them all.

It is helpful to keep in mind the words of William Temple: "In a sense it is required that every existing Christian communion should die in order to rise again into something more splendid than itself." This is certainly no harder to accept than the view of some that there already exists the perfect form of Church and that all others must conform to it if there is to be not only unity but union in the fullest sense. Yet a third view sees organic union as not of itself a necessity, since variety in unity is possible and desirable, and "The Coming Great Church" need not be envisaged as organizationally integrated any more than the various parts of the Anglican communion are integrated organizationally today— yet see themselves, as they are seen by others, in a framework of undeniable unity.

It requires both faith and insight to labor in the cause of unity. But that faith feeds on the insight many American thinkers have shared with William Temple who said: "In the end the reunion of the Church will not be something fabricated by us at all; it will be the work of God resulting from a deeper devotion in all parts of the Church, and all members of all parts of the Church, to the one Lord of the Church." Not skill in debate or negotiation, not the power of philosophical analysis or theological insight, but devotion to the will of Christ is the utterly essential element. We cannot too often be reminded that Jesus said: "Follow me"—not "find the perfect theology and the ideal Church order." More and more the ecumenical movement in the first half of the century has demonstrated the truth of the statement frequently on the lips of its leaders: "The closer we come to Christ, the closer we come together." The primary loyalty which will unify in the future that which is now divided is not institutional but personal and the resulting sense of spiritual community is what gives and will give reality to the dream of "The Coming Great Church."

BIBLIOGRAPHY

Brown, William Adams, *Toward a United Church* (New York, 1946)

Dun, Angus, *Prospecting for a United Church* (New York, 1948)

Horton, Walter M., *Toward a Reborn Church* (New York, 1949)

Hutchison, John Alexander, *We Are Not Divided* (New York, 1941)

Leiper, Henry Smith, editor, *Christianity Today* (New York, 1947)

Macfarland, Charles S., *Christian Unity in Practice and Prophecy* (New York, 1933)

Morrison, C. C., *What Is Christianity?* (Chicago, 1940)

Pittinger, William Norman, *Historic Faith in a Changing World* (Chicago, 1950)

——, *Sacraments, Signs and Symbols* (Chicago, 1949)

Van Dusen, Henry P., *World Christianity, Yesterday, Today and Tomorrow* (New York, 1947)

Wedel, Theodore O., *The Coming Great Church* (New York, 1945)

Zabriskie, Alexander C., *Bishop Brent* (New York, 1948)

CHRISTIANITY AND
OTHER RELIGIONS

John A. Mackay

JOHN A. MACKAY was born in Scotland in 1889. He studied at the University of Aberdeen, the University of Madrid, the University of Bonn, and Princeton Theological Seminary. He spent several years in South America as principal of the Anglo-Peruvian College in Lima, Peru, where he was also Professor of Philosophy at the National University. After living for several years in Montevideo and Mexico City as a continental lecturer under the auspices of the Y.M.C.A., he became Secretary of the Presbyterian Board of Foreign Missions in the U.S.A. in 1932. Since 1936 he has been Professor of Ecumenics and President of Princeton Theological Seminary. Among the many offices which he now holds in the worldwide movement of the Christian Church are those of President of the Presbyterian Board of Foreign Missions, U.S.A., and Chairman of the International Missionary Council. He is also a member of the Central Committee of the World Council of Churches and the Editor of the quarterly review, *Theology Today*. His published contributions, both in Spanish and English, have been considerable; his best-known books, perhaps, being *The Other Spanish Christ* and *A Preface to Christian Theology*.

XII

WHAT is the essential nature of the Christian religion, that which differentiates it from the other religions of mankind? What should be the attitude of Christians to other religions and towards the people who adhere to them? What constitutes the justification, and what are the prospects, of Christian missions in the non-Christian world? In the course of the twentieth century, these questions have engaged the thought of some of the most virile and representative minds in Protestantism. They have also been the subject of pronouncements of world gatherings of Protestant churches.

At the turn of the century, two books of symbolic significance were published in the United States. The author of the first, which appeared in 1899 under the title *A Handbook of Comparative Religion*, was Samuel Henry Kellogg, an American missionary to India. The other book was published in 1900 by John R. Mott and entitled, *The Evangelization of the World in This Generation*. The former of these volumes is important because it was the first "handbook" of comparative religion printed in any country which was specifically designed to promote popular interest in the subject. That the book should have appeared in the United States is significant for, as has been pointed out by Louis Henry Jordan, a British authority on the literature of comparative religion, it was in America that the science of comparative religion was born.[1] The second book is significant because it constituted a resounding call to the Christian churches and, in particular, to youth, to carry forward the great task of world evangelization which had been the most significant spiritual feature of the nineteenth century, and in which American Christianity had played an important part. Its

[1] *Comparative Religion*. A Survey of Its Recent Literature, by Louis Henry Jordan. Second Edition. Oxford University Press, London, 1920. Vol. 1, p. 25.

author was destined to become the century's dominant statesman in the promotion of the Christian religion throughout the world.

1. World Forces which Affected the Status and Relations of All Religions

During the period which has elapsed since the above-mentioned books were written, great world forces have affected every religion, both as to its outlook and the conditions of its existence. These forces have been represented mainly by applied science or Technology, and by basically conflicting views of life, that is, by one ideology or another. Technology made the world a global physical unity, a planetary world, an "ecumenical" organism. During the same period Ideology caused two world wars, accentuated differences between peoples and nations, divided mankind into three major political systems and produced an unparalleled revolutionary situation.

Technology and Ideology affected the non-Christian religions, as well as the missionary thought and activity of Christianity. Because of the new global unity it became possible for Christian missionaries to reach the whole world as never before. It also became possible for Islam and Buddhism and the theosophical derivation of Hinduism to take on world significance. Scientific skepticism had an opportunity to propagate its doubt and negations in all the centers of ancient religion and culture. Because civilization tended to become one, there grew up in certain circles the illusion of a common world culture, of a "grand cultural synthesis." But the new physical unity in whose development millennia had been packed into decades, and as a result of which, all men had become neighbors and contemporaries, was held together exclusively by technological advancement. There existed a common civilization, but the basis for a common culture was lacking.

Ideology has brought about unprecedented disunity in this physically united world. Secularism, spear-headed by scientific skepticism, had emptied human life of all spiritual content, and produced a total emptiness. But men and nations had to live. The double urge for spiritual meaning and for daily bread created in the void new positive forces, which were religious in character. When God and the transcendent were banished from life, new "gods" appeared to take their place. Out of the depths of the human soul, out of the national soil where people lived, out of the historical tradition of which they were a part, new divinities emerged. In the absence of a common transcendent loyalty, a spiritual loyalty was provided by some concrete heritage. God was banished and the "gods" returned; the whole polytheistic litter of deities returned whose exorcism from human life the poet Milton had described in his "Ode on the Morning of Christ's Nativity."

The rampage of the new "gods" seeking world dominion produced the Second World War. The struggle lasted six years. The eventual destruction of militant Fascism left Russian Communism, with its theory of a Messianic Proletariat, sponsored by a Messianic people, as the strongest and most integrated world force. A nihilistic spirit became rampant, which Russian Communism was interested in promoting, both in the lands of democracy and in the lands where the ancient religions had their seat.

As the first half of the twentieth century draws to a close, several things become plain. We witness the passing of the European world hegemony. Europe, where for nearly two millennia, the traditional centers of Western culture and of the Christian religion had been located, occupies now a secondary position. Asia is resurgent. The time-honored relativism, native to the East, has succumbed to new secular absolutes. Under the influence of these absolutes, Confucism and Shintoism tend to disintegrate. Challenged by them Islam, Hinduism and Buddhism make basic adjustments, and by every means in their power, seek to rehabilitate themselves and strengthen their ancient position. Russia, the homeland of Communism, and the United States, the chief center today of both Protestant and Roman Christianity, have emerged as the two leading world powers. Added to these, as the brightest single feature of the contemporary situation, is the reality of the Ecumenical Church, a world-wide fellowship of Christians who are united in faith and love across all the dividing frontiers of a revolutionary epoch.

II. The Sources of Protestant Thought on the Relation of Christianity to the World Religions

The study of Protestant thought during the five decades of the present century, upon the subject of Christianity and its relations to the other religions, is best undertaken in close connection with a series of international conferences which were held during this period. Those gatherings, convened between 1910 and 1949 to consider the missionary responsibility and task of Christianity in relation to the non-Christian religions and to the world as a whole, are landmarks in the realm of missionary policy and theology. They became occasions for the crystallization of thought on many important issues. Not a few of the studies written in anticipation of those meetings were the work of eminent Christian thinkers who took part also in the actual conference deliberations. For that reason the printed reports of the gatherings in question constitute a primary source of information regarding representative Protestant thought on the theme of this chapter. It is important, therefore, that I should begin with a panoramic view of those uniquely significant meetings.

In 1910 a great international missionary gathering was held at Edinburgh, Scotland. Its chief objective was to formulate Christian missionary strategy on a world scale. The vast majority of those present were representatives of the Western churches, for the new Christian churches of Asia and Africa had not yet sufficiently developed to send many representative figures. Quite apart, however, from that circumstance, the idea was latent in the mood and deliberations of this epoch-making assembly that the East was destined to be permanently dominated by the West. Out of the Edinburgh Conference grew the International Missionary Council which became the first ecumenical body of modern times. Four years later the First World War broke out.

Ten years after the War came to an end, that is in 1928, the Protestant missionary forces of the world met again, this time in Jerusalem, on the Mount of Olives. Nearly half of the delegates to this gathering were Christian nationals from the "younger" churches. The message of the Conference, familiarly known as the "Jerusalem Message," was drafted by a Committee whose chairman was the late Archbishop Temple. The meeting was dominated by the conviction that secularism was the most sinister and potent force which affected the spiritual life of mankind. It, therefore, called upon the non-Christian religions, as well as the Christian churches throughout the world, to combat the sway of the secularistic spirit. Taking place in the heyday of optimism regarding the possibility of a true international order, the Jerusalem Conference lacked somewhat the intensity and the tragic sense of life which its successors were to reflect.

When it was already clear that a Second World War was inevitable, representatives of Protestant and Eastern Orthodox Churches came together at Oxford, England, in 1937, to consider the topic, "Church, Community and State." It was at Oxford that thought began to be focussed upon the Church and its great importance in the witness and expansion of the Christian religion. At this conference, too, came into contemporary vogue a new use of the term "ecumenical." After Oxford, Protestant Christians began to speak of the "Ecumenical Church," that is, of the Church which is "coextensive with the inhabited globe." This conference, meeting as it did so shortly before the outbreak of the Second World War, prepared the Christian forces in thought and in life for the six years of world struggle that were to follow. Its spirit, moreover, and the decisions to which it came regarding the indestructible bonds by which Christians are bound together in Christ, made possible a speedy resumption of relations between Protestant Christians in the warring nations, as soon as hostilities came to an end.

During the Christmas season of 1938, not many months before the War actually broke out, another great gathering was convened in the Orient. It took place at Madras, India. The great majority of those present at Madras were representatives of the "younger" churches. Special consideration was given in the deliberations to a tension long latent in Protestant thought with respect to the true nature and function of the Christian religion in relation to the other world faiths. Two viewpoints had been expressed during the previous decade. One stressed the continuity between Christianity and the other religions. This view was associated with a book published in 1932, as the result of a study of the Missionary movement in the Orient by a commission of American Christians, mostly laymen, and entitled, *Re-thinking Missions*, or *A Layman's Inquiry After One Hundred Years*. The now famous report was closely linked with the name of the distinguished Harvard philosopher, Professor W. E. Hocking, who had been the Chairman of the Commission and the chief author of the resultant volume. The other viewpoint, the one which dominated thought in the Madras Conference, was that expressed in a book published in 1938 entitled, *The Christian Message in a Non-Christian World*. Its author was H. Kraemer, Professor of the History of Religions in the University of Leyden, Holland, and a former missionary to Indonesia. Dr. Kraemer, a layman like Dr. Hocking, had been specially asked to write this volume in preparation for the Madras meeting. The book, which reflected the movement in Protestant theology associated with the names of Kierkegaard and Barth, insisted upon the total discontinuity between Christianity and the non-Christian religions. Over against the universal fact of Religion it set the dynamic reality of Revelation.

Eleven years later, in the summer of 1947, that is, two years after the Second World War came to an end, representatives of the "older" and the "younger" churches met at Whitby, Canada. Made aware, by the experiences of the War, that the only spiritual force which is capable of weathering the horrors of war, revolution and persecution is a witnessing church, and deeply conscious that the world was in the midst of a new revolutionary era, the Conference set in high relief the "witness of a revolutionary church."

At Whitby a new slogan emerged: "partners in obedience." The representatives of Christian churches from the whole world pledged themselves to become "partners in obedience," so that, transcending all divisions, pooling all resources and working in perfect comradeship, they might make a common approach along a world front to the spiritual problems of the age.

A year later there took place at Amsterdam, Holland, the most significant ecclesiastical event of the century. A World Council of non-Roman Churches was constituted. One of the most significant constitutional actions which the Council took was to "associate" itself officially with the parent ecumenical body, the International Missionary Council, which had been organized some twenty-five years before. In this way the fact was symbolized that the whole Church in its official capacity now recognized the missionary obligation of the Christian religion. This obligation had previously been regarded as very largely the responsibility of missionary societies which might, or might not, be sponsored officially by the churches to which their members belonged.

The last of the great series of ecumenical gatherings which marked the first half of this century, was held in the city of Bankok, Thailand, in December, 1949. The new emergent region of East Asia was in a ferment. A Communist regime was in control in China from which no official delegates could come to this Conference. The gathering recommended the appointment of an Asian Christian to be an apostolic pastor-at-large for the Protestant Churches of East Asia, to function under the joint auspices of the two ecumenical bodies which had become officially associated at Amsterdam.

III. Interpretations of Christianity and Its Relation to the Other Religions

After this survey of secular world forces and of Christian world gatherings, we come now to representative answers that have been given during the present century to the question, What is Christianity? Wherein lies the uniqueness of the Christian religion?

a. *Christianity as one religion among others.* Comparative Religion as a special branch of study has veered between two extremes. As expounded by Dr. Kellogg, author of the first "handbook" on the subject, the comparative study of religion should chiefly establish the superiority of the Christian religion and so provide an apologetic for Christianity. Such an approach, however, is open to the criticism that it destroys the objectivity of Comparative Religion as a science and makes it merely an introduction to and a handmaid of Christian theology.

The other extreme is that represented by the new W. M. Birks, Professor of Comparative Religion in the Faculty of Divinity of McGill University, Montreal. In his inaugural lecture on the subject, *The Comparative Study of Religion*, Professor W. C. Smith recognizes that the study of religion is important, because as he says, different ways of worshipping God have very basic implications for the economic, the political, the agricultural, the medical, and the industrial life of peoples. Religious differences, moreover, affect cultural relations and human understanding between peoples. But Comparative Religion should neither define religion nor say what it ought to be. It is not interested in ascertaining the essence or essential structure of a religion, nor will it venture to formulate value judgments regarding the religions. To be a Christian from the view point of Comparative Religion, thus conceived, is simply to belong to the Christian tradition. What is important is simply the empirical historical reality of a religion. Such an approach to the study of religion, being hindered by considerations of scientific objectivity to seek the essence of a religion, and forbidden by the demands of academic neutrality, to show a marked preference for one religion over another, leaves untouched and unanswered all the great concerns which make people religious and make religious people want to propagate their faith.

We move therefore into a realm of interpretation where religious essences are sought, and where religious commitment is held to be indispensable for the true study of religion.

b. *Christianity as the highest religion.* That the Christian reli-

gion is the highest, though not the absolute religion, is the view expressed by Professor W. E. Hocking, in the book already referred to, *Rethinking Missions,* and in a subsequent volume by the same distinguished author, *Living Religions and a World Faith.* Religion is defined as "a passion for righteousness and for the spread of righteousness, conceived as a cosmic demand." It is religion's supreme role to establish a civilization and to keep the civilization sound. Thus the real absolute is culture whose servant religion is to be. *Rethinking Missions* was convinced that events the world around were moving in the direction of the emergence of a common world culture. Religion's task was to provide that coming world culture with a soul. For those seeking to fulfil this task, Jesus, the greatest religious genius who ever appeared, would become in spirit their "Companion and Master" in the great adventure. They who accepted His leadership would not be interested in displacing one religion by another, even by Christianity. They would not be interested either in a mere synthesis of religion, but would exercise a virile intolerance of all those aspects of religion which are unwholesome. This method would be one of "reconception," giving time for their faith to be considered under the most favorable circumstances by peoples of other faiths. Renouncing as futile all private proprietorship in truth, they would live and work for the expression of the final truth. That final truth, whatever it may be, is "the New Testament of every existing faith." This represents the so-called "liberal" view of the Christian religion.

From this viewpoint, Christianity, while being the highest religion which has yet appeared, as Christ is the greatest religious figure, is not the final religion. We must look forward to a still more perfect and adequate religion, which, as already stated, will constitute the soul and inspiration of a universal culture. But the expectation of an emergent world culture has proved, in the light of subsequent events, to have been purely illusory. To remove, moreover, from a religion the sense of being related to an absolute truth, and to divest it of an apostolic urge to make that truth known, has led, and can only lead, to religious formalism and

spiritual stagnation. For the essence of a potent religion is not to believe that it has a truth, but that it is related to the Truth. For a religion to admit the relative into what it regards as its essence is to destroy its character as religion.

c. *Christianity as the absolute religion.* In striking contrast to the view that Christianity contains the highest truth is the view that it presents the *absolute* truth, because it presents Jesus Christ who is the Truth. During the first half of this century, the absolute character of the Christian religion has been set forth in "orthodox" Protestant thought under two forms or, one might say, with two distinctive emphases. For some, Christianity is the absolute religion because in Jesus Christ, who is the perfect revelation of God, the absolute meaning of life, and so life's absolute value, has appeared. Others in stressing the absolute character of the Christian religion put the emphasis upon the activity of the everliving God as that appears in the Bible. This view stresses not so much the quality of life which appeared in Jesus Christ, as the expression of the divine activity which became manifest when He appeared. In both views there is a high Christology. The one is impressed, however, by the significance of Christ as the supreme Value for life; the other, with Jesus Christ as the supreme Lord of life.

The former of these viewpoints was given classical expression in the Jerusalem Message of 1928. The Message said: "Our message is Jesus Christ. He is the revelation of what God is and of what man through Him may become. In Him we come face to face with the ultimate reality of the universe. He makes known to us God as our Father, perfect and infinite in love and in righteousness."

Those who met at Jerusalem were convinced that Christianity stands or falls with the conviction that the revelation of God in Jesus Christ is something unique. What we have in Jesus Christ is not simply the highest idea of God, but God Himself in His self-giving love. Inasmuch, therefore, as Christ is the Truth, a Christian must necessarily be missionary and pass on the Truth. When, however, we speak of the "superiority" of Christianity we are not saying that Christians have been more "religious" than the great

men of the East. As a matter of fact oriental mystics have done much more spiritual climbing in a religious sense. The superiority of the Christian religion lies in the fact that God comes to meet man in Jesus Christ. The Christian, therefore, can glory only in this, that he owes everything to Christ. For that reason he must ever feel humble. It is by God's grace that he is what he is. The fact was emphasized at Jerusalem that the superiority of Christianity, for example, over Islam, could not be grounded in its culture or in its theology, but only in the fact that the "Spirit of God was in Christ." It was the manifestation of this living Presence which Islam lacked. For at bottom, religions differ not so much in their trappings as in their essence. When all is said and done they differ "in their view of the character of God." Or more concretely, the true division between religions is not between the East and the West, but, as Archbishop Temple expressed it in one of the Jerusalem documents, "between Bible and non-Bible." The inescapable fact is that "salvation is of the Jews." It is at this point that the Jerusalem emphasis passes into that which, in Christian thought on the subject of Christianity and the non-Christian religions, has become associated with the name of H. Kraemer.

Kraemer, then a missionary in Java, was present at the Jerusalem Conference. Several years before the Conference at Madras, and in preparation for it, he was asked to prepare a special study on the Christian Message. The fruit of years of thought and travel is the now famous and influential volume, *The Christian Message in a Non-Christian World.*

According to Kraemer, it is not enough to think of the Christian religion in terms of values, however great the values. A comprehensive view of life is needed. Such a view we derive from the Bible, or as Kraemer puts it, from "Biblical realism." "Biblical realism" is not interested merely in spiritual values, but in the dramatic saving events which the Bible presents. Christianity is essentially the religion of the Incarnation, of the fact that God became man for man's salvation. That being so, Christian truth is not eternal truth or the expression of eternal values, it is rather truth that *became*. Its central affirmation is that God became man. The most purely divine dimension of the Christian religion is the Resurrection. Because of this mighty act of God, Jesus Christ is Lord. That earliest Christian creed is "the pith of the Biblical revelation." In the Risen Christ, God began a new order of life of which Jesus Christ Himself is the center and head. Christianity is, therefore, not so much Religion as Revelation. Christ as the ultimate standard of reference becomes the crisis of all religions, not only of the non-Christian religions, but also of empirical Christianity, that is, Christianity as we know it in history. That being so, all natural religious superiority dies.

Thus Kraemer, under the influence of Kierkegaard and Barth, in stressing the special Divine activity of God in the Bible, affirms the discontinuity between Christianity and the other religions. The viewpoint takes issue with that viewpoint in Christian theology associated with the name of Clement of Alexandria, which, by stressing the principle of continuity, regards Christianity as essentially the supreme and ultimate wisdom. No, says Kraemer, Christianity is never a mere perfecting of what went before. The non-Christian religions are not schoolmasters which bring people to Christ. Christianity differs from them not merely in value but in the fact that the living God was active in Christ and in the drama associated with Christ, as He was not active in the leaders and the history of other religions.

IV. The Missionary Approach of Christianity to the Other Religions

What kind of missionary approach should Christianity make to the other religions? An adequate and representative answer to this question involves consideration of the missionary *objective*, the missionary *motive* and the missionary *attitude*.

a. *The missionary objective*. Two main answers have been made in the course of the present century to the question of the missionary objective. One is the view advocated by *Rethinking Missions* and subsequently enlarged on by Professor Hocking in

Living Religions and a World Faith. Christianity must ever maintain the point of view of world culture, which was believed to be emerging in the late twenties and early thirties of the century. A general desire existed in the world for the voice of Christianity to be heard. The authentic spirit of Christ would always be welcome. That being so, it should not be necessary to "sell" Christianity any more than it was necessary to sell the other wares of world culture. All that was needed was that the good things of Christianity be presented in order to be sympathetically received. Christian missionaries should, therefore, share with the representatives of other religions such certainties as they themselves had in the sphere of religion. Such an approach, however, should not involve any undue or embarrassing haste on the part of the preacher or of the philanthropist. Haste would be in order only when it appeared to the missionary that there was a danger of local customs changing too rapidly as the spirit of world culture loosened the sanctions and ancient customs of religion. He must never work towards the displacement of another religion, but towards the growing together of Christianity with it, or the continued existence of the other religion alongside Christianity. For, after all, the devotees of all religions are brothers in a common quest. It is for Christians, therefore, to share with the representatives of other religions the spiritual resources of Western civilization, those things which they have learned through Christ. This will be done best through a living philanthropy and education, rather than through evangelization in the traditional sense.

This point of view led to the organization in the U.S.A. in the mid-thirties of a movement called "The Modern Missions Movement," renamed soon after, "A Movement for World Christianity." It aimed to substitute for "Foreign Missions," a "Christian International," which would aim to build a Christian civilization. The rapid disintegration of this movement was a demonstration of the fact that its leaders had faced neither the realities of the world situation nor the realities of the Christian religion. The distinguished men and women who after a long period of close study of

Christian missions and the other religions in the Orient, wrote *The Layman's Inquiry*, seemed to be totally unaware that, quite apart from Christianity, there was a force present in many lands, namely Marxist Communism, which was bent upon the most radical transformation of ancient life and faith.

The other view, the view which is inherent in the nature of Christianity and responsible for its expansion in the world, has been that Christians should devote themselves to the evangelization of all mankind irrespective of nationality, religion, class, or race. The Edinburgh Conference of 1910 gave classical expression to Christian concern for world-wide evangelism. The Gospel, said the Edinburgh Convention, must be carried to all the non-Christian world. The world situation should be studied with a view to making the Gospel known to all men. The sense of urgency should be all the greater in view of the fact that the non-Christians were attempting to adapt themselves to modern conditions. Christians must make haste. It was a spectacle "of singular interest and grandeur," it was said, to think of the Christian Church advancing along many lines of action "to the conquest of the five great religions of the modern world." In these words becomes evident the tremendous crusading surge of missionary enthusiasm that dominated the great gathering in the Scottish capital. But it should be borne in mind that this conquest was to be the conquest of Jesus Christ who "fulfills and supersedes all other religions."

Some three decades later the Christian missionary forces, meeting at Madras on the edge of the Second World War, and representing the "older" and the "younger" churches, with the representatives of the "younger" churches predominating, made world evangelism the keynote of the gathering. It was pointed out that Christianity had come to a point in human history where it was in a fighting situation comparable to that in which the early Christians found themselves in the Roman Empire. In such a case the kind of missionary objective towards which Christians should look was not any goal inherent in the other great world religions. The true religious goal was no "return to totality," no "serene ecstasy or liberating gnosis," no "aristocratic mysticism," no "static conservatism," no "national self-deification," but a submission to the "Lordship and sovereignty of God, the Eternal."

b. *The missionary motive.* But granted that Christianity by its very nature must pursue the evangelization of the world, what is the motive of true missionary effort?

The motivation of Christian missionary activity was classically expressed in the "Jerusalem Message," which said, "Christ is our motive and Christ is our end. We must give nothing less and we can give nothing more." Christians, therefore, in their approach to other people, must be inspired by the "good news" of Christ. They must repudiate all ulterior purposes. They must eschew imperialism in every form. And never must they confer benefits on other people in order to be in a position to manage their souls. Let them reject "theological charity;" doing good to people must not be contingent upon their acceptance of certain theological ideas or their adoption of certain religious practices. To be a Christian and a missionary should be synonymous, for Christian witness is the supreme manifestation of self-giving love.

Pearl Buck in *Fighting Angel,* a book which describes her father, has a description of the intensity of the early missionaries: "To go forth, to cry out, to warn, to save others, these were frightful urgencies upon the soul already saved. There was a very madness of necessity and agony of salvation." Those who drafted the Jerusalem Message went on record as saying that, although they were as concerned as their fathers about the implications of men dying without Christ, they were still more concerned about the fact that multitudes were living without Christ. So they addressed themselves to the whole world; to all the Christian Churches; to all non-Christian religions; to all who enjoyed the benefits of Western civilization, that they might face the fact and its implications that "Jesus Christ is indeed the Saviour of the world."

It is an impressive fact that this sense of apostolic obligation towards God and the world has taken on new meaning and intensity in these last times. Those who attended the Madras Conference were aware that there was nothing left for many Christians save "purely religious and moral suasion." They were, therefore, being forced back to fundamentals. Impotent to use education or medicine, or to engage in philanthropy, nothing remained for many Christians but the simple proclamation of the Lordship of Jesus Christ over all life. As Kraemer has expressed it, "The former ideas of recommending Christianity as the bringer of enlightenment and freedom, as a capital, national and social tonic to make powerful nations, as the infallible guide to progress, had come to naught. . . . Sharing religious experience, even service to men, Christianizing the social order, or the economic and political order, though necessarily included in the living act of man's full missionary expression, cannot be the real motive and ultimate purpose. The real motive and ultimate purpose are not in anything that man or civilization call for. As Kagawa has said, 'The starting point of missions is the Divine Commission to proclaim the Lordship of Christ over all life.' "

A decade later, after the Second World War had ended, the men and women who met at Whitby, Canada, proclaimed two insistent needs: "The desperate need of the world for Christ; the unsatisfied yearning of Christ for the world." These together constitute the expression of the missionary motive in the best Protestant thought of the twentieth century.

c. But if evangelization is the missionary objective and if the Christ whom the world so desperately needs and who so yearningly loves the world, is the motive, what should be the personal attitude of the Christian missionary towards those belonging to other religions?

The missionary attitude. In the missionary thought of the nineteenth century it was not uncommon to regard any show of sympathy with the ethnic religions as a very great blunder on the part of the Christian missionary. The Edinburgh Conference, however, amid the surge of crusading passion which dominated it, and the world-wide strategy which it developed, advocated a sympathetic approach to the other religions. Missionaries, it was said, should proceed with knowledge and charity, looking always for the nobler elements in the other faiths. Such a sympathetic study would introduce them to "hitherto undiscovered riches in Christ who is the absolute revelation." Some considered that, in view of the fact that the Eternal Word had been active in other religions, they would find, as they penetrated within their structure, that Christ was no stranger there. Much would be found there which was expressive of His influence; people would be found there who would be responsive to His Lordship.

The ideal missionary approach has been finely expressed by Kraemer as the combination of "a prophetic, apostolic heraldship of truth for Christ's sake, with a priestly, apostolic ambassadorship of love for His sake." The real point of contact with those of other religions would thus be the missionary himself. Everything depends upon the missionary's disposition and attitude. The foreign word must become indigenous flesh. Recognizing that he is not the possessor of a truth, but rather the witness to a truth which God has mercifully revealed, the Christian missionary can have no ground for pride or conceit.

When the problem was raised at the Bangkok Conference of 1949 as to the relationship between Christianity and the cultural heritage of East Asia, emphasis was laid upon the fact that it was the Christian, whether missionary or national, who was the true answer to this problem. The way to proceed, especially in the present situation, was not to formulate a theoretic statement of Christianity in relation to the Asiatic cultural heritage. What was required or suggested was that the true Christian working in those areas should sympathetically absorb and identify himself with all that was best in the cultural heritage of East Asia, and, thereafter, express in relation to it the unsearchable riches of Christ. The Christian who knows Christ and loves Him, and who desires to impart that knowledge and love to others, will relate himself sympathetically to other people and their culture. Then, in terms of that culture, and in a manner intelligible to those who belong to it, he will communicate the knowledge of Christ. He will study the Bible with representatives of other faiths not as if they were merely non-Christian, but taking into account that they are human beings he will treat them as such. A Hindu who experienced Christian love in a mission hospital in Fategahr, India, made the statement, "There is more healing in the dust of Fategahr than in all the waters of the Ganges." That expression was born out of the patient's contact with Christlike personalities, inspired and molded by the great Physician.

As a contribution to this point of view, and in illustration of it, the distinguished Indian Christian, P. D. Devanandan, made a remarkable contribution to the thinking of the Bangkok Conference. He showed how three of the central ideas stressed by Mahatma Gandhi could be realized adequately only by Jesus Christ. The sense of the sacredness of personality, expressed in *Ahimsa*, could only be secured by the belief that God had become manifest in the flesh. The soul force or passion for righteousness, expressed in *Satyagraha*, could only be achieved by a religion whose founder could say, "My Father worketh hitherto and I work," and which proclaimed that "God was in Christ reconciling the world unto Himself." An order of society in which all political and economic relationships between people would acknowledge the ultimate sovereignty of God, expressed in Gandhi's idea of *Ramrajga*, could only be realized by the worship of a God who was both omnipotent and actively concerned about righteousness.

V. The New Emphasis in the Christian World Outlook

What does the future hold for the Christian religion? Have the missionary days of Christianity come to an end? What does the emergence of the East in world politics, and the specter of Communist domination in the Orient, bode for a religion whose chief centers for nigh two millennia have been in the West?

These questions can only be answered when we consider the new status of the Christian Church in the world of today. We have witnessed in these last years the emergence, or better, the resurgence, of the Church both as a living world reality and as a principle topic of Christian thought.

In the early days of the Christian missionary movement the Church was taken for granted. It meant simply the local congregation or some form of organized Christianity. There was practically no theological thinking about it. But a new sense of the Church has been born; and the new reality of the Church has appeared. This new reality has come into being on a worldwide scale as the result of Christian missions. The Oxford Conference of 1937 gave birth to the slogan "Let the Church be the Church." Let it be itself and not something else. Shortly after Oxford, a new science, the science of Ecumenics, was formulated. Ecumenics has been defined as "the science of the Church universal, conceived as a World Missionary Community—its nature, functions, relations and strategy." Representatives of the Church universal have accepted and become committed to the new watchword, "partners in obedience," which involves the transcendence of everything in race, money, or administrative policy, which would prevent the fullest missionary cooperation between the "older" and the "younger" churches. It involves also the "association" of the two great Ecumenical bodies.

"Let the Church be the Mission." This is the slogan which is emerging. The Church was designed by God to be the mission and must take its calling seriously. World evangelism is its main task. It is "inherent in the nature of the Church as the Body of Christ, created by God to continue in the world the work which Jesus Christ began in His life and teaching, and consummated by His death and resurrection." So spoke the Madras Conference. "The Missionary Obligation of the Church" will be the theme of the next meeting of the International Missionary Council scheduled, world conditions permitting, to convene in 1952. Now that the Christian Church is "coextensive with the inhabited globe" it was never in a more favorable situation to evangelize the world, even "in this generation."

The Church must become the mission, because it finds itself everywhere in a missionary situation. It lives literally in a strange

world. Many churches live in a post-Constantine situation where
the Church has been deprived of privileges which it formerly enjoyed. In other countries churches live in a post-Christian situation
where life is no longer dominated by the Christian ethos. In many
regions of the modern world Christians have become in a wholly
new sense "pilgrims and sojourners." That being so, the Church's
missionary work must, therefore, be begun all afresh. The new
situation gives significant meaning to the title of Kraemer's prophetic book, "The Christian Message in a *Non-Christian World*."

As the mission, the Church is summoned to a new task. No
longer can the representatives of the Christian religion think in
terms of a global Christian strategy as was done by the men and
women who attended the Edinburgh Conference in 1910. "To talk
about global missionary strategy," says a distinguished Christian
thinker and missionary statesman,[2] "is to surrender to the intoxica-
tion of verbiage. It is to fall a victim to Titanism. Decentraliza-
tion of the missionary enterprise, not centralization is the clamant
need of today." This means that the Christian churches in their
great dispersion around the globe, while maintaining close ecumenical unity, must speak and act in their several national and
regional situations as circumstances require.

In some parts of the world it becomes necessary for the Church
to proclaim and to stand in a very special way for the dignity and
integrity of man and of human nature. Never was it so urgent, in
view of the enserfdom and debasement of man, to outline a true
Christian anthropology. Beyond that the significance must be
worked out for life of the living reality of Jesus Christ and of the
"new man in Christ." This "new man" alone can meet the pagan
dynamism of the new religions. He can meet it because the Comrade of his new frontier life is the Lord of the Frontier.

It is no less a part of the missionary task of the Christian Church
today to manifest the meaning of true community. The Christian
community, on the one hand, indigenous and national, and, on the
other, loyally ecumenical because rooted in the Christian tradition

[2] Max Warren in *The Truth of Vision*

and related to other Christians throughout the world, has a missionary task of a communal nature to fulfil. "The Church herself is the leaven by which Christ transforms the life of society and nations. There can be no true Christian action which is not rooted in full participation in the worship of the Church and animated by zeal for the expression of true community in things both spiritual and material." So said the Oxford Conference, and Whitby added, "The Church alone offers the only concept adequate to furnish focal unity for corporate existence."

In his book *Living Religions and a World Faith,* Professor Hocking has expressed disdain of a plan of the ages. "The idea of a divine plan considered as a dated product of God's wisdom and goodness, wholly unimaginable to man, is, I fear, an ingenious invention of St. Paul. To take it up again today is to place a halter around the neck of Christianity for those to tug at who are disposed to work upon the more graven fears of the human heart. It is time for a robust and honest Christianity to have done with all this rattling of ancient moral chains." So writes the distinguished professor. Yet it is precisely the vision and understanding of this divine plan which is needed by the Christian Church today. Such a plan we find in Paul's Letter to the Ephesians, the greatest of all Biblical documents. It is the book of the Church Universal, the most contemporary book in the Bible. Here is found the only vision and theory of history which can match the Marxist dream.

Happily the vision of the "Mystery," the "Unveiled Secret" of God, is breaking upon the Church, which braces itself with militant faith for a wilderness life, on all the frontiers of the world. To build the Church, to make it a missionary instrument in God's hand is the great task of our time. For the Church is the one indestructible community which shall outlive the waxing and the waning of all political systems and religious organizations. Let the Church, therefore, be in a new sense the Mission, in the knowledge that Jesus Christ is Lord, and in the hope that all men everywhere shall one day acclaim His sovereign Lordship.

BIBLIOGRAPHY

Kellogg, Samuel Henry, *A Handbook of Comparative Religion* (Philadelphia, 1899)

Mott, John R., *The Evangelization of the World in This Generation* (New York, 1900)

The Missionary Message in Relation to Non-Christian Religions, Report of Commission IV, World Missionary Conference, 1910 (New York, 1910)

The Christian Life and Message in Relation to Non-Christian Systems of Thought and Life, Volume I, Jerusalem Meeting of the International Missionary Council (New York, 1928)

Hocking, William Ernest, Editor, *Re-Thinking Missions: A Laymen's Inquiry After One Hundred Years* (New York, 1932)

Kraemer, H., *The Christian Message in a Non-Christian World* (New York, 1938)

Hocking, William Ernest, *Living Religions and a World Faith* (New York, 1940)

Jurji, Edward J., Editor, *Great Religions of the Modern World* (Princeton, 1946)

Ranson, C. W., Editor, *Renewal and Advance: Christian Witness in a Revolutionary World* (London, 1948)

Ranson, C. W., Editor, *The Christian Prospect in Eastern Asia* (Report of the Bangkok Conference, 1949) (New York, 1950)

THE FUNERAL

THE WESTMINSTER SOURCE BOOKS
FOR MINISTERS

The Funeral . . . . . . *by Andrew W. Blackwood*

The Christian Sacraments . . *by Hugh Thomson Kerr*

Pastoral Work . . . . . . *by Andrew W. Blackwood*

(*Other volumes in preparation*)

The Funeral

A Source Book for Ministers

ANDREW WATTERSON BLACKWOOD

Chairman of the Practical Department
The Theological Seminary, Princeton, New Jersey

The Westminster Press · *Philadelphia*

Dedicated
to my students
past and present

Acknowledgments

THE writer is indebted to the following for permission to quote. If he has neglected to secure permission from any other, he will rectify the error when it is called to his notice.

American Tract Society: Poems from *Bees in Amber*, by John Oxenham.

Barnes, A. S., and Co.: Two cuts from *Song and Service Book for Ship and Field*, ed. by Chaplain Ivan L. Bennett. 1941.

Coolidge, Mrs. Grace: A poem, "The Open Door."

Freeman, Mrs. Margery: Two poems by Robert Freeman.

Houghton Mifflin Co.: "The Butterfly," from *A Marriage Cycle*, by Alice F. Palmer; "Resignation," by H. W. Longfellow; two poems by J. G. Whittier.

Little, Brown and Co.: "Going to Heaven," from *Poems by Emily Dickinson*.

Macmillan Company, The: Excerpt from *The Art of Ministering to the Sick*, by R. C. Cabot and R. L. Dicks; four poems by C. Rossetti; two poems by Alfred Tennyson; "At a Burial," from *Poems* by William Watson.

Methodist Publishing Company: Two prayers from *The Ritual*.

Osborn, H. F.: A poem by his brother, Will C. Osborn.

Scribners: "Emancipation," from *Thoughts for Every-day Living*, by M. D. Babcock; a selection from *Poems* by Sidney Lanier; two selections from *The Poems of Henry van Dyke*.

The author is grateful for implied permission to quote from many sources, notably prayers, not under copyright. Other obligations appear in the text. The chief is to the one who suggested the writing and helped with the plans.

Contents

Contents

Foreword

THE request for this book has come from the publishers. They report that many pastors desire a comprehensive treatment of the funeral and related matters. Especially do young ministers wish such a guidebook. Out in the laboratory of life they are learning by trial and error what they should have known in part before they were ordained. "In every art there is a knack that is not a gift."

Fortunately, it is possible to master any practical subject during the first few years in the parish. That is what the majority of us have had to do. In my early pastoral experiences I should have welcomed a book showing how mature clergymen solve problems relating to the funeral. Strange as it may seem to lovers of theory, the most perplexing questions that come to the parish ministers have to do with the old word "How?"

Many pastors feel that the teaching of practical theology has been too theoretical. Some of the ablest lecturers and writers in the field steer away from things practical. They speak of the "how-to" books as superficial, and keep writing about other things. Surely someone ought to prepare ministerial treatises as scholarly and readable as are at hand in the field of medicine. In that profession things practical enjoy prestige.

In medicine no names are more revered than those of Cabot and Osler, each of whom has written about practical methods of healing. In our field the problems are more elusive, but still we can learn from the masters of medical literature. We too should prepare the student to deal with the person who is in need; we should stress the normal rather than the abnormal; we should make large use of typical cases; and we should provide clinical training under expert supervision.

"What can be learned can be taught." In years to come the minister will be trained for his practical duties as thoroughly as his brother who studies medicine or surgery. Meanwhile my sympathy goes out to young men of promise who have entered the greatest work in the world with little concern about the mundane matters that must occupy many of their waking hours. Nowhere does the lack of training seem more glaring than when a young minister stands face to face with death, and knows not what to do.

Such are the practical problems and ideals that have led to the writing of the book. The work of preparation has enlisted my heart. I have enjoyed recalling the days when I was a parish minister and becoming familiar with the work of masters now on the field. I believe that on the average the ministry today is stronger than at any time in recent years, and that the pastors of tomorrow will be still better trained. I hope that this book about the funeral will cheer and help many a man of God in his ministry of Christian comfort and hope.

ANDREW WATTERSON BLACKWOOD.

The Theological Seminary,
Princeton, New Jersey.

I. The Funeral Problem

AMONG all the problems of the parish minister few are more baffling than those that concern funerals. Not every occasion proves difficult, but in the course of the year any pastor is likely to face perplexing problems. This is especially true of the first few years. If a man learns as he goes along he will gradually become accustomed to meeting each situation as it arises. Meantime, the difficulties connected with funerals should help to make a man humble. They should also send him to his knees.

How can a minister hope to solve such problems? Before we turn to suggestions about ways and means, we ought to think further about the basic principles. Since we are approaching the matter from the viewpoint of the pastor, we shall start with him. But we should remember that the interests of the sorrowing friends are of vastly more concern. Most vital of all are the claims of God.

THE MINISTER

What is expected of the minister at a funeral? Instead of thinking abstractly, let us consider a case. When William James died, his widow sent a note to George A. Gordon, of the New Old South Church in Boston: "I want you to officiate at the funeral, as one of William's friends, and also as a man of faith. That is what he was. I want no hesitation or diluted utterance at William's funeral." What an ideal for any pastor: to be a friend, as well as a man of faith, with no hesitation or diluted utterance!

Conversely, when Robert Burns lay dying he spoke about his obsequies. Referring to a company of ill-trained vol-

unteer soldiers, he said: "Don't let that awkward squad fire
a salute over my grave." While the poet was not thinking
of any clergyman, every minister should take these words to
heart. Otherwise he and the others who share in the final
ceremonies may seem like members of an awkward squad.
From this point of view there are two kinds of ministers:
the one knows how to conduct a funeral; the other does not.

The difficulties are of many sorts. Some of them relate to
time. The call from the home of sorrow may come without
warning. For weeks the pastor may toil with little to break the
daily routine. Then there may be a succession of funerals.
Even though there is nothing unusual, every such experience
ought to move his heart. Sometimes he scarcely knows what
to do or say. If he had a week or two he might be able to
solve the new problem, but meanwhile he must act, once
for all.

These perplexing situations are not so common as the
present discussion makes them appear. But they do come.
Among the harrowing experiences which the writer has had
at funerals, the most perplexing were in his early ministry at
Pittsburgh. Within half a year, owing to the character of the
neighborhood surrounding the church, he officiated at the
obsequies of six persons who had come to death through
violence.

Each case was different. In none of the six was there anything especially reprehensible. Still the young pastor longed
for the wisdom of a Solomon and the heart of a shepherd. As
he grew older, the annual number of funerals increased, but
the proportion of perplexing situations became smaller. Like
the family physician, the minister who is faithful learns how
to heal the broken in heart. Even so, it should never seem
easy to make ready for a funeral, and thus to lead the sorrowing friends close to the heart of God.

The following experience was unique. A graduate of a
divinity school had never officiated at a funeral, and he knew
practically nothing about the subject. In August he went out

to his first charge. For two weeks he was the only clergyman in town. During the first ten days he had ten funerals. In each situation he found something different, and in most cases he was perplexed. To this day he doubtless feels that someone back in the seminary should have forewarned him about what he might soon have to face.

No small part of the problem may be due to the shortness of time for preparation. Before his first funeral the writer had only fifteen minutes. During that interval he felt that he should shave and dress as for a vital ceremony. He did not wish to seem less suitably attired than the mortician. Before the young parson was ready the carriage was waiting at the door. As for spiritual preparation, he had never learned to pray while shaving, but he did have a few minutes of quietness on the way to the home.

Like Abraham, the young minister went out by faith, not knowing whither. He claimed the promise: "It shall be given you in that same hour what ye shall speak." But on the way home he resolved that by God's grace he would never again go to a house of grief so totally unprepared. As for the way to get ready for unexpected funerals, that is shown throughout the present book. It represents what the writer wishes someone had taught him while in the seminary.

Even in the case of a normal funeral there may be only a little time for preparation. If a person falls asleep on Wednesday evening local custom may call for services on Thursday afternoon. This is all the time that usually elapses between death and burial in certain parts of the South. Meanwhile the pastor has other things to do. How can he get ready for what is to be a neighborhood event?

When there is an opportunity to prepare there may be a paucity of suitable materials. Even at the seminary library, with half a day at his disposal, a man who is familiar with the books in the practical department may not know where to lay his hands on what he wishes to use at a complex funeral. Much more likely is this to be the case early in a man's first pastorate. For a year or so books may be few. There may not be near at hand a friendly older minister to whom the young man can telephone for advice. This is the pastor's zero hour.

If there are materials there may be no plan. The more facts and ideas a man has in mind, the more he may become bewildered. Unless he has had experience in using such resources to meet human needs, he may not know how to prepare a simple program. If he is able, after a fashion, he may not feel that he has time without neglecting his other duties. Doubtless he will muddle through. But a death comes only once; there should be no ministerial muddling. Our God is not a muddler.

Is there in the ministry anything vital that receives as little attention as making ready for many a funeral? In preparing to preach, the clergyman mulls over his subject for days, if not for weeks or months. In looking forward to the celebration of the Lord's Supper, he is even more zealous about making ready in advance. He may not know that his prestige, locally, depends largely on his ability to do and say the right thing at every neighborhood funeral.

We are taking for granted that the pastor is a sincere Christian, and that he has been called of God to be a minister. Even so, at times he may have psychological handicaps. For instance, he may be called into the home of strangers. There he may feel unready to administer comfort. Then if ever he needs to serve as a friend and a man of faith, without hesitation or diluted utterance. Instead of cherishing an inferiority complex, he ought to cultivate a holy self-respect.

Whether in the study making ready or in the home conducting the service, no man is able to do his best work when he is bothered, and feels conscious of his mental processes. At a funeral people wish to know that the minister in charge is master of the situation and of himself. It is so with the engineer in a railway locomotive. In the recent autobiography of Irvin S. Cobb, *Exit Laughing,* he says that of all the craftsmen in America the locomotive engineer makes the strongest impression of mastery. It is much the same with the captain of an ocean liner. He knows. He is able. He is ready. Should it not be so with the pastor in the presence of death?

The most experienced clergyman may receive a summons that will cause him perplexity. He may know the books, and he may have solved many problems in ways all his own. But the present case is unique. Like the physician when he finds conditions that differ from anything in the textbooks, the minister feels that under God he must work out his own salvation. There is no one stereotyped way of ministering to friends or strangers in sorrow. There are no patent formulas. Every funeral should be somewhat unique. Herein lies much of the difficulty.

Without pausing now to consider possible solutions of these problems, let us fix in mind two texts. Each of them has to do with using available resources in meeting the heart needs of men. The first text is from the spiritual autobiography of the Apostle Paul. The other passage is from the most tender and moving of all his letters to Christian friends.

"My grace is sufficient for thee: for my strength is made perfect in weakness" (II Cor. 12: 9a). Here is abundance of divine power for all a minister's needs. The other text voices a man's faith, which is human weakness laying hold on divine power to supply his needs: "I can do all things through Christ which strengtheneth me" (Phil. 4: 13).

THE SORROWING FRIENDS

Still more serious may be the questions that concern the friends who have just parted from their loved one. As a matter of course they may be strangers, but in alluding to them as friends one is holding up the ideal. After the funeral they should be loyal supporters of the pastor and the local church.

Whether strangers or not, they are likely to feel confused. At times they seem to be beside themselves. For weeks or months they have been wearing themselves out in attendance on their loved one. In another kind of situation, still more difficult for the pastor to meet, the blow has fallen without warning. Yesterday the husband and father was hale and happy. He had never known what it meant to be weak and ill. In his office today just before noon he dropped dead. Is it any wonder that the widow cries out, "My God, my God, why?"

Even if the circumstances are not exceptional, still the bereaved may be confused. They may never have had a death in the home. They know nothing about morticians, burial plots, and funeral services. The widow may never have handled any money of her own. She may never have made an important decision without first consulting her husband. As she sits among the ashes of her hopes for the morrow she is in no condition to decide about what must be done today.

Some of the perplexities relate to money. In one case there is little or none. The long illness has eaten up the household savings. The person in charge does not know which way to turn. If the pastor is aware of the circumstances he may suggest to the deacons that they consider extending financial aid. The situation, however, is delicate. Even in the hour of sorrow self-respecting folk do not wish to think of themselves as on relief. Really they are members of the church household, and they should be ready to receive what they would gladly give if the facts were reversed. In any case, the minister himself should not become mixed up in matters relating to money.

In another home of sorrow there may be more money for disposal than ever before. If the husband has been frugal there may be various sorts of insurance funds. When these resources become available all at once, the inexperienced widow may lose her head. She may say to herself, "This is all I can do now for my dear husband." Around her may be a small host of relatives and neighbors who keep proffering advice. As each new group arrives there may be still more counsel that seems new and strange. If it is not followed in detail there may be ruffled feelings.

The most officious neighborhood advisers make it their business to visit any home in sorrow. This is more likely to be the case in a rural community, or in the residential district of a city, than among those who dwell in vast apartment buildings, where the feeling may be one of isolation. In either case, the attention of the persons who mourn may be fixed upon things of the earth.

In an occasional household there is only a semblance of grief. At heart the relatives are relieved. Although they strive to conceal their feelings, they find it hard not to look happy. Privately they say, "At last the old man is gone; now we can get his dough." Who but the pastor knows how an elderly man lingers on in a family circle where his room and his money would be more welcome than his presence? Perhaps the only real religion beneath the roof has been in the heart of the aged invalid.

Whatever the background, the funeral is likely to be an event in the community. The good name of the Lord Jesus, the prestige of the local church, and the influence of the pastor, all depend in part on the minister's ability to conduct a funeral. If he is wise he devotes a good deal of spare time to making ready for such a ministry. If he becomes a master of every funeral assembly, his influence for good will be widespread.

At many a service of farewell the throng is cosmopolitan. More than at any other time men and women come home from afar. They feel that the occasion is unique; to each friend death comes only once. Many of those present never attend church. Except for an occasional funeral service, they have no contact with religion. They are as sheep without a shepherd. If the minister is able to move their hearts God-ward, they will remember him as long as they live. But in less than thirty minutes it is far from easy for the pastor to supply the needs of all the waiting hearts.

THE MYSTERY

We have thought about the difficulties that concern the minister and the sorrowing friends. Still more serious are the problems that have to do with death itself. It is a mystery. Who can tell what is the meaning of death? It is the end of a man's life on earth, and the beginning of his eternal existence elsewhere. But what is life, here and hereafter? No one can tell. According to the Anglo-Saxons, a man's sojourn on earth is like the flight of a bird at night. Out of the darkness and the unknown the winged one comes into the banquet hall, circles for a while amid the shadows above the central fire, and then flies out again into the darkness and the unknown.

According to the Christian faith, a human soul comes from God at birth and goes back to God at death. This way of looking at the facts is religious. It stresses the other world. In recent years such an old-fashioned view of life may seem outmoded. Whatever the reason, many a man never thinks or speaks about death unless he must. In large measure he seems to have adopted the Christian Scientist's attitude towards the final mystery of earth: "There is no such thing as death." But still the fact and the mystery persist.

The spirit of our time is secular. For instance, compare the best sellers among present-day novels with the tales of Charles Dickens. Where among current fiction is there so much stress on deathbed scenes as in Dickens? He may have kept his readers too long at the deathbed of Little Nell. If so, the novelist was a man of his day.

The same contrast appears in the pulpit. Where among published sermons today can you find such emphasis on death as in the printed discourses of Spurgeon? For example, in his most famous message, "Songs in the Night," there are two deathbed scenes. In his preaching, as in his choice of hymns and in his public prayers, Spurgeon was a man of his time. He believed with William Sanday, the Oxford scholar, that in the New Testament the center of gravity is beyond the grave.

Doubtless Spurgeon and Dickens went too far. Nevertheless, neither was afraid to face the mystery of death. If the present-day minister would give the subject the prominence that it has in the New Testament, he would help to prepare each of the friends for the change that is sure to come erelong, either in his own case or in that of one who is dearer than all else on earth. When shall we Protestant ministers learn that the glory of the Christian faith lies veiled in mystery?

The mystery is not so much about death as what lies beyond. Perhaps this is why the Book refers to the experience in terms of motion and the forward look. Here are some of the Biblical figures for death: starting on a journey, crossing a river, going home, falling asleep, or being transformed from an earthly seed into a heavenly flower. Whatever the figure, wrapped up in it lies a fact. The fact concerns the life everlasting.

The word "mystery" points to a lofty Christian truth that no man is able to discover for himself, but that God makes known through his Holy Bible. Among all the mysteries of the Christian faith, some of the most precious cluster round the reality of heaven. From the human point of view these are the most glorious truths that the Lord Jesus came to reveal. At a funeral service the question is, how can the minister hope in so brief a time to make eternal verities clear and luminous in the eyes of men and women who may be thinking about things of time and space?

Even in the light of the Resurrection, and of the New Testament which makes it known, there are many questions that the minister cannot answer. Some of the most perplexing have to do with heaven. Is it a place? If so, where do its islands lift "their fronded palms in air"? If the body sleeps in the grave until the resurrection, how does the soul survive without a personal habitation? Will the children of God recognize each other in the Father's home? How can the redeemed in glory be at peace if they know that loved ones who tarry on in the flesh are not making ready to live forever with God?

The facile way to deal with such issues is to ignore them. In any funeral there is sure to be something interesting on the human level. At the services in memory of a businessman the front part of the church was filled with flowers and the rest of the sanctuary was thronged with neighbors and friends. Downtown he had been highly esteemed and in the church he had been active as a trustee. Without referring directly to him, the minister spoke for ten or twelve minutes on "The Religion of a Businessman."

The text was one of the supreme verses in the Old Testament: "What doth the Lord require of thee, but to do justly, and to love mercy, and to walk humbly with thy God?" (Micah 6: 8). The heart of the message was that a businessman's religion starts with justice. He determines to be right with God, right with men, right with self. Such religion expresses itself in kindness, and reaches its culmination in humility. For the Christian the way to achieve such a standard is through Christ and the Cross.

That evening the treasurer of the church, also a businessman, said to the minister, "If you can give me as good a final send-off, my friends will feel that I have not lived in vain." The pastor was pleased. But the next day when he called at the home to which sorrow had come he changed his mind about that funeral message. He decided that he had dodged the real issue, and that he had missed the mark.

At the door the first member of the household to greet him was the daughter, ten years of age. When she saw her friend, the minister, she ran to greet him, and exclaimed, "Where is my daddy today?" What did she care about the religion of a businessman? For the first time in all her happy days she had come face to face with the eternal mystery. She wished to be sure that her father was safe in the keeping of the Lord Jesus.

Fortunately, the evasive attitude toward death and the hereafter is not so common now as a few years ago. Many a pastor has rediscovered the value of the individual soul. In the songs of the sanctuary and in the prayers of the pastor there may be much about the forgiveness of sins, the resurrection of the body, and the life everlasting. In the pulpit work, also, from time to time there is luminous teaching about heaven as home. Throughout both prayers and preaching there is a spirit of mystery and wonder.

Thus we have thought about the funeral problem. It relates to the minister who officiates, to the people who mourn, and to the mystery that envelops death. In view of these facts it is not strange that the conduct of a single funeral takes out of the pastor untold energy. From such an experience he will emerge either a better man or a worse. His purpose in conducting the service is to glorify God and thus help the sorrowing friends. To his own heart also the experience should be a means of grace.

The funeral ceremony brings out whatever there is in a man of strength or of weakness. The content and the spirit of all that he does and says reveal the truth or unreality of his doctrinal beliefs, the warmth or coldness of his spiritual experience, the breadth or narrowness of his Biblical knowledge, the sincerity or sham of his sympathies, and his resourcefulness or lack of skill as a leader in worship.

Despite all the difficulties, or perhaps because of them, there is nothing that the retired clergyman misses more than the privilege of being among people who stand face to face with the last great enemy, and are sore afraid. Next to the satisfactions of being a parish minister, the veteran would welcome the opportunity to confer with any young pastor who is perplexed about funeral problems. Happy is a young minister if in his first charge there is near at hand such an older brother who is ready to sympathize and confer in any time of need.

The spirit of the retired clergyman may be that of Lyman

Abbott. When he wrote the following he was eighty years of
age: "I enjoy my home, my friends, my life. I shall be sorry
to part from them. But I have always stood in the bow looking forward with hopeful anticipation. When the time comes
for me to put out to sea, I think I shall still be standing in
the bow and looking forward with eager interest and glad
hopefulness to the new world to which the unknown voyage
will take me" (II Tim. 4: 7, 8).

Inspirational Readings

Brown, Charles R., *The Making of a Minister*. The Century Co.,
1927. Chapter XI.
McAfee, Cleland B., *Ministerial Practices*. Harper & Brothers, 1928.
Chapters XIX, XX.

II. The Christian Pastor

THE man who has the shepherd heart knows what to do at a deathbed or a funeral. The minister who is not helpful at such a time is probably not a diligent pastor. To these broad statements there is one exception. They do not refer to the man who has had little experience. During the first year or two in the active ministry the majority of us belonged to the awkward squad. Nowhere else did we seem so little at home as in the presence of death. But if a man trusts the Lord and loves people he can learn how to be helpful at a deathbed and in the funeral service.

Failure to be useful at such a time may be due to no lack of ability. In one of our largest cities an active lay officer is devoted to his minister, a brilliant preacher. But when the layman's wife was on her deathbed, he wished that he could invite a neighboring clergyman who excels in pastoral sympathy. After the funeral services, which were coldly intellectual, the layman went in private more than once to the home of the man with the shepherd heart. A real pastor approaches a deathbed or a funeral as a friend, not as a plenipotentiary.

For the neglect of the pastoral office some of us older ministers may be responsible. We have stressed other things. According to Charles R. Brown, of Yale, the favorite form of indoor amusement for clergymen a few years ago was to poke fun at the habit of ringing doorbells. In a city church the present custom is to have the people come to see the pastor. That is good. Somehow or other he should care for the sheep. Meanwhile no one has accepted Dean Brown's challenge: "Will someone be good enough to find me strong, stable, growing, generous, spiritually-minded churches where no pastoral calling has been done in the past ten years? I do not know of any such."

Fortunately, the Protestant Church is witnessing a revival of the pastoral ministry. Theologically, there has been a rediscovery of the individual soul. At the same time there is a feeling that the prospective pastor should be as well trained for his duties as his brother who expects to become a physician. The man who ministers to the soul ought to enter the home as a personal friend. In the presence of death there is no room for mere professionalism.

What, then, are the traits that mark the helpful pastor? At present we are thinking about him as he ministers in the presence of death. We shall consider seven qualities, each of which the minister can cultivate. We shall begin with the most vital and come down to the most external.

SPIRITUALITY

To be an effective pastor a man needs to be filled with the Holy Spirit. The reference is to no esoteric experience, and to no extreme theory. The meaning is that he ought to have had a personal experience of God's redeeming grace, and that he should be renewing the experience from day to day. Body and soul, he should belong to the Lord and the people in the local church. Whenever there is a call to an upper room where death is near, or to a home where it has come, he should be ready to serve as the man of God.

Such a pastor is a living epistle. He is known and read by everybody in the community. Day after day the minister shows the meaning and glory of Christian manhood. Because he lives in constant fellowship with Christ, the pastor's life is radiant. By his daily ministry he shows what the Fourth Gospel means when it says that for the child of God the life everlasting has already begun. Such a radiant personality was Phillips Brooks. In his presence it was not difficult to believe in the reality and nearness of the spiritual world. At a deathbed, in a funeral service, or anywhere else, such a pastor is a living benediction.

SYMPATHY

The man filled with the Spirit of God is a lover of people. He becomes increasingly like God, and God is Love. The man with the shepherd heart knows his sheep one by one. He is eager to share sorrows as well as joys. Especially does his heart go out to the friend who is dying, and to the loved ones after the end has come. Into the home of grief he comes as a personal friend, not as a professional stranger.

Such a man wins his way into the hearts of people while they are hale and active. When he first enters a field he resolves that by God's grace he will almost never be called into a home where he is a stranger. If he knows and loves the people, one by one, he will be able to help in any zero hour. If he prays with them in normal times he will know how to intercede at a deathbed, or a funeral service. If he has spoken on behalf of Christ to every unsaved person in the community, the minister will know what to say in the presence of death. At such a time it is the shepherd's heart that counts.

The helpful pastor is like his Saviour, a friend that sticketh closer than a brother. On the manward side, the chief fact about such a minister is sympathy. That means putting oneself in the other person's place, looking at his world through his eyes, feeling as he ought to feel, and doing all one can to bring him out into the sunlight of God's love. Sympathy is only another name for personal Christianity in action. That in turn is the meaning of the Golden Rule.

Pastoral sympathy calls for the use of imagination, or insight. How else can the unmarried minister, such as Phillips Brooks, comfort a young mother who has lost her little babe? How can a man, even though a husband and father, enter into the experience of a mother who knows there will never be another babe to fill the arms that are empty now? When the pastor's heart is overflowing with sympathy quickened daily at the Cross, he can enter into any "life situation." Better still, he can bring to the broken heart God's healing balm.

Even when the minister is called into a home where he is a stranger, he should know what to do and say. Through no fault of his own he is not as yet a personal friend. But he will be from this time forward. Just now he is present as one who longs to bring these persons close to the heart of God. Once again the secret of being a good pastor is sympathy. It was at the grave of Lazarus that the Lord Jesus wept. While the pastor may not weep, he should make clear how much he cares when any heart is broken.

Such a minister expresses sympathy by sending personal letters. Early in his lifework he learns to put into permanent form anything that his friends in sorrow may wish to preserve. Even though he may live near by he wishes them to have in their home a visible token that he has loved and revered the father who has gone home to God. In later years no minister has ever regretted the time and care devoted to the writing of pastoral letters.

A few years ago a schoolmaster died. In going through his papers the loved ones found a number of personal messages from the pastor. Whenever anything worthy of note had come into the life of the schoolman, or into his family circle, the minister had sent him a note of felicitation or sympathy. Perhaps because that was the pastor's custom with all his friends, he did not remember those letters. But when the husband and father was no longer with them in the flesh, the other members of the household cherished those visible signs of the place he had occupied in the heart of the minister.

In short, when a pastor trusts the Lord and loves the people, one by one, he knows what to do and say at a deathbed or in a funeral service. He feels that he is among friends. When there is an opportunity to make ready, he does so as well as he can. He wishes to represent the Lord worthily.

Beneath all his intellectual preparation is the willingness to let the heart have its way. Would that there were in every parish a minister excelling in the fine art of Christian sympathy!

INTELLIGENCE

The effective pastor needs also a high degree of intelligence. The surest proof of mental acumen is the ability to solve each problem as it arises. The reference here is only to the funeral and related matters. If a man is able to do and say the right thing in one service after another, he evidently possesses a high degree of intelligence. If he had time for extended research among books, and for conference with brethren of piety and experience, it might be possible to employ collective wisdom. But as a rule the minister must rely on himself, as the servant of God. When the time comes for him to act, he must be ready.

Many of the problems that test a man's intellectual powers will appear in later chapters. If he were content to treat every situation according to a set of principles worked out by somebody else, he would be like a physician who has only one way of treating all sorts of diseases. But if the physician of souls is to be an expert in sizing up each new situation, and in using holy words to heal human hearts, he must know how to think, and that with precision.

From a different point of view, the minister needs to have a sound philosophy of life. If he is to serve as the local interpreter of the Christian faith, especially as it relates to death and the hereafter, he must know what the Scriptures teach about time and eternity, and what reason there is for the hope of life everlasting with God. In the presence of the last great enemy, if the minister is not to seem like a blind leader of the blind, he must know the truth that makes men free. He must have brain power, and use it all for the glory of God.

MATERIALS

All that we have seen thus far has a bearing on the choice
and use of materials. If a man is spiritual, sympathetic, and
intelligent, he is able to employ the Scriptures and other materials—notably the words of prayer—as God-given means
for expressing the desires of stricken hearts and as the channels for bringing comfort from on high. However brief and
simple, the funeral services ought to be worthy of note for
helpfulness.

In the pastor's study the materials for an approaching service may be arranged like pieces of lumber in a merchant's
yard. But in the hands of a minister with a definite purpose
they should be joined together for the glory of God and the
solace of his children. Sometimes there is singing. Again
there is a stanza or two of a poem. But the chief reliance,
under God, is on the reading of the Scriptures and the words
of prayer.

Ofttimes the question is where to find the materials for
the coming funeral. If the minister is forehanded he has
many such things ready for use. In his files or somewhere
else he has them classified, so that any needed item is available at once. In the hands of a bungler, a filing cabinet might
do more harm than good. But if a man has piety and brains
enough to be in charge of a funeral, he will be able to use
mechanical helps without becoming their slave. At best such
things are secondary.

The time to begin making ready for unexpected funeral
calls may be during the slack season in midsummer. In fact,
such preparations ought to start while a man is in the seminary. As a help in getting under way a student may resort
to books. But the most helpful materials, as a rule, are those
that a man discovers for himself, preferably in the original
settings. Not only do they mean much to the finder's soul;
they also lend themselves readily to his needs as a pastor.

If a man has the shepherd heart he enjoys these hours of

preparation for pastoral leadership. During the early summer, when sickness is somewhat rare, he may be getting ready for funerals that are sure to come. In his files there may be a growing number of cards with texts for such occasions. There should be passages appropriate for the funeral of a child, or of an aged saint. Even if there never is an opportunity to employ some of these texts, the work of compiling them is good for a man's soul.

Much the same suggestion applies to hymns, poems, and illustrations, as well as words of prayer. Whenever a man runs across anything precious he can store it in his treasure chest. Ten years later one of these items may be a very present help in trouble. It is better to have abundance of materials that one does not need than to feel desperate because certain materials are not at hand. In short, the pastor should be able to bring out from his treasure chest things new and old.

EXPRESSION

If a minister has these other qualities he probably knows how to speak in public. The pastor who thinks clearly articulates distinctly. As an educated man, he is able to voice thoughts and feelings with clarity and interest. There may also be a touch of beauty. Hence the clergyman may choose as a motto a few words from the Prophet Isaiah: "The Lord God hath given me the tongue of the learned, that I should know how to speak" (Isa. 50: 4).

The emphasis just now is on public address as well as mastery of written words. People today are accustomed to hearing over the radio diction that is correct and pleasing. They are beginning to insist that the local clergyman use the King's English for the glory of God. Just as thoughtful folk do not listen long to the radio speaker who lacks signs of culture, so do they prefer the local minister who is a master of public speech.

Later we shall consider the purpose of the Scripture readings, as well as the content of the funeral sermon. At present the stress is on the form of all these utterances. Spiritually, the value lies mainly in the substance of what is spoken. Practically, the effectiveness is due more largely to the literary form and the vocal expression. In reading the Bible the pastor should bring out the meaning and the beauty. If he chooses to read the short opening prayer, he should call no attention to himself or to the fact that he is using words drawn from a well of living English, pure and undefiled.

At a funeral the chief test of the minister's ability to speak comes in the pastoral prayer. While never long, it should include much. There ought to be a modest pattern. The words should be clear and pleasing. The sentences should flow. With no evidence of nervousness or tension, the man who is leading others to the throne of grace should be uttering words that are full of Christian feeling. According to psychology, when a man's heart is moved his words flow in rhythmical beauty. Such a spirit of prayerfulness should communicate itself to the people. When the minister is leading, everyone should pray.

If there is a sermon, short and simple, it should be a blending of Biblical thought and pastoral feeling. If there is little time to prepare, the man who spends many waking hours in working with words should be able to use them for the glory of the God from whom they come. The fact that he prepares whenever he can ought to encourage him to speak with holy boldness whenever there is need of a message from the God of all comfort and grace.

SELF-CONTROL

Equally apparent is the need of self-control. At a deathbed or a funeral service, when everyone else may be nervous and distraught, the minister should be calm and dependable. When no one else seems to be certain what to do, the pastor should know what the Lord requires of a leader. He should have such poise and self-possession that his quiet confidence will become infectious. Erelong people should begin to say of him, lovingly: "He never loses his head. He never does or says anything not in keeping with the spirit of the hour."

Self-mastery appears in the conduct of every funeral. Into the home or funeral parlor the minister can come without calling attention to his entrance. He is able to sit still as long as he should remain seated. When at last the mortician indicates that the time has come for the minister to take charge, he moves slowly. He speaks in tones that are low but clearly audible. He controls his voice, as well as his tears. At times they may be near the surface, but they must not flow. Even if others break down and weep, this man's heart is fixed on God. Nothing on earth can disturb the poise of the ideal pastor.

Above all is self-control imperative in an emergency. No man has any more powers of leadership than he is able to use in a moment of crisis. If a surgeon is worthy to perform an operation, he knows what to do when the chief assistant faints or when the hospital catches fire. So should it be with the minister.

Once in a rural district of Oklahoma the funeral procession was fording a creek, because the recent floods had swept away the bridge. In the midst of the stream the rear axle of the hearse gave way. The man in charge commandeered a passing wagon, placed the casket in it, then led the procession to the cemetery. To the young minister officiating at one of his first funerals such resourcefulness was an object lesson of how to meet an emergency. On the way home that afternoon he prayed that he might be granted like wisdom to act in any crisis.

PRESTIGE

The last quality of which we shall think is prestige. Such a suggestion may seem strange. Should the minister of the Gospel think about his local reputation? No, not selfishly.

But neither should he forget that he represents God and the Church. When the clergyman first comes into the community he is accepted, temporarily, for the sake of the institution he serves. In a few months he will have to stand on his own feet.

Sooner or later a minister is likely to receive all the honor he deserves. Sometimes God's people do not appreciate a pastor until he has gone away, perhaps to glory. Occasionally they think more highly of a man than the facts warrant. But as a rule you can rely on the judgment of godly people when they revere a certain minister and hold aloof from another. In the time of grief they long for the guidance of a friend who has journeyed far into the King's country. They know that he can lead them close to the heart of God.

From this point of view a pastorate may be too short. On other grounds it may be wise for a man to move after four or five years. On the contrary, when people have to walk through the valley of the shadow where they bid farewell to one whom they love, they wish to receive comfort from a trusted friend. "A stranger will they not follow, but will flee from him: for they know not the voice of strangers" (John 10: 5). The minister to whom their hearts go out with longing is the one who in other days has led them safely through the dark valley.

Nonetheless, if the new pastor knows how to visit the sick and how to conduct a funeral, he can quickly win for himself a place in the hearts of the congregation. The fact that he trusts the Lord and loves people, one by one, will help to bridge every gap. After they have been with him at his first funeral, and at his first celebration of the Lord's Supper, they will know that he is a man of God.

Every minister has some sort of reputation, locally. Why should it not be worthy? Why should not his new friends thank God for sending a leader who is master of his calling? Such a man has a heart as well as a head. He knows. He cares. He is able to do the will of God on any occasion. In all the afflictions of his friends he too is afflicted. He is God's messenger of mercy.

In short, the funeral service is probably the chief test of a man's helpfulness as a pastor. For a living object lesson of such prestige, won by ceaseless toil, read *Ian Maclaren, the Life of John Watson,* by Sir William Robertson Nicoll. Over in Liverpool for years John Watson was a beloved pastor. Both as a preacher and as a writer he won distinction. To the world at large he became known as the author of *Beside the Bonnie Brier Bush* and other tales of rural Scotland. But in the eyes of those who knew him best and loved him most, John Watson was supreme as a pastor. He excelled as a comforter in the hour of grief.

There is a popular impression that a shepherd of souls is born, not made. But it was not so with John Watson. Under God, that man became a helpful pastor. Little by little he transformed himself into a messenger of mercy. Never did he find the work easy, perhaps because he was not of the outgoing temperament. Instead of starting on his afternoon rounds with joy, often he would have preferred to tarry at home and read. Some households he hesitated to enter. Certain people he did not easily like.

By faith and patience the man called of God to be a pastor rose above his personal handicaps. He learned how to employ all his gifts and graces in the service of people, especially anyone in sorrow. Throughout his home city and far beyond he became like the shadow of a great rock in a weary land. In such an achievement there is nothing magical. Rather is there a triumph of faith and perseverance.

Many a humble pastor has learned how to be helpful at all times, and especially at a funeral. His name never appears in books but it is known in heaven. His experience is heartening to other ministers. It shows that the one called of God can become worthy to wear the mantle of a Christian shepherd. Earth has no higher honor. Of any such clergyman it might be written, as of Goldsmith's "village parson": "Allured to brighter worlds, . . . [he] led the way."

Inspirational Readings

Adams, Hampton, *Pastoral Ministry*. The Cokesbury Press, 1932.
Jefferson, Charles Edward, *The Minister as Shepherd*. T. Y. Crowell Company, 1912.

III. The Dying Friend

IF A friend is dying, what should the pastor do? How quickly should he respond to the call? How should he deal with the doctor, the hospital authorities, the nurse? How should he greet the members of the family? How enter the room of the dying friend? Once there, what should he do and say? How long should he tarry? If the friend rallies, and lingers on in the flesh for weeks, how often should the minister call? At what hour of the day or night? After the last expiring breath, what should he do and say?

These questions may not loom so large now as in grandfather's day. In many circles then it was the custom to summon the minister whenever death seemed near. On his arrival he felt that he knew what to do and say. Sometimes his course of treatment was heroic. Occasionally it ran counter to present-day ideas of Christian kindness. That may be one reason why the pastor today does not often minister at a deathbed.

However, such experiences do come. As a minister gets older, if people discover that he has a message from the heart of God, they wish him to be present when death is drawing near to one whom they love. Whether these calls be many or few, in each case there is an appeal to the pastor's heart. The first time or two he may have a feeling akin to terror. But if he keeps his emotions under control, and simply tries to be helpful, spiritually, as a Christian friend, he will gain confidence in the Lord's power to use him as a messenger of comfort. This is no small part of what it means to be a physician of souls.

THE BASIC CREED

What a minister does at the deathbed depends much on what he believes. In the case of a godly man or woman, the pastor may stress the thought of heaven as home. If the dying friend is not a Christian, there may be more about Christ and the Cross. The underlying assumption at present is that God can save any sinner, even if death is drawing near. While such experiences are rare, the writer has witnessed a few conversions which seemed as real as that of the dying thief (Luke 23: 39-43).

In the old-time hymn "There Is a Fountain Filled with Blood," many of us shrink from the figure in the opening stanza. But in the song as a whole we find the truth of God's redeeming grace, as revealed in the Cross:

> "The dying thief rejoiced to see
> That fountain in his day;
> And there may I, as vile as he,
> Wash all my sins away."

A case will throw light on the matter of deathbed repentance. One night a young minister responded to the call of a dying stranger, an aged Scotsman. What occurred in the humble upper room was substantially as follows: The dying man whispered: "Dominie, I want to get in." The pastor thought the stranger referred to the Brotherhood of St. Andrew. "No, I want to go hame." Again the minister did not understand. He supposed that the other man's mind was wandering and that he wished to cross the ocean. But at length the stranger made it clear that he wanted to find the way back to his mother's God.

The clergyman told the dying man about the beauty of our Saviour's life and the simplicity of his teachings. But the hearer protested, feebly: "No, dominie, I'm dying, and I need the Saviour!" At last the minister forgot about his up-to-date ethical culture and started to tell the old, old story of the Cross. He spoke about the love of God for the weakest and worst of men, about the death of Christ, about the pardon of sins, and the cleansing from their guilty stains.

"That's it! That's what I need!" said the stranger. "But does it mean a mon like me?" Then the minister quoted in part the most blessed of all our evangelistic hymns:

> "Just as I am, without one plea,
> But that thy blood was shed for me."

After a while the aged Scotsman breathed his last. On the way home that night the minister felt as though he were treading on air. He was sure that he had witnessed the birth of a soul. At the same time the clergyman had found his own way back to the Cross.

In a sense this type of conversion is sudden. But on second thought it seems to be only the turning of the wandering child back to the God of mother and father. Whatever the explanation in terms of psychology, the Christian minister should have a message for a wicked man who is close to death. If the Christ of the Cross could save the penitent thief, is there any limit now to the grace of God?

> "Dear dying Lamb, thy precious blood
> Shall never lose its power
> Till all the ransomed Church of God
> Be saved, to sin no more."

THE SUMMONS

Let us turn to details, some of which are by no means spectacular. In the work of the pastorate there is far more drudgery than drama. When there is a call to a deathbed, it may not be convenient to drop everything else and respond at once, but that is the path of duty. The minister should be as alert and prompt as the family physician.

Like the weary doctor, the clergyman occasionally responds to a false alarm. Instead of a dying friend there may be only a case of hysterics. Almost every pastor of middle age has had the experience of being awakened out of sleep and hastening to a home to prepare for death a person who proved not to be critically ill. Nevertheless, the rule is to go at once, and that graciously. The minister should thank God that the people wish him to be with them in trouble, whether it be real or imaginary.

The call is likely to come from a hospital. There the minister should co-operate with those in charge. He should previously have established friendly relations with the superintendent and the office force. If at other times he has deferred to their way of doing things, they will help him when he comes to minister at a deathbed. With few exceptions these friends are religiously minded. They soon learn to trust the minister who knows how to deal with sickness and death.

In an emergency case the minister has the right of way. Ordinarily he secures permission from the doctor before calling on one of his patients who is critically ill. But the hospital authorities know when to waive formalities. As soon as the minister arrives at the office someone escorts him to the sick chamber. On the way he learns as much as he can about the case. Especially does he wish to know if the friend seems to be conscious and if the end appears to be imminent.

Within the room the pastor moves and acts quietly. He knows that a sick person is sensitive to new noises and that anything sudden may cause a shock. On the other hand, the minister should be natural. He ought never to walk on tiptoe or speak in a sepulchral tone. He should not look funereal or afraid. Without glancing to the right or the left, he should go to the bedside. There he may kneel, or else be seated, if there is a waiting chair. He should not bend over the patient. If the friend holds out his hand, the minister takes it, but scarcely otherwise.

If the sick person is conscious, and is not breathing his last, there may be a few moments of silence. The pastor is waiting for a whisper. When there is no word, he may ask, gently and slowly, if there is anything for which he should pray. In any case there is a brief word from the Scriptures, such as Matt. 11: 28-30, and a short prayer. Both the passage from the Bible and the prayer should be spoken, not read. If there is no immediate crisis, it may be expedient to repeat the Apostles' Creed. But as a rule that would involve too much of a strain. It is usually better to close with The Lord's Prayer, uttered deliberately, and then pronounce the benediction.

If every moment seems likely to be the last, take less time. Get at once to the heart of the Gospel. Over in England when Bishop J. Taylor Smith was chaplain general he had a final test for each ministerial applicant: "I am dying. In a few words tell me what I must do to be saved." What appeal could be more vital, and more difficult? Here is one way of speaking. It assumes that the dying man is conscious, somewhat familiar with Christian truth, and aware of his approaching end:

"My brother, God is your Father; he loves you. Christ is your Friend; he died for you. Only his Cross can save us sinners. 'If we confess our sins, he is faithful and just to forgive us our sins' (I John 1: 9). Do you want me to pray for you?" If so, there are a few simple petitions, based on God's promises of forgiveness. There is time for only one truth, the pardoning love of God, made known in the Cross. There is need of only one response, with which the prayer may close. From his heart the dying man should say with the minister a portion of the old hymn, especially one stanza:

> " 'Just as I am! Thou wilt receive,
>   Wilt welcome, pardon, cleanse, relieve;
>   Because thy promise I believe,
>   O Lamb of God, I come!' "

However short the time, be sure to speak slowly. If the words must be few, still they ought to be clear. In case the dying man seems not to be conscious, speak as though he were able to follow every word. Especially in the case of a paralytic stroke, although there may be no evidence that the patient is aware of what is going on about him, the pastor may find that his few words have touched the heart and that there is meaning in the pressure of the hand.

As a rule, however, such moments are more helpful to the members of the family circle than to the one who is dying. If only for their sakes, the pastor should be careful about what verse of Scripture he quotes and what other forms of worship he employs. Especially if they are from Scotland, he may repeat part of a psalm, notably the Twenty-third. Many a golden passage he ought to know by heart, word for word. If the people attach value to symbolism, he may put his hand on the forehead while pronouncing the benediction. Whatever the procedure, it should center round the dying friend.

In a home there is usually less routine than in a hospital. If a nurse is in charge, a few words with her outside the door will help to guide the clergyman. However, there should be no whispering where the patient will hear, and feel that he is the subject of conversation. Within the room the minister speaks to no one save the dying man. It is easier to do that aright if few others are present. Indeed, a deathbed confession should be made in private. Everyone should leave the dying one alone with the pastor and his God. In a rural community, however, a suggestion that the members of the family retire might be counted an affront.

An illustrative case will show what not to do at a deathbed. The writer's first experience was with a family who belonged to a neighboring congregation. Their minister, who was out of town for the day, had until recent years been a blacksmith. While he knew nothing about school and little about books, he had accumulated a wealth of practical wisdom. In circumstances less awesome the contrast between him and the young graduate of university and seminary would have been ludicrous.

When the young man arrived at the house he was stiff with fright. He found the large front room downstairs filled with curious neighbors. On the bed in the far corner lay the aged father. His every gasp seemed likely to be his last. The death rattle had already begun to sound. On the table near the door, fifteen feet from the bed, was a lighted oil lamp. Taking his station there, the young minister began to read the Ninetieth Psalm, as at a funeral service.

Before he had gone far with his formalism, there was a stir near the door. The people opened up the way for the older minister to come through. Going at once to the bed, he knelt there and commenced to pray. In a few words, slow and clear, but not loud, he committed the unconscious man to the keeping of the Father God. Then this older minister pronounced the benediction. Someone brought him a chair. Without looking to the right or left, there he sat, watching the face of the dying man. Erelong came the end. Rising to his feet, the pastor spoke quietly to his assembled neighbors, suggesting that they retire so that he could be alone with the members of the family.

Meanwhile, fortunately, everyone had forgotten about the young clergyman. As soon as the pastor arrived, the young brother had taken refuge in silence. During the next minutes he learned from an untutored lay preacher certain lessons that someone might have taught back in the seminary. To this day the "educated" minister wonders why he and his classmates were ordained to the ministry without having served some sort of apprenticeship. On the other hand, he knows that in many a situation the pastor must rely upon God and thus meet the unexpected without fear.

THE LINGERING ILLNESS

The case reported above was exceptional. In fact, our books may give the impression that the pastoral ministry is largely a succession of crises, whereas it is chiefly a matter of routine. For instance, an elderly woman has a way of hanging on to life long after the end seems to be at hand. If the patient lingers at death's door for weeks, how often should the pastor call? Whenever he is in doubt, probably he should go. In no other way can he invest time and energy more profitably than in unremitting devotion to one who is dying by degrees.

Even in a large parish the writer made it his rule to call on a dying member once a day. Whenever the minister could do so, he planned to go each time at the same hour; for example, in the hospital, probably at five thirty in the afternoon; in the home, perhaps at nine thirty at night. In a hospital, the latter time would not be convenient for the nurses.

Whatever the hour, as a rule the call should be short. In days to come the family will remember the number of visits, not their length, unless the minister stays too long. If there is a special reason for his lingering, he lets the claims of the dying one have precedence. Ordinarily, it is best for the patient that the pastor come in quietly and steal out soon. At the bedside he may kneel, and there wait, in silence. This brief time should be precious. If there is anything on the heart of the dying one, what he whispers will guide the minister as he prays.

At each call, if the way be clear, there should be a verse of Scripture, spoken from the heart, and not read from a book, unless it is the patient's Bible. Some one verse may be especially fitting with the same person day after day. If so, there may also be a new word from God each time. The verse should be short, simple, and easy for the friend to recall. If at times he cannot sleep, the few words from the Book should keep singing in his soul. They are more likely to do so if they form the basis of the prayer. It too should be brief, and the rate of speech deliberate. When a patient is weak in body he is scarcely able to think fast or long. Especially in repeating The Lord's Prayer, the minister should speak so deliberately that the patient can join, at least in his heart.

On successive days there should be different forms of benediction. Fortunately, the Bible has various words of blessing.

The following case is somewhat typical. Dr. X., fifty years of age, was dying at his home with inoperable cancer. He knew that he had not long to live. All through the day he kept looking forward to nine thirty, when he knew that the minister would call. If there was a church meeting, the hour might be a little later. In that case the minister would explain the matter the night before. After the call, if the patient could not sleep, he would keep saying to himself whatever he remembered most clearly: a verse of Scripture, a sentence from the prayer, or a stanza of a hymn. In selecting these materials the pastor aimed to leave something easy to recall.

From such visits to an upper room the minister often receives far more than he gives. He learns afresh the meaning of human pain, and Christian courage, as well as divine grace. In his autobiography George A. Gordon, of Boston, tells of lessons that he learned at a bedside in Maine during his first pastorate. A gentlewoman of early middle age was wasting away with tuberculosis. Three times a week he talked with her about life and death, the Judgment Day, and the life everlasting. One night when the thermometer was thirty degrees below zero he was summoned to her deathbed. As long as he lived he thanked God for those revelations in the upper room, where the dying friend brought her young pastor near to the heart of God.

Such experiences cause a man to know his Bible and his hymnbook as never before. He has a new incentive for intercessory prayer. As his heart becomes filled with the Spirit of God there is new power and radiance in the pastor's everyday life. In the pulpit also there is a new note of triumph. The older people thank God and say one to another: "What has come over our minister? He preaches and prays better than ever before." The answer is that he has found at the bedside of a dying friend the inner meaning and the glory of the Christian religion.

In an occasional experience there is need of rare wisdom and tact. For instance, there is the case of Mrs. G. At the hospital, after an operation for cancer, this woman of middle age was dying. Despite the fact that she was a devoted Christian, her pastor insisted on conducting daily inquisitions into the state of her soul. One afternoon he stayed so long that the nurse asked him to leave. The patient was wrought up nervously. That night she could not sleep. Her physician, not a churchman, was furious. He forbade the pastor to return. The next morning the husband requested another minister to call on the dying woman.

This clergyman, being new in the town, consulted with his senior elder, who advised him to go and not to confer with the pastor. (The latter part of the advice seems to have been an error in judgment.) The physician, when approached by the husband, reluctantly gave his consent for a single call, not to exceed three minutes. After it was over he sent word to the new minister, "You can see any of my patients whenever you desire." Through this doctor, as well as the nurses, the report went round. Henceforth that minister had free access to almost any sickroom he wished to visit.

It is seldom wise or necessary to call on a person who belongs to another parish. In the case before us the lay adviser knew all the parties concerned. He felt that the new minister should give the needs of the dying woman precedence over ministerial etiquette. A few days later he advised that the minister who had brought her comfort should accept the invitation to conduct the funeral services. Meanwhile the family as a whole had severed all connection with the church whose pastor had tried to dangle their dear mother over the bottomless pit. Doubtless he was a good man, but he was not a wise pastor.

THE DEATHBED CONFESSION

The following case is still more delicate. The facts are disguised, because the author agrees with Dr. R. C. Cabot, in

The Art of Ministering to the Sick: "Don't preach about the sick, or repeat stories about them. Like the doctor, the minister hears confidences and becomes conversant with many secrets. Some of them would make admirable illustrations. Most of them feed people's idle curiosity about their neighbors. People soon find out who keeps confidences and who does not. We believe that a minister's experiences with the sick should enrich his sermons, as all experience does, but this need involve no violations of confidence, and no anonymous stories. They are sure to be recognized."

John Doe, sixty years of age, was a victim of pernicious anemia. Despite repeated transfusions of blood, he was dying. Erelong he was likely to lapse into unconsciousness. This he learned one afternoon from the physician, whose business it is to inform the patient about the probable course of his disease. That evening when the minister called, the dying man asked his wife and the nurse to leave the room. A little later, with tears in his eyes, he whispered, "Will God pardon me for my sins of long ago?" Then he explained as much as the pastor needed to know.

The minister was shocked. He had been preaching much about the forgiveness of sins, but seldom with reference to a member of the church, a man of repute in the community. To hear this friend confessing his sins made the pastor shudder. Fortunately, he had the grace to keep silent until he knew what he should say. Without referring to the facts in the case, and without showing how he had felt at first, he quoted slowly a few texts, which his friend had often heard in the sanctuary:

"Come now, and let us reason together, saith the Lord: though your sins be as scarlet, they shall be as white as snow" (Isa. 1: 18). "If we confess our sins, he is faithful and just to forgive us our sins, and to cleanse us from all unrighteousness. . . . The blood of Jesus Christ his Son cleanseth us from all sin" (I John 1: 9, 7). Then the minister spoke to his friend by his Christian name: "John, are you sincerely sorry for the sins that you have confessed, and all others that you have committed? Trusting solely in the merits of Christ and his Cross, do you now receive God's pardon and his cleansing grace?"

To each question the dying man whispered, eagerly, "Yes!" The minister, knowing him to be a man of his word, formally assured him that his sins had been forgiven. In fact, they had probably been pardoned years before. But they had left on the conscience such a stain that he found it difficult to be sure of God's redeeming mercy. If there had been time and strength it would have been fitting for him to receive the Sacrament. At any rate, through the official representative of God and the Church that penitent received assurance of pardon and peace.

No two cases are alike. If that man's disease had been farther advanced, it would not have been wise to keep him listening so long. The conversation required perhaps six or eight minutes. On the other hand, the easing of his conscience had a tonic effect. As for administering the Sacrament, the writer would do that only when the members of the family make the request. Even then he would consult with the physician. Ordinarily the individual Communion set is for use with the shut-in friends who are not critically ill. As a rule it is not necessary to administer the Sacrament at a deathbed.

THE SYMPATHETIC PASTOR

There are scarcely any rules about ministering to the dying. When the clergyman enters a home where death is near he almost never knows what he will find. But the Lord knows and he will guide his servant who trusts and obeys. At the deathbed the loving heart knows what to do and say. In fact, the pastor may do almost nothing. He may keep quiet. When he has nothing to say, he says it. Silence may be golden.

For years a minister felt that he had failed at a certain

deathbed. Being at the time without pastoral experience, he had not known what to do or say. He had simply sat by the bedside and waited with the dying friend and his wife. In later years he learned from the widow that she had always cherished the recollection of the way he had led her husband down through the valley of the deepening shadows. Especially did she appreciate the minister's tactfulness in keeping silent. Somehow he had made it clear that he cared, and that God cared vastly more.

In a sense the main service that the minister renders is in being with his people when they need him most. In the room with the one who is dying, the pastor gives heed only to him. If the last moment is approaching, the minister stays. Usually he tarries at the bedside. But it may be more convenient for the nurse to have him wait in an adjoining room. If he has pressing duties elsewhere he informs the nurse how she can reach him by telephone, and then he steals away.

Why all this solicitude? One reason is that the minister represents Christ and the Church. Another is that in the presence of death some people expect unusual attention from their pastor. If he is sympathetic and untiring they will love him as long as he lives. If he seems disinterested and neglectful he will lose their esteem. However, they should remember that he has countless obligations and that his time is precious. If people love their pastor they are almost always reasonable in their demands on his time and strength.

Concern about the deathbed has much to do with the minister's preparations for the funeral service. In his mind and heart, at least unconsciously, he begins to make ready before the hour of his friend's demise. In each of the cases reported above there was no difficulty in deciding what to do and say at the services of farewell. Rather was there a feeling of thankfulness because everything was right between the friend and God. There was also a sense of relief because the hours of pain and weakness were at an end. Hence the memorial services could be radiant with the joy and the hope that God alone can give and the world can never take away.

In short, the minister should be much concerned about the person who is dying, and about those whom he loves. If the pastor feels at home in the upper room where a child of the King is breathing his last, the same spirit of trust in God will carry over into the funeral service. If any minister, therefore, longs to excel in this vital part of his work, let him resolve to become a good shepherd.

At the end of the chapter are a few pages that show how clergymen of various beliefs quote a word from the Book and pray in the presence of approaching death, or else after it has come. The last few examples have to do with a child's going home to God. Through study of these texts and prayers, and countless others like them, any pastor can learn much about the theory of ministering at the bedside of a dying friend. But when the call actually comes, leave at home the funeral source book. At the deathbed speak to God out of a heart that overflows.

"Depart out of this world, O Christian soul, trusting in the name of God the Father Almighty, who created thee;
In the name of Jesus Christ, who redeemed thee;
In the name of the Holy Ghost, who sanctifieth thee.
May thy rest this day (or night) be in peace, and thy dwelling-place ever be in the Paradise of God.   Amen."

FOR USE IN THE SICKROOM

Be still, and know that I am God. Ps. 46:10.

Fear not: for I am with thee. Isa. 43:5.

Why are ye so fearful? how is it that ye have no faith? Mark 4:40.

There is no fear in love; but perfect love casteth out fear. I John 4:18.

What time I am afraid, I will trust in thee. Ps. 56:3.

I will trust, and not be afraid. Isa. 12:2.

I will fear no evil: for thou art with me. Ps. 23:4.

The Lord is my shepherd; I shall not want. Ps. 23:1.

God be merciful to me a sinner. Luke 18:13.

Though your sins be as scarlet, they shall be as white as snow. Isa. 1:18.

The blood of Jesus Christ his Son cleanseth us from all sin. I John 1:7.

Him that cometh to me I will in no wise cast out. John 6:37.

Believe on the Lord Jesus Christ, and thou shalt be saved. Acts 16:31.

Lord, I believe; help thou mine unbelief. Mark 9:24.

In quietness and in confidence shall be your strength. Isa. 30:15.

As one whom his mother comforteth, so will I comfort you. Isa. 66:13.

Rejoice in the Lord alway: and again I say, Rejoice. Phil. 4:4.

Blessed are the pure in heart: for they shall see God. Matt. 5:8.

All things, whatsoever ye shall ask in prayer, believing, ye shall receive. Matt. 21:22.

Come unto me, all ye that labour and are heavy laden, and I will give you rest. Matt. 11:28.

Thou wilt keep him in perfect peace, whose mind is stayed on thee: because he trusteth in thee. Isa. 26:3.

I sought the Lord, and he heard me, and delivered me from all my fears. Ps. 34:4.

Also Ps. 4:8; 23:6; Isa. 43:2; John 14:27; Rom. 8:28; 8:32; Phil. 4:6, 7; I John 1:9; Rev. 3:20; 21:4.

☙ ☙ ☙ ☙

Most merciful Father, look graciously upon this Thy servant in *his* sore distress. Through the precious blood of Christ cleanse *him* from all sin; visit *him* with Thy salvation, and sustain *him* by Thy tender love. Grant *him* the assurance of the Saviour's presence, so that by laying hold of the hand which was pierced *he* may be led into Thine everlasting light. O Lord, in Thy mercy receive *him*. Into Thy hands we commend *his* spirit. Keep *him* safe forevermore, through the merits of Christ our Redeemer. Amen.

⚜ ⚜ ⚜ ⚜

O Lord our God, Thou alone hast the issues of life and death. Look in mercy upon this our *brother* who lies upon a bed of weakness and pain. Grant *him* the grace to repent for all *his* sins, and to rest upon Jesus Christ as Saviour and Lord.

When Thou hast finished Thy plan for *him* here on earth, give *him* an abundant entrance into Thy heavenly home, that *he* may ever serve Thee in fullness of joy, through Jesus Christ, our Lord. Amen.

⚜ ⚜ ⚜ ⚜

Merciful Father, we commend unto Thee the soul of Thy servant, that *he* may die unto this world and live unto Thee. Whatsoever sins *he* has committed we implore Thee to pardon. Whatsoever stains *he* has acquired we beseech Thee to wash away, through the cleansing power of Thy Holy Spirit. Amen.

⚜ ⚜ ⚜ ⚜

Holy Father, Thou dost not desire the death of any sinner. Here is one of Thy servants who needs Thy forgiving love. Look upon *him* in mercy. Set *him* free from sin. Prepare *him* for the life everlasting with Thee in Thy heavenly home, through Christ our Saviour. Amen.

⚜ ⚜ ⚜ ⚜

O Lord our God, Thou dost hold all souls in life and in death. Thou hast spared this our friend through long and gracious years. Receive our thanks for all Thy gifts on *him* bestowed. Grant *him* an entrance into the house not made with hands. There *he* shall serve Thee with powers equal to *his* tasks, through Jesus Christ *his* King. Amen.

✠ ✠ ✠ ✠

Grant, O Lord, faith and courage to these Thy servants who have said farewell to their beloved *brother*. Give them strength and courage for the days to come. Forbid that they should sorrow as those who have no hope. Enable them to live in the assurance of a family reunion in the Father's home, through the merits of Jesus Christ. Amen.

✠ ✠ ✠ ✠

O Lord Jesus, who didst weep at the tomb of Lazarus, Thou dost love Thy friends in this family circle. Assure them of Thy presence and comfort them in their grief. Show them that all things are working together for their good and for Thy glory. Guide them by Thy Spirit while they live and afterward receive them into glory. There they shall sing praises unto Thee, the Redeemer, with the heavenly Father and the Holy Spirit. Amen.

✠ ✠ ✠ ✠

Our heavenly Father, we beseech Thee to solace Thy children in their sorrow. As Thou didst send Thy Holy Spirit to be the Comforter of Thy people, strengthen them by His gracious indwelling, that they may be enabled to contemplate the joy of that better home where Thou art seen and worshiped in the light of all whom Thou keepest in Thine everlasting love, through Jesus Christ our Lord. Amen.

[From the Ritual of the Methodist Church, 1940.]

✠ ✠ ✠ ✠

O our God, we beseech Thee, by that love which brought
Thy Son from heaven, have compassion on the soul of this Thy
servant: forgive *him* all *his* sins and failings, and supply all
his defects. Let *him* now experience the multitude of Thy
tender mercies, and be sensible how good a God Thou art.
Grant *him*, we implore Thee, true patience and perfect resignation in *his* pains and anguish. Confirm *his* faith, strengthen
his hope, and perfect *his* charity that, departing hence, *his* soul
may be received into Thy mercy, through Jesus Christ our
Lord. Amen.

[From the Office of the Roman Catholic Church.]

☙ ☙ ☙ ☙

O blessed Redeemer, by that distress which Thou didst suffer
on the Cross, when Thou didst cry out to Thine Eternal Father,
show mercy to this Thy servant in *his* extremity; hear the desires
and petitions of *his* heart; and since *he* cannot speak for *himself*, intercede Thou for *him*, we implore Thee, for Thou art
the Eternal Word, and the Father will refuse Thee nothing.

Let those hands, which once were nailed to the Cross, now
plead for *him*, and, obtaining *his* pardon, conduct *him* into
Thine everlasting rest. Amen.

[From the Office of the Roman Catholic Church.]

☙ ☙ ☙ ☙

Into Thy merciful hands, O heavenly Father, we commend
the soul of Thy servant now departing from the body. Acknowledge, we humbly implore Thee, a sheep of Thine own fold, a
lamb of Thine own flock, a sinner of Thine own redeeming.
Receive *him* into the arms of Thy mercy, into the blessed realm
of everlasting peace, into the glorious estate of Thy chosen
saints in heaven.

O most merciful Saviour, that soul cannot perish which is
committed to Thy charge; receive, we beseech Thee, this spirit
in peace. Amen.

[From the Office of the Roman Catholic Church.]

☙ ☙ ☙ ☙

O God, whose most dear Son did take little children into His arms and bless them; Give us grace, we beseech Thee, to entrust the soul of this child to Thy never-failing care and love, and bring us all to Thy heavenly Kingdom; through the same Thy Son, Jesus Christ our Lord. Amen.

[From *The Book of Common Prayer*, According to the Use of the Protestant Episcopal Church.]

✿ ✿ ✿ ✿

O Lord Jesus Christ, the only-begotten Son of God, who for our sakes didst become a babe in Bethlehem, we commit unto Thy loving care this child whom Thou art calling unto Thyself. Send Thy holy angel to bear *him* gently to those heavenly habitations where the souls of those who sleep in Thee have perpetual peace and joy, and fold *him* in the everlasting arms of Thine unfailing love, who livest and reignest with the Father and the Holy Ghost, one God, world without end. Amen.

[From *The Book of Common Prayer*, According to the Use of the Church of England.]

✿ ✿ ✿ ✿

O Almighty God, and merciful Father, to whom alone belong the issues of life and death, look down from heaven, we humbly beseech Thee, with the eyes of mercy upon this child, now lying upon the bed of sickness. Visit *him*, O Lord, with Thy salvation; deliver *him* in Thine appointed time from *his* bodily pain, and save *his* soul for Thy mercy's sake. If it be not Thy good pleasure to prolong *his* days on earth, receive *him* into those heavenly habitations where the souls of those who sleep in the Lord Jesus enjoy perpetual rest and felicity. Grant this, O Lord, for Thy mercy's sake, through Thy Son our Lord Jesus Christ, who liveth and reigneth with Thee and the Holy Ghost, ever one God, world without end. Amen.

[From *The Book of Common Prayer* . . . as Amended by the Presbyterian Divines . . . 1661.]

✿ ✿ ✿ ✿

Informative Readings

Balmforth, Henry, and Others, *Introduction to Pastoral Theology*.
  The Macmillan Company, 1937. Part II, Chapter V.
Bonnell, John Sutherland, *Pastoral Psychiatry*. Harper & Brothers,
  1938. (In the closing chapter note the manner of using a brief
  text.)
Cabot, Richard Clarke, and Dicks, R. L., *The Art of Ministering to
  the Sick*. The Macmillan Company, 1936.

IV. The Funeral Arrangements

WHEN death comes to a home the pastor may be present. If so, he tarries for a little while to give comfort. As for the practical arrangements, he may suggest that he return at an hour convenient to the family. Meanwhile they should consult with the mortician and otherwise determine what they wish to do. Both pastor and mortician will help them to carry out their plans.

As a rule the minister is not present when a death occurs. If the people are considerate they notify him almost immediately. But they have many other things on their minds. The word may reach him through some of the neighbors. In some communities, unfortunately, the notice comes only through the mortician. Practically all the plans are complete before the pastor is informed about what is expected of him as the representative of the Church.

After a minister has been in a parish for a year or two he should experience little difficulty in learning of any death among his people. If he takes care of the sick folk he will know when a certain member of the flock is about to die. If the end comes without warning there should be in the district some officer or member who will keep the pastor informed. If the work is properly organized for keeping him informed about newcomers and sick folk, the same channels will bring to the manse tidings about any death. At least that is the ideal.

Such a call takes precedence over everything else. However, the minister must be careful not to rush into any home where the people belong to another congregation. Even if they are his personal friends, courtesy suggests that he tarry at home until they have completed the arrangements with their pastor. Then one can express the sympathy of a Christian neighbor. While a call would be in order, a note of sympathy is less likely to be misinterpreted by watchful folk across the street. To these ethical matters we shall refer later. At present we are thinking about a normal situation, where there is no question about ministerial courtesy.

At the first call after a death there may not be much for the minister to do. If the neighbors report at once, he may arrive before the mortician. The ensuing call is pastoral. As a rule it should be short. The minister volunteers no advice about the approaching services. He expresses his sympathy. If he is to be in charge of the funeral he may suggest that he return at a later hour. Meantime the family can determine what they wish to do. They should understand that the mortician is in charge of everything except the religious exercises.

In an exceptional case there is much for the pastor to do at the first call. If the people seem helpless they probably need advice about things practical. The best person to counsel with them may be some wise deacon or friendly woman, whom the minister can ask to represent him and the church. Only in a case of extreme necessity should he advise the securing of any particular mortician. Neither should he have much to do with other practical details that do not concern him as the leader of worship.

Let the clergyman be a clergyman. Otherwise he may come to be known as the congregational errand boy, who is glad to render jitney services without charge. If his predecessor has been unduly accommodating it may not be easy for the new minister to confine himself within his own province. But it is always possible for a pastor to enlist others for what he has not time and strength to do himself. Then if things go wrong he personally is not to blame. If they go well, as they usually do, he should give others the credit, and be careful to express his thanks.

THE PRIVATE INTERVIEW

At a time convenient to the friends the minister calls again in the home. He confers, preferably, with one or two members of the family circle. The plans should be the result of previous consultation in the family group as a whole. But at the interview with the pastor it is easier for him to talk things over with one or two persons, perhaps the widow and the oldest son. Otherwise it might be as difficult to make specific arrangements as at a wedding rehearsal, where there are many women with many minds. Any single procedure may be proper, but in the end there can be only one way to carry out each part of the service.

Prior to the interview the mortician will have come and gone. Before he decides about the place and the time of the funeral service he should have conferred with the minister by telephone. At least that is the custom when the two are on friendly terms, as they ought to be. In matters relating to funerals the minister defers to the mortician as an expert in his art. As for morticians of the baser sort, the writer has had little experience. Those of the profession whom he has known best have been Christian gentlemen. Each of them has been glad to co-operate with any minister who is worthy of his calling.

In his own sphere the pastor should be as skillful and careful as the mortician. At the end of the interview now in mind, the minister should be in possession of certain facts. Obviously there are cases where some of the items below would be superfluous. Even so, it is wise to have a check list, and to keep it in mind,—if not on a card in hand,—during the interview. If it seems strange for the minister to be writing down such items, he can explain that he wishes to preserve accurate records.

Where will the services be held?
On what date? At what hour? (Repeat this to verify.)

Will the exercises be public or private?
Is any other minister to share in the services?
If so, which parts should he take?
Who is to invite the other minister?
Is any fraternal order to be present? to take part?
Is there to be music? If so, of what kind?
Who is to secure the musicians?
Is there a favorite hymn to be sung or read?
Is there a favorite text or passage of Scripture?
Is there to be a formal obituary?
If so, who will prepare it?
If the minister prepares it, what are the facts?
Where will the interment take place? Is it to be public or
    private?
Should the deacons arrange for extra automobiles?
Is there anything else that the church can do?
Is there any suggestion about the services?
Do the friends have the minister's telephone number?
"Is there any special request now before we pray?"

In some cases it is not easy to secure the needed information. Even at the minister's second call the people may be
distraught. What do they know or care about this or that
detail? They wish a service that will bring them heart's ease.
Perhaps they also desire to impress the neighbors. Nevertheless, if the pastor proceeds without reference to household
desires he may discover too late that he has run counter to
the traditions. Within the limits of truth and good taste
every family has the right to a service that will lead to abiding satisfaction.

THE OTHER MINISTER

The most delicate question may concern the desire to have
another minister take part. In fact, the people may wish him
to do everything. On the other hand, the pastor feels that he
should be in charge, and that, since the service must be short,
there should be only one leader. Such an attitude may be far
from selfish. The presence of two or three clergymen tends

to make a funeral service seem more human than divine. There may be more of ministerial display than heavenly comfort.

Nonetheless, the desires of the family should prevail. Since they may hesitate to offer such a suggestion, the pastor should open the way. If they inform him, hesitantly, that they wish the former minister to take practically all the service, the pastor should acquiesce, graciously. He should volunteer to communicate with the brother concerned. If the members of the family prefer to extend the invitation, they should do so in the name of the pastor. Except in an extreme case they are willing that he arrange for the services, and that he take the brief opening part himself. That is all he has a right to expect.

Occasionally the person who represents the family ignores the pastor. If so, there may be no opportunity for him to have an interview. The predecessor or some other clergyman may assume charge. In these circumstances there is little for the present minister to do, except to hold his tongue and pray for grace. At the home of sorrow he should call to express his sympathy. Perhaps he should attend the public services, and even go to the cemetery. However, if he has an engagement calling him out of town that afternoon, no one can find fault.

The writer has had no such experiences. He always found the former pastor, and other clerical brethren, eager to follow the Golden Rule. Sometimes it leads the former minister to decline the invitation. When he feels free to accept, he defers to the present pastor, even if he is young and inexperienced. In what is said during the service neither of them should refer to the other. With one accord they should strive to comfort the friends in their sorrow.

Such is the ideal. Sometimes the facts are the reverse. After a minister leaves a parish he can make his successor's pastorate a series of perplexities. Without intending to do so, the older clergyman can prevent his friends from falling in love with the younger brother, partly because his ways are different. If the two ministers are to share in a funeral service, the visiting brother may embody in his opening prayer what the young minister plans to do later in the half hour. Partly for this reason, the man in charge usually takes the opening parts himself.

In all these matters, where there may be a clash of ministerial personalities, the interests of the sorrowing friends should be paramount. If the new minister is patient and kind, even when a family here or there ignores him, gradually he should win all the favor that he deserves. Meanwhile he should resolve that by God's grace he will never seek to outshine or outwit—not to say outkick—any other clergyman. At the root of such difficulties between two ministers there is likely to be jealousy, as well as pride. Neither spirit has any place in the heart of God's servant, above all when he stands in the presence of death.

THE FINAL ARRANGEMENTS

Elsewhere we shall consider what to do when a fraternal order is to take part in the funeral services. Under normal conditions the interview we have in mind need last only fifteen or twenty minutes. When the minister has all the facts in hand he may suggest that the household assemble for a word of prayer. Or he may think it better to have brief devotions with the person who has helped to make the plans. In either case, unless the family traditions call for some other posture, it is good to pray while standing. Then one can steal away at once, and without a word, though there ought to be a firm clasping of each right hand.

The idea is to depart from the home as the pastor, not as a man of affairs. In the same spirit of prayer the minister goes to his study at the church, or else to his home. Then he sets in motion whatever is necessary to carry out the plans for the use of the church, the securing of singers, and the arranging for extra automobiles. If there is an office secretary, she can relieve the pastor of such details. If not, perhaps his wife can do the telephoning. In any case, the minister needs to check up on the final plans. Before the hour for the funeral everything should be in readiness.

Meanwhile the pastor alone can prepare for what is far more vital than all those details. He is to be in charge of the religious exercises. If he is to lead aright, he should plan to be alone with his God. There let us leave the man with the shepherd heart. The Lord bless him and use him as a means of grace to the friends who on the morrow will look to him for light in all their darkness.

"Comfort ye, comfort ye my people, saith your God. Speak to the heart of Jerusalem" (Isa. 40: 1, 2 from the Hebrew).

Practical Readings

Hathaway, Helen, *Manners*. E. P. Dutton & Co., seventh edition, 1934. Pages 138-150.

Odgers, J. Hastie, and Schutz, E. G., *The Technique of Public Worship*. Methodist Book Concern, 1928. Chapter X.

V. The Public Services

THE funeral services should be Christian throughout. What our religion calls for in any one case depends on many factors. Most of them appear in this book; some do not. The man called of God to lead must be resourceful. He should adapt means to ends. Before we turn to practical methods, let us think about the purpose. What are the reasons for holding a funeral service?

The chief aim is to glorify God. The best way to do that in the presence of death is to administer comfort. As the root idea of the word makes clear, to comfort means to strengthen in the Lord. Both in making the arrangements and in carrying them out, the pastor strives to bring the people into right relations with God, so that they will accept his plan for their altered lives.

There is need also of setting before them certain truths and ideals that will help in days to come. Hard as they may find it to accept sorrow now, they will need still more of God's sustaining power in days to come. As long as they live they should remember with thanksgiving the services that bring them close to God and persuade them one by one to lay hold on the hand that was pierced.

At times there may be an opportunity for evangelism. Certain members of the family circle may not yet be consciously and gladly children of God. Others among the throng of relatives and neighbors may be still farther from the Lord and his Church. Thus the need for the Evangel is real. But as a rule the appeal should be indirect. Within the brief limits of time allotted for the service it would be unwise to attempt much more than to comfort those that mourn and prepare them for unknown morrows.

As for the funeral services, their character will depend in part on where they are held. This matter deserves more attention than it usually receives.

THE APPOINTED PLACE

As a rule local custom goes far to determine the choice of the place for the services. In a current issue of *The New York Times* are fifty-eight death notices. Twenty-four call for services at funeral parlors; twelve, in churches, chiefly Catholic; six, in private residences. Most of the other notices indicate that the services will be in private, or else not in New York City. Needless to say, conditions there are not normal. In a small town funeral parlors would not be much in demand.

The logical place for many a funeral is in the home. That is where the deceased has lived. It has been the place dearest to his heart. The ties there are personal and enduring. Everything is familiar. The atmosphere is friendly. Amid such surroundings it should not be difficult for anyone to think of heaven as home, and of death as falling asleep at the end of life's little day. However, a funeral service may not be feasible in a tiny cottage, or a vast apartment house.

When the exercises are to be held in a Christian home it may be comparatively easy for the minister to make his plans. If the departed has been a believer in Christ, the occasion calls for uplifting worship. The spirit of the services ought to be that of Christian peace and hope. There need be nothing about "death's cold, sullen stream," or "Hark! from the tombs a doleful sound." As a rule that sound is pagan. In a Christian service of farewell why pitch the worship in a minor key?

The exercises in the home should be short. In making the plans it is good to think of twenty minutes as the upper limit. If the people desire a number of hymns, the time may be thirty minutes. But as a rule it is not wise to keep everyone on a strain for half an hour. According to a familiar saying about a sermon, few souls are saved after the first twenty minutes. In a memorial service few hearts find comfort during the latter portion of a thirty-minute service.

On the other hand, there should be no haste. If the minister speaks and acts deliberately, no one will leave or fall asleep. If he is to make a lasting impression for time and eternity, he will need fifteen minutes or more. Whatever the length of time, he ought to make every word count. In such circumstances it is an almost unpardonable offense to be loquacious. Even if there has been little opportunity for immediate preparation, the clergyman should school himself in speaking directly to the point.

In keeping with the spirit of the home, everything should be simple. The appeal should be more to the heart than to the head. The emphasis should be on the expression of Christian feeling rather than the teaching of religious truth. At other times and places there is a call for instruction about the meaning of death and the assurance of everlasting life, but just now the need is for spiritual comfort. It comes best through uplifting worship that has to do with the living Christ. Once he died on the cross. Some day he is coming in glory. Meanwhile he is here in our midst. He is tender to sympathize and mighty to save.

The appeal to the heart should be personal. However, the feelings should be under firm control. There is not likely to be any emotional disturbance if the minister keeps away from personalities. If there is an obituary it should be factual rather than laudatory. Otherwise nothing need be said directly about the deceased. There need be no mention of any other person, except the Lord Jesus. At a Christian service of farewell he should be all in all. In the light of his presence the friends should find peace for the present hour and hope for the days to come. The leader's aim, therefore, is to bring them one by one face to face with the living Christ.

Such a time of worship ought to be beautiful. The reference here is to nothing striking or flamboyant, but rather to the sort of spiritual beauty that breathes through the Crusaders' Hymn, "Fairest Lord Jesus." In every part of the service, notably in the readings from the Bible and in the prayers, the beauty of the Lord should shine forth. If there is music, or any other added feature, it should have a beauty all its own. In making ready for a funeral service this is a wise motto: "Let the beauty of the Lord our God be upon us."

The simplest way to test words for their beauty is to repeat them aloud. If they flow along with a quiet motion, whether it be that of poetry or of prose, they are probably worthy of a place in a funeral service, but not otherwise. If the leader is a lover of the beauty that dwells in words, he is able to read them so that they will move the heart Christward. If he can read from the Book, and then speak from the heart when he prays, he will cause the friends to feel that God is near and that he is good. If the beauty of the Lord is to remain with them, it should shine forth through the leader of the service.

There is a sort of somber beauty that has little place in a Christian funeral. For example, in the Bible few books have more of rhythmical movement than certain portions of Lamentations, but they are more in keeping with the gloom of the Wailing Wall in old Jerusalem than with the spirit of the celebration when a saint goes home to God. Then if ever the Gospel is good tidings. The call is for the children of the Most High to cast the mantle of forgetfulness over the days and weeks of waiting, the hours of agony and tears, the sadness of farewell. They should learn to look upward, not down; and forward, not back.

Throughout the services there should be a sense of motion. If there is to be no evidence of haste, neither should there be any appearance of delay, or of marking time. Since there is in the leader's mind and heart only one controlling purpose, that of bringing comfort, he can keep moving on from stage to stage. Each successive part should be fairly short. But there should be no break from beginning to end. Step by step he should lead all so close to God that erelong they will be ready to receive the most beautiful of the benedictions (Num. 6: 24-26).

One reason for having a benediction at this service, with another at the grave, is that some persons will be present at one time and not at the other. A more cogent reason is that the benediction should be the crowning feature of any religious service. When the minister solemnly pronounces these words of blessing they should bring to trustful hearts the healing balm of heaven. On those who have faith to receive the divine blessing, these last few words bestow "the manifold helpfulness of the Triune God."

Even when the exercises at the home lead up to the benediction there is still a sense of incompleteness. As the friends go out from beneath the family roof they should look forward to the services at the cemetery. Beyond that they should set their hearts on the open gates of heaven. They should be thinking of the family reunion in the Father's home.

Such was the spirit that prevailed throughout the services in memory of Mrs. L. For months she had been wasting away. At last she was free from her weakness and pain. Since the interment on the morrow was to be at her old village church forty miles away, the services were held in the home at night. The house was filled with loving neighbors and friends. The season was a day or two before Christmas. At first the young minister had wondered how he could blend the beauty of yuletide with the thought of death. Then he thought to himself, "In each case the spirit is that of homegoing." Few of those present will ever forget the resulting vision of heaven in terms of Christmas Eve at home by the fireside.

THE CHURCH FUNERAL

Sometimes funeral services ought to be held in the main sanctuary. If the throng of relatives and friends is too large for the home, the logical place for the ceremony of farewell is at the church. Especially is this the case if the departed has been a lay officer or a leader in the women's work. What is the sanctuary for if not to shelter God's children in their time of sorrow as well as of joy? If the church doors are open wide for many a wedding, should they not also be open for a funeral?

The time to make these facts clear is when no member has recently died. Every once in a while, through the bulletin or in other ways, the minister can announce that the church is available for funerals as well as weddings. When there is added expense for heating the building, the members of the congregation will understand without being told. In dealing with strangers it may be necessary occasionally to fix a moderate fee. But if it is financially possible the church should be open for any funeral service, without money and without price.

When the throng is not large, a more fitting place may be the chapel. Every church of any size ought to have a small sanctuary, as beautiful as the large one, and likewise dedicated to worship. At the First Presbyterian Church in New York City the chapel is perhaps the most pleasing part of the entire edifice. At the Old First Church of Orange, New Jersey, the smaller sanctuary is known as "The House of Prayer." Either of those chapels is large enough to accommodate comfortably the normal funeral party. Such a setting is almost ideal. It is churchly without seeming cold. In the main sanctuary the people might feel lost.

It is more difficult to plan for a funeral at the church than in a home. One reason is that people expect more. Another is that the arrangements must include two places, rather than one. Some ministers make it their rule to be present at the home, with a brief service in private, before the funeral party goes to the church. That is entirely proper, if the members of the family so desire. Ordinarily it is easier for the pastor to greet them at the main entrance to the church. Thus there need be no haste in getting from the home to the sanctuary and in putting on the pulpit gown.

For ten or fifteen minutes before the funeral party is expected there may be meditative music from the organ. As the people assemble there should be no conversation in either the lobby or the pews. Above all the minister should refrain from chatting with those who enter. He does well to tarry in the study until one of the ushers notifies him that the funeral party is arriving. Without haste he should go to the front entrance. Step by step with the mortician, the minister should lead the procession toward the chancel.

All the while the organist should be playing softly. No music is more fitting than the melodies of familiar hymns about Christ and the Cross. When the procession enters the people should rise and remain standing until after the members of the family are seated. In some churches it is the custom for the minister, as he precedes the casket down the center aisle, to repeat the words of our Lord: "I am the resurrection, and the life: he that believeth in me, though he were dead, yet shall he live: And whosoever liveth and believeth in me shall never die" (John 11: 25, 26).

The members of the funeral party take the front pews reserved for them on the right. The pallbearers go to the front pews on the left. Meanwhile the minister walks to the pulpit, or other place from which he plans to conduct the service. If the funeral party is seated in front of the lectern, he may wish to stand there. From this point forward the service may follow much the same order as at a private residence.

A church funeral, however, differs from one in a home. In fact, unless the leader is a master of his art, there may be coldness and stiffness. If the sanctuary is dark by day, there should be artificial light, though not much. Where the atmosphere of the home would lead to emphasis on things personal, the spirit of the sanctuary may suggest something more churchly. This is one reason why the minister does not wear a pulpit gown in the home, but always does in the church, if that is counted proper. When there is a message, it may be about the communion of saints, both on earth and in heaven.

As a rule services in the sanctuary last a little longer than they would in a home. Even if there is singing and a sermon, it is wise to think in terms of half an hour. Still more than in a home, the appearance of haste or of undue brevity might make the occasion seem inconsequential. Within thirty minutes, however, it should be possible, ordinarily, to greet the party at the door, conduct the service as a whole, and then escort them from the sanctuary.

Before the minister goes from the church he can step into the study and remove his pulpit gown. Then he should precede the party all the way to the funeral car. The pace should be slow, not only because the occasion is solemn, but also because those in charge of the casket need time. At the funeral car the minister stands in the street, facing the rear of the hearse, and far enough away so as not to interfere with the bearers. Unless the weather is inclement or cold, his head is uncovered. However, it is proper for an elderly man to wear a skullcap.

While the members of the family are being escorted to their motor cars the minister takes his seat in the automobile appointed for him. It may belong to the mortician, who is always glad to send for the minister at his residence and later deliver him there. In such a case the pastor may ride to the cemetery with the pallbearers. Less frequently, he goes with the mortician, or the chief assistant. Occasionally, the minister rides with the bereaved family. Whatever the arrangement, it is made by the mortician. He in turn carries out the wishes of the family.

In such matters one defers to the mortician. If he thinks

that the minister should ride in a stately conveyance, that is the part of wisdom. Otherwise the pastor may prefer to use his own car, provided it is presentable. On the way home from the cemetery he can make several calls at the hospital or elsewhere. Funerals are most frequent at the time of year when illness is most prevalent. They usually come in the afternoon, which is the best time for calling.

If the people concerned know that the minister has on his heart other folk who need his tender care, they will scarcely object to slight informality. Even if they should, the responsibility for the arrangements lies with the mortician. Whatever the minister plans to do, it should be clear to the man in charge. Neither at the church nor at the cemetery should the clergyman cause any inconvenience or delay. When everything else moves according to schedule, the public representative of the Most High should be ready for each step when it is due. "Let all things be done decently and in order" (I Cor. 14: 40).

The church funeral that the writer remembers most vividly was that of Mother W. Throughout the parish for years she had been known as "the flower lady." In person she was as dainty as a rose and in life she was as fragrant. Apart from her duties at home, her chief concern was for the flowers in the sanctuary. On Sunday night or Monday morning she sent pulpit flowers to persons who were sick or in distress. Whenever there was serious illness in a home, or a church member in the hospital, she ordered, in the name of the congregation, a box of flowers or a plant in bloom. During times of convalescence she made many a cheery call.

Such a messenger of beauty may be worth more to the parish than the average assistant pastor. The flower lady was so beloved that the services in her honor had to be held in the main sanctuary. Since the interment was to be at her girlhood home far away, the time for the assembly was in the evening, as the sun was about to set. The season was early in summer, when flowers were most lovely and profuse.

From gardens near and far came such old-fashioned flowers as she had loved. They filled the front portion of the sanctuary.

During the afternoon anyone who wished to look upon the face of this dear friend could do so in the church, where she seemed to be sleeping among the roses. As the time drew near for the services the organist began to play softly the melodies of the flower lady's most beloved hymns. Erelong the casket was closed, not to be opened again in the church. Soon the pews were filled. On the way home from work the men joined with the women who had come from their homes. The spirit was that of a family reunion among those who loved each other in the Lord. Within the throng were more than a few from other congregations.

In the services the dominant note was that of beauty. The deceased had been seventy years of age. She had come to her death through a painful accident. Hence it would have been easy to stress what was dark and hard and awful. But the prevailing spirit was thanksgiving for the memories of by-gone years, and rejoicing because of her going home. The readings and the prayers had to do with "mother, home, and heaven." The songs were such as she had loved to sing at home and in church. Instead of the conventional obituary there was a loving tribute prepared by the officers of the church and read by the pastor in their name.

Since the members of the family desired a brief message, it was on the words, "The beauty of the Lord our God be upon us" (Ps. 90: 17). After the services of farewell, as the people departed from the sanctuary, they loved to think of their departed friend in terms of beauty. Many of them felt that heaven was nearer than it ever had seemed before.

The order of service that appears below was prepared especially for the occasion. Although the congregation joined with the choir in singing the hymns, there was no announcement. The numbers were on the bulletin board. Since the interment was to be elsewhere, the services in the sanctuary included a few items that usually belong at the grave. Since the occasion was memorable, owing to the years of service rendered by the departed, the exercises were slightly longer than is customary.

Organ Music: Favorite Hymn Tunes

Hymn of Entreaty: "Abide with Me" . . . . *Monk*

The Reading of Psalms 103; 23

The Prayer of Adoration and Confession

Hymn of Thanksgiving: "Now Thank We All Our
God" . . . . *Crüger*

The Apostles' Creed

The New Testament Readings

Music by the Choir: "Unfold, Ye Portals" . . . *Gounod*

The Tribute Prepared by Officers of the Church

The Message by the Pastor

Hymn of Exultation: "Hark! Hark, My Soul!" . . . *Smart*

The Covenant Benediction

Organ Music: "Our Father Who Art in Heaven" . . *Bach*

THE FUNERAL PARLOR

One of the most difficult places in which to conduct a Christian service of farewell is at a funeral parlor or cemetery chapel. Such places are doubtless essential. If present trends continue, the majority of funerals may be held in rooms set apart exclusively for the purpose. For that very reason the atmosphere is likely to seem sepulchral. The associations are with death, not with life everlasting. No matter what is said or done, the services may seem hollow, if not hopeless.

Nevertheless, it is possible to be a minister of comfort and hope in the most conventional funeral parlor. God is there, and he is waiting to bless all that is done for his glory. In like manner it is feasible to have a Christian burial on a battlefield by night, as the chaplain stands by the grave of a young soldier who has recently been slain. All the while everyone feels that the situation is abnormal. But by faith the servant of God can rise above his feelings.

At a funeral parlor the problem is unlike that in the home or church. There the minister would conduct a service in harmony with the loftiest traditions and ideals of the hallowed spot. It has been the scene of love and joy such as we associate with heaven. But in a funeral parlor the Christian leader must strive to foster a spirit foreign to the surroundings. The very name "parlor" suggests something conventional and stiff. It makes one think of a marriage parlor, which is a sorry place for a wedding ceremony.

Some of the up-to-date rooms for funerals are models of architecture and interior decoration. Even so, the associations are with death. Never does the place ring with the shouts of children. Never does it sound forth the bells of Christmas or the notes of the wedding march. Hence there is little to suggest the mercies of God in the past or his promises for years to come.

It may be that all this is unfair. Each man's experience is his own. As for the writer, he does not recall with satisfaction any exercises that he ever conducted or attended at a funeral parlor. He wishes that it were feasible to have every Christian service of farewell in the living room of a home or within the confines of a church.

In time, however, it should be possible to change the atmosphere of many a funeral parlor. As a rule the services there are in the hands of Christians. In the early centuries of the Church at Rome the saints filled the catacombs with emblems of Christian hope and joy. In like manner, if the minister is in close touch with the Lord, he can rise above the conventional gloom and cold formality of any funeral parlor.

The way to transform such a place is to change the temper of our funeral customs. If in days to come every Christian funeral is in keeping with our holy faith, the places set apart for such services will be suggestive of peace and joy, with many foregleams of heaven. Meanwhile the pastor can say to his sorrowing friends, as they sit in a room given over to gloom, "Lift up your hearts." A fitting response would be: "We lift them up unto the Lord."

At a funeral parlor both pastor and people should remember what a man of old learned at a spot that had seemed to him God-forsaken: "Surely the Lord is in this place; and I knew it not. . . . This is none other but the house of God, and this is the gate of heaven" (Gen. 28: 16, 17).

THE PAGAN CUSTOMS

Thus far little has been said about unseemly funeral customs. One of them is the wearing of black raiment. Wholly apart from the cost, which may be heavy, the practice is pagan. Black is suggestive of night, gloom, despair. If there must be special funeral garments, let them be white. That is a symbol of the day, of purity, and of hope. Even more laudable is the custom of putting on the best attire at hand, provided it calls no attention to itself. Fortunately, the whole matter is righting itself, and that without ministerial pressure. More and more is common sense likely to prevail.

Another reform has been still more striking. A generation or two ago the favorite time for holding a funeral was on Sunday afternoon. Now the custom is almost extinct. Except when the body is to be taken elsewhere for burial, a Sunday funeral is almost unknown. Here again, common sense has prevailed.

A third practice is gradually disappearing. It is that of letting the public services culminate with "viewing the remains." The most harrowing scenes that accompany death may occur at this juncture. As the curiosity seekers parade past the open casket, the members of the family may have to look on. How can they keep back their tears? If they desire to be alone once more with the body of their beloved, that may be their privilege. But they ought to be shielded from the gaze of the curious.

Unfortunately, in many a rural community there is little that the minister can do, at least directly. Seldom does anyone ask what he thinks about such practices. However much his soul may revolt, he should hold his peace and bide his time. As a rule reforms are more effective if they come about gradually, in response to the desires of the people concerned.

If the clergyman were so disposed he could request the official board to forbid viewing the remains after a service in the sanctuary. In more than a few churches pagan music is no longer allowed, whether at a funeral or a wedding. The same principle would apply to this other practice. It is better, however, to work slowly and indirectly. In conference with the mortician the minister can suggest a more fitting plan. Whether the services are to be held in the church or elsewhere, the neighbors who find satisfaction in such things can see the body beforehand, at a time convenient for all concerned.

However much the pastor may deplore viewing the remains, he has no right to protest unless the practice interferes with the religious exercises. He has a right to arrange that these shall culminate with the benediction and silent prayer, to be followed by gentle music from the organ.

From beginning to end everything in such farewell services ought to be in harmony with the spirit of the Christian religion. Later we shall consider what to do when the departed has not been a believer. At present we are thinking about a normal ceremony, in memory of one who has loved the Lord and the home church.

At such a time the souls of believers should be filled with thanksgiving as they recall God's mercies in the past. Their hearts ought also to be full of peace as they trust in the ever-present Saviour. Their spirits should rejoice as they look forward to a family reunion in the Father's home.

Funeral Manuals

Halsey, Jesse, *A Living Hope*. The Abingdon Press, 1932 (loose leaves).

Harmon, Nolan Bailey, Jr., *Pastor's Ideal Funeral Manual*. Abingdon-Cokesbury Press, 1942.

Leach, William Herman, *Cokesbury Funeral Manual*. The Cokesbury Press, 1932.

VI. The Homemade Ritual

EVERY pastor ought to have some sort of funeral ritual. The word, as here employed, refers to a regular way of leading in the worship of God, time after time. In general, there are two kinds of ritual: the one is prescribed by a man's Church; the other is made in the home study. The one is adopted; the other is adapted. The question about which is better does not concern us now. In describing the one that is made at home there is no desire to disparage the one that is prescribed.

The merits of the prescribed ritual are well known. The majestic cadences of the Protestant Episcopal burial service are second to nothing of the sort. The corresponding portions of the Lutheran liturgy are equally worthy of honor. More ancient than either are the burial rites of the Roman Catholic Church. With such examples of liturgical art every clergyman should be familiar. Sooner or later a minister will be asked to read the Episcopal burial service. If so, he should be able to do it with distinction.

The pastor should be still more intimately acquainted with the book of forms issued by his own denomination. In one branch of the Church the title is *The Book of Common Worship*; in another body, *The Book of Service*. Almost without exception, these volumes of late have been well edited. Each of them is in accord with the traditions and ideals of the denomination. Whenever a minister is in doubt concerning what to do and say at a funeral, he can fall back on his official book. The fact that the suggested funeral forms are somewhat general makes them fitting when it would be unwise to deal directly with the "life situation."

In many another funeral, also, the pastor can draw from his favorite book of forms. But as the months go by he may feel a longing for an order of his own. For instance, he may think that the readings from the Bible should call forth words of prayer more often than in some of the rituals that he finds in books. If he conducts many funerals he will tend to follow much the same order time after time. If so, there may be no reason why he should change what he has found most helpful to his people. But it can do no harm for him to check up once in a while.

What, then, is the philosophy undergirding this kind of "free worship"? The principle is that the funeral service should employ spiritual materials in meeting human needs. Since they are much the same from one occasion to another, the general order may be fairly well fixed. But since in almost every funeral certain conditions are unique, the content should vary somewhat widely. For example, at the funeral of an aged saint who has fallen asleep after long months of weary waiting, the readings and the prayers would not be like those at the services over a young brakeman who has met his death in a railroad collision.

THE PRACTICAL DIFFICULTIES

It is far from easy to make a funeral ritual of one's own. One difficulty is that the service must all be related to the idea of death. Hence it is hard to avoid monotony. While there are certain to be readings and prayers, and there may be additional elements, all of them have to do with one grim subject. The tone color throughout is likely to be somber, if not doleful. Even if the service lasts only twenty minutes, the time may seem long. There are few contrasting hues, with lights and shades. There may be no alternating currents of thought and feeling. In short, there may be need of a better plan.

A kindred difficulty is that there may be only one leading

voice. If there were singing by the congregation, or the repetition of The Lord's Prayer and the Apostles' Creed in unison, there would be a measure of corporate worship. But ordinarily the pastor must be the spokesman for both God and people. In no other kind of worship, except a sermon, does the minister speak for twenty or thirty minutes uninterruptedly. In the Sunday message there is more variety of spirit and substance than in many a funeral service. Partly for this reason, such exercises may seem long.

If the services were like a land of hills and valleys, the effect would be cumulative. But there is difficulty in providing for two or three climactic stages. Instead of having everything on a dead level, there should be two or three places where the thought and feeling culminate. At any such climactic stage the wise thing to do is to pause for a moment, and then proceed, perhaps with a lower tone of voice. Without seeming hurried or jerky, the movement should be progressive. Variety is restful. If it is lacking, the basic plan may call for revision.

The chief difficulty is not in devising the program but in using it as a means of comfort and not as an end in itself. Instead of thinking further about the theory, therefore, let us glance at a homemade ritual. It scarcely deserves such an imposing title, for the chief mark of it all is simplicity. In a service lasting little more than twenty minutes, and intended to reach the heart rather than the head, anything except simplicity would seem out of place.

Sometimes the list is shorter than the one below. It is easier to omit than to add. But if there is singing, the list needs to be longer. With three musical selections, have one at the beginning and one after each prayer; with two, omit the first; with one, have it after either of the prayers.

The Call to Worship

One or Two Short Psalms

A Brief Prayer—Adoration and Confession

The New Testament Readings

Brief Remarks (Omit?)

A Brief Poem (Omit?)

The Pastoral Prayer

The Lord's Prayer

The Priestly Benediction

THE PRACTICAL WORKINGS

Let us watch the plan at work. The call to worship should
be deliberate. The tone should be low in pitch, but with no
little volume. Strive as a man will to keep his voice down,
it tends to rise. The effect is more pleasing if he starts with
a tone that is low but clearly audible. In reading the two
short psalms, or else a longer one, the rate of speech depends
on the spirit of the words. The Ninetieth Psalm, for instance,
requires more deliberate utterance than the Ninety-first. As a
rule the latter is more in keeping with the uplift of a Christian service.

The first part of the worship may reach its climax at the
end of the brief prayer, which ought to require less than a
minute. After a brief pause come the New Testament readings. Here too the impression should be that of deliberate-
ness and dignity. While clearly audible, the voice need not
be loud. It should never seem boisterous, but it should be
masculine and authoritative. The readings from the New
Testament are the most vital portion of the service. If the
passages are arranged in due order, they lead up to another
climax. A certain minister always closes with a part of the

fourteenth chapter of John; another, with a passage from the Apocalypse.

If there are remarks they should be short. There is time to bring out only one luminous idea. It should appeal to the heart. Much more important is the pastoral prayer. It should lead up to The Lord's Prayer, which comes at this stage more fittingly than near the beginning of the service. According to the plan before us, this is the only part of the main service in which everyone present takes part. The fact that The Lord's Prayer is dear to every heart makes it all the more fitting here. In a funeral it is often the old rather than the new that brings people close to God. After The Lord's Prayer they should receive the benediction.

For services in the sanctuary, or elsewhere with music, there may be need of a longer list. Still the basic pattern is much the same. It calls for alternate emphasis on speaking to God for the people, and then addressing the people in the name of God. If there is singing by the people, however, they can speak for themselves. Likewise there is a wholesome sense of corporate worship when they join in repeating the Apostles' Creed and The Lord's Prayer. Thus the exercises need not be merely a ministerial monologue.

Whatever the order, the value of the service depends far more on the spirit of the leader and on his selection of materials than on the sequence of the parts. In fact, one could follow an ideal order in a wooden way, just as one might have a helpful service without much semblance of a pattern. But since there are sure to be many funerals in the course of a man's ministry, he will save time and energy if early in his career he determines how he will conduct a service of farewell. In any one case, however, he may have to vary his plans so as to meet human needs.

Thus it appears that a minister who follows a ritual of his own devising ought to be something of a poet as well as a seer. The spirit of worship is closely akin to the beauty of verse. When love for God and his sorrowing people fills the heart of the minister as he makes his plans, and then carries them out, materials that in other hands might seem wooden become vital and moving. At times there may be a touch of splendor. From this point of view look at the following plan for a funeral in the sanctuary. The time is summer, early in the afternoon.

Organ Music—Familiar Hymn Tunes

Hymn by the People: "Our God, Our Help in Ages
Past" . . . . *Croft*

The Reading of Psalm 91

The Prayer of Adoration and Confession

Hymn by the People: "Beneath the Cross of Jesus" . *Maker*

The Apostles' Creed

The Readings from the New Testament

The Obituary (Omit?)

The Pastor's Message (Omit?)

Special Vocal Music: "God So Loved the World" . *Stainer*

The Pastoral Prayer

The Lord's Prayer

The Priestly Benediction

Organ Music: "Jerusalem the Golden" . . . . *Ewing*

THE LOOSE-LEAF NOTEBOOK

For use at funerals and elsewhere, the minister should have a loose-leaf notebook. It ought to be small enough to fit snugly in a side pocket, and large enough to hold leaves or cards four by six inches. In the portion set aside for funerals there should be room for any brief prayer that he wishes to read, as well as Scripture lessons, poems, and other materials. As a rule there is need of no other book, either during the main services or at the cemetery. If he always writes out such materials, he will keep them from being long.

When the materials are not in use they can repose in the files. The heading may be "Funerals." There may well be separate listings for each kind of material, so that the readings suitable for a child's funeral will not become confused with those for an aged saint. When the call comes to make ready for an unexpected service, the minister can turn to his files, take out what he wishes to use, and then arrange the parts according to his purpose. On his return from the cemetery he can replace all the materials in the files. If he wishes to note where he has used any item, such information belongs on the reverse side of the card.

The description makes the matter seem mechanical. But really it is only a common sense way of conserving time when every moment is precious. However, this way of working is not so simple as it seems. No worthy plan operates automatically. In some circumstances it may require most of the morning to prepare for a funeral that will last only twenty minutes. In any case it is a source of satisfaction to have at hand, available instantly, the fruitage of past reading and thinking. It is also convenient to have the notebook ready to receive the materials as they come out of the treasure chest.

Such a method would not be safe in the hands of a literalist or a worldling. But if the minister has a heart as well as a head, and if he employs both for the glory of God, in order to comfort his children, the use of a basic plan, with fresh materials each time, will enable him to find in this part of his work enduring satisfactions. Nevertheless, he must ever be on his guard lest he substitute a working method for a living faith.

VII. The Available Music

NOWHERE in the funeral service is there more need of a reform than in the music. In some circles the tendency has been to sweep away everything of the sort. But when those who mourn express a desire for hymns or other music, the request is reasonable. Did not the Protestant Reformation encourage God's people to sing? If the selections are wisely made and properly rendered, even by amateurs, music has power to bind up the broken in heart.

The right sort of music goes far to insure variety and spiritual helpfulness. Like the flowers that some of the fathers used to ban from the funeral service, music affords the children of God "beauty for ashes, the oil of joy for mourning, the garment of praise for the spirit of heaviness" (Isa. 61: 3).

There need not be music at every funeral. In the writer's experience there has often been none. But it so happens that there has been something of the kind in almost every funeral that he recalls with satisfaction. This may be due to the fact that he is a lover of music, especially hymns. So are many others who attend funeral services.

In arranging for such services the author made it a rule to ask whether or not the friends desired music. He was careful not to express an opinion one way or the other. Except in summer, when funerals were few, he was asked for music two or three times a month. If the people wished for the presence of expert musicians, who received compensation on the Lord's Day, he explained the situation, and had nothing to do with securing their services. But if volunteer singers were acceptable, he offered to provide them, without cost.

In every congregation of any size there are godly women who are glad to sing at funerals. In each of his parishes the writer found at least two volunteer singers, either of whom could play the tunes on the piano. If one of them could not be present on a certain afternoon, she was able to send a substitute. These volunteers seldom ventured to sing anything but hymns. That was what the members of the family desired. Those who wish music at funerals are old-fashioned folk, who love hymns about Christ and the Cross.

THE LIMITED RANGE

In such circumstances the range is likely to be limited. The people usually ask for the old stand-bys. If so, the minister accedes to the desires of the family. Without seeming facetious, one might say that the minister should remember that this is to be "their funeral." But if at heart he is a home missionary of music he can promote the cause at certain funerals. While the hymns that are usually asked for include some of the noblest in the English tongue, there is need of a wider range.

When the services are held in the sanctuary the singing may be by the people. With a capable organist and someone to lead the congregation there can be effective choral music, with no special numbers. Consequently there may be a sort of variety out of the question when the minister alone takes part from beginning to end. There is also the feeling of restfulness and uplift resulting from the right sort of Christian songs. There may even be exultation.

It was so one afternoon in Miller Chapel at Princeton Seminary. At the services in memory of former President Stevenson the sanctuary was thronged. No one was dressed in mourning. There were three hymns, each sung by the congregation, and there was no other music save that of the organ as the people entered and as they departed from the sanctuary. The list below is due to the loving-kindness of the

one who chose the songs as expressions of her husband's
devotion to Christ and the Church:

> "The King of Love My Shepherd Is."
> "O Saviour, Precious Saviour."
> "Ten Thousand Times Ten Thousand."

At the funeral of President Stevenson's brother-in-law,
Professor J. Y. Simpson, of Edinburgh University, the two
hymns were chosen in much the same manner and for exactly
the same purpose. They were: "Be Still, My Soul: the Lord Is
on Thy Side" and "Ten Thousand Times Ten Thousand." A
study of the first hymn will show the spirit with which the
lonely believer faces the future, unafraid. When the words
are sung to "Finlandia" the appeal is all the more plaintive.
Toward the end of the service the second hymn would be
glorious by contrast. Together the two come close to the
heart of the Christian faith.

As a rule our funeral music is melancholy. It need not be
so. Within the same family circle as above, farewell services
were held at Indianapolis in memory of the aged father. For
years he had served as a leading Christian layman. At last
a host of his friends came together in the sanctuary to cele-
brate his home-going. The concluding song was the "Halle-
lujah Chorus" from Handel's "Messiah." Surely that is closer
to the heart of our holy faith than the sort of lugubrious
music that used to be common at funerals. At other services
it may be wholesome to stress the somber side of our mortal
existence, but at the home-going of an aged saint the call is
for peans of triumph. "For all the saints who from their
labors rest, . . . Alleluia!"

Whoever selects the hymns ought to know music as well as
poetry. While there is room for pleasing variety, each song
ought to be the best of its kind. By the best, one refers only
to what is available and feasible. The range may be limited
to the hymns in the church hymnal. The choice there is restricted to those that the available musicians can render for

the glory of God. Not many amateurs can play or sing acceptably the creations of Beethoven and Bach. Obviously, the more limited the ability of the musicians is, the more care will be necessary in making the selections.

If the pastor does not know how to choose hymns, he can secure help from his wife, or someone else who is at home in realms of beauty. Gradually he can learn how to select songs that will voice the various moods appropriate at a funeral service. From his treasury the pastor can bring forth songs old and new. As a rule the old will predominate. Many of the people, especially among the aged, prefer the old favorites. In time he will learn how to keep the balance between the old songs and the new. Gradually he can increase the range.

THE OLD HYMNS

By the old hymns one means those that are common at funerals. In this respect local customs vary. In the writer's experience the repertoire has been much as follows: "Abide with Me"; "Asleep in Jesus"; "He Leadeth Me"; "In the Cross of Christ I Glory"; "Jesus, Lover of My Soul"; "Jesus, Saviour, Pilot Me"; "My Faith Looks Up to Thee"; "Nearer, My God, to Thee"; "Peace, Perfect Peace"; "Rock of Ages"; "The Old Rugged Cross"; "There Is a Land of Pure Delight"; "What a Friend We Have in Jesus"; and "When Peace, Like a River."

To most of these songs there can be little objection. Doctrinally, nearly all are in line with the teachings of the New Testament. Without some of them at hand, the pastor might often feel at a loss. Putting them together, however, one feels that something more is needful. Speaking broadly, one finds too much about "death's cold, sullen stream," and too little about the joys of the New Jerusalem. With certain exceptions, the music is neither restful nor uplifting.

In funeral services there should be a place for songs like

those listed above. But the range should be wider. In the additional hymns there should be more stress on what is dominant in the New Testament, as it deals with the last great enemy, death. Instead of attempting to define the difference, let us look at the lists below. No one of the three groups is better, perhaps, than the list above. But by making selections from the old favorites and these other groups one can secure wholesome variety.

If anyone wishes to sense the difference, let him spend an evening with his wife at the piano. Together let them sing a stanza or two of each hymn listed above, and then do the same with the songs that appear below. In each case the list is suggestive, rather than exhaustive. It merely shows some of the possibilities. With the help of the church organist and the leader of the choir, the pastor and his wife can make lists more suitable for the home parish.

The songs listed below are in the standard hymnals of the various Churches. The order of arrangement is alphabetical. The first list includes hymns that may come early in the funeral service. The second group consists of those that may be more fitting in the heart of the worship. The third section comprises those that may be suitable just before the benediction. But these groupings are subject to various modifications.

When a funeral service calls for three hymns, each should be somewhat different from the other two. The choice and the arrangement depend on the basic pattern of the service. If in his spare time the pastor makes up lists of hymns appropriate at the beginning, the middle, and the end of such a service as he often conducts, he will have in his files a treasure store on which he can draw in the hour of need.

The compiling of the lists will deepen the minister's love for the hymnbook. Apart from the Bible, the church book of praise is the most precious thing in any man's study. Through the hymnal the pastor will come close to the God who loves to reveal Himself in the beauty of holiness.

"Angel voices, ever singing" [for a child]
"Brightly gleams our banner" [for a child]
"Come, thou almighty King"
"Come, thou Fount of every blessing"
"Come, ye disconsolate, where'er ye languish"
"Come, ye thankful people, come"
"Gloria in Excelsis" (Old Scottish chant)
"Hark! hark, my soul! angelic songs are swelling" (evening)
"Now the day is over" (evening)
"Now thank we all our God"
"Our God, our Help in ages past"
"Unto the hills around do I lift up" ("Sandon")
"Upward where the stars are burning"

⚜ ⚜ ⚜ ⚜

"Beneath the cross of Jesus"
"Brief life is here our portion"
"Come, O thou Traveler unknown"
"How firm a foundation, ye saints of the Lord"
"I heard the voice of Jesus say"
"I'm but a stranger here"
"Love divine, all loves excelling"
"My God, my Father, while I stray" (a chant)
"O God of Bethel, by whose hand"
"O Love that wilt not let me go"
"O sacred Head, now wounded" (tune difficult)
"Saviour, like a Shepherd lead us" [for a child]
"The King of love my Shepherd is"
"The Lord's my Shepherd, I'll not want"
"There is a green hill far away"
"When I survey the wondrous cross" ("Hamburg")

⚜ ⚜ ⚜ ⚜

"Around the throne of God in heaven" [for a child]
"Crown Him with many crowns"
"For all the saints who from their labors rest"
"Guide me, O thou great Jehovah"
"I heard a sound of voices"
"Jerusalem the golden"

"Lead, kindly Light, amid th' encircling gloom" ("Sandon")
"Now the laborer's task is o'er"
"One sweetly solemn thought"
"O Jesus, I have promised"
"O mother dear, Jerusalem"
"O what their joy and their glory must be" (O Quanta Qualia)
"Sunset and evening star"
"Ten thousand times ten thousand"

THE ORGAN MUSIC

A funeral service in the sanctuary calls for music from the organ. If the friends wish for silence, save when the minister is speaking, they should have their way. But few will object to soft, meditative harmonies as the people come into the House of Prayer, and something more uplifting as they go out toward the cemetery. Like the beauty of the flowers and the stained glass windows, the right sort of music from the organ tends to foster the spirit of Christian peace and hope.

Sometimes there need be nothing more than the melodies of standard hymns. The appeal of music is to the heart. The spiritual value comes chiefly through association. Hence there should be a blessing when the organist plays tunes like those in the list below. At any one service the choice of the tunes depends on various factors. For instance, the melodies played while the people are assembling should be more meditative than the music while the throng is leaving the sanctuary. With such a setting of beauty there is abundance of room for lights and shadows. As a rule the lights should prevail.

The list that follows is suggestive, not exhaustive. It does not include the tunes of the "old" funeral hymns: Adeste Fideles, Alford, Aurelia, Austrian Hymn, Beecher, Bentley, Diademata, Dundee, Evening Praise, Eventide (Monk), Finlandia, Hamburg, In Babilone, Love Divine (Le Jeune), Morecambe, Old 124th, O Quanta Qualia, Palestrina, Passion Chorale, Pilgrims (Smart), Portuguese Hymn, Saint Anne,

Sandon, Schönster Herr Jesu, Sine Nomine (R. V. Williams), and Vox Dilecti.

For simple music from the organ the pastor may rely on a volunteer who loves to play for the glory of God. When the regular organist is present there may be special music that is more difficult. In either case the idea is to afford the service a background of quiet beauty. Otherwise the atmosphere of a church partly filled may seem cold and desolate. At a funeral parlor, also, the right sort of instrumental music tends to soften hearts and prepare them to receive the ministry of words.

When a volunteer plays hymn tunes on the organ she will be glad if the pastor makes the selections. But when there is to be special music the organist wishes to decide what she shall play. However, she will appreciate from the minister a statement of what he has in view. As a lover of beauty she knows that the tone color of the organ music ought to be in harmony with the spirit of the hour. Hitherto she may have ministered with clergymen whose conduct of the services called for a funeral march by Chopin or Grieg. She will be relieved to learn that it is proper to render selections pitched in a major key.

Among melodies suitable for funerals there is endless variety. However, there are certain restrictions. Each number should be restful or uplifting. The associations ought to be Christian. For aid in compiling the list below the author is indebted to friends at the Westminster Choir College, notably Alexander McCurdy, D. Mus.; Mrs. Harry Krimmel; James Weeks; and Philip T. Blackwood. For the final selections, however, the writer alone is responsible. Among the various proposals he has retained numbers that are likely to be available for the organist of the average church.

Bach, J. S. . . . . . "Hark! a Voice Saith, All Is Mortal"
"O God, Have Mercy"
"Our Father, Thou Art in Heaven Above"
*"Our Father, Who Art in Heaven"

Brahms	"Deck Thyself, My Soul"
	"A Lovely Rose Is Blooming"
	"O Sacred Head Now Wounded"
	"O World, I Now Must Leave Thee"
Dupré	"Cortège et Litanie"
	"He, Remembering His Great Mercy"
Franck, César . . .	Andante from "Grande Pièce Symphonique"
Greenfield	"Prelude in Olden Style"
Guilmant, A. . . .	"Funeral March and Song of the Seraphs"
	"Prayer and Cradle Song"
Karg-Elert	"Adorn Thyself, O My Soul"
	"O God, Thou Faithful God"
	"Rejoice Greatly, O My Soul"
Mendelssohn, F. . .	Adagio from "The First Organ Sonata"
Muffat, G.	Adagio from "Toccata"
Purvis	"Communion"

THE SPECIAL SONGS

The special vocal music is likely to cause more concern than all the hymns and organ numbers combined. If the members of the family secure the singer, the resulting solo may be "Beautiful Isle of Somewhere," or another number equally non-Christian. When sweetly rendered by a gifted soprano such a song may be pleasing, but there may be in it scarcely a word or a suggestion that would be out of place in a Hebrew synagogue or a gathering of secular humanists. Quartet numbers may be equally lacking in Christian content and spirit.

In the course of time many of these conditions will right themselves. Sensitiveness to what is proper in worship seems to be growing. Other branches of the Church are beginning to follow the Protestant Episcopal practice of forbidding in the sanctuary vocal music that is non-Biblical. At marriages the Roman Church has recently issued a ban against such songs as "Oh Promise Me." The same principle, when applied to funerals, will go far to remedy the present musical secularism. As a rule it is wise to bring about reforms gradually, with no blaring of trumpets.

The way to promote the use of worthy special music at funerals is to guide in the choice of such numbers as those that appear below. In compiling the list the author is indebted to the friends named above. The majority of the following selections are only moderately difficult. Nevertheless, they ought to be attempted only by persons who can sing correctly and with skill. Unless real musicians are available, it is much better to have simple hymns than to suffer while well-meaning members of an "awkward squad" are doing their utmost to "rend the anthem."

In time it should also be possible to use chants. Especially do the psalms lend themselves to this kind of uplifting worship. After the singers have learned how to chant, and the people have become accustomed to this way of ascribing glory to God, nothing will add more distinction to the funeral service than to have the chanting of such a psalm as the Fifteenth, Twenty-third, Twenty-fourth, Twenty-seventh, Thirty-ninth, Forty-sixth, Ninetieth, Ninety-first, One Hundred and Third, or One Hundred and Twenty-first.

ANTHEMS

Bach, J. S. . . . . "Now Let Every Tongue Adore Thee"
"Ah, How Fleeting"
Barnby, J. . . . . "Crossing the Bar"
Barnby-Lewis . . . "Now the Day Is Over" (men's voices)
Chadwick, G. W. . . "When Our Heads Are Bowed with Woe"
Gaul, A. R. . . . . "Great and Marvelous" ("The Holy City")
"No Shadows Yonder" ("The Holy City")
Gounod, C. . . . . "Forever with the Lord" (quartet)
"Unfold, Ye Portals Everlasting" ("Redemption")
Grieg, E. . . . . "Jesu, Friend of Sinners"
Haydn, F. J. . . . "Lo, My Shepherd Is Divine"
Matthews, J. S. . . "I Heard a Voice from Heaven"

Mendelssohn, F. . . .	"Forever Blest Are They" (men's voices)
	"Happy and Blest Are They"
	"He That Shall Endure to the End"
Noble, T. Tertius .	"The Souls of the Righteous"
Parker, H. W. . . .	"The Lord Is My Light"
Spohr, L.	"Blest Are the Departed"
Shelley, H. R. . . .	"Crossing the Bar" (solo, low voice, with chorus)
Stainer, J.	"God So Loved the World"
	"My Hope Is in the Everlasting"
Tschaikowsky-Cain .	"O Blest Are They"

SOLOS AND DUETS

Christiansen, F. M.	"I Know a Home Eternal" (baritone)
Franck, César . . .	"O Lord Most Holy"
Gaul, A. R. . . .	"They Shall Hunger No More" (soprano and alto)
Gounod, C. . . .	"Forever with the Lord" (duet, high and low)
Handel, G. F.	"Come Unto Him" (soprano)
	"He Shall Feed His Flock" (alto)
	"I Know That My Redeemer Liveth" (All from "The Messiah")
Handel-Milligan .	"Immortal Love" (high)
Kingsley, R. . . .	"Immortality"
MacDermid, J. G. .	"In My Father's House"
Shelley, H. R. . . .	"Hark, Hark, My Soul"
Ward-Stephens . .	"In My Father's House"
Willeby, C.	"Crossing the Bar" (duet, high and low)

Informational Readings

Breed, David Riddle, *History and Use of Hymns and Hymn-tunes.* Fleming H. Revell Company, 1934.

Gilbert, Harry, Editor, *Gilbert's Manual for Choir-Loft and Pulpit.* Charles Scribner's Sons, 1939.

Hjortsvang, Carl, *The Amateur Choir Director.* Abingdon-Cokesbury Press, 1941.

Randall, Mallinson, Editor, *The Choirmaster's Guide to the Selection of Hymns and Anthems.* H. W. Gray Company, 1911.

VIII. The Scripture Readings

THE simplest way to better the average funeral service would be to improve the selection of the Scripture readings. Sometimes there is music; often there is not. But there is always at least one passage from the Bible. Usually there are several. If there is no sermon, the readings from the Book afford the only opportunity to throw light from above on the mystery of death. If the pastor chooses aright, and reads with distinction, portions of Holy Writ will reach and bless many a heart. What could be more vital?

But, alas, the selections are often unwise. Instead of choosing passages that throw light on present needs, a man may pick up a book of forms and without preparation stumble through a succession of passages that have little continuity, no climax, and no power to soothe. In one of the older books there are on two small pages fifteen varied passages, from nine books of the Bible. Even if the reader were well prepared, how could he secure any harmony of tone color?

In the older books of forms the funeral readings were often melancholy. In the New Testament after the resurrection of our Lord there is from the lips of a believer scarcely a note of pessimism. But in some of our funeral services most of the Scripture passages are gloomy, not to say despairing. "Man that is born of woman hath but a short time to live, and is full of misery." "He heapeth up riches, and knoweth not who shall gather them." "Vanity of vanities, saith the Preacher, all is vanity and vexation of spirit."

All of that is true, and it ought to be told. But there are other occasions when one can speak about "the dark line in God's face." When the sun is shining and the south wind is blowing softly, there may be need of warning the mariner that the winter is drawing nigh. But when the tempest has broken forth in fury and all seems likely to be lost, there is a call for words of sympathy and hope. Especially if the deceased has been a radiant Christian, the emphasis at his funeral should be on the glory of our holy faith.

In recent years the books of forms have been largely free from such faults. They have put in the forefront psalms like the Twenty-third and the One Hundred and Third. The other selections are mainly from the New Testament. As a rule each passage is a unit. While it may not be long, there is completeness of thought and feeling. There is little of the old "hop, skip, and jump" reading that used to make the Scriptures seem disjointed. Consequently, if a clergyman is in doubt concerning what to read at a funeral service he can fall back on his favorite book of forms.

SELECTING THE PASSAGES

Ordinarily the minister wishes to select passages inspired of God to meet the sort of needs that will face him in the approaching funeral. In the Scriptures not only does he look for certain strains of thought and feeling; he likewise notes the tone color. Even within any one book each literary unit is likely to have a tone color all its own. By careful choice of materials he can produce harmony of effect, and increasing warmth of spirit, as the succession of beautiful words leads the hearers closer and closer to God.

The first reading is usually from The Book of Psalms. If each of them is short, there may be two. But if the selection is the Ninety-first, or the One Hundred and Third, a single psalm is enough. At an occasional funeral, where the departed is aged, the Ninetieth Psalm may be in order. But as a rule the Ninety-first is more in keeping with the spirit of the hour. At other times the minister should stress the solemn truths voiced by the Ninetieth Psalm. But when those whom he loves are sitting under the shadow of death they need to lift up their hearts as in one of the more radiant songs.

As a rule there need be no other selection from the Old Testament. But if it seems wise to have a passage from any other part of the Old Testament, this comes as the first of what we designate as "New Testament Readings." For instance, at the funeral of a practical woman whose name was Martha, the pastor read ten or twelve verses from the closing chapter of Proverbs. In that prose poem there are twenty-two verses, but only ten or twelve may be of special interest at a funeral today. By careful selection of verses one can secure continuity and likewise preserve the tone color.

After a slight pause, and with a change of tone, the minister read from the Gospels about the way the Lord Jesus loved Martha, as well as Mary. Then came another brief pause, with a shift of tone, after which he read a passage from the Epistles and one from the Apocalypse. The entire service, including the Ninety-first Psalm at the beginning, called for five readings, no one of which was long.

As a rule it is wise to have only a few separate passages. Five or six is a good upper limit. If the number were higher there would probably be a scattering of interest. Even when the total number is not large, each passage ought to be fairly short. In dealing with the fifteenth chapter of First Corinthians, for example, one scarcely knows what to do. To read it aloud as a whole would require perhaps seven minutes. Even if one started with verse 20, the remainder of the chapter might seem heavy. In the lists that appear below, this golden chapter is broken into a number of passages, each of which seems to form a complete unit.

The same principle of feeling free to select certain parts applies to other chapters, such as the fortieth chapter of Isaiah or the fourth chapter of Philippians. In the latter passage the writer would begin with verse 4, read through verse 8, and then pass on to verse 13, finishing with verse 19. By this means he would have in seven verses the heart of all that the apostle here tells about Christian contentment. At a funeral there is seldom any announcement of what passage one is reading; hence there need be no reference to the omissions.

As a rule the best version for use at a funeral is the King James Version. While it has minor flaws, the language is notable for beauty. Even the prose has a pleasing rhythm. The diction has a dignity and elevation rarely found in recent translations. The fact that the old version is familiar makes it welcome in the time of sorrow. That is when the heart cries out for the old faith and the familiar landmarks, as they appear in mother's Bible.

A case will show how the principle works. At services held in memory of an aged friend the minister read a few of her favorite psalms. That was the kind thing to do, as she had been a lifelong singer of the psalms. The list had been prepared by her daughters, who singled out the Twenty-third as the psalm that their mother had loved most. But to their dismay the minister began the reading with the words, "Jehovah is my Shepherd." At such a time a little thing may loom large. To her dying day each of those daughters will think of that reading as the only unfortunate feature of their mother's coronation service.

Without being spectacular or bizarre, such readings ought to be memorable. They should appeal to the heart and likewise kindle the imagination. They should suggest something for the eye to see, for the heart to feel, and for the will to do. Erelong the sorrowing friends should go out feeling that they have been with the Lord Jesus on the mountaintop and that they will walk with him on earth until their traveling days are done.

PREPARING TO READ

Whenever there is time to make ready for a funeral, a good deal of thought should go into the study of the Scripture readings. One way to prepare would be to learn them by heart and then recite them without glancing at the printed

page. Every minister should commit to memory golden portions of the Book, the more the better. But as a rule the pastor
who best knows the Book prefers to read the Scriptures. One
reason is that the interpreter should call attention to the
Bible, not to himself. Occasionally, however, one hears a
clergyman who can recite the Scriptures without an air of
showmanship. Down in his heart every minister should determine that he will read so as to exalt the Saviour and not
the self.

Whatever the method, the pastor should be prepared. He
ought to understand each passage. Without pausing for
comment, he should be able to interpret the revealed will
of God. Hence he should know which words to stress, and
when to pause, as well as how long. Otherwise the emphasis
might fall on the wrong word. Instead of singling out the
verb and the noun, the reader might thump the preposition
and the pronoun. Instead of stressing a single word in a
clause, he might attempt to make every syllable stand out.
Instead of bringing out the prose rhythm of the old King
James, he might resort to a singsong swing.

One difficulty about interpreting the Bible is that each passage calls for a different treatment. How else could the minister bring out the tone color? Such excellence in reading is
rare. It comes through living with the words until the soul
is in accord with their mystic harmonies. When a wise interpreter comes to the funeral service he makes everyone feel
that the Lord is the Good Shepherd, here and now; and that
in the Father's home there are many rooms for the redeemed
children of God. With a few passages interpreted by one who
can read, there may be no call for a sermon.

A good way to prepare in general is to make a loving study
of each passage that is likely to be needed at a funeral. The
man who dwells at "the house of the Interpreter" spends a
good deal of time each day in mastering some part of the
Book. When the study of any passage is complete, the words

themselves may be written on a separate card or a loose-leaf sheet, all ready for his files. If there is a secretary, she can do this work; but if the minister does it himself, he will love the words all the more. How could he spend his spare time more profitably than in working over luminous passages about the life everlasting?

When there is a call for a funeral, with little time to make ready, the interpreter can quickly select from his files a few passages inspired to meet the present needs. Then he can read them, one by one, so as to bring the hearers close to the heart of God. Even in a service that lasts only twenty minutes, he can guide his sorrowing friends into the mountaintop. There they will behold the Lord Jesus and begin to be transformed into his likeness.

Such is the theory. The lists following show how the plan works. In time a minister ought to have ready for use passages of various kinds. The arrangement here is Biblical rather than topical. It matters little how a man stores his treasures, provided he can quickly lay his hand on what he wishes to use. The writer has found it best to file such material according to the book, the chapter, and the verse in the Bible. However, he is vastly more concerned with the meaning and the use of the Scriptures than with any method of classification.

Psalm 1.	The Blessedness of Being Good.
Psalm 15.	The Portrait of a Godly Man.
Psalm 16.	The Song of the Saint.
Psalm 23.	The Goodness of the Shepherd.
Psalm 24.	The Glory of Our King (use at the grave?).
Psalm 27.	The Psalm of the Soldier.
Ps. 34: 1-19.	The Goodness of Our God.
Psalm 39.	The Gloom of the Grave (use seldom).
Ps. 42: 1-5.	The Shadow in the Soul.
Psalm 46.	The God of the Battlefield.

Psalm 90.	The Shadow of Eternity (for an aged person).
Psalm 91.	The Security of the Saint.
Psalm 103.	The Loving-Kindness of the Father.
Psalm 116.	The Sorrows of the Saint.
Ps. 119: 9-16.	The Religion of a Young Man.
Psalm 121.	The Song of the Pilgrim (use at the grave?).
Psalm 130.	The Prayer of the Desolate.
Psalm 139.	The Cry of the Lonely Soul (use only a part).

❦ ❦ ❦ ❦

Gen., ch. 50.	The Burial of a Godly Father.
Ruth 1: 16-22.	The Loyalty of the Loving Heart.
II Sam. 12: 16-23.	The Home-Going of a Baby.
Job 14: 1-14.	The Hope of Immortality.
Job 19: 23-27.	The Assurance of the Resurrection.
Prov. 31: 10-31.	The Portrait of a Godly Woman.
Eccl. 12: 1-7, 13, 14.	The Dissolution of the Body.
Isa. 40: 1-11, 28-31.	The Message of God's Comfort.
Isa. 43: 1-3a.	The Power of God to Redeem.
Isa. 63: 7-9.	The Grace of God for the Sorrowful.

❦ ❦ ❦ ❦

Matt. 5: 1-16.	The Blessedness of God's Children.
Matt. 6: 19-34.	The Security of Heavenly Treasures.
Matt. 7: 18-27.	The Christian Secret of Security.
Matt. 11: 25-30.	The Master's Gift of Rest.
Matt. 18: 1-6.	The Saviour with the Child.
Matt. 18: 10-14.	The Shepherd with His Lambs.
Matt. 25: 1-13.	The Meaning of Religion as Readiness.
Matt. 25: 31-40.	The Surprises of the Judgment Day.
Mark 5: 22, 23, 35-43.	The Death of a Growing Girl (aged 12).
Mark 10: 13-16.	The Lord's Blessing on Little Children.

Luke 7: 11-15.	The Death of an Only Son.
Luke 10: 38-42.	The Joys of Being with Jesus.
Luke 23: 33-47.	The Love of the Dying Saviour.
Luke 24: 13-35.	The Fellowship of the Risen Lord.
John 10: 7-16.	The Goodness of Our Shepherd.
John 11: 11-26.	The Promise of the Resurrection.
John 14: 1-18, 25-28.	The Meaning of Heaven as Home.
John 15: 1-17.	The Christian Secret of Fruitfulness.
Rom. 8: 18-28.	The Wonders of God's Providence.
Rom. 8: 31-39.	The Power of God over Death.
I Cor., ch. 13.	The Supremacy of Christian Love.
I Cor. 15: 20-28.	The Beginning of the Eternal Harvest.
I Cor. 15: 35-49.	The Glory of the Heavenly Harvest.
I Cor. 15: 50-58.	The Power of Christ over the Grave.
II Cor. 4: 5-18.	The Power of God in Man's Weakness.
II Cor. 5: 1-10.	The Hope of Going Home.
Eph. 6: 10-18.	The Completeness of the Christian Armor.
Phil. 2: 5-11.	The Glory of the Incarnate Lord.
Phil. 3: 7-16.	The Power of Christ's Resurrection.
Phil. 4: 4-9, 13, 19.	The Christian Secret of Contentment.
I Thess. 4: 13-18.	The Promise of the Second Coming.
I Thess. 5: 1-11, 23, 24.	The Comfort of the Christian Hope.
Titus 2: 11-14.	The Gospel of Christian Hope.
Heb. 11: 1-10.	The Title Deeds of Heaven.
Heb. 11: 32 to 12: 2.	The Faith of Our Fathers.
Heb. 12: 1-14.	The Meaning of God's Chastening.
I Peter 1: 1-9.	The Glory of the Christian Hope.
I Peter 2: 11, 12, 19-25.	The Beauty of Christian Suffering.
I John 1: 1-9.	The Glory of God as Light.
I John 2: 12-17.	The Religion of the Family.
I John 3: 16-24.	The Meaning of Religion as Love.
I John 4: 7-21.	The Victory of Love over Fear.
Rev. 7: 9-17.	The Joys of the Heavenly Host.
Rev. 21: 1-7.	The Glory of the Heavenly City.
Rev. 21: 22-27.	The Lights of the Eternal City.
Rev. 22: 1-7.	The River of Life Everlasting.

Informational Readings

Blackwood, Andrew W., *The Fine Art of Public Worship*. The Cokesbury Press, 1939. Chapter VII.

Curry, Samuel Silas, *Vocal and Literary Interpretation of the Bible*. Doubleday, Doran & Co., 1910.

IX. The Pastor's Prayers

THE most difficult part of the funeral service is the prayers. Except for the Scripture lessons, nothing else begins to be so vital. In fact, the minister often dispenses with everything except the readings and the prayers. In a Christian service this is usually the minimum. There may be nothing more, but there should always be a word from the heart of God, as well as a prayer addressed to him. In all Christian worship, and not least at a funeral, these two belong together. Either without the other would be incomplete.

In the plan for the service each prayer may follow a reading from the Bible. If so, the principle is that of alternating. In the readings the minister is speaking for God to the hearts of his children. In the prayers the pastor is addressing the heavenly Father on behalf of his sons and daughters. While it is not easy to interpret the Scriptures so as to bring out the tone color, and thus use them in meeting the needs of human souls, it is even more difficult to voice the desires that should fill the hearts bowed down in grief.

In a funeral service there may be five acts of prayer. This number includes what is done at the home, or in the church, as well as at the grave. The list also includes the two benedictions. Really a benediction is not a prayer, but it belongs in the same lofty realm. If we include only a single benediction, the one at the grave, the acts of prayer in a funeral service are somewhat like those in a regular hour of morning worship.

According to the plan in mind, the first prayer comes after the reading from The Book of Psalms. The mood of the words addressed to God should be in keeping with the tone color of what has just gone before. The minister voices the feelings of adoration and awe that should fill the hearts of God's children as they come into his presence and seek his blessing. While these words are brief, they are difficult to prepare. It is seldom easy to pray at the beginning of public worship, and most of all in the presence of death.

For the opening prayer the minister often employs a collect. If the people are not accustomed to the use of written forms, he should close his eyes and speak out of his heart. But if the friends are not averse to form in worship they should be ready to follow a historic prayer of the Church. In deciding whether or not to read a collect, the minister should ask whether or not his doing so will call attention to how he is praying.

The number of suitable collects is large. This is one: "Eternal God, who lovest us with an everlasting love, help us now to wait upon Thee with reverent and submissive hearts, that as we hear the words of eternal life, we may through the comfort of the Scriptures have hope in Jesus Christ, and be lifted above our darkness and distress into the light and peace of Thy presence, through Jesus Christ our Lord. Amen."

After a brief pause there may be a few words of confession. This part of the funeral service is usually omitted. If the minister does not refer to sin he may displease no one save himself and God. Nevertheless, if he is striving to voice the feelings that should fill the hearts of God's children as they bow down in the presence of death, he should remember that the cause of human woe is sin.

This part of the service, while clear and impressive, should be short and moving. A few words are enough: "Hear us, O Father, as we confess our sins. 'If we say that we have no sin, we deceive ourselves. . . . If we confess our sins, he is faithful and just to forgive us our sins, and to cleanse us from all unrighteousness. . . . And the blood of Jesus Christ his Son cleanseth us from all sin' " (I John 1: 8, 9, 7).

Even with two elements, the prayer as a whole should be short, without seeming abrupt. If the minister speaks deliberately, as he should, the time may still be less than a minute. Even if the words are those of the minister, they may well be down in the notebook. Here again, he should read only if he can do so without calling attention to how he is praying. As a rule there is more of spiritual uplift in the opening prayer that is read, or else committed to memory, than when he speaks extempore. There is also a saving of time, which is precious.

The second prayer is usually somewhat longer. It may require two or three minutes. This prayer may come after the readings from the New Testament. The purpose is pastoral. In the earlier prayer the minister leads his friends into the presence of God and voices their feelings of penitence because they are not worthy to be called his children. In the pastoral prayer the aim is to express their emotions after they have heard from the New Testament the Gospel of peace and hope.

The pastoral prayer may begin with thanksgiving. If so, it should center round the goodness of God and the grace of the Lord Jesus Christ. Unlike the former prayer, which is somewhat general, this one should be more specific. Without resorting to eulogy, and with no attempt at appraisal of the deceased, the minister should thank God for all his goodness to the departed, and to the family circle. Needless to say, it is seldom necessary or wise to go much into detail.

It is difficult to give thanks at a funeral. A man is likely to say too little, or else too much. Unless this part of the service is planned with tenderness and taste, as well as sincerity and truthfulness, it is better not to be specific. If everything is to be general, why not read from a book? That is what one often does at a problem funeral. But if a man has the shepherd heart, he wishes to give somewhat specific thanks at the services in memory of a sainted friend.

After the brief words of thanksgiving there may be a

pause. In a different tone, somewhat lower, come the petitions for the members of the household and for others who share the sorrow. Without referring to anyone by name, the minister can present the heart needs of his friends. In these matters of the soul there are no rules. The man who knows how to pray for his people at other times will be able to intercede for them when they must walk through the dark valley.

After the petitions there should be another brief pause. Then there may be short, meaningful supplications for others who mourn. Often the minister omits this part of the service, if only because the time is limited. But if he excels in prayer, he can foster the spirit of sympathy with suffering hearts elsewhere. He knows that grief is likely to make his friends self-centered, and that they ought to share in the sorrows of the world.

Since this part of the service is pastoral it should lead up to The Lord's Prayer. If these familiar words come in the heart of the service, or else toward the end, they give everyone an opportunity to take part. If the minister is new in the parish the people may not understand that they are to join in the act of family devotion. At the first funeral or two, before the service begins, he may request the singers and a few other friends to join with him both in The Lord's Prayer and in the Apostles' Creed. These words may prove to be the climactic parts of the service.

The benediction that is most likely to accord with the service is the most beautiful of all. It comes from the Hebrew Bible. The fact that the words of blessing do not issue from the New Testament, with its triumphant assurance of the resurrection and the life everlasting, may suggest that the services thus far must be incomplete:

"The Lord bless thee, and keep thee: the Lord make his face shine upon thee, and be gracious unto thee: the Lord lift up his countenance upon thee, and give thee peace" (Num. 6: 24-26).

At the grave the prayer is usually brief. The dominant truth in this part of the service is the resurrection and the life everlasting. In view of such a blessed hope the minister voices the desire of each waiting person as he dedicates himself to God. Since life is never to end, and there is to be a family reunion in the Father's home, everyone at the grave should put himself anew into the hands of God.

Among the prayers in the funeral service, this one may be the most individual. At the opening of the exercises in the home or the church the pastor voices the feelings that should fill the hearts of God's people as they worship together. Even in the pastoral prayer, they should think of themselves as a group of the Father's children, who are looking to him for grace to supply all their needs. But at the grave each person, individually, should dedicate himself anew to the service of God and men.

At the grave the most suitable benediction is that of the covenant God (Heb. 13: 20, 21). Among all the Biblical benedictions, this one alone has to do with the Resurrection of Christ and the perfecting of the saints while they are still in the flesh. As with the words of blessing at the home or the church, the benediction at the grave is for the group as a whole. In the assurance of God's covenant peace the sorrowing friends should turn homeward and face the future unafraid.

If we look back now we shall see that the prayers over the body of a departed friend conform to a definite pattern. From funeral to funeral the content may differ widely, according to the circumstances. But the order of the prayers, as a rule, should be much the same. Whatever the circumstances, there are certain needs that the minister should have in mind as he makes ready to pray, and certain feelings that he should voice at every funeral.

In preparing to lead others as they worship God at such a time, it may help the young minister to remember the suggestion from Dean L. A. Weigle, of the Divinity School at

Yale. He says that in public prayer there should be five elements, and that the order should always be the same: adoration, confession, thanksgiving, supplication, and submission. Under supplication he includes petitions for those present and intercessions for others. By submission he means what we have termed dedication.

As an aid to the memory, Dean Weigle suggests the homemade word "Actss." While such a mnemonic device may seem wooden, if it leads to more carefully ordered prayers in public worship, especially at the funeral service, everyone should thank God. Even the most experienced pastor may need to check up on his prayers, to see if there is either overlapping or overlooking.

When the minister leads in prayer at a funeral there should be a basic plan for the service as a whole. Near the beginning, and only once, he should voice the feelings of the friends as they come consciously into the presence of God. Once, and only once, he should express their sorrow for their sins. In the longer prayer, and then only, he should give thanks for whatever the occasion warrants. Here, and here alone, he should ask for what the sorrowing friends need most. At the grave, and there only, he should give thanks for the fact of the Resurrection, and then lead his sorrowing friends as one by one they give themselves anew into the hands of the heavenly Father.

The chief fact about any of these prayers is the purpose. In each of them the aim is primarily to express feeling. According to the Westminster Shorter Catechism, "Prayer is an offering up of our desires." Whether the dominant mood be that of adoration or confession, thanksgiving or petition, intercession or dedication, that is what the friends should be feeling. In psychological terms, the minister is striving to "induce a desired response."

If the pastor is to lead, the people should be able to follow. If they are not in a mood to pray, there is all the more reason why the minister should "condition the desired response." If he is really praying, and not simply repeating words, his spirit should lead others to pray. If he knows whither he is going, and how he expects to reach the goal, he will not have to proceed alone. Otherwise there is likely to be the blind leading of the blind.

At a funeral, as elsewhere in public worship, every prayer should have a pattern. There should be a clear beginning and a strong ending. There ought to be definite stages, clearly marked. The prayer should move forward by paragraphs, each of which ought to be fairly short. Throughout the prayer as a whole the same tone color should prevail. In short, the form of a prayer ought to be somewhat like that of a poem. The spirit should be much like that of a psalm.

The language of prayer differs from that of preaching, much as the words of poetry differ from the diction of prose. In either case all that a man says ought to be clear and easy to follow. In a prayer there should be even more of quiet beauty than in a sermon. There should also be a sense of motion. Whenever a man's heart is full of feeling his words tend to flow in a pleasing rhythm. In the presence of death the minister's prayers ought to be luminous with spiritual beauty. They should also be radiant with Christian hope.

There is time to mention only four of the many faults that may mar the prayers at a funeral. One fault is excessive length. The cause may be lack of preparation. Another fault is undue loudness, as though God were far away and dull of hearing. A third is excessive speed. A fourth is impropriety. For instance, at the church funeral of a young deacon the minister pleaded with God that the vacant place in the home might soon be filled. Incidentally, the comely young widow was married again in less than a year.

The gist of the matter is that the minister's culture and his training, or his weaknesses in both, appear whenever he leads in prayer at a funeral. In view of these facts the young clergyman may exclaim, "How can I learn to pray at such a time?" By way of reply there is nothing novel. The one who leads others to the mercy seat ought to be a good man, a hard student, and a diligent pastor. A holy man of God who has no time for special preparation can pray more acceptably than a worldling who knows almost everything except the grace of God. On the other hand, the man who loves the Lord resolves with King David: "Neither will I offer burnt offerings unto the Lord my God of that which doth cost me nothing" (II Sam. 24: 24).

Since prayer is sacrifice to God, any such exercise of the soul is costly. In other words, the minister may think of "prayer as a battlefield." When he is alone with God, he should pour out his soul. Of course he should pray often with his people, and for the nations, near and far. But first he should offer sacrifices for himself. That was what the Hebrew priest did before he dared to intercede for others. In short, if a man wishes to excel in public prayer, especially at a funeral, the training school is in the closet. Before a man tries to lead others, he himself should know the way to God.

Anyone who is troubled by wandering thoughts may form the habit of writing out a prayer each morning. At first the task may seem mechanical. But it need not be so. A written prayer may be as real as a love letter. The oftener a young man writes to the one he expects to wed, the more is he able to pour out his heart to the beloved whom he cannot behold. In prayer, as in a love letter, it is the spirit that counts. When a man's heart is overflowing with love his words are full of beauty.

Unfortunately, the more prayers a man composes, the worse he will write, unless he works carefully. In order to keep up a sense of the style that is worthy in prayer, the minister ought to own and use a number of liturgical masterpieces, beginning with *The Book of Common Prayer* of the Protestant Episcopal Church. He ought also to saturate his soul in the devotional classics, if only because their language is that of heaven come down to earth.

Among the devotional classics every man has his favorites. Those of the writer include Bunyan's *The Pilgrim's Progress* and *Grace Abounding to the Chief of Sinners*, Augustine's *Confessions*, Bishop Andrewes' *Manual of Private Devotions*, Richard Baxter's *Saints' Everlasting Rest*, and Austin Phelps's *The Still Hour*.

"There is a language of devotion," says J. Oswald Dykes,[1] "in which the young minister does well to steep himself. It has been the product of centuries of devout life. It is not a mosaic of Bible phraseology but it is modeled on Scripture examples and even more on its spirit and tone. It is a rare essence, distilled from the experience of all saints, fragrant with their concentrated devoutness.

"With classic expressions of its literature, which are not numerous, a man would need to be conversant who would catch the mingled dignity and simplicity, depth and sweetness, boldness and reverence, gravity and cheerfulness, warmth and chaste reserve, which befit the temper of Christian piety at its best."

Such is the spirit of the cloister. But if a minister is to pray aright at a funeral he ought also to be an indefatigable pastor. With his people in their homes, and likewise welcoming them one by one at his study, he should rely largely on prayer for the cure of human souls. If he prays often with his people when they are not in distress, he will know how to intercede for them when they stand face to face with the mystery of death.

In short, the minister who lives close to God and human beings will know how to make ready for leadership in prayer at a service of farewell. However brief the time to make ready for a funeral, he will spend most of the passing minutes in preparing to pray.

[1] From *The Christian Minister and His Duties*, p. 142. T. and T. Clark, Edinburgh, 1908.

On the next few pages are a number of funeral prayers. They show how ministers of various types lead sorrowing friends to the mercy seat. The prayers that come first are suitable for the early part of the service. The longer ones are more pastoral. The fifth page has a number of prayers that show what men do at the funeral of a child. Another page gives forms that have been used at the grave.

The purpose in showing these examples is to suggest that the reader start making a collection of his own. The most searching test of any such prayer is the spiritual quality. Does it move the heart Godward? Does it lead the worshiper to lift up his soul? Another test is quiet beauty. In making such a collection, as in assembling funeral poems, the minister should find refreshment for his soul.

The most suggestive and fruitful of the next few pages ought to be the last one. It contains doxologies and benedictions. The difference between the two is worthy of note: the doxology is addressed to God; the benediction, to the people. Each kind of holy words is especially fitting in the sickroom or the funeral service. Nowhere else, even in the Scriptures, can the leader of worship find so much of blessing in so little space as in some of the doxologies and benedictions. In order to use these words aright, the pastor himself ought to be a living benediction.

PRAYERS USED AT FUNERALS

Dearly beloved, seeing it hath pleased Almighty God to take unto Himself the soul of our *brother* departed, let us beseech Him to grant us His Holy Spirit, the Comforter, that our hearts may not be faint or be troubled, but may find in Him their refuge and strength. Let us pray.

Almighty God, whose will is sovereign and whose mercy is boundless, look upon us in our sorrow, and for the sake of Thy dear Son, who Himself was partaker of flesh and blood, enable us to listen to Thy Holy Word, that we through patience and comfort of the Scriptures may have hope; and grant us the consolations of Thy Holy Spirit, that, humbly confessing our manifold sins, we may hold fast the assurance of Thy favor and the hope of life everlasting, through Jesus Christ our Lord. Amen.

[From *The Directory for Public Worship*,
The Presbyterian Church of England.]

✿ ✿ ✿ ✿

Eternal God, our heavenly Father, who lovest us with an everlasting love, and canst turn the shadow of death into the morning: help us now to wait upon Thee with reverent and submissive hearts, that as we read the words of eternal life, we through patience and comfort of the Scriptures may have hope, and be lifted above our darkness and distress into the light and peace of Thy presence: through Jesus Christ, our Lord. Amen.

[From *The Book of Common Order*, 1928,
United Free Church of Scotland.]

✿ ✿ ✿ ✿

O God of Peace, who hast taught us that in returning and rest we shall be saved, in quietness and in confidence shall be our strength; By the power of Thy Spirit lift us, we pray Thee, to Thy presence, where we may be still and know that Thou art God; through Jesus Christ our Lord. Amen.

[From *The Book of Common Prayer*, According to
the Use of the Protestant Episcopal Church.]

✿ ✿ ✿ ✿

O holy Father, whose mercies are from everlasting to everlasting, to Thee alone can Thy children flee for refuge in their afflictions, trusting in the assurance of Thy love. From the grief that burdens our spirits, from the sense of solitude and loss, from the doubt and fainting of the soul in its trouble, we turn to Thee. Strengthen our feeble faith, we implore Thee; comfort our hearts, and by the Gospel of Thy beloved Son speak peace to our souls. Grant this, O heavenly Father, for Jesus' sake. Amen.

[From *The Directory for Public Worship*,
The Presbyterian Church of England.]

☘ ☘ ☘ ☘

Father of all mercies and God of all comfort, who healest the broken in heart and bindest up their wounds, in mercy behold the sorrows of Thy children. Leave them not without comfort, we implore Thee, but sustain them by Thy Holy Spirit, and through His witness in their hearts enable them to rest in Thy fatherly love. Teach them Thy way, and lead them in a plain path. Hear our prayer, for the sake of Thy dear Son our Saviour. Amen.

[From *The Directory for Public Worship*,
The Presbyterian Church of England.]

☘ ☘ ☘ ☘

Grant, O Lord, to all who are bereaved, the spirit of faith and courage, that they may have strength to meet the days to come with steadfastness and patience, not sorrowing as those who have no hope, but in thankful remembrance of Thy great goodness in the past, and in the sure expectation of a joyful reunion in the heavenly places. This we ask in the Name of Jesus Christ our Lord. Amen.

Almighty and eternal God, who amid the changes of this mortal life art always the same, we frail children of earth do humble ourselves in Thy presence. We bow in reverence before Thy judgments, saying, "The Lord gave, and the Lord hath taken away; blessed be the Name of the Lord." In the silence of this hour speak to us of eternal things, and comfort us with the assurance of Thine everlasting love, through Jesus Christ our Lord.

God of all grace, who didst send Thy Son our Saviour Jesus Christ to bring life and immortality to light, most humbly and heartily we give Thee thanks that by His death He destroyed the power of death, and by His glorious resurrection opened the Kingdom of heaven to all believers. Grant us assuredly to know that because He lives we also shall live, and that neither death nor life, nor things present nor things to come, shall be able to separate us from Thy love which is in Him.

Help us now to wait upon Thee with reverent and submissive hearts, that as we read the words of eternal life we through patience and comfort of the Scriptures may have hope, and be lifted above our darkness and distress into the light and peace of Thy presence, through Jesus Christ our Lord. Amen.

[From *The Ordinal and Service Book*,
The Church of Scotland.]

❦ ❦ ❦ ❦

O Lord Jesus Christ, who by Thy death didst take away the sting of death, grant unto us Thy servants so to follow Thee in faith as Thou hast led the way that we may at length fall asleep peacefully in Thee, and awake after Thy likeness, through Thy mercy, who ever livest and reignest with the Father and the Holy Spirit, one God, world without end. Amen.

Father of mercies and God of all comfort, who hast brought life and immortality to light through the Gospel, we thank Thee for the messages from Thy Word and the promises that break upon our vision with the light of heavenly hope. We praise Thee for the assurance that to depart and be with Christ is far better, and that to be absent from the body is to be at home with the Lord, so that our thoughts are not turning downward to the grave but upward toward the glory. We thank Thee that "life is ever lord of death, and love can never lose its own," for since Jesus died and rose again, even so them that fall asleep in Jesus wilt Thou bring with Him, that we all may be forever with the Lord.

We thank Thee for the boundless blessings that attend our earthly pathway; in a world full of anguish our sheltered lives are brightened with sunlight and beauty. We praise Thee for the inspiration of Christian friendships; especially do we thank Thee for the one whose memory we are here to honor. For the gentleness of *his* character, the breadth of *his* sympathies, the power of *his* convictions; for *his* patience and courage, *his* genius for friendship, *his* loyalty to a great tradition; for *his* devotion to Christ and His Church—we give Thee thanks.

Now that for a time we have parted, we beseech Thee to bless the family circle that is severed, and the comrades who are bereft. Grant that we all may be worthy of our friends, and true to those who trust us. Send us back to our tasks with new cheerfulness and hope, gladly to accept whatever Thou dost give us to do or endure. As we wait for the cloudless day to dawn when the shadows shall flee away, give us unquestioning confidence in Thy holy will; and unto Thee shall be the glory forever. Amen.

[Charles R. Erdman.]

Our loving Father, comfortingly look upon us in our sorrow, and abide with us in our loneliness. O Thou who makest no life in vain, and who lovest all that Thou hast made, lift upon us the light of Thy countenance, and give us peace. Amen.

We pray that Thou wilt keep in tender love the life which we shall hold in blessed memory. Help us who continue here to serve Thee with constancy, trusting in Thy promise of eternal life, that hereafter we may be united with Thy blessed children in glory everlasting, through Jesus Christ our Lord. Amen.

[From The Ritual of The Methodist Episcopal Church, 1936.]

✠ ✠ ✠ ✠

Heavenly Father, we thank Thee for that happy Home above, of which the children sing, and for that place of heavenly joy, where children with their unstained hearts grow in stature and beauty amid scenes of peace and blessedness, and where their angels do always behold the face of their Father in heaven.

We thank Thee that for a little space Thou didst grant to Thy servants this gift of Thy love, to be to them now a sanctifying and blessed memory, lifting their thoughts above the things of earth, to that abode where the child of their love is waiting to welcome them home. May this memory and hope remain with them in their hearts, and lead them to the dedication of their lives to Thee, their Father.

Help us all, O God, amid the trials and temptations of this our earthly life, to preserve within us the spirit of little children, for of such is the Kingdom of Heaven. Hear this our prayer for Jesus' sake. Amen.

[From *A New Pulpit Manual*, James Burns, editor.]

✠ ✠ ✠ ✠

Almighty God, the Father of our Lord and Saviour Jesus Christ, in this hour of sorrow, with the burden of our mortality heavy upon us, we bow before Thee. We bless Thy name for the promise of everlasting life which Thou hast given to all who believe on Jesus Christ Thy Son. Open our eyes, we beseech Thee, to behold Him present with us, as He was with sorrowing men and women in the days of His flesh, sharing their grief, comforting them in distress, revealing unto them the Father. So comfort and strengthen our faith in Him Who is the Resurrection and the Life, that neither sorrow nor death shall have dominion over us. . . .

To Thee, O Father, who pitiest Thy children, we commend those on whom this loss most sorely falls. Comfort them, we pray, as Thou alone canst comfort. Be Thou their Friend and their Helper. Grant unto them that even through their tears they may see Thy face and have assurance of Thy love. To all who are here grant Thy grace that we may learn the lessons of Thy providence. So teach us to number our days that we may apply our hearts unto wisdom.

Go with us as we are to lay this body in the ground. Let not our thoughts linger there with the dust of *him* whom we love. Rather do Thou open to us the vision of heavenly places in Christ Jesus, of the assembly of just men made perfect, where they are who have washed their robes and made them white in the blood of the Lamb, and where they ever praise Thee with unclouded vision and undivided love. All this we ask for the sake of Christ our Redeemer. Amen.

[From *The Directory for Public Worship*,
The Presbyterian Church of England.]

✿ ✿ ✿ ✿

O Lord God, Light of the faithful, Strength of the toilers, and Repose of the blessed dead, we remember before Thee all Thy servants who have departed this life in faith and fear, and especially *him* whom Thou hast now taken unto Thyself. For all Thy loving kindness to *him* throughout *his* earthly life we give Thee thanks. We bless Thee that for *him* all sickness and sorrow are ended, that death itself is past, and that *he* has entered into the rest that remaineth for Thy people, through Jesus Christ our Lord.

We beseech Thee that being inspired by the example of those who have gone before, we may run with patience the race that is set before us, looking unto Jesus, the Author and Finisher of our faith, so that when this changeful life shall have passed away we may meet with those whom Thou hast loved, in the Kingdom of Thy glory, through Jesus Christ our Lord.

Father of mercies and God of all comfort, in tender love and mercy, we beseech Thee look on Thy servants who are in sorrow. Enable them to find in Thee their Refuge and Strength, and to know the love of Christ which passeth knowledge, that their faith and hope may be in Him, who by death hath taken away the sting of death, and rising again hath opened the gates of life everlasting.

Now be with us as we follow to the grave the body of our *brother* here departed, not sorrowing as those who have no hope, but believing that as Jesus died and rose again, so them also who sleep in Jesus wilt Thou bring with Him. Amen.

[From *The Ordinal and Service Book*,
The Church of Scotland.]

❈ ❈ ❈ ❈

Almighty and eternal God, we give Thee thanks for all those redeemed by Thy grace, who, having fallen asleep in Jesus, have entered into the rest that remaineth for the children of God.

Especially do we remember Thy grace to this our *brother*, whom Thou hast taken to Thyself. We praise Thee for Thy goodness and mercy to *him*, for guidance bestowed, for strength renewed. We bless Thee for *his* knowledge of Thee, the living and true God, for *his* experience of Thy redeeming grace, and for *his* fellowship with Thy church and people.

Above all do we give thanks because Thou hast granted *him* deliverance from pain and death, and hast brought *him* from the temptations of this life to the inheritance that is incorruptible and undefiled and that fadeth not away.

Give us grace, we beseech Thee, O Lord, to be followers of them who through faith and patience have inherited the promises. Enable us also to endure unto the end, to be more than conquerors through Him that loved us, to whom be glory and praise for ever and ever. Amen.

[From *The Directory for Public Worship*,
The Presbyterian Church of England.]

❧ ❧ ❧ ❧

O Lord, support us all the day long of our troublous life, until the shadows lengthen and the evening comes, and the busy world is hushed, and the fever of life is over, and our work is done. Then in Thy mercy grant us a safe lodging, and a holy rest, and peace at the last; through Jesus Christ our Lord. Amen.

[John Henry Newman.]

❧ ❧ ❧ ❧

O the depth of the riches both of the wisdom and knowledge of God! how unsearchable are his judgments, and his ways past finding out! Rom. 11: 33.

Unto him that is able to do exceeding abundantly above all that we ask or think, according to the power that worketh in us, unto him be glory in the church by Christ Jesus throughout all ages, world without end. Amen. Eph. 3: 20, 21.

Unto the King eternal, immortal, invisible, the only wise God, be honour and glory for ever and ever. Amen. I Tim. 1: 17.

Unto him that is able to keep you from falling, and to present you faultless before the presence of his glory with exceeding joy, to the only wise God our Saviour, be glory and majesty, dominion and power, both now and ever. Amen. Jude 24, 25.

Unto him that loved us, and washed us from our sins in his own blood, and hath made us kings and priests unto God and his Father; to him be glory and dominion for ever and ever. Amen. Rev. 1: 5, 6.

The God of all grace, who hath called us unto his eternal glory by Christ Jesus, after that ye have suffered a while, make you perfect, stablish, strengthen, settle you. To him be glory and dominion for ever and ever. Amen. I Peter 5: 10, 11.

The peace of God, which passeth all understanding, keep your hearts and minds in the knowledge and love of God, and of his Son Jesus Christ; and the blessing of God Almighty, the Father, the Son, and the Holy Ghost, be amongst you and remain with you always. Amen. (Derived from Phil. 4: 7.)

The peace of our Lord Jesus Christ be with you. Amen.

The grace of our Lord Jesus Christ be with your spirit. Amen. Gal. 6: 18.

The familiar benedictions are II Cor. 13: 14; Heb. 13: 20, 21; Num. 6: 24-26.

Informational Readings

Blackwood, Andrew W., *The Fine Art of Public Worship*. The Cokesbury Press, 1939. Chapters VIII, IX.

Noyes, Morgan P., Editor, *Prayers for Services*. Charles Scribner's Sons, 1934.

Suter, John W., Editor, *The Book of English Collects*. Harper & Brothers, 1941.

X. The Formal Obituary

AMONG all the things that the minister does at a funeral, probably the least vital is the reading of the obituary. It is also the most questionable. At best the obituary is a concession to local custom. At worst the practice is far from Christian. The obituary may be a tissue of half-truths or lies. But it need never be so.

When the pastor has his heart's desire, there is no obituary. The reading of it, however brief, consumes time that is precious. The assembling of the facts may not prove easy. The phrasing of them in good literary form is much more difficult. If someone else does the writing, there may be too much or else too little. If commonplace, the production will sound flat. If well written, it may not be religious.

Nevertheless, it is possible to secure a worthy obituary. In order to prepare it aright, or else advise someone else what to include, the minister needs to ascertain facts that will later help him in making ready for the vital parts of the service. After he has thought about the obituary he is more likely to remember that in the approaching funeral there should be the human factor, as well as the divine. Into the facts as they are to appear in the obituary he can read a wealth of meaning. Shining through them all he can see the goodness of God.

The preparation of the statement calls for care in composition. There should be no attempt at appraisal of the departed, and no suggestion of a eulogy. As a rule there need be only a single, short paragraph. If the obituary is factual rather than panegyrical, it may seem cold and dull. If so, the fault may be partly in the reading. If the minister knows how to use words for the glory of God, the facts may shine.

In the family circle there may be someone who can write the obituary. If so, the minister should delegate the privilege. In such a case he leaves the content to the discretion of the writer, or else he suggests some such items as those that appear below. At the funeral, before the pastor reads the obituary, he says, "The following statement has been prepared by a friend in the family circle." If the minister himself is the author, there need be no word of explanation. In the obituary the facts are much as follows:

> The full name of the departed.
> The names of *his* father and mother.
> The place and date of *his* birth.
> The schools from which *he* graduated.
> The facts about *his* marriage (the last, if two).
> The facts about *his* children.
> The facts about *his* church life.
> The facts about *his* lifework.
> The facts about *his* military service.
> The facts about *his* fraternal affiliations.
> The time and the place of *his* death.
> The words of *his* favorite Scripture verse.
> The first stanza of *his* favorite hymn.

If the service is to include a poem this may come immediately after the obituary, thus leading up to the pastor's brief message or to the main prayer. By selecting certain hymns, as in choosing the text and the Scripture lessons, the minister can indirectly say about the departed anything that is true and worthy. Still there need be no mention of his name, except at the beginning of the obituary.

For instance, at the funeral of a schoolmaster who has been deeply beloved by successive generations of boys, the pastor might use part of the poem written by Matthew Arnold in praise of his father, Thomas Arnold, headmaster of Rugby School for Boys. Before the reading there should be a few words of explanation. Even then, the poem might be clear only to people with a rich cultural background. The words are difficult to interpret:

"O strong soul, by what shore
Tarriest thou now? For that force,
Surely, has not been left vain!
Somewhere, surely, afar,
In the sounding labor-house vast
Of being, is practiced that strength,
Zealous, beneficent, firm!

"Prompt, unwearied, as here!
Still thou upraisest with zeal
The humble good from the ground,
Sternly repressest the bad!
Still, like a trumpet, dost rouse
Those who with half-open eyes
Tread the border-land dim
Twixt vice and virtue; reviv'st,
Succorest!—this was thy work;
This was thy life upon earth.

"We were weary, and we
Fearful, and we in our march
Fain to drop down and to die.
Still thou turnedst, and still
Beckonedst the trembler, and still
Gavest the weary thy hand.

"Strengthen the wavering line,
Stablish, continue our march,
On, to the bound of the waste,
On, to the City of God."

Sometimes the indirect obituary assumes a striking form. At the Webb School in Bell Buckle, Tennessee, the idol of the boys was one of the founders, John Webb. Largely because of his influence as a teacher, more Rhodes scholars

are said to have come from that school than from any other
in America. When he died at an advanced age the funeral
services were not sad. As they culminated at the grave and
the body was being lowered to its last resting place, a group
of his boys sang the hymn that he liked best: "O Love That
Wilt Not Let Me Go."

At the funeral of a man less distinguished, but equally
loyal to Christ and his loved ones, one might read the following tribute from a saintly widow in the second or the
third century. If so, a word of explanation would be in
order. The inscription appears in one of the catacombs at
Rome. The translation is by Gilbert Murray. It has been
slightly altered:

> "Pass hence, beloved, at the call divine,
>   Leaving the path we twain have trod;
> Pass, and the soul that still is one with thine
>   Through grief shall learn the way to God."

After the services are over, the pastor may send the family
a copy of the obituary, the poem, or whatever in the service
has been most distinctive and memorable. It would be easy
to hand the token in person before leaving the cemetery,
but there is some advantage in waiting until the morrow and
then writing a note by hand, enclosing a visible evidence of
the pastor's love and esteem for his friend who has fallen
asleep.

The minister who day after day receives letters from near
and far may not know how much it means in many a home
to receive a personal message from the pastor. That is one of
the countless ways in which kindness should be God's messenger of comfort. According to "Tintern Abbey," by Wordsworth, "the still, sad music of humanity" is never sweeter
than in

> ". . . that best portion of a good man's life,
>   His little, nameless, unremembered acts
> Of kindness and of love. . . ."

XI. The Elusive Poem

THE writer has long been a lover of poetry. But he questions the wisdom of using it constantly in sermons and at funerals. As a rule such effusions are of a low order as literature. Sometimes they are not delivered with distinction. Occasionally they are not clear. If so, they tend to distract. Hence there is a saying that the minister quotes poetry to please himself, not to help the people.

These observations have nothing to do with the right sort of verse. To every minister there comes a time when he is eager to lay his hands on a bit of poetry that will voice a certain mood. If only to brighten the heart of the funeral service, he may wish to read a few golden words from a master of song. The fact is that the minister with taste would read funeral poems more frequently if he could discover exactly what he desires.

At present we are to consider what a man should look for in such a poem. Later we shall think about the wisdom of the minister's having a homemade anthology. We shall assume that he already knows his hymnal better than any other book save the Bible, and that he enjoys using materials which he finds for himself. What, then, should he have in mind as he starts on his quest?

A funeral poem should be short. In the original form it may not be so. But unless the minister can use only a part, he should make some other selection. Within two or three stanzas, perhaps only one, he should be able to bring out a luminous truth, and thus give a glimpse of heavenly glory.

If it seems wise to use a part of a long poem, such as *In Memoriam,* there should be no explanation or apology. If the fragment is clear, and if it contributes to the end in view, all is well. While it would be possible to carry the idea of brevity too far, one often feels that, whether in the pulpit or at a funeral, a poem would be twice as effective if it were half as long.

But mere lack of length is not enough. There must be positive merit. It is not easy to tell what sets a worthy poem apart from prosaic rhymes. Perhaps the nearest approach is to say that a poem for use at a funeral ought to sing. The technical name for this kind of verse is a lyric. When every heart is sad, the call is for words that sing.

As a rule the poem should be fairly new to the hearers. With a hymn the reverse is often the case. In the hour of grief, if there is singing, the best is likely to be what the friends have long known and loved. The same is true of the readings from the Bible. But if there is a poem, it should be so new and pleasing that it will illumine what might otherwise be a dark corner.

The chief fact about any funeral poem is the spiritual quality. It should sing about the ways of God in the soul of man. This quality is what our twentieth-century verse most lacks. As our neighbor Albert Einstein often says about present-day music, "Much of it has no message, because there is no soul." Where some of the Victorian bards sang about the being of God and the spirit of man, the meaning of death and the hope of heaven, contemporary poets often excel in describing the petty things of earth. This is why the larger number of the poems in the anthology appended to this book are not of recent birth.

On the whole there is a vast deal of religious verse that the minister should know. Like Phillips Brooks, he may not often quote poetry in his sermons, but he should have it ever singing in his soul. He can saturate his spirit in the work of one bard after another, until he too becomes a master in the use of words. Then he will be able to read and pray out of a heart that is a wellspring of beauty.

The man who loves poetry has a soul that feels. Again he is like Phillips Brooks, who could see the promise of goodness in the heart of a little child and hear the song of the angels in a bit of fugitive verse. If in these coming days our sons keep close to the hearts of human beings, and at the same time grow in their love of beautiful words, the ministry of tomorrow should include more than a few pastors like Phillips Brooks.

There is no short cut to this kind of excellence. A man who has not as yet learned to recognize poetry when he hears it singing cannot acquire a love for the best in verse by dipping into anthologies. The richest of them, such as *The Oxford Book of Christian Verse,* should grace the shelves of a man's study. As for the "poems" that appeared in some of the older books made up for preachers, the words seldom sang. In a work that might be known as *An Up-to-Date Funeral Made to Order,* there were eighty-seven pieces of "poetry." Only two or three were able to meet the tests before us now.

THE PASTOR'S ANTHOLOGY

The part of wisdom, therefore, is for each pastor to start making his own anthology. At first he may keep in one place all sorts of religious verse; but when this part of his files begins to overflow he should set off by themselves the songs that are especially appropriate for funerals.

The best way to start a collection is to read poetry. If the quality is high, it does not matter much what the minister reads in his hours of rest. A good deal of the poetry need not be directly religious. But it should be verse about whose beauty there is no question.

For a while the minister can saturate his soul in the writings of a certain poet. It may be Dante, Milton, or Wordsworth. While the poems of Wordsworth are uneven, they contain much that the minister should know and love. In order to do so, he should read the choicest portions again and again. Better still, he should commit many of the golden words to memory.

It is good, likewise, to know the best of modern poetry, such as the work of Edwin A. Robinson or Emily Dickinson. Here too the minister finds snatches of beautiful song, though ofttimes little that is religious. In almost every magazine of the better sort there are sure to be a number of poems. Once in a while there is something that the reader wishes to preserve. If the windows of a man's soul are ever open, it is amazing how many words of beauty will keep blowing in from near and far.

After all this labor there may seem to be little fruit. With few exceptions the golden portions of Wordsworth or Milton are too long for the purpose now in view. With still fewer exceptions the excerpts from Robert Browning or John Donne will not be clear to lay friends whose favorite rhymester is Eddie Guest. No matter how lofty the song, and how much it moves the heart of the minister, if the words will not sing their way at once into the souls of the people for whom the service is being planned, the poem should have no place in the funeral service.

Nevertheless, there is value as well as joy in the quest for words that sing. Such a course of reading at home is sure to increase the sense of rhythm. That in turn affects the choice of words and the form of sentences. At Harvard, Dean L. B. R. Briggs used to say that by following a man's paper work for three or four minutes he could tell whether or not the writer had ever studied Anglo-Saxon. In like manner, by listening to a man's spoken words, especially in prayer, the discerning spirit knows whether or not the minister is a lover of poetry.

Whenever the reader discovers a treasure in verse, much of the joy comes through making it his own. One way of doing so is to write out the words and put them away with others of their kind. In the storehouse the poem may nestle for years without being used. But every once in a while the minister will take out his treasures and renew the rapture that filled his soul when he first discovered these words that sing.

The sort of poetry that a man uses at a funeral is a test of his culture. His homemade anthology likewise reveals him as a human being. After the aged minister has gone home to his God, when his loved ones turn through his papers to decide which ones to preserve, they will be wise if they keep treasures of three sorts: the pastoral prayers that he has composed, the loving letters that he has received, and the spiritual poems that he has collected if not composed. Where else on earth, save in his Bible and hymnbook, can those who tarry on in the flesh come so close to the inner spirit of the father who has fallen asleep?

Collected Poems

Cecil, Lord David, Editor, *The Oxford Book of Christian Verse.* Oxford University Press, 1940.

Clark, T. C., Compiler, *Poems for Life.* Willett, Clark & Company, 1941.

Hill, Caroline M., Editor, *The World's Great Religious Poetry.* The Macmillan Company, 1923.

XII. The Funeral Message

Is IT wise to have a short funeral sermon? In each parish the answer depends largely on local custom. In one community every person expects a sermon. In an occasional Dutch congregation the tradition calls for a message that lasts thirty minutes or even longer. In another neighborhood a funeral sermon is rare. In general there is more likely to be such a message in a rural community than in a city, and in a small congregation than in a large one. But there are all sorts of exceptions.

The writer does not recommend a return to the practice of preaching at a funeral. But he feels that the minister should be ready to give a brief message whenever that seems best. In any community he should follow the best local custom. He should be especially careful to honor the most worthy traditions of his congregation. Early in each new pastorate it is good to confer with the senior elder or deacon. The response to one inquiry of the sort was as follows:

"Your predecessor almost always had something to say at a funeral. The people heard him with satisfaction, largely because they loved him. He was a man with a heart like that of God. The preceding pastor almost never spoke at a funeral. But the people said that his reading of the Scriptures and his prayers were more than enough to fill the service with light and glory. As for the neighboring ministers, most of them preach; the best of them do not. In every case do as you deem best."

In that parish the decision was not to have any funeral sermon unless there was a request from the family. With them the minister would invariably raise the question. If they thought of a funeral in terms of the former pastor who always spoke, that was the sort of service most likely to do them good. If they preferred the simple ways of the earlier minister, there was no formal message. In time the new leader began to create traditions of his own.

Before he makes any such decision, the pastor should pray. If he follows the guidance of the Holy Spirit, there may be no speaking at nine funerals out of ten, but there may be a brief sermon once in a while. "Where the Spirit of the Lord is, there is liberty" (II Cor. 3: 17). When the minister is in doubt, he had better preach. If he believes in the power of the spoken word, and if he has a healing balm for broken hearts, he may at times be glad that local custom allows him to bring words of comfort to those in distress.

Why has the funeral message been largely discontinued? The reference here is not to problem funerals; we shall think about them later. In the farewell service for a saint of God, why should there be no sermon? Doubtless because such a message in the past has not always been well prepared and properly delivered. Often it has been too long, too trite, too dull. It has seemed conventional, lifeless, impractical. In the worst sense of the word, the funeral sermon has been other-worldly.

When a minister should be his best self, he is likely to do his worst work. Time after time he may say much the same things in much the same ways and with much the same boredom. Such "sermonizing" is worth little more than it costs, which may be next to nothing. A man might as well use his breath in blowing on his hands when they are cold. If such a description seems harsh, let any pastor review some of his own preaching at funerals. Seldom does the good man have an opportunity to prepare a real message.

At the other extreme is the old-fashioned sensationalist. In most parts of the land, fortunately, he is only a local tradition. In a certain village of the Middle West a self-trained lay preacher was noted for his funeral oratory. From far and near curious folk would come to listen spellbound as he let his fancy roam through the corridors of the home on high. Despite the fact that his effusions were certain to be lengthy, the services had to be held in the largest church. As the lurid discourse went on and on, everyone kept waiting for the grand finale, which was sure to be thrilling.

For instance, take the funeral of a little girl who had met a tragic death. Near the end of the funeral discourse, in which he had recounted the details of the accident, he began to picture her as leaning from the window of her little room in the heavenly home. Through the minister, as God's messenger of mercy, she was sending words of cheer to her mother and father, her brother and sister, as well as each little playmate or friend.

Naturally there was an emotional upheaval. The man in the pulpit was so schooled that he could talk while he wept. But as he pointed to one person after another and spoke of the tender ties that had bound each heart to the little girl, the people lost control of themselves. There were constant sobs and occasional shrieks. From those nerve-racking experiences some of the victims doubtless never fully recovered. Fortunately, that kind of exhibitionism is as rare today at a funeral as in a revival service. Almost without exception, ministers now are free from such excesses.

THE SPIRIT OF THE MESSAGE

If there is a funeral message it should be worthy. What, then, are the practical tests? The most important one relates to the purpose. It is pastoral rather than evangelistic. The aim is to comfort the friends who mourn, that is, to strengthen their hearts in God. In a case where the minister can find no ground for Christian comfort, he is fortunate if he is not expected to speak.

"Whenever you preach at a funeral," said a Southern gentlewoman to the pastor of a neighboring church, "you always try to bring the comfort of God." The minister expressed his thanks, and then he asked, "Pardon me, but what else could I attempt to do?" "I scarcely know," was the reply, "but you are the only clergyman in town who always uses a funeral service as a means of bringing Christian comfort."

The spirit of such a message is like that of the meditation prior to the Lord's Supper. In each case, if there is anything approaching a sermon, it should be short and full of meaning as well as of light and beauty. The appeal should be mainly to the heart, not the head. In this respect many a funeral message misses the mark. It is coldly intellectual. It attempts to prove what the heart already feels. There is little appeal to what Bunyan calls the ear-gate. Such a sermon would be better if left unspoken.

The funeral message ought to be short. Even at the services in memory of a lay officer in the church, ten minutes may be the upper limit for the sermon. As a rule six or eight minutes should prove ample. Still there need be no appearance of haste. There is no time for a preamble. The occasion calls for only a single truth. That one should shine. If it is about "Heaven as Home," there need be no proof, no argument, no elaboration. The reliance should be on the words of the Lord Jesus: "In my Father's house are many mansions" (John 14: 2). In terms of today one can use a paraphrase: "In the Father's home there are many rooms."

Whatever the minister says at a funeral should be interesting. In this respect the call may be for something like a junior sermon. When grief fills the hearts of men and women, they often become as meek as little boys and girls. There is a clear pathway into every heart. The door is open wide. Without taking time to arouse interest, the pastor begins at once to use divine truth in meeting human needs. From the opening words to the closing syllable, his heart is speaking to their hearts. "Deep soundeth unto deep."

Think of a specific case. A boy twelve years of age had always been frail. He was the only child, and because of his birth there could never be another babe. For the lad's sake the parents had moved to the suburbs, where they had built a home, so that he could play in the sunshine. Gradually he was growing more robust. But one morning, while taking his bath, he was electrocuted. He died at once. In making ready for the funeral the pastor found that the father and the mother wished a brief message.

The question was how to bring them comfort. If the minister had stressed the facts in the case there would have been needless anguish. At last he determined to start with the text: "The broad places of the city shall be filled with boys and girls playing in the broad places thereof" (Zech. 8: 5, in the orginal). Strictly interpreted, that text does not refer to heaven. Nevertheless, the striking words enabled the pastor to make clear what was in his heart. He spoke about the City of God as a place of beauty where the heavenly Father knows how to make a growing boy feel at home from the very first. In the Father's house everyone is well and strong, being filled with the spirit of eternal youth.

The appeal should be mainly to the imagination. In a few minutes there is time for only a single truth. It should be luminous. It should appeal to the friends where they are, in a home that seems to have lost its reason for being. The message should lead them to lift up their hearts unto God. The healing grace is in him, and in his promises.

Since the time is short, there should be little exegesis, and no argument. Even if there were time for a logical discourse about immortality, the hearers would be in no condition to think hard and long. But still their eyes may be open, perhaps as never before. Both in the text and in the words that follow there should be something for them to see and feel. There should also be something tangible that they will remember. Whatever the circumstances, there is always some word from God for those who need him sorely.

For example, at the funeral of an aged farmer the dominant note may be that of the harvest. If the deceased has been a godly leader, an officer in the church, the minister can have the people rise to sing,

> " 'Come, ye thankful people, come,
> Raise the song of harvest home.' "

In the sermon the text may be one of the many that speak about death in terms of gathering the harvest, e.g., Gen. 15: 15 or Job 5: 26. Ideally, the resulting message should be somewhat like a lyric poem.

The funeral sermon ought to have a beauty all its own. Throughout the service, from the organ prelude to the benediction, and beyond that to what is done at the grave, everything should move in the realm of mystic beauty. In all that the Bible teaches about the death of the believer there is naught save beauty. Everything relating to ugliness is of the earth earthy, and that has all been done away through the death of Christ. To be in keeping with the facts, the farewell message should be radiant with the beauty of the Lord.

From one funeral to another the shades of beauty should vary. In a bed of pansies the appeal to the heart is not the same as in a bank of climbing roses. In a farewell service for a little girl the tone color should be different from that when her grandfather has fallen asleep at the end of golden years. "There is one glory of the sun, and another glory of the moon, and another glory of the stars: for one star differeth from another star in glory. So also is the resurrection of the dead" (I Cor. 15: 41, 42).

THE CHOICE OF THE TEXT

At least among friends who love the Lord, the easiest way to start well is to quote a text. Nothing else on earth is so sure to touch and move the heart as a few words from mother's Bible. Just as in singing the hymn "Holy, Holy, Holy," the first six notes of the melody sound the motif of it all, so in a funeral message the opening words from the

Bible should voice the dominant theme. As long as any hearer lives, these words from the Book should keep ringing through his soul.

It may not prove easy to select a passage that is sure to meet the needs of the approaching hour. In one case the text may come to mind without effort. Again, the pastor must search and be patient. But if he knows the Book, and if he waits upon the Lord, in due time the text will appear. When once it knocks at the door, there need be no question about credentials. Neither should there be any thought about a second choice. When once the golden text has found its way into the heart of the preacher, the work of preparing the message has well begun.

As a rule the text should be short. Provided it makes complete sense, the shorter the text, the more it will shine. For instance, if the friends are in love with the sea, they will respond to words about hope as "an anchor of the soul" (Heb. 6: 19). In such a case the idea is to interpret the figure as it sets forth the facts, and then to speak of the facts in the light of the figure. The reference is to the olden time when every vessel of any size had sails.

When a large ship drew near to a harbor that was difficult to enter, the captain would send a seaman ahead in a little boat. Within the bay he would drop the anchor, to which was attached a rope extending back to the ship. Then little by little the sailors on board would draw the vessel safely into the harbor. Thus it should be in the Christian life. Within the haven our Forerunner, Jesus Christ, has gone to drop the anchor. Day by day we should be drawing nearer to the time when we shall be with him beyond the reach of earthly storms. Meanwhile we should work out our own salvation, with fear and trembling.

As a rule the text should be more nearly self-evident. If it is not clear and luminous, one should make it so with a few simple sentences; otherwise, it is better to choose some passage that is more obvious. If the words are in the form of a question, it should be clear. For instance, "If a man die, shall he live again?" (Job 14: 14). Whatever the text, there is little time for interpretation. In other sorts of preaching there is a place for careful instruction, but in a funeral sermon the chosen words should shine in their own light.

The text should be striking. It should arrest attention, and fix itself at once in the memory. Even if the friends are all worn out, after weeks of anxious waiting followed by hours of frenzied activity, they should respond to a striking text. So it ought to be in the funeral of a soldier: "If this earthly tent is taken down, we have a building of God, a house not made with hands, eternal in the heavens" (II Cor. 5: 1, in the original). The figure may be that of a soldier who for months has been living in a tent. At last the call comes to fold up the tent and sail home.

Such a text appeals to the imagination. It makes the hearer think of death as the supreme adventure. He should look forward to the hour when he too shall hear the call, "Westward-ho!" If there were time for a teaching sermon it might be about the resurrection of the body or, rather, the glory of the heavenly abode. But since the time is brief, all that the minister can do is to leave in the waiting heart the picture of the life everlasting as the home of the warrior.

In the classic chapter about the life to come there are many striking texts. One of them speaks about dying as putting off earthly garments, and about entrance into the other world as putting on heavenly attire. "This corruptible must put on incorruption, and this mortal must put on immortality" (I Cor. 15: 53).

When such words start to sing in the hearer's soul they will suggest to him far more than the minister has time to say. They should help the man in sorrow to feel sure that from a mortal body, with all its frailties and shortcomings, the loved one has gone to be with the Father God. What He has in store for his children in the world to come no person here can begin to tell. But this we know: the One who fashioned our present bodies is able to prepare something better by far in a world where sin never dares to enter. He knows how to make heaven seem like home, and how to make us worthy to dwell with him and his saints forevermore.

THE FORM OF THE MESSAGE

The form of any funeral sermon must depend in part on the length of time that the minister has for preparation. If in a single day he must speak at two or three funerals, each of which calls for a sermon of a different kind, obviously he cannot make ready as he desires. But in the farewell service for a beloved officer in the church, who has been wasting away for weeks, there is every reason why the pastor should be prepared.

The style of the message should be that of quiet charm. If everything else in the service has a beauty not of earth, the pastor's sermon ought also to be

"Instinct with loveliness, and sweet and rare,
The perfect emblem of its Maker's care."

Especially should he be watchful about the first few sentences. They should flow from the text and have much the same tone color. In fact, the entire message should have a pleasing rhythm. When the heart of the pastor is being moved, his words ought to have a rhythm like that of the King James Bible. So they will if he knows how to write and speak.

The effectiveness of the funeral sermon depends much upon the delivery. If the services are in a private home, and if the friends are seated in another room, there is no reason why he should not read the most vital parts of the message. But in the sanctuary, or whenever the members of the family are looking up into the face of their pastor and friend, with the hope of catching a glimpse of light from God, there ought to be no glancing down at a notebook. Especially since the sermon is brief and simple, one should be able to talk without any "helps."

In a funeral message the voice ought to be audible but it should never seem loud. The rate of utterance should be deliberate without seeming to be slow. At times the way of speaking should attain distinction. If ever on earth a man is able to serve as a herald of the King, it should be in the presence of death. The need is evident, as the friends look to him for the light that he alone can bring. The message is in his heart, for it has come from the Book. All that he needs now is unction from the Most High God.

From one funeral to another, at least within the congregation, there should be a wholesome variety of messages. If at times the minister follows a familiar trail, the people will understand. But in view of the manifold needs of human hearts, and the boundless resources within the Bible, there seldom needs to be any sameness that will call attention to itself. In order to keep from saying much the same things again and again, the pastor ought to form the habit of preparing messages to meet human needs.

The current name for this kind of preaching is the "life situation sermon." While the name is new, the idea is not. Some of us have been doing this kind of sermonic work for years. We prefer to call it "divine power for human needs." Whatever the title, such preaching is in order whenever there is a call for a funeral message. If any minister wishes to become a master in the art of preparing "life situation sermons," the secret is simple. Live by faith, and learn by doing.

XIII. The Sermonic Seed Plot

IN A parish where every funeral calls for a brief message, how does the minister find his materials? Partly by preaching from the Bible, and also by being forehanded. No matter how many calls there may be, and how many people are present at almost every funeral, there is always something new to say. The pastor needs to think of only one sermon at a time. For that one he should trust in the God who has stood by him before.

Ofttimes the minister scarcely knows how he first discovered the text that leads to the funeral sermon. The seed thought may have come during one of the visits at the bedside of the dying friend, or else in the later interview with the family. The idea may have emerged while they were telling him the facts for the obituary. Just as in a coal country every boy knows the meaning of the "blossom" on the hillside, so in our calling the minister often says to himself: "If I dig into that bank I shall get what I need." All that he finds necessary is a "lead."

Sometimes the sermonic idea has to do with the season of the year. If the time is just before Christmas or Easter, the thought of the Incarnation or the Resurrection will help the friends to find peace in the face of the last great mystery. During the spring one can speak about the seedtime, and in the autumn there is the glory of the harvest. In the depths of winter, everyone can behold "The Gospel in the Snow." It affords a way of contact between the sorrowing hearts and the God who sends the snow.

It is good, also, to consider the lifework of the deceased. Without descending to personalities, the minister can speak

144

of religion and the life everlasting in terms of the builder or the athlete, the soldier or the sailor, the musician or the traveling man, the schoolmaster or the housemother. Again, the facts about the departed may suggest the crossing of a river or the sailing of a ship, the moving to a new home or the return to an old one, the coming of sleep or the sowing of seed for the eternal harvest.

When once the facts about the deceased have suggested the trail that the minister is to follow, his problem should be transformed into an opportunity. For instance, take the idea of a voyage. This is how the truth shone out in a sermon by an old-fashioned preacher who loved to journey through Eastern waters:

"We make too much of death. We do not dwell enough on the soul and its ongoing might. As one sails the Mediterranean, round whose shores much that is greatest in history has taken place, one shrinks from leaving it. Then too the sea contracts toward the west; the shores gather together; in the way of the ongoing mariner the straits are narrow; apparently they are impassable; they are like the end of a man's life.

"But as you advance, the illusion vanishes The straits are wide enough for the mightiest ship. On past the great rocks at the portal, your ship goes out into the vaster sea. From the horizon comes the call of loved ones, and the tender welcome home.

"Such is a man's voyage on the sea of time. In the narrow passage there is room for the greatest soul. Let him go forward in confidence and hope. Beyond is the Infinite, and out into it the soul is moving to find the welcome of the Father's love and the light of his eternal home."

In this kind of semipoetic preaching a man should be on his guard. Otherwise he may follow his fancy and depart from good taste. For example, think of the funeral service in memory of a church officer who for years had been worthy of note for loyalty and meekness. The choice of the text was worthy: "Well done, good and faithful servant" (Matt. 25: 23). But the dominant figure was open to question. The minister had recently returned from a trip to the Northwest, and he spoke about the departed in terms of "Old Faithful." Some of those present could not see the resemblance between the layman who had been notable for humility and a geyser that intermittently spouts hot water.

THE SEED PLOT

The minister is less likely to depart from good taste if he lets the seed thought grow for weeks or months before he brings it out in public. Whenever an idea relating to death or the hereafter comes into mind, the part of wisdom is to put the seed thought away to mature. In the homiletical garden the idea may grow for years. When at last the need arises, the resulting message will have back of it all that long brooding. In such a case the work of preparation may call for only a little time and energy.

The following suggestions have to do with starting a seed plot for funeral sermons. In any one example the writer could indicate how he would deal with the germinal thought. But such a development might deprive someone else of the joy that comes through thinking for himself. If any minister wishes to find satisfaction in the hours of study, he should use his intellectual muscles. Then the funeral message will come chiefly from the Book, and will meet the needs of burdened hearts.

After he becomes accustomed to working this way, any thoughtful pastor can make a seedbed of his own. Culture of such a garden will enrich his whole ministry and make him more Christlike.

The Funeral of a Child

I Sam. 1: 28a.	The Giving of a Child to God.
II Sam. 12: 23c.	The Hope of a Reunion in Heaven.
Isa. 11: 6c.	The Influence of a Little Child.

Isa. 40: 11.	The Shepherd with His Lambs.
Matt. 18: 2.	The Lover of Little Children.
Matt. 19: 14.	The Friend of Little Children.

Of a Boy or a Girl

II Kings 4: 26c.	The Death of a Growing Boy.
Zech. 8: 5.	The Joys of Children in Heaven.
Luke 8: 52.	The Meaning of Death as Sleep.

Of a Youth or a Maiden

Gen. 22: 12.	The Love of a Father for His Son.
I Sam. 20: 18b.	The Vacant Chair in the Home.
Job 1: 21.	The Grief of a Father for His Sons.
Eccl. 12: 1.	The Meaning of a Young Man's Religion.
Luke 7: 14.	The Sympathy of the Lord Jesus.
I John 2: 14b.	The Glory of Young Manhood.

Of One of Middle Age

Job. 19: 25a.	The Hope of a Personal Resurrection.
Ps. 90: 12.	The Passing of the Years.
Matt. 11: 28-30.	The Gift of Rest for the Soul.
Matt. 12: 20.	The Compassion of the Lord Jesus.
Matt. 20: 12b.	The Laborers in God's Vineyard.
John 11: 25, 26.	The Giver of Life Everlasting.
John 14: 27.	The Secret of the Untroubled Heart.
I Cor. 15: 58.	The Power of Christian Hope.
Rev. 14: 13.	The Reward of Work Done for God.

Of One Who Is Old

Gen. 5: 24.	The Joys of Walking with God.
Gen. 15: 15.	The Gathering of the Heavenly Harvest.
Num. 23: 10b.	The Death of the Godly Man.
Ps. 90: 17.	The Beauty of God's Older Children.
Ps. 91: 16.	The Glory of a Godly Old Age.
Luke 2: 29.	The Prayer of an Aged Believer.
Phil. 1: 21.	The Joys of Being with the Lord.
II Tim. 4: 7, 8.	The Faith of a Christian Veteran.

Of One Who Has Suffered Long

Deut. 33: 27a.	The Secret of Security in God.
Job 1: 21.	The Afflictions of a Godly Man.
Ps. 16: 11.	The Joys of the Life to Come.
Rom. 8: 18.	The Contrast Between Earth and Heaven.
Rom. 8: 28.	The Basis of Christian Optimism.
II Cor. 4: 7.	The Glory of Earthen Vessels.
Rev. 7: 14.	The Cleansing Power of Christ.
Rev. 7: 17.	The Felicity of the Redeemed.

Of One Who Has Been Friendly

I Sam. 18: 1.	The Pattern of Abiding Friendship.
II Sam. 1: 26.	The Glory of Human Friendship.
John 11: 11b.	The Friend of the Master.
John 15: 15.	The Meaning of Religion as Friendship.

Of a Pious Father

Gen. 18: 19.	The Best Thing About a Good Father.
Ex. 20: 12.	The Way to Honor a Father.
I Kings 2: 2, 3a.	The Spirit of a Father's Loyalty.
II Kings 2: 9c.	The Mantle of a Father's Service.
Ps. 103: 13.	The Sympathy of the Father God.
Isa. 38: 1b.	The Way to Prepare for Death.
John 14: 2.	The Hospitality of Heaven.
Heb. 12: 1, 2a.	The Inspiration from the Departed.

Of a Godly Mother

Prov. 31: 30, 31.	The Bible Picture of a Godly Mother.
Isa. 66: 13.	The Loving Kindness of Mother's God.
John 14: 2.	The Welcome to the Heavenly Home.
II Tim. 1: 5.	The Influence of a Pious Mother.

Of a Godly Farmer

Job 5: 26.	The Farmer's Hope of Heaven.
Ps. 1: 3.	The Fruitfulness of a Godly Life.

Micah 6: 8.	The Religion of a Farmer.
John 12: 24.	The Seed Corn of Heaven.
I Cor. 15: 20.	The Beginning of the Eternal Harvest.

Of a Christian Businessman

Matt. 6: 19, 20.	The Treasures of a Good Man's Heart.
Matt. 25: 21.	The Rewards of Faithful Service.
Phil. 1: 21.	The Inventory of a Good Man's Life.
James 4: 14b.	The Mist on God's Mountain.

Of Some Other Friends

I Sam. 20: 3c.	A Victim of Foul Play.
Mal. 2: 5-7.	The Pastor of the Church.
Matt. 25: 23.	The Religion of the Average Man.
Matt. 25: 34.	The Rewards of Christian Kindness.
John 11: 3.	The Brother in the Christian Home.
John 11: 28.	The Sister in the Godly Home.
Acts 6: 5b.	The Religion of a Deacon.
I Peter 5: 4.	The Elder in the Church.
Dan. 12: 3.	The Rewards of the Godly Teacher.
(R. V., margin)	

A Cluster of Golden Texts

Ps. 23: 6.	The Joys of the Heavenly Home.
Ps. 116: 15.	The Death of God's Saints.
Ps. 127: 2b.	The Sleep of God's Beloved.
Mal. 3: 17.	The Jewels of the Lord.
Matt. 6: 20.	The Treasures of God's Children.
II Cor. 5: 4.	The Garments of Immortality.
I Tim. 4: 8.	The Rewards of Godliness.
I Tim. 6: 19.	The Foundations of Life Eternal.
Heb. 13: 14.	The City of the Redeemed.
Rev. 21: 4.	The City Without Tears.
Rev. 21: 25.	The Gates of the Heavenly City.
Rev. 22: 5.	The City of Everlasting Light.

XIV. The Sunlit Grave

THE funeral services ought to reach their climax at the grave. All that has gone before should lead up to the final emphasis on the resurrection of the body and the life everlasting. In this assurance everyone present should join. On all sides are the resting places of departed friends. To the redeemed children of God even the gloomiest tombstones ought to serve as emblems of eternal life. It was so in the catacombs at Rome.

At the cemetery the setting is usually one of beauty. The place of burial is likely to be among the hills. Here and there are trees. On every hand there is grass, and in the summer there are flowers. Far in the distance may be a river, which makes one think of the trumpet sounding for Bunyan's Pilgrim. Perhaps the sun is about to set. In all God's outer world everything saith, "Glory!"

Despite the beauty of the background, the services are sometimes disappointing. Occasionally they are almost pagan. More often they are perfunctory. If there is dignity, there may be coldness, as well as stiffness. The prevailing spirit may be that of unreality. The burial rites over a saint may be the same as for a scoundrel. In recent years, however, there has been a marked improvement. If at times there is still something unseemly, it is doubtless due to lack of taste or of proper training.

Thus far we have assumed that the minister in charge of the services elsewhere should also be God's spokesman at the grave. Some books suggest that he ask to be excused. If that is necessary, because the parish is vast or because he is feeble, everyone will understand. But if he is able to be with the family at the cemetery, he can invest an hour or two most profitably. There is no easy pathway to being a good minister of Jesus Christ.

At the grave the length of the services should depend in part upon the weather. The suggestions here relate to a time of year when the air is balmy and to an hour of the day when the sun is shining. In such a case there is no reason for cutting the services short. There is time for a well-rounded ritual, which ought to be climactic. The idea is to send everyone home thinking about life instead of death, and the joys of heaven rather than the desolateness of earth. Throughout every syllable the services ought to be vibrant with Biblical energy and luminous with Christian hope.

The exercises need not last longer than five or six minutes. When the weather is foul the time should be shorter. Once in a blizzard, when the thermometer stood at zero, the writer simply pronounced the benediction. The way to show respect for the dead is to have concern for the living. Otherwise a single funeral may lead to a number of deaths. Physically, people are in no condition to withstand exposure. Even if there is a canopy over the grave, some may become chilled if the services last more than a very few minutes, the fewer the better.

Whenever the clergyman deems it wise to depart from custom because of inclement weather he should consult beforehand with one or more of the family. Whereas it is customary for the minister, as well as the other men, to stand at the grave with head uncovered, that would be foolhardy when there is rain or snow. Through the mortician the pastor can notify the pallbearers that they are free to wear their hats. They will be relieved to learn that common sense prevails.

At the historic Princeton Cemetery on a wintry afternoon Clarence E. Macartney, of Pittsburgh, stood by the grave of his predecessor and personal friend, Maitland Alexander. Assisting in the service was President John A. Mackay, of

Princeton Seminary. Without explanation or apology each of
them wore his hat. That was a present-day version of the
Golden Rule.

Whatever the weather, the minister should be at hand
when the pallbearers remove the casket from the funeral
carriage. When they are ready to move he should walk
slowly with the mortician as together they lead the procession. At the grave the minister stands a little to one side until
the pallbearers have deposited the casket on the descending
device. Meanwhile he should have ascertained from the
mortician which is the head of the grave. As a rule that is
where he stands. However, if the mortician suggests otherwise, it makes no difference.

When everything is ready the mortician indicates that the
clergyman is to take charge. A good way to begin is to read
the One Hundred and Twenty-first Psalm. Afterward, if the
departed has been a Christian, it is good to repeat Rev. 14:
13. Meanwhile the mortician is beside the grave. He is waiting to strew on the casket either flowers or dust. As he does
so, the minister slowly repeats the committal service. In an
occasional service the people prefer that there be no such
form of committal. If so, one can substitute a reading from
the New Testament, e.g., Rev. 21: 1-7 or ch. 22: 1-5. Some
of us think that this sort of reading is much better than the
stereotyped committal ceremony.

When custom calls for words of committal it is more
effective to recite than to read from a book. No matter how
many funerals there may be, with some of the same people
present almost every time, the pastor needs to vary the form
of committal only when the deceased has not been known as
a consistent Christian. Then, if the matter were not serious,
one might say facetiously that the words of farewell should
be "noncommittal." The following is one of various forms
that are suitable when the departed has been an unbeliever:

"Here we commit the body to its kindred dust—earth to
earth, ashes to ashes, dust to dust. The spirit we leave with

God. May the living lay it to heart. As we know that God will bring us every one to the grave, let us here dedicate ourselves to do with our might what our hands find to do. May our trust be in Him who says, 'I am the resurrection, and the life: he that believeth in me, though he were dead, yet shall he live: and whosoever liveth and believeth in me shall never die.' "

In the burial of a believer, after the committal service may come the Apostles' Creed, in which everyone present should join. During the committal ceremony and the recitation of the Creed it is wise to keep the loose-leaf notebook open at the proper page. Then if the memory falters, as it may, the thing to do is to read until the trail again becomes clear. If one is speaking deliberately, an involuntary pause may be impressive. But as a rule there need be no such interruption. If all goes well the saying of the Creed in unison may be the climactic part of the entire ceremony.

After the Creed there should be a prayer. It need not be long. The underlying truth may be the assurance of the resurrection. On this basis, because the Lord Jesus arose from the tomb and is alive forevermore, the minister should lead his friends as one by one they dedicate themselves anew to the service of God, who alone can make anyone feel secure about the resurrection of the body and the life everlasting.

If the services elsewhere have not included The Lord's Prayer, it may come now. In the spirit of the familiar words, "Thy will be done in earth, as it is in heaven," the people should be ready to receive the benediction. At times it may be better to use some other form, such as the Apostolic Benediction, but as a rule the Covenant Benediction (Heb. 13: 20, 21) seems to be most fitting at the grave.

When it is spoken aright, this unique benediction may be more moving than a sermon. The words of blessing actually bestow on the hearts of believers the covenant mercies of the Almighty: "The God of peace, that brought again from the dead our Lord Jesus, that great shepherd of the sheep, through the blood of the everlasting covenant, make you perfect in every good work to do his will, working in you that which is wellpleasing in his sight, through Jesus Christ; to whom be glory for ever and ever. Amen."

In most communities, after the benediction it is the custom for the members of the family circle to go at once to their carriages. If they prefer to tarry for a while and mingle with loved ones who have come home from afar, the pastor should not interfere. But if there is any evidence of uncertainty about what is proper, he should offer to escort them to the waiting vehicles. He should know, as they do not, that the mortician has work to do elsewhere. The minister, likewise, has calls to make at the hospital. Then, too, the people most concerned need to go home, where they can relax.

In an occasional community, however, the custom may be different. In certain parts of the South, whenever the skies are balmy, the funeral party tarries near the grave until it is filled. Meanwhile there may be quiet snatches of conversation, but as a rule everyone is silent. The minister should not talk. When everything is in readiness, loving hands drape the sunlit mound with flowers fresh from the gardens back at home. Then as the loved ones depart from the cemetery their last recollections of the services are in terms of beauty.

At such an impressive funeral the filling of the grave may come immediately after the psalm and the committal service. Then the Apostles' Creed and the short pastoral prayer, with the benediction, should be the culminating part of the exercises. When all these things are ordered aright, this sort of ceremony is the most memorable that the writer has witnessed at the grave.

PRAYERS USED AT THE GRAVE

Heavenly Father, look in mercy upon these our friends as they leave the earthly form of their loved one resting beneath the beauty of Thy flowers. Be with these Thy children as they go again to their home. Grant them faith to believe in the communion of saints, the forgiveness of sins, the resurrection of the body, and the life everlasting. Through Thy Spirit enable them to be steadfast, unmoveable, always abounding in the work of the Lord, forasmuch as they know that their labor is not in vain in the Lord (I Cor. 15: 58).

[Adapted.]

✿ ✿ ✿ ✿

Almighty God, who by the death of Thy dear Son hast destroyed death, by His rest in the tomb hast sanctified the graves of Thy saints, and by His glorious resurrection hast brought life and immortality to light; receive, we beseech Thee, our unfeigned thanks for that victory over death and the grave which He hath obtained for us and for all who sleep in Him; and keep us ever in communion with those who await Thee here upon earth and with those who stand around Thy throne in heaven: in union with Him who is the Resurrection and the Life, who liveth and reigneth with Thee and the Holy Spirit, ever one God, world without end. Amen.

[From *The Ordinal and Service Book*, The Church of Scotland.]

✿ ✿ ✿ ✿

Grant, O Lord, to all who are bereaved, the spirit of faith and courage, that they may have strength to meet the days to come with steadfastness and courage; not sorrowing as those without hope, but in thankful remembrance of Thy great goodness in past years, and in the sure expectation of a joyful reunion in the heavenly places; and this we ask in the Name of Jesus Christ our Lord. Amen.

[From *The Book of Common Prayer* According to the Use of the Church of England in Ireland.]

XV. The Possible Cremation

EVERY minister should be familiar with the facts about cremation. The term relates to the practice of committing the body to the flames and then preserving the ashes. Another term is incineration. In that process, which is not so common as cremation, the body is exposed to intense heat, but not directly to the flames. The final effect is the same. By weight ninety-seven per cent of the body disappears in the form of vapors; three per cent remains in the form of gray ashes.

The place where all these rites occur is called a crematory. The receptacle for the ashes is an urn. The place where the urns repose is a columbarium. Literally the word means a resting place for doves. In Roman history the columbarium was a vault lined with recesses for cinerary urns. Anyone who visits an up-to-date columbarium will see the resemblance to a vast dovecote. Ordinarily the crematory and the columbarium are housed beneath a single roof.

It is worth any young minister's while to visit such an establishment. In Greater New York there is one at Ferncliff, near Ardsley, in Westchester County. In the suburbs of almost every large city there is a like institution. In the Far West the practice of cremation is more common than in the East or the South. But now that cemeteries are becoming crowded, and it is legally impossible to set apart land for these purposes within the limits of a city like New York, there will likely be an increasing trend toward cremation.

Personally, the minister may or may not approve of such proceedings. Privately, he is free to hold any opinion that he will. But officially he should keep an open mind. In the Christian religion there is nothing that frowns upon cremation or requires burial. If a body is lost at sea or consumed in a burning building, the remains are still in the keeping of the Father God. So it is if the relatives prefer cremation in lieu of burial; they alone have the right to determine the disposition of the dear body.

Sooner or later a minister is likely to be consulted about the services over a body that is to be cremated, or else about what to do with the ashes that remain. There is no special difficulty about his part in such services. The reason for discussing the matter now is to forestall any feeling of uncertainty or dread. As a young clergyman approaches his first ceremony of the sort, let him trust in God and not be afraid.

The difficulties are chiefly psychological. The minister who has always thought of death as leading to burial may find in these other circumstances nothing but unreality. If so, let him remember three truths. Each is spiritual and vital.

First, God is as near to sorrowing people in a columbarium as at a cemetery. Secondly, his children are as much in need of comfort before and after the cremation of the body as though it were to be buried. Thirdly, the minister of the Gospel should fix his eyes on the things that are unseen and eternal. Thus only can he bring to needy hearts the solace that comes from the Father God, through the old, old way of the Cross, which is ever new.

When the body is to be cremated the services may be held at the residence the evening before. That time of day is convenient for all concerned. If the throng is likely to be large the exercises may be held elsewhere. For some reason, however, a church funeral almost never occurs after dark. Hence the services there might be late in the afternoon.

Whatever the time and the place, the exercises are much the same as though the body were to be buried. Instead of having the final services at the grave, however, they are at the columbarium. They are held, as a rule, after the cremation, and are private. If the pastor's other engagements permit, he plans to be with the friends when they go to the crematory.

He makes a special effort to be with them when they put the urn in the columbarium. Any such ceremony must be at an hour when the gates are open and the attendants are on duty.

Still another plan is to hold the chief funeral services in the chapel under the same roof as the crematory and the columbarium. What the minister says and does in the chapel is much the same as at a funeral parlor. If he thinks about the matter calmly, and makes his plans carefully, all should go well. After the services are over he may wonder at his previous perturbation.

What the minister says and does at the columbarium is much the same as at a grave. However, it is advisable to make a few slight alterations in the committal service. When the exercises are held before the cremation the Scottish *Book of Common Order* suggests the following:

"Forasmuch as it hath pleased Almighty God to take unto Himself the soul of our *brother* here departed, we therefore commit *his* body to be dissolved, ashes to ashes, dust to dust, in sure and certain hope of the resurrection to eternal life, through our Lord Jesus Christ."

When the ceremony takes place after the cremation the same rites will serve, with a single change. Instead of saying, "We therefore commit *his* body to be dissolved," the minister declares, "We therefore commit *his* ashes to this resting-place." In no case should there be any use of the word "flame," or "fire."

If the deceased has been a Christian, the minister may add these triumphant words from the Apocalypse: "I heard a voice from heaven saying unto me, Write, Blessed are the dead which die in the Lord from henceforth: Yea, saith the Spirit, that they may rest from their labours; and their works do follow them" (Rev. 14: 13).

XVI. The Fraternal Order

SOMETIMES there is a question concerning the part in the services to be taken by a fraternal order. If the deceased has been a member of the Masons, or some other secret society, the family may wish the lodge officials to share in the public exercises. If so, the minister should gladly assent to whatever the people desire. If their spokesman is not aware of what is customary, the pastor should explain the possibilities. The decision about what to do, however, should rest with the family. Obviously, the rest of this chapter applies to only an occasional funeral.

In most communities the custom now is for the lodge to have services in the home, or at the funeral parlors, on the evening prior to the day for the exercises conducted by the pastor. The notice about the lodge services appears in the daily newspapers. The officers and members can be present without losing time from their regular work. The chaplain of the lodge is more likely to be available than at the funeral on the following day. As a result, there are two distinct services, which differ in character. Each of them may be almost a model of its kind.

Another plan is still less common. In it the representatives of the lodge share with the minister in the exercises at the home, the church, or the funeral parlors. In such a case the lodge officials usually prefer to come last. If so, the clergyman carries out his part in the services and then gives way to the official who is to assume charge. Of course the clergyman keeps his part of the exercises fairly short. He should also do his best to make them shine. He does not wish to have the Church overshadowed.

At the proper time it is the part of courtesy for the minister to introduce the chief representative of the lodge. Previously these two should have held a private conference.
In it the pastor should have written down the requisite facts.
Then he can state them with clarity and precision. The announcement may be as follows: "The remainder of the
services will be in charge of Mercer Lodge Number Fifty,
Free and Accepted Masons, under the leadership of the
Grand Master." During these ceremonies the minister should
remain, giving reverent attention to all that is said and done.

Another procedure is even less common of late. It is for the
lodge to take part only at the grave. In fact, the officials may
be willing to excuse the clergyman from attendance at the
cemetery. The fraternal burial rites are often impressive,
not to say spectacular. That is likely to be the case when the
Knights Templars perform. On each side of the grave stands
a row of comrades, with swords upraised and crossed,
thus forming an arch of steel athwart the open tomb. Then
the chaplain intones the stately ritual. If he has a sense of
rhythm and knows how to read, the effect may be picturesque.

Friction between the minister and the officials of the lodge
is most likely to occur with reference to the benediction at the
grave. Just as professing Christians in the Holy Land quarrel
about the reputed sites of the Saviour's birth and death, so do
his followers in our homeland sometimes squabble about the
holiest words that mortal lips can utter. Fortunately, such
spectacles are rare today. If the lodge officials like the minister personally, they usually ask him to pronounce the benediction. If they prefer to have it spoken by their own chaplain, who may not have been ordained, why should there be
any dispute? At the grave let there be peace and good will
among men.

In this connection it is interesting to note the official
regulations for chaplains in the Army. At a military funeral
the regular services by the grave precede the rites of any
fraternal organization. If the lodge ceremonies are semi-

military, they come immediately after the Army religious service. Then there may be the firing of muskets and the sounding of taps. Nonmilitary rites conducted by a fraternal organization are held at the conclusion of taps. Since the Army services may be in the hands of a civilian clergyman, if the family so desires, it is clear that the Army gives the place of prominence to the regular religious exercises.

However, it is not wise for a minister of the Gospel to be concerned about his personal "rights." If he is tactful and considerate he need anticipate no difficulty in making satisfactory arrangements with the officers of any recognized fraternal order. With few exceptions they are Christian gentlemen. They have worthy ideals, as well as tolerance. Unfortunately, they must sometimes deal with a clergyman who is unwilling to budge an inch, or even allow them a minute of "his" time, as though he were the Almighty! Since no rites can make any difference to the deceased, both pastor and lodge officials should accede to what the family desires.

The occasional clergyman does not understand how important the funeral obsequies seem to the officials of the lodge. During any month except August he conducts religious services of various kinds. He may have more than a few funerals. Does he realize that among the Masons, for instance, the only ceremonies held in public, as a rule, are at a funeral or at the laying of a cornerstone? Is it any wonder that those in charge wish to magnify their offices?

XVII. The Military Funeral

A LOCAL pastor may be invited to take part in a military funeral. Even if he is not, he should be able to advise people who are concerned about the subject. For instance, he should know who may be the officiating clergyman. In the Army the regulations prescribe that the one in charge may be a regular chaplain, that he may be assisted by a civilian clergyman, or that the latter may serve alone. The choice of the minister rests chiefly with the family of the deceased.

The present discussion concerns the Army, with burial by land, not by sea. In the Navy many of the same principles operate. The parish minister is much more likely to take part in a military funeral. What makes a funeral military is the presence of officers and soldiers in a body, showing honor to a fallen comrade, and the carrying out of certain symbolic actions prescribed by the regulations of the Army. Such is the information that has come most graciously from the Office of the Chief of Chaplains at Washington, D. C.

The regulations simply provide for "a decent and orderly way of handling the persons present and of rendering the honors prescribed for the deceased." As for the character and the conduct of the religious services, both elsewhere and at the grave, the regulations are silent. The leader is free. In the prescribed parts of a military funeral, if the clergyman is not a chaplain, he should ask for instructions and then do exactly what he is told by the officer in charge, who is normally the chaplain.

The chaplain in the Army must know many things that do not concern us now. For example, he should be able to serve as the burial officer on the battlefield. If he does so, he must be exceedingly careful about identifying each body, and then marking it for future investigation. He must keep exact and detailed records, far more minute and painstaking than those herein suggested for a parish minister. Years after a hasty burial at night, the chaplain's loving attention to detail may help distraught parents to locate the resting place of their soldier son.

From a study of such regulations any minister can learn the importance of doing the Lord's work decently and in order. Without lack of spirituality or loss of sympathy, the local pastor should be able to do his part in a military funeral with as much skill and precision as the chaplain displays. If any clergyman is unable to qualify, save as a member of an "awkward squad," he should ask to be excused from taking part. Better still, he can learn how to excel in such a Christian ceremony.

According to the regulations, military funerals are of three different kinds. These distinctions are prominent in the literature that guides the Army chaplain. If a civilian clergyman is invited to take part in a military funeral, he should adapt himself to one of the three plans.

The most elaborate procedure is that of the "chapel service." The word "chapel" is interpreted to mean the church, the home, or any other place where funeral services are held, prior to the exercises at the grave. After the chapel service, or, rather, as a vital part, there is a procession to the cemetery, with a military escort. According to this plan, all that is done reaches its climax at the grave.

In the second type of military funeral the procession forms at or near the entrance to the cemetery and marches to the grave. As a rule some kind of religious ceremony has been held previously, perhaps at a distance. In any case it would probably not be military. If it does not seem wise to have military exercises both at the chapel and at the grave, what seems to matter most according to the Army regulations is the service within the cemetery.

The third plan is much more simple. The exercises are only at the grave, with no procession. Since the first type of military funeral really includes the other two, the discussion here relates chiefly to what is known as the "chapel service."

A military procession with full honors affords an awesome spectacle. It consists of the following, in the order prescribed: (1) band, (2) military escort, (3) colors, (4) clergy, (5) caisson or hearse and casket bearers, (6) caparisoned horse (if the deceased had been mounted), (7) honorary pall-bearers, (8) family, (9) patriotic or fraternal organizations, (10) friends.

At the "chapel" the band, the escort, and the colors form in line facing the edifice. The band is on the flank toward which the procession is later to move. Before the bearers remove the casket from the conveyance, the members of the family enter the chapel, followed by their friends. The honorary pallbearers stand at attention, in two ranks, facing each other, so as to form an aisle through which the casket will be borne from the conveyance to the entrance of the chapel.

When all is in readiness the band plays and the procession moves into the chapel. As at a civilian's funeral, the clergyman leads. Within the chapel he does as at other times. He takes his place wherever he is to stand during the service—it may be in the pulpit or at the altar. When everyone is seated and all is hushed he is free to do what his church and his conscience dictate. But woe be to him if he is not prepared to read and speak with a touch of distinction!

After the exercises in the chapel the clergyman leads the procession to the funeral conveyance. There he stands with head uncovered, unless the weather is cold or inclement. When the casket is in place he goes to the front of the caisson or hearse. At the cemetery the clergyman leads the procession to the grave, where he should take his position at the head. After the bearers have deposited the casket on the descending device, they remove from the casket the flag that has been reposing there, and hold it in a horizontal position, waist-high, until the conclusion of taps.

During the procession to the grave the band keeps playing. When all is in readiness for the religious services, the music ceases. Then the clergyman takes charge. He is as free as at any other funeral. If he is wise his words will be few and memorable. After the benediction he moves two steps to the side or the rear so as to make room for the bugler. After the appointed squad has fired three volleys of blank cartridges, the bugler sounds taps.

Thus the military funeral practically comes to an end. The soldiers march from the grave, but no music is prescribed. In fact, there may be a military funeral without a band or certain other features that have been mentioned. In a case where the family of the deceased wish to eliminate nonessentials, all that the regulations of the Army require is the presence of the clergy, the casket bearers, the firing party, and the bugler.

THE RELIGIOUS SERVICES

In planning for his part in a military funeral the clergyman may have difficulty in deciding what to say. Naturally he will follow the customs of his denomination. If they permit a measure of freedom, he may choose between two procedures. The one is more or less military in spirit; the other is not. The one follows the principle of likeness; the other, of contrast. In explaining them both, there is no desire to disparage either. When well done, each is worthy.

According to the first plan, things military enter into practically all that the minister says and does. If the religious exercises consist of nothing more than readings and prayers, they may be about life in terms of Christian warfare, and about death as the warrior's folding up his army tent and the sailing west toward home. This kind of service may call for a poem about facing the last foe without yielding to fear. For instance, take the latter half of Browning's "Prospice." Unfortunately, the words are hard to read well: "I was ever a fighter, so—one fight more."

If there is music, either instrumental or vocal, the spirit may be that of the martial hymn, "The Son of God Goes Forth to War." If the members of the family desire a brief sermon, it may be from one of the many texts that speak about religion and life in terms of Christian warfare. Especially do such passages abound in the writings of Paul. By his use of military and other masculine metaphors he shows how to reach the hearts of stalwart men.

Rom. 13: 12c.	The Armor of Eternal Light.
I Cor. 15: 57.	The Victory of Christ's Warriors.
Eph. 6: 11.	The Armor of God's Soldiers.
I Tim. 6: 12.	The Good Fight of Faith.
II Tim. 2: 3.	The Discipline of God's Soldier.
II Tim. 4: 7, 8.	The Farewell of the Christian Warrior.
Heb. 2: 10.	The Captain of Our Salvation.
Rev. 2: 7.	The Fruits of Christian Conquest.

Such a sermon may well be factual. Here is a case in point. According to *The Christian Century*, April 9, 1941, the father of Martin Niemöller sent the following message through a newspaper correspondent who was returning to the States:

"When you go back to America do not let anyone pity the mother and father of Martin Niemöller. Only pity any follower of Christ who does not know the joy that is set before those who endure the Cross, despising the shame.

"Yes, it is a terrible thing to have a son in a concentration camp. Paula here [the mother] and I know that. But there would be something far more terrible for us: if God had needed a faithful martyr and our Martin had been unwilling."

> " 'Tis man's perdition to be safe,
> When for the truth he ought to die."

In the spirit of Emerson's lines the clergyman may feel led

to stress things military. Again he may be prompted to follow the other plan. Instead of being like what has gone before, and what will follow after, the religious services may stress the love of the Father God and the assurance of the life beyond. In the prayers the minister will remember the soldiers who are present and the cause that they represent. But he will be chiefly concerned about bringing comfort and hope to sorrowing hearts.

Such a service is difficult to plan and still more difficult to carry out. Unless the minister knows how to lead in worship there may seem to be no connection between what he is doing and what the soldiers stand for. In their presence it may require courage for the clergyman to speak out boldly for Christ and the Kingdom. On the other hand, there is nothing that Army men admire more than courage. There is nothing that they need so much as personal friendship with Jesus Christ. Since he is the Saviour and Lord, now and forever, what Christian warrior need fear the worst that death can do?

As a rule this second plan is the procedure that the writer prefers. During the World War I, he ministered to as many soldiers and officers as almost any pastor in the South. Hence he has an abiding concern for the spiritual welfare of Army men. Now that his son and namesake is serving as a chaplain in the Navy, that work is equally dear to his heart.

Any minister who is specially interested should secure the literature recommended below. The small book listed first contains wise suggestions about the leadership of worship among enlisted men of various faiths. There are drawings to make clear the correct procedure at a military or naval funeral.

Informational Readings

Bennett, Chaplain Ivan Loveridge, *Song and Service Book for Ship and Field*. A. S. Barnes & Co., 1941. 75 cents.

The Chief of Infantry, *Basic Field Manual 22-5*. Government Printing Office, Washington, D. C., 1941. Chapter IX. 50 cents.

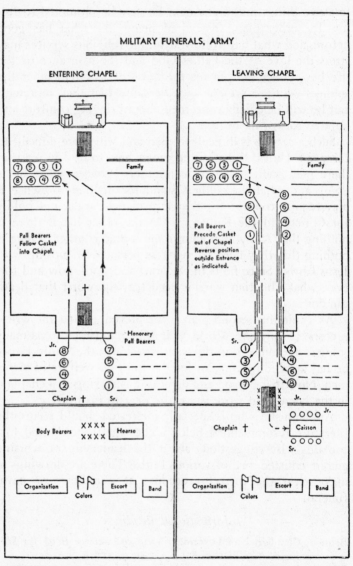

From *The Song and Service Book for Ship and Field.* Edited by Lt. Col. Ivan L. Bennett. Copyright, 1941, by A. S. Barnes and Company, New York, New York.

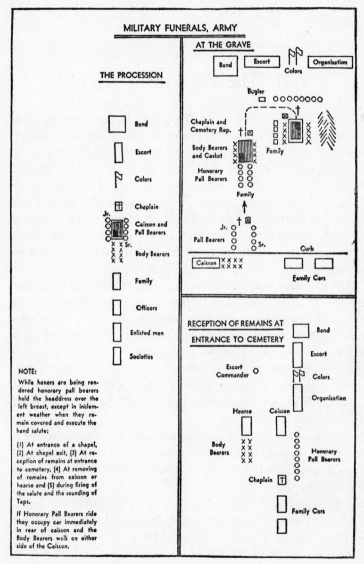

From *The Song and Service Book for Ship and Field.* Edited by Lt. Col.
Ivan L. Bennett. Copyright, 1941, by A. S. Barnes and Company, New
York, New York.

XVIII. The Permanent Records

THERE should be two sorts of records about funerals. One set is for the pastor, and is personal. The other is in charge of the church secretary, and is a part of the office equipment. If there is no office or church secretary, still there should be an official record of every funeral that is conducted on behalf of the congregation. There should also be a clear statement of the facts about the death of any member whose funeral has occurred elsewhere. The pastor's records, however, need to include only the funerals that he conducts in person.

Let us begin with the church records. They are even more important than those kept by the pastor. The official records should be available for future reference by any person who has a sufficient reason. Any minister who has secured such information from the sexton or the rector of a parish church in Great Britain, and has then tried to duplicate the feat in a corresponding situation here at home, will determine that henceforth in his parish such things shall be done decently and in order.

The minister himself should not keep the church records. If he did so, they might lapse when he moved away. But he should instill in the minds of the lay officers the ideal of having the facts available. They may be kept either on filing cards in a suitable case or else in a permanent book. Each entry should show the family name and the given name of the deceased, the time and the place of death, the place of burial, the name of the officiating clergyman, and, as a rule, the age of the person at the time of death. These are the facts that may some time be needed to settle an estate or to com-plete a genealogical table.

As a rule the church has a weekly calendar or bulletin. If so, on the Sunday following each funeral there should be a brief memorial notice concerning the departed. From time to time the notices should be much the same. Since space is limited, there need be only a simple heading, such as "In Loving Memory," "In Memoriam," or "Entered Into Rest." Immediately below, on three separate lines, carefully centered and spaced, should appear the name of the deceased, the date of death, and a few words of Scripture. If the verse is long, the citation will be sufficient. Occasionally the motto may be the first line of a hymn.

If the departed friend has been an officer in the church, or a leader in the women's work, a more extended statement is fitting. In order to keep from praising one person more than another, the minister can arrange for the memorial notice to appear in the name of the board or society con-cerned. The paragraph in the bulletin need not be long. The memorial should not be fulsome. But it ought to record permanently the gratitude of the living for the services rendered by their former comrade. Incidentally, such notices, when properly prepared and carefully edited, lend interest and value to a church bulletin. Often it lacks human warmth and a spiritual glow.

If there is an office secretary, she should mark on the cal-endar for the coming year the anniversary date of each death among the people. When the black day comes round again, there should go to the family a note of loving sym-pathy or a bouquet of flowers. Better still, there should be a call by the minister or some other tactful person.

The carrying out of such a plan calls for thoughtfulness and care. The marked calendar should be accessible only to the secretary and the pastor. It should be as complete as possible. It is better not to single out any such anniversary than to make much of one and then ignore another. Occasionally there are conditions where any reference to events of a year ago would be embarrassing. In the meantime the vacant place in the home may have been filled by a comely woman who has already heard too much about her angelic predecessor.

In the following case the blackest day of all the year was February 28. Years before, while cleaning his gun, David F. had accidentally killed himself. He had been the only child in a home where the parents were beginning to grow old. Twenty years later, after there had been three changes in the pastorate, a deacon told the new minister that these two friends needed him more on that one day than on any other. While the pastor had never seen the son, there was need that day of a messenger from God. Should not such information be available to each incoming pastor?

PASTORAL RECORDS

The minister also should keep accurate records of each funeral that he conducts. A single card, perhaps four by six inches, affords ample space for all the facts. They are much the same as for the church records. On the pastor's card, however, there should be a record of additional facts that he may wish to recall in later years: for instance, the name of the other minister, the important passages of Scripture, the text and subject of the sermon, the first line of each hymn, and the title of the poem.

Some of these items may go on the other side of the card. In nine cases out of ten the data will never be used. Even so, there can be no harm in having them at hand. If ten years later the minister has to conduct a funeral in the same family circle, he may wish to remember clearly what he said and did the other time.

The cards can be filed either alphabetically or chronologically. In any one pastorate there is an advantage in having the materials arranged according to families, alphabetically. The man who has a shepherd heart thinks of his people by name, not by numbers on the calendar. In later years he will recall each funeral occasion because it concerned human beings whom he loves. When he removes to another field he will set all these records off by themselves, and then make a new start. But there should be no private bonfire.

At first a man shrinks from such clerical detail. Even if there is a church secretary or two, the pastor needs to supply some of the data. He must also supervise the keeping of the records. As time goes on, the number of funerals will increase. If the pastor thinks he is too busy to keep records, he should call on a friendly physician and ask how he keeps countless items accurately. The doctor can immediately bring out from his files a card showing the facts about any case, past or present. Should not the physician of souls be equally careful?

LEGAL PROBLEMS

Occasionally the pastor must appear in court to testify as a witness. In the presence of a judge and other attorneys, as well as a jury, all of whom attach importance to precise records, the clergyman may have to testify that he ministered at a certain deathbed or in the funeral service. He need never divulge what he has learned in confidence—unless by keeping silent he would violate the laws of God and man. But he should be able to produce the exact data, and provide the requisite proofs.

Such legal problems seldom arise. Nevertheless, the pastor should be informed about the laws of the commonwealth where he resides. (Such information is even more vital in the case of marriages than with reference to funerals.) The following statement has been prepared with the help of Robert B. Knowles, Esq., who for years has been a ruling elder in Central Presbyterian Church, Summit, New Jersey. He is a prominent member of the bar in New York City. He assumes that the laws of that commonwealth are typical of such statutes elsewhere.

1. The Public Health Law regulates and controls the duties and responsibilities of those who have to do with births and deaths. Such control includes the physician, the surgeon, the nurse, the mortician, and the clergyman.

2. A physician licensed by the state and duly registered must issue a death certificate, which must be filed with the authorized city or state official. The filing is done by the mortician. He must be registered by the state as an embalmer.

3. The authorized city or state official then issues to the registered embalmer a permit for burial, cremation, or removal to another state. In Massachusetts the state laws require that a body be embalmed before it can be cremated.

4. In the case of a suicide, a death by accident, or when there is a suspicion of foul play, the city or state officials have the right to withhold the permit for burial until the matter has been investigated to their satisfaction. The procedure may include a post-mortem, as well as an inquest under the coroner, who may or may not summon a jury.

5. After the proper authorities have issued the permit for burial or cremation, the mortician and the minister may proceed with plans for the funeral.

These are the facts, legally. Within his own parish, and often elsewhere, the minister can ignore them all. But he should be careful to keep his records straight. He should exercise caution in dealing with strangers. For example, if the body is cremated, it is vital that all the legal formalities be observed. If the minister knows and trusts the mortician, there is little need for anything more than accurate records. But some day, if the man of God is concerned exclusively about things beyond the clouds, he may wish that he had kept his feet on the ground.

The following case was unique. In it no one was to blame. In a capital city a minister conducted the services over the body of a derelict found floating in the river. Before the interment there had been a careful investigation. A few weeks later the clergyman received a visit from an aged widow who lived in a distant part of the state. She brought a letter from her pastor, who joined with her in the plea that the body be disinterred. The widow and her minister felt certain that it was the body of her son.

The local pastor was a busy man. But his heart went out to the widow. He learned that her son had been a lifelong imbecile. He had been confined in the state hospital, from which he had escaped. The mother wished to know whether he was dead, or was wandering helpless among strangers, some of whom might be cruel. She knew that the hospital authorities had measured the derelict's body with care. They insisted that it could not be her son. Nevertheless, she was importunate. By persistence she and the minister gained permission to have the body exhumed.

At length, to the satisfaction of all concerned, she established her son's identity. Despite the fact that the body taken out of the river had been six inches longer than the person whom the attendants at the hospital had measured, there could be no doubt concerning the identity. The superintendent acknowledged that he and his staff had been mistaken. He supposed that the body must have swollen while in the river. The minister suspected that some careless attendant had guessed at the height and missed it by six inches.

To that one case, involving complete strangers, the pastor devoted much of his time for two days. In the end he had the satisfaction of bringing peace to a troubled mother's heart. He had likewise learned much about legal technicalities and still more about human fallibilities. In after days he wondered if he would have been willing to have some of his other funerals investigated by the legal and medical authorities of the city where he was a pastor. To the best of his knowledge he had never officiated at services where he was helping to conceal a crime. But he could visualize such a possibility.

The minister concerned does not object to cremation. But he has often wondered how that widow could have found peace if her son's body had been burned. The obvious inference is that the authorities should be able to disinter the remains of any person about whose death there can ever be any question. A more personal consideration is that no legal inquiry ought to involve the fair name of the minister who conducts the funeral. If he must come into court, he should have clean hands and a calm heart. The heart will be more peaceful if the hands are holding adequate records.

Informative Readings

Brand, N. F., and Ingram, V. M., *The Pastor's Legal Adviser.* Abingdon-Cokesbury, 1942.

XIX. The Rising Costs

SOME of the most perplexing problems relating to funerals have to do with the rising costs. In modern parlance the subject of this chapter would be "The High Cost of Dying." Unfortunately, there seems to be little that the minister can do. His hands appear to be tied. As a rule he has no share in making funeral arrangements that require money. With minor exceptions, he seems powerless to change local customs, however pagan. Nevertheless, he should be aware of what often goes on behind the scenes.

The costs come all in a heap. After a protracted illness, which has drained the household treasury, there is need of money for the purchase of the burial plot or the niche in the columbarium; the digging of the grave; the purchase of the casket (this item usually includes other professional services); the buying of wearing apparel for the body and mourning garments for the widow as well as for other members of the family. Then there may be the expense of securing carriages for relatives and friends. Later will come the bill for the headstone or other marker at the grave.

The list is not complete. It makes no mention of the flowers purchased by sympathetic friends or of such items as telegrams and long-distance calls, and the entertainment of guests from a distance. In one case a Negro family in Alabama shipped the body of the deceased father to Pennsylvania and back. Thereby they escaped the expenses incident to a gala funeral at home. Even so, those simple-minded folk probably fell victims to some undertaker like the one who advertised the following rates for professional services:

"For composing the features, $1.00.
"For giving the appearance of quiet resignation, $2.00.
"For giving the appearance of Christian hope, $5.00."

Prior to the collapse of the boom in 1929, "the high cost of dying" had become so notorious that there were various investigations. The findings were disconcerting. One research specialist discovered that certain undertakers were charging the patron six times the original cost of the casket. The calculation did not include the cost of professional services. Those the statistical expert computed separately.

THE MORTICIAN

There is much to be said for conscientious morticians. Those whom the writer has known best have been high-minded Christian gentlemen. In his last congregation there were two, representing different firms, each of which had a code of honor. On the other hand, there were in the city a few undertakers on a level with quacks among doctors and ambulance chasers among lawyers. As a rule shysters and tricksters do not belong to a reputable association, such as "The National Selected Morticians."

Such a businessman faces a financial problem. His income is intermittent. In summer funerals may be few. In late winter, when his work is most difficult and costly, there may be many deaths. In an establishment of any size there may be several funerals at the same hour of the afternoon. In summer as well as winter the equipment and the staff must be ready for an emergency. For all this someone must pay.

The overhead is high. The annual budget must provide for the equipment and maintenance of funeral parlors, costly conveyances, a number of drivers, and a staff of experts, one of whom must be a licensed embalmer. There are also expenses for clerical help, and many other items. Even if every bill were paid at once and in full, the financing of the concern might not be easy. From year to year the expense of doing business has kept rising.

From the mortician's point of view the secret of keeping down the costs lies in co-operation among competitors. From the minister's standpoint the question concerns the friends who must meet the funeral expenses, often unexpectedly. With unpaid bills from the physician and the surgeon, the hospital and the nurses, the druggist and the grocer, the person in charge at the home must face a number of other accounts, some of which call for cash. Meanwhile the household expenses may have doubled, temporarily, and the income may have stopped, permanently.

In another home the conditions are quite the reverse. There is a lot of new money. Sometimes the situation is complicated by the life insurance agent. As a rule he too is a Christian gentleman, but when he is not, there may be an awkward situation. As far back as 1905 abuses among industrial life insurance agents had become so glaring that the chief company in the field, the Metropolitan, forbade any of its agents to have business dealings with an undertaker. The company also urged every agent to warn the patron against incurring needless expenses for the funeral. Unfortunately, such counsel is usually wasted. Local custom prevails. It leads to extravagance.

Think of a case, which is not unique. The widow has had no experience in handling large sums of money. At times she has felt that too much of the family income has been going into life insurance and not enough into making the home happy. Soon after her husband's death she discovers that she has at her disposal thousands of dollars, where she has been thinking in terms of dimes.

In the hour of grief the widow is surrounded by sobbing friends who tell her that nothing is too good for the funeral of her dear husband, and that she must keep up with the standards of other people who live down the street.

Into this milieu comes the mortician. He also is human. He feels sure that the money will soon be scattered. He is not averse to a funeral that will compare with the work of his competitors. In short, while neither the widow nor the mortician may be consciously at fault, the funeral is likely to help to negative the plans of the deceased for the future comfort of his family.

THE PASTOR

A little later the pastor confers with the widow about the approaching services. He brings her the Gospel of comfort and hope. He is thinking about the world to come, not about funeral costs. He may wonder why he finds it difficult to keep his friend's attention fixed on the things that are unseen and eternal. If he becomes aware of the struggle between God and Mammon, he may wonder if there is not something he can do to stress laying up treasures in heaven.

It is not easy to deal with such a situation. Theoretically, it should be possible for a pastor to train his people so that they will use all their money for the glory of the God from whom it comes. Practically, it is hard to promote trusteeship at any time, and doubly so when there is a death in the home.

The subject of trusteeship is too large for us to consider now. In the case just mentioned the wife should long since have had a share in the larger concerns of household finance. The basic need here is justice. There is also a place for the use of money as an expression of love. What else did the Lord Jesus have in view when he commended Mary for her lavish gift of ointment? "She did it for my burial. Verily I say unto you, Wheresoever this gospel shall be preached in the whole world, there shall also this, that this woman hath done, be told for a memorial of her" (Matt. 26: 12, 13).

On the other hand, it is hard to invoke the blessing of God on the pagan display that marks many a funeral. For instance, think of the flowers. Somewhere between niggardliness and prodigality there is a Christian way of showing love for the one who has fallen asleep. In as far as the minister has any influence he will exert it in the promotion of simplicity.

He will foster the feeling that the funeral service should call no attention to itself, but turn every eye toward God.

It is almost never wise for the pastor to mention "the high cost of dying." No matter what the occasion, he is likely to be misunderstood. Unintentionally, he may hurt the feelings of a mortician or a florist who does his best to prevent extravagant display. There may also seem to be a criticism of church members who were responsible for a funeral months before. After a few futile attempts to change non-Christian customs, the minister will probably decide that he must leave the whole problem to his successor.

A concrete case will show part of the difficulty. In California a public-school teacher learned by telegraph that an aunt had died back in Virginia. While he scarcely knew her, he sent word that she should be properly interred at his expense. In a few weeks he received a bill for $400, which represented his salary for two months. At the same time, in 1940, the United States Army regulations for the funeral of a soldier read in part as follows:

"Burial expenses proper are restricted to undertaker's services, cost of casket, cost of outside box or shipping case, and hire of hearse. The general limitation on these expenses is $85. The amount may be extended to $100 on authority of the quartermaster general." After having had more or less to do with military funerals, the writer can testify that the financial provision has always seemed adequate.

THE FUNERAL FEE

One thing the minister can do from the very first day in the parish. He can refrain from exacting payment for his own services. Among the members of the congregation he may decline to receive compensation for anything that he does in the presence of death. If some of his people have abundant means, and if they insist on his receiving a token of their gratitude, he can take their gift with thanks. If it is money, he can apply it to some part of the church work. In that event he may ask the treasurer or the church secretary to write the donors a letter of thanks.

In dealing with persons who were not as yet affiliated with the local church the writer adopted much the same procedure. Year after year the funeral fees were larger than those at weddings. The latter went to the mistress of the manse; the former, into the treasury of the church or of some society. Whenever he was offered a funeral fee, the pastor explained that there was no charge. But if the people insisted on paying, and if they were able to do so without hardship, the minister felt that it was a kindness to let them aid in supporting the church. Thus the use of money may be a means of grace.

Throughout the community the pastor should become known as a neighbor and friend upon whom any person can call for ministerial services that are absolutely free. His time and strength belong to Christ and the home church. If an exceptional case arises, when he does not know whether or not to receive money on behalf of the congregation, he ought to solve the problem in the light of a golden text. One of many is the key verse in the Gospel of service:

"The Son of man came not to be ministered unto, but to minister, and to give his life a ransom for many" (Mark 10: 45).

Informational Readings

Dowd, Quincy Lamartine, *Funeral Management and Costs.* The University of Chicago Press, 1921.

Gebhart, John Charles, *Funeral Costs.* G. P. Putnam's Sons, 1928. Report of an investigation under a committee appointed by the Metropolitan Life Insurance Company.

XX. The Funeral Code

THE heading above represents an ideal. There is in print no official code of honor to guide a young Protestant clergyman with reference to funerals or to any other part of his pastoral work. While certain branches of the Church have drawn up ethical codes, no one of them has any binding force. As a rule they are general, and do not touch the funeral. Hence it is the part of wisdom for each minister to formulate his own personal code, which may not be in writing. It should include such items as the following:

1. The Christian minister is the servant of the community, not merely of his parish.

2. The physician of souls responds at once to the call from a dying man, whether he is a friend or a stranger.

3. The ministering shepherd goes at once to the home where there has been a death.

4. The Christian minister carries out these principles in the spirit of the Golden Rule. It forbids the stealing of sheep.

5. The pastor is directly responsible for the spiritual ministry at any deathbed or funeral service in his congregation.

6. The Golden Rule leads any minister to confer with the pastor before rendering any service in the other man's parish.

7. The former pastor accepts such an invitation, if at all, only when it comes through the present minister.

8. In an emergency the Christian clergyman responds to the call of human need and afterward makes his peace with any other minister concerned.

9. The Christian clergyman never submits a bill for services rendered, and never indirectly solicits payment. How-

ever, he is entitled to receive money sufficient to defray his
traveling expenses.

10. The pastor holds inviolate everything that he learns in
confidence, notably a deathbed confession.

PRACTICAL SUGGESTIONS

1. Be patient. In the time of critical illness or sudden sorrow the shortcomings of human nature are likely to be inten-
sified. People who are in suspense, or else all let down, may
say and do strange things. They sometimes make impossible
demands. Whatever the provocation, the minister of Christ
should control his temper, keep his poise, and hold his
tongue. The secret of doing so is to pray.

2. Remember that the mortician is in charge of the preliminary arrangements and the public services. He has practically nothing to do with the religious exercises, but he is
responsible for everything else. The wise minister is glad to
be released from concern about business arrangements and
practical details. If things go awry he should not interfere,
even to proffer advice. As in dealing with a physician, the
clergyman keeps to his own field. However, when the mortician does an excellent piece of work, a note of appreciation
from the minister is a kindness.

3. In public as in private treat the mortician as an equal.
He too has his professional honor. Do not refer to him as an
"undertaker." When you first enter a parish become acquainted with the reputable morticians. If a certain family
is in financial straits, suggest to the deacons that they confer
with the mortician in charge about extending the time for
payment. He may even reduce his bill, especially if the
deacons are willing to help him to defray the actual costs. In
short, treat the mortician as a human being with a heart.
Erelong he should become a personal friend.

4. When in doubt concerning a matter beyond the congregation, it may be wise to consult with the mortician. Here
is a case in point. Two young men requested a Protestant

clergyman to officiate at the funeral of their mother. From birth she had been a Catholic, but she was not in good standing with her priest. Because she had been attending another Roman church, and had not kept up her pew rents, he refused to perform the burial rites.

The Protestant minister was young and inexperienced. He wished to help the young men but he was dubious about conducting services in a Catholic home and cemetery. He thanked the young men for coming, assured them of his desire to do all he could, and suggested that they talk things over with the mortician in charge.

A few days afterward the clergyman asked the mortician what had taken place. The latter replied: "I told the young men that there would be hard feelings if you buried their mother in holy ground. Since they much preferred a Catholic funeral I offered to intercede for them with the German priest. I took them to his home, where I held a private interview with him. He protested that the woman had been untrue to her parish church. I agreed with him but I pleaded for leniency. At last, grudgingly, he said: 'Tell the boys to bring the old woman to the church tomorrow for eight o'clock mass. If they hand me ten dollars, the matter will be closed.' " Both the mortician and the minister knew that no other priest in that part of the city would have been so heartless.

5. A much more timely suggestion relates to the presence of a second clergyman. As a rule the practice should be discouraged. Especially in a brief service, a single leader is almost always preferable to more than one. On the other hand, the pastor cannot ignore the desire of the family that there be another minister or two. The pastor should extend the invitation heartily, and any brother who accepts should feel sure that he is welcome.

6. When two ministers are conducting a service, the home pastor should be in charge. He should make the plans. He himself should take the opening part. He should ask the

other minister to do whatever the friends desire. In any case, each man should be brief, and confine himself strictly to what has been agreed upon in private conference. For instance, it is embarrassing if the one who utters the opening words of prayer does all that the other one plans to do later in the service. Here again, follow the Golden Rule.

7. When a minister relinquishes a pastoral charge, he relinquishes the privileges as well as the responsibilities. As soon as his successor enters the field, the former minister should give the other man the right of way. Especially during the first year or two of the new regime, the part of kindness is not to accept invitations to assist at funerals in the former parish. Of course there may be exceptions. In each case the determining factor should be the advancement of the Kingdom in the congregation that both the ministers love.

8. A still more personal warning relates to professionalism. It manifests itself whenever a minister can look on death with heart unmoved, and whenever he can conduct a funeral without the expenditure of nervous energy. At such a time self-control and a gift of leadership are sorry substitutes for spirituality and sympathy. Especially in a day when the world is at war, the heart of a Christian minister ought to be full of love.

Professionalism may also lead the clergyman to relate amusing incidents about a deathbed scene or funeral service. In fact, there has often been a temptation to do so in this book. Blessed is the pastor or physician to whom God has given a saving sense of humor. But neither of them ought ever to tell a joke about death and the grave. Like Phillips Brooks, the clergyman today should be a lover of fun, but not a clerical jester. In brief, let the clergyman be a clergyman.

9. The best time to prepare the people of God for sickness and sorrow is while they are well and strong. That is when their spiritual mentor should interpret the Ninetieth

Psalm and other Biblical teachings about time and eternity, the great white throne, and the Judgment Day. "The wages of sin is death; but the gift of God is eternal life." "Watch therefore, for ye know neither the day nor the hour wherein the Son of man cometh." Whenever he appears, be ready to meet him with joy and to serve him in glory. Such are the teachings of the good pastor.

10. Much the same principles apply to the preparation by the minister. The time to make ready for usefulness at a deathbed or in a funeral service is long before the call has come. If it were necessary for people in sorrow to choose— as it is not—between the prepared heart without an orderly program and the orderly program without the prepared heart, they would prefer the man whose heart is right with God.

Informational Readings

Harmon, Nolan Bailey, Jr., *Ministerial Ethics and Etiquette*. The Cokesbury Press, 1928 (bibliography).

Jefferson, Charles Edward, *Building of the Church*. The Macmillan Company, 1910.

Post, Emily Price, *Etiquette*. Funk & Wagnalls Company, 1937 (25th Edition).

XXI. The Problem Funeral

A CERTAIN funeral may cause the pastor more concern than a dozen others. In such an event books may be of little help. Naturally, they deal with the dozen cases that are normal rather than the one that is unique. In our work, as in medicine, facts have a way of defying theories. Under the guidance of the Holy Spirit, therefore, the minister has to work out his own salvation. Often there may be fear and trembling.

If a man trusts God, and works hard, he will find out what to do and say at each problem funeral. Fortunately, such occasions are likely to come seldom, and at intervals. Instead of discussing the problems abstractly, let us look at a number of actual cases. The principles that emerge should prove helpful in deciding on a course of action amid still other circumstances. The main thing, on the human level, is to sympathize. Even when one of the bereaved cries out, "My God, my God, why?" the minister should know how to "trace the rainbow through the rain."

A SUICIDE

John Doe, forty years of age, was highly esteemed. He was the cashier of a prominent bank and the treasurer of his church. One day, without warning anyone, he shot himself and died instantly. When the authorities investigated, they discovered that he had been gambling on the stock market. He had appropriated large sums from the bank and had used up the small vested holdings of his church. Doubtless he knew that the facts were about to be revealed. Hence he took what the man of the world styles "the easy way out." Out to what?

From this point onward the statements are hypothetical. While the minister is hastening to the home he is wondering what he can say. He has never had occasion to question the integrity and honor of the deceased. Much as the pastor knows that the congregation will feel the financial loss, far more does he dread the spiritual effect on the family and the community. Once again, as with Judas, a strong man has given way to the lure of silver. But still the pastor should not judge or condemn.

The first thing he does is to pray. Long since he should have learned that it is possible to do so while hastening to the home of sorrow. If he goes in faith, as the servant of the Lord, the Spirit will guide. At such a time the rule is, "A minister has no more religion than he displays in an emergency."

Within the home the pastor expresses his sympathy. At first he may have little or nothing to say about the facts in the case or about the departed. Probably everyone is too distracted for coherent thinking. If the minister makes any remark, however harmless, he may be misunderstood. At such a tragic hour he should be careful about the neighborhood purveyor of gossip, as well as the ever-present reporter.

If the household is in turmoil, the presence of one man who is calm may serve as a spiritual stabilizer. As soon as the pastor can do so, he arranges to talk alone with the widow, or some other person who ought to be in charge. Speaking for the sake of the family, he may advise that the funeral services and the interment be private. If he does not know the people well enough to proffer advice, he may get in touch with the mortician, directly or by telephone, and ask him to make the suggestion. Any such conversation should be strictly confidential.

At first the widow is likely to be overcome. She may be under the care of a physician, who has to administer a sedative. But sooner or later there will be an opportunity for her to talk at length with the pastor. If he is comparatively a stranger, she may send for his predecessor, or some neighboring clergyman. With her may be the daughter, and perhaps other members of the family circle.

As a rule it is wise to let the widow, or it may be the oldest son, keep on talking until there is nothing more to be said. Like Job's wife in her extremity, the widow's words may be wild and bitter. Justly or unjustly, she may reproach her husband. Perhaps mistakenly, on the other hand, she may feel that she herself has been chiefly at fault. It may be that both have had wrong attitudes toward money and toward God. Fortunately, the pastor is not their judge. He commits all these matters to the only One who knows; that is the Lord.

After the widow has exhausted herself, and everyone has become silent, the pastor should speak. Perhaps the kindest thing to say is this: "Your husband was my friend. So are you. Let us both remember about him all the good that we can recall. At the last he probably was not himself. He must have worried so long over his wrongdoings that temporarily he lost control of himself."

Gradually the pastor can encourage the widow to forgive the most tragic injustice that she has ever endured. He may succeed in persuading her to recall whatsoever things have been true and pure and beautiful in the life of the deceased. Even if the pastor feels certain that the banker stole in order to meet increasingly exorbitant demands from his wife and grown children, the hour has come for Christian mercy. If there ought to be a sterner note about justice, in due time the conscience will speak.

In the funeral services, whether they be private or public, there should be no allusion to suicide. It would not be hard to read up about Judas, or King Saul, and then consult *The Pilgrim's Progress*, where Bunyan discusses Doubting Castle and Giant Despair. From Bedford Jail come ten reasons why a man should not be guilty of self-murder.

To the sensationalist the facts would suggest a lurid discourse. But the heart of a pastor revolts against any suggestion that he make capital out of human sorrow. The circumstances call for a brief service of Christian comfort. Fortunately, at other times he has led his people not to expect a funeral eulogy. He may have established the reputation of doing nothing more than read from the Bible and then pray to God. If so, he brings the family to the foot of the Cross, and leaves them there, close to the heart of the heavenly Father.

After the funeral there is much for the pastor to do. Gradually, in the home, or perhaps in his study, he can guide the widow as she makes her readjustments, spiritually. Indirectly, he can see that the most winsome and tactful women of the parish go out of their way to show their sister in Christ friendship and esteem. Instead of treating her as a social outcast, and thus permitting her to develop an inferiority complex, he and the others can make it clear that the congregation is a household of faith, and that God's children never desert a loved one in need of Christian sympathy.

A STREET FATALITY

James X, twelve years of age, was a communicant member of the church, which he had recently joined through confession and baptism. His parents were adherents. While riding on his bicycle at dusk he was struck by an automobile. Soon afterward he died. The driver of the car was eighteen years of age, and a member of the same congregation; so were his parents. A few weeks later at the trial the young man narrowly escaped being convicted of manslaughter. A deacon in the home church testified that he had been an eyewitness and that the young man had been blameless.

On the part of the little boy's parents and friends there

was bitterness. They felt aggrieved at the church to which both the driver and the chief witness belonged. On the side of the young man there was bewilderment. The father, who was an invalid, made generous financial arrangements with the people who were bereaved, and did everything in his power to show them sympathy. But the young man's relatives felt that he could not have avoided hitting the boy, who had been riding on the wrong side of the street, and with no lights on his wheel.

To the theorist, who concerns himself only with supernal mysteries, these details may seem inconsequential. But to the pastor of a neighborhood church, life is made up largely of relations among people who are far from perfect. In that prolonged dispute the pastor took no part. He admired the restraint of the young man's relatives and he shared with everyone in sympathy for the victims of a mechanized "civilization." In vain the minister strove to have the differences settled out of court. To no avail he pleaded with the boy's parents to be reconciled to the young man's people.

In this case, as in a number of other problem funerals, the pastor felt that he had partially failed. As a rule the books for ministers record only the writers' successes. But candor compels any pastor to confess that his attainments often fall below his ideals. His failures ought to keep him humble. They should likewise lead him to consult with other ministers so as to learn from their experiences how to meet trying situations. From the medical fraternity we should learn the value of frequent consultations with masters in the same profession.

As for the funeral services, they were held in the boy's home. Because of the newspaper publicity, there was a throng of curiosity seekers. Everyone wondered what the minister would say. To the disappointment of many, he did not allude to the tragedy. Rather did he stress the fact that the Father God knows how to make heaven seem like home to a growing boy, and how to bring forth all "the full-grown energies that suit the purposes of heaven." Whether or not that kind of comfort was what the family desired he never felt sure. At least he held their friendship and he made them aware of God's unfailing love.

A PROFLIGATE

Samuel M. was sixty-five years of age. He was accounted the most wicked man in his part of the city. He had been guilty of almost every sin except murder. While he was dying with pneumonia the woman in attendance was his latest paramour. Years before, by cruelty and abuse, he had caused his wife to seek refuge elsewhere, and he had helped to break the hearts of other women. In short, if in the other world there were no place for such a person, there would need to be some extra provision. At least he was not consciously a candidate for heaven.

Somewhere in the entourage, however, there was a vestige of religion. When the neighboring pastor was called in, he found in the dying man no evidence of repentance or remorse for broken vows, bruised hearts, blasted hopes. Each evening he called but apparently without avail. The dying man seemed to appreciate the presence of the clergyman and to be willing for prayer, or anything else. But in as far as the minister could see, there was no change in the heart of the sinner. He died as he had lived, without God.

In that community everyone expected a funeral sermon. For a while the minister was at a loss about what to say. At last he recalled a conversation with the woman of the ménage. She had told him that the deceased was passionately fond of flowers. At heart a man of that type is often a lover of beauty. This may be partly why he can appeal to women. Much as they have to endure at his hands, they respond to his quest for beauty.

In the services the clergyman read the Ninetieth Psalm. A little later he spoke about the God of the flowers (Ps. 103: 15). In the most beautiful of all the psalms the stress is on the loving-kindness of the Father God. In the heart of the song there is a strain about the frailties of man.

At such a time the man of God wonders why there should be a funeral sermon. When his heart has its way, there need be nothing more than the reading of Biblical passages and prayers that he finds in his favorite book of forms. At first glance such a procedure may seem unsympathetic, or even cowardly. But this is a wise rule: when there is nothing good to say, say nothing specific.

A more delicate case was that of Susan N. She was thirty-five years of age, and presumably a widow. Because of her sins, she was dying with tuberculosis. Before her final illness she had been comely. She had appealed especially to men. In the neighborhood for years she had been known as a prostitute.

Perhaps because of her childhood training, she was much concerned about religion. After she was confined to her bed she sent for the same minister as in the case just reported. Again and again he called, but never when he would be alone with the dying woman. Always he found her responsive to his readings and his prayers, as well as his words about the way back to God. But never could he note any sign of penitence and change of heart.

After she died the clergyman was asked to officiate at the services in the home. In that back street any funeral was a neighborhood event. This time the little house was sure to be filled to overflowing. Everyone wondered what the parson would say. So did he for he was young. Never before in his life, to his knowledge, had he spoken to a prostitute.

Sitting in his study he was thinking about what he had learned of the woman's childhood in a Christian home. Then he looked out upon the snow that covered the earth and made even the city slums look white and clean. In the gospel of the snow he found a message from the heart of God (Isa. 1: 18; Ps. 51: 7b; or Isa. 55: 10, 11). While he did not use the poem in the services, he read to himself more than once from Palgrave's *Golden Treasury* the familiar words of Thomas Hood in "The Bridge of Sighs." This is a brief portion:

"Touch her not scornfully,
Think of her mournfully,
Gently and humanly;
Not of the stains of her—
All that remains of her
Now is pure womanly."

On the way to the cemetery the pastor rode with the only two relatives who were present. These brothers had come from a neighboring city, where they had left their aged parents, broken in heart. With eyes full of tears the brothers thanked the minister for his sympathy and his message. They explained that even in girlhood their sister had resisted the efforts of her godly mother and father to keep her from going astray. In every sense she had seemed to be a prodigal daughter, except that she never repented.

The brothers were Christian men, and active in the home church. They were glad that the minister had held high the standards of the Christian faith, and that he had not spoken directly about their sister. They loved to think that she might have repented ere she fell asleep, and thus fulfilled the vows with which she had long since been dedicated to the Lord. They said that as long as they lived they would think of God and his redeeming grace whenever they looked out on the sermon in the snow.

A YOUNG CRIMINAL

The following case is perhaps the most perplexing of all. John R. was twenty-two years of age. He had been reared in a humble home where both his parents feared the Lord and loved the Church. Early in life he had broken loose, partly because they were of foreign birth and speech. He had gone from bad to worse and had become a professional criminal. One night he took a leading part in the robbery of a bank.

A few days afterward he was arrested for the murder of the night watchman.

During the trial, which was speedy, the parents attended daily. They heard the judge pronounce the final sentence and they watched their son walk out toward the death chamber. Then they went back to their home. Meanwhile the penitentiary chaplain had striven to comfort them, and had promised to deal with their son on behalf of Christ. But all that minister's efforts seemed to be fruitless. The young man went to his death as he had gone through life, defying God.

At the home town of the parents, in a distant part of the state, the pastor was new on the field. He had never seen the son, and knew of him only through the newspapers and also through the parents. When the minister learned that the young man had been condemned to die, the man of God did his best to prepare the mother and father for the oncoming shock. The pastor suggested that the funeral services be private. Even so, he wondered what he should say to those childlike people.

On the afternoon when the parents were at the railroad station waiting for the train that was to bring home the body of their son, the pastor was by their side. Since he did not know what to say, he kept silent. In later years he has often wondered what he could have said or done to show his sympathy and faith in God.

To such a question, there may be no answer, at least on the human level. According to the *British Weekly*, during the first World War a Christian widow was watering her roses one morning while she was praying for her soldier son, the only child, who was in the front-line trenches across the Channel. She loved to think of him as the living image of the young father whom he had never seen.

Then she saw a lad coming up the hill on his bicycle with a telegram. When she opened the envelope, she learned that her son had been slain in battle. Seeing that the messenger was waiting for a reply, she said to him softly, "There is no answer."

But that is not the last word. It must come from God. Silent sympathy has its place. When the time comes for his servant to speak, the words may be few and faltering. Even so, they should have to do with the compassion of God: "Like as a father pitieth his children, so the Lord pitieth them that fear him" (Ps. 103: 13). "As one whom his mother comforteth, so will I comfort you" (Isa. 66: 13).

While passing these cases in review, almost every minister is sure to recall others equally perplexing. Whatever the circumstances and the difficulties, one fact is clear: the pastor should respond immediately to any such call for his services. Not to do so might come close to the unpardonable sin. In the autobiography of George A. Gordon, *My Education and Religion,* is the account of an experience that must have been without a parallel:

"A man of very bad repute had died, and the Episcopalian, Presbyterian, Methodist, Baptist, and Congregationalist ministers declined to officiate at the funeral, on account of previous engagements. The only minister available was the Unitarian. The widow of the deceased refused to let him conduct the service, declaring with warmth of feeling, 'No minister is fit to conduct that service who does not believe in hell!' "

What the widow had in mind no one can say. But surely it should not have been necessary for her to go shopping round for a clergyman who was willing to assure her that God cared for her soul. In the funeral of a man whose life has been wholly evil, the services are for the sake of those who survive. Whatever the circumstances, the minister of Christ should respond, and that willingly.

In the service there need be no allusion to the departed, or to the facts in the case. If the exercises must be in public, the clergyman can read from his favorite book of forms. The fact that the Scripture passages and the prayers are somewhat general makes them all the more suitable for a problem funeral. If a man has a shepherd heart, he will also utter petitions of his own. All the while he will deal tenderly with those that are bruised.

"THE GOOD MORAL MAN"

Much the same principles apply when the deceased has been indifferent to religion, rather than depraved in morals. At the funeral the clergyman is likely to swing to one or the other of two extremes. If he is a "jolly good fellow," he may give the impression that it makes little difference whether or not a person had been loyal to Christ and His Church. On the other hand, if the pastor prides himself on his Puritanism, he may seem to be standing in judgment where God alone has a right to speak. What, then, shall the minister say?

At a county seat in North Jersey a young pastor reports that half of his funerals are in circles with no semblance of religion. For instance, the head of the household may have had a vague conception of a "grandmotherly God." The man may have held a churchless creed about being a jolly good fellow. He may have boasted, "I get my religion from the Sermon on the Mount," by which he meant a mild humanitarianism. When death has struck him down custom calls for a funeral service to be in charge of a Protestant clergyman who is sure to be "safe." There may even be a request for a sermon.

Amid such surroundings two things are clear, negatively. One is, do not discuss ethics. Another is, do not deal with eschatology. What, then, is left? The basic truth about God! If the deceased has been a husband and father, that may be a good place to begin. The text may be from the Sermon on the Mount, and from The Lord's Prayer, "Our Father." Since there is time to make clear and luminous only a single truth, let it be about God as Father. That is the bedrock in our religion. Everyone present at the funeral needs to know God and love him as Father.

If such a line of thought raises more questions than it

answers, is it not good for worldly folk to start thinking about God? As for the answers to their questions, there should be more than one quiet personal conference soon after the funeral obsequies. The physician of souls almost never does his most effective work in public and en masse.

Whatever the immediate facts, it is possible for the Christian clergyman to speak out for God. Let him do it boldly, and yet kindly. On the human level there may be little that he can say without being misunderstood. But why should the man who represents God in the community have to tarry long on the human level? Without being a disciple of Karl Barth, any minister should agree with the most famous words from that master of paradox:

"As ministers we ought to speak of God. We are human, however, and so cannot speak of God. We ought therefore to recognize both our obligation and our inability, and by that very recognition give God the glory. This is our perplexity. The rest of our task fades into insignificance in comparison."

Let no one think of such positive preaching as an evasion, or defense mechanism. After all, God alone can change the hearts of those who hear a funeral message. His Word shall not return unto him void. After a funeral service in the far Middle West, when the deceased had been a pronounced unbeliever, but never known as a "bad" man, the pastor was able to lead into the fellowship of Christ and the home church the various members of the household, every one of whom had hitherto been devoid of religion.

In the services over an unbeliever it is possible to make God seem so real, and Christ so precious, that some of those assembled will long to know God better and love him more. Erelong, under wise pastoral leadership, such persons should find their way to the foot of the cross. The evangelistic appeal, however, should come in private, not in public. Evidently, there is no cheap and easy way for a minister to do his duty at the funeral of a "good moral man."

Another word of caution is needful. Only God knows the

facts about the deceased. He may have been living a double life. Fortunately, the clergyman is not the judge. But neither is he the advocate. Every word that he utters should be true in the sight of God. The call is not merely for good intentions and veracity. A man must be certain about any facts to which he refers. For instance, at the obsequies of a widow who had supported her household by living in adultery, the visiting clergyman prayed that the two growing daughters might follow in their mother's footsteps!

In such a case the fewer one's words, the less are they likely to be untrue. Fortunate is the pastor who has trained his people never to expect a funeral eulogy or any appraisal of the departed. Even more to be envied is the man who has won the reputation of never delivering an address except where the deceased has been a pillar in the church. If the minister knows how to read the Scriptures, and how to guide others up the mystic altar stairs, he will cause everyone present to feel that God is near and that he is waiting to bless.

Ideally, it should be possible to solve any such problem. That is how a man feels after he goes through many of the books on other aspects of pastoral theology. In the printed accounts of cases the physician of the soul seems almost invariably to bring about a cure, ofttimes speedily. The writer's experience does not accord with such glowing accounts. Of course they are strictly true, but they are selective, not representative. In actual life a minister often feels that he has done the will of God. Sometimes he is not certain. Occasionally he knows that if he were a surgeon he could be sued for malpractice.

Whenever a clergyman fails at a funeral there are likely to be two causes, which are closely connected: he has not depended on God for personal guidance and has not kept on working until the plans are complete. By looking back, therefore, he can see the necessity of being humble, and of depending on God in prayer.

Every case that has been before us required hours of toil, as well as all a man's God-given ability. There is no quick and easy way to comfort the people who are most concerned in a problem funeral. If the modern method of dealing with cases, one at a time, has taught us anything at all, it is that to be a good physician of souls takes a vast deal of time, as well as ability. Except during his annual vacation period, a man has to stay at home and work hard.

On the other hand, there is an untold opportunity to advance the Kingdom of God, and win friends throughout the community. Immediately after the service the results may seem to be negative, but, as we shall see erelong, the door into the hearts of the people concerned should be open wide. When others throughout the neighborhood learn that the minister is the untiring helper of everyone in distress they will think of him as the shadow of a great rock in a weary land.

The substance of the whole matter is unexpectedly simple. The man who is called of God and eager to work is sure to be guided in solving each funeral problem as it arises. If that is an ideal to which none of us has yet attained, does not the spirit of our holy faith lead the servant of the Most High to attempt the impossible?

> "Ah, but a man's reach should exceed his grasp,
> Or what's a heaven for?"

XXII. The Pastoral Opportunity

IT IS unwise to think much about pastoral problems. To the Christian minister every one of them is an opportunity. In the normal parish the problem funeral comes only occasionally. Amid all its perplexities the man of God should make ready in the spirit of accepting a privilege to serve. Such difficulties ought to call out the best that is in a minister. They should lead him to say with the apostle, "I can do all things through Christ which strengtheneth me" (Phil. 4: 13).

The pastor's opportunity starts when he comes into a new field. From the very first day, indirectly and unconsciously, by his presence and influence, he can help the new friends prepare for sorrows sure to come. Without being gloomy he can live and serve in the light of eternity. Then it will never seem strange when people in sorrow call for his ministrations as death hovers near, or if it has already come to the home.

Especially in a day when the world is at war, the pastor's main concern with believing men and women may be to comfort. At the City Temple in London, Joseph Parker used to say, "In every pew there is at least one broken heart." That is the case wherever the pews are reasonably well filled. They are more likely to be filled if the man in charge of the service brings into it at least a glimpse of the life everlasting.

In a pastoral ministry of comfort nothing is standardized. In a normal hour of worship the Christian hope may sound forth in one of the hymns or in the responsive reading. Again, there may be a New Testament lesson that breathes the assurance of peace in the presence of the last great enemy. In the pastoral prayer there should always be some word of thanksgiving for "the saints who from their labors rest," or else an entreaty for those who sit under the shadow of unexpected sorrow.

Hope is one of three notes that should dominate every hour of worship. The other two are faith and love. Just as in a painting of the Madonna by Raphael there is sure to be a glimpse of the sky, so in the public worship of God there should always be a vista of the Father's home. Especially should this be the case when the world is full of woe, and fearful of something worse to come.

TEACHING SERMONS

From time to time the regular sermon ought to deal with "the last things." As a rule this kind of preaching comes at the evening service or at vespers. If there were more teaching of Christian doctrine on Sunday evening, so that every vital truth in its turn would be as luminous now as in the Early Church, there would be less difficulty in persuading people to attend the second service. In every community there are many who wish to be sure that it is possible for the modern man to believe in the life beyond.

One way to present these Christian truths is to have a series about the Apostles' Creed. In fact, there may be two series. In the sermons that deal with the closing words of the Creed there is an opportunity to preach about "The Communion of Saints." One Sunday afternoon at the Fifth Avenue Presbyterian Church in New York City, when John S. Bonnell was speaking on the subject, everyone seemed to be hanging breathless on his words. It is good to know that while still in the flesh believers can commune with the spirits of just men and women made perfect in glory.

As for heavenly recognition, that is largely a matter of inference. About the matter no one has spoken more wisely than the aged woman in Scotland: "Mon, do ye think we'll be bigger fules in heaven than we are on earth?" Of course we shall know and love those who have been dear. We shall likewise need no introduction to the saints and martyrs of olden times. In the heavenly home there will be no formalities and no social barriers. There will be fellowship with the Father and the Son, as well as with all the children of light.

Another sermon may be about "The Resurrection of the Body." Like many a modern youth, the writer once questioned this teaching of the Scriptures. He wondered if it were possible to believe in the resurrection of the soul, but not the body. Later he discovered that there must be a death ere there can be a resurrection. Since the only part of a man that dies is the body, how could there be a resurrection of the soul?

Whether or not a man believes the doctrine, the New Testament teaches the resurrection of the body. According to the Westminster Shorter Catechism, which is in keeping with the Scriptures, "The souls of believers are at their death made perfect in holiness, and do immediately pass into glory; and their bodies, being still united to Christ, do rest in their graves, till the resurrection."

The doctrine now is the same as in days of old. But the way of presenting the truth today should be different. Doctrine is teaching. In the best schools now a good deal of the instruction is by the use of cases. Why should we not employ this method in teaching what the New Testament makes known concerning the state of the soul after death? The dying thief affords an object lesson. If his soul went at once to God, the same must be true of everyone who believes in Christ (Luke 23: 43).

Again, the text may be from Paul's classic words about the life to come. Through him we learn that the heavenly body will be spiritual, not physical (I Cor. 15: 44-49). What the nature of the spiritual body will be no one can tell. Surely there will be no such limitations as beset the present earthly tenement, in which for a few score years the soul of man finds a local habitation. For the eternal dwelling place of every redeemed soul the Lord God will provide a spiritual body like that of Christ Jesus after he arose from the grave.

Here again the teaching is partly by inference. If reverent and humble, surmise is far from wrong. When the late William G. Moorehead was seventy-seven years of age he shared with a group of us his conception of the resurrection body. For years that eloquent preacher and lecturer had been frail. Every once in a while he had been forced to undergo an operation for the removal of glands from his neck. Whimsically he told us: "Whenever I read in the Apocalypse, 'There shall be no more pain,' I paraphrase the words to read, 'There shall be no glands.' "

These popular teaching sermons ought to include one about "The Final Return of Our Lord." Here again we move in the realm of mystery. Much about the Second Coming we on earth cannot know. But, in fairness to the facts as they shine out from many a page of the New Testament, the Christian interpreter should proclaim the central truth. In some way that we do not understand, and at a time that we cannot foretell, our Lord is coming in glory, to complete the work for which he died upon the cross. "Wherefore comfort one another with these words" (I Thess. 4: 18).

In the pulpit and elsewhere the minister should make clear the Christian attitude toward death. For the child of God this experience is a sort of sleep. Beyond the sleep is the awakening in the Father's home. All these terms about death are figurative. The only way that we can speak about heaven is in the language of earth. But beneath every such figure should be a solid fact. It is that the Father God promises to take care of every redeemed child, both in death and the life that follows.

PASTORAL CARE

The same spirit of loving concern for God's children enables the pastor to care for the household when sorrow comes. After the funeral services are over, his ministry of love has only begun. On the same evening, if the way is clear, he may call at the home and lead at family prayers. In a week or ten days he may call again and see if he can help in the new adjustments. If the friends ask his advice about matters of business, he need not become involved, but he should suggest a wise counselor. In short, the pastor should be a personal friend of the family.

In the case of those whose church membership has lapsed there is an opportunity for the renewal of their old-time vows. In the home of the boy who was electrocuted accidentally, the father and mother had long been nominal Christians. But after he was with them no more, they united with the local church. They were always in their pew ahead of time on the Lord's Day, and especially at the Communion. Little by little their lives became transformed. In short, bruised hearts call for pastoral care.

After another kind of funeral there may be an opportunity to win a person or a household where religion has been practically unknown. If a man has been making money his god, or if a woman has been living for pleasure, the death of an only child may reveal the soul's need of God. In every congregation some of the saintliest persons have come to him through the sacrament of sorrow.

In a certain downtown church the membership has kept growing, despite the fact that the tides of population are away from that district. One day the sexton asked the minister if he had noticed how the church was securing the majority of the new members. The pastor thought that he knew but still he asked the sexton for an opinion. The reply was unexpected:

"Whenever people enter the church for a funeral they are likely to come back for church membership." Is it any wonder that the congregation is growing in spiritual power? Under God, one reason is that the minister knows how to conduct a funeral service, and how to follow it up by winning the new friends for Christ and the parish church. In short, he is a good shepherd.

The presence of death opens to the pastor many a door that might otherwise remain closed. If at all times he cares tenderly for the flock, and especially when there is sorrow, he should have comparatively few problem funerals among his own people. But when others out in the community learn that he has a shepherd's heart, they will turn to him in the hour of need. Gradually he should win more than a few of them for the fellowship of Christ and the church. Who save the parish minister has so many golden opportunities?

Is it any wonder that many of us look on the work of the local pastor as the most vital and the most difficult in the modern world? Nowhere else does the man of God meet such a test of his ability and training as in many a funeral. But let him not falter; the grace of God is far more than sufficient for all the needs of his ministering servant.

"The elders which are among you I exhort, who am also an elder, and a witness of the sufferings of Christ, and also a partaker of the glory that shall be revealed:

"Feed the flock of God which is among you, taking the oversight thereof, not by constraint, but willingly; not for filthy lucre, but of a ready mind;

"Neither as being lords over God's heritage, but being ensamples to the flock.

"And when the chief Shepherd shall appear, ye shall receive a crown of glory that fadeth not away" (I Peter 5: 1-4).

Inspirational Readings

Green, Peter, *The Man of God*. Hodder & Stoughton, Ltd., London, 1935.

APPENDIX

Appendix

A FUNERAL ANTHOLOGY

THE following pages show some of the funeral poems that one is able to assemble in spare hours during a few months. When the writer left the pastorate he foolishly discarded such materials. Now he welcomes the opportunity to start another anthology.

The order of the poems is somewhat mechanical. It depends in part on the number of lines that can appear on a page. There is little endeavor to put in one section the verses that deal with a given subject. Each poem bears a serial number, to aid in using the topical index.

However, the order is somewhat progressive. By watching each poem that appears at the top of a page, and ignoring the shorter verses that appear elsewhere, it is possible to trace an increasing purpose. Even so, the arrangement is dictated by personal feeling, not cold logic. The same is true of more worthy collections, such as the first series of *The Golden Treasury*, by Francis T. Palgrave.

The ensuing anthology should encourage the reader to start one of his own. The majority of these poems are worthy to appear in any garden of spiritual verse. However, a few are here for personal reasons. Many others of recent vintage would be included if the costs for such use were not prohibitive. Fortunately, there is no barrier to their being in any private anthology.

The present collection affords variety enough to suit different tastes. In any case the poem for use at a funeral should be so clear and luminous that it will impart light and beauty, if not a touch of splendor.

1.   THE BUTTERFLY

I hold you at last in my hand,
    Exquisite child of the air.
Can I ever understand
    How you grew to be so fair?

                .   .   .   .   .

Now I hold you fast in my hand,
    You marvelous butterfly,
Till you help me to understand
    The eternal mystery.

From that creeping thing in the dust
    To this shining bliss in the blue!
God give me courage to trust
    I can break my chrysalis too!
                                —*Alice Freeman Palmer*
[I John 3: 2a]

2.   DEATH IS A DOOR

Death is only an old door
Set in a garden wall;
On gentle hinges it gives, at dusk
When the thrushes call.

                .   .   .   .   .

There is nothing to trouble any heart;
Nothing to hurt at all.
Death is only a quiet door
In an old wall.
                                —*Nancy Byrd Turner*

[John 19: 41a]

3.　　　　　　　SEEDS

We drop a seed into the ground,
A tiny, shapeless thing, shrivelled and dry,
And, in the fulness of its time, is seen
A form of peerless beauty, robed and crowned
Beyond the pride of any earthly queen,
Instinct with loveliness, and sweet and rare,
The perfect emblem of its Maker's care.

This from a shrivelled seed?—
—Then may man hope indeed!

For man is but the seed of what he shall be,
When, in the fulness of his perfecting,
He drops the husk and cleaves his upward way,
Through earth's retardings and clinging clay,
Into the sunshine of God's perfect day.
No fetters then! No bonds of time or space!
But powers as ample as the boundless grace
That suffered man, and death, and yet in tenderness,
Set wide the door, and passed Himself before—
As He had promised—to prepare a place.

　　　　.　　.　　.　　.　　.

We know not what we shall be—only this—
That we shall be made like Him—as He is.
　　　　　　　　　　　　—*John Oxenham*

[John 12: 24]

4.   WHERE TO FIND GOD

As the marsh-hen secretly builds on the watery sod,
Behold I will build me a nest on the greatness of God:
I will fly in the greatness of God as the marsh-hen flies
In the freedom that fills all the space 'twixt the marsh and the skies:
By so many roots as the marsh-grass sends in the sod
I will heartily lay me a-hold on the greatness of God:
Oh, like to the greatness of God is the greatness within
The range of the marshes, the liberal marshes of Glynn.
                                                    —*Sidney Lanier*

[Isa. 40: 28]

5.

" 'Tis the weakness in strength, that I cry for! my flesh, that I seek
In the Godhead! I seek and I find it. O Saul, it shall be
A face like my face that receives thee; a Man like to me,
Thou shalt love and be loved by, forever: a Hand like this hand
Shall throw open the gates of new life to thee! See the Christ stand!"
                                                    —*Robert Browning*

[Heb. 4: 15]

6.

So, through the thunder comes a human voice
Saying, "O heart I made, a heart beats here!
Face, my hands fashioned, see it in myself!
Thou hast no power nor mayst conceive of mine,
But love I gave thee, with myself to love,
And thou must love me who have died for thee!"
                                                    —*Robert Browning*

[I Peter 2: 21]

7.   BEYOND THE HORIZON

When men go down to the sea in ships,
'Tis not to the sea they go;
Some isle or pole the mariners' goal,
And thither they sail through calm and gale,
When down to the sea they go.

When souls go down to the sea by ship,
And the dark ship's name is Death,
Why mourn and wail at the vanishing sail?
Though outward bound, God's world is round,
And only a ship is Death.

When I go down to the sea by ship,
And Death unfurls her sail,
Weep not for me, for there will be
A living host on another coast
To beckon and cry, "All hail!"

—*Robert Freeman*

[Ps. 107: 23]

8.   THE ETERNAL VOYAGE

Is this the end? I know it cannot be.
Our ships shall sail upon another sea;
New islands yet shall break upon our sight,
New continents of love and truth and might.

—*John White Chadwick*

[II Tim. 4: 6-8]

9.   IN ANOTHER ROOM

No, not cold beneath the grasses,
    Not close-walled within the tomb;
Rather, in our Father's mansion,
    Living, in another room.

Living, like the man who loves me,
    Like my child with cheeks abloom,
Out of sight, at desk or schoolbook,
    Busy, in another room.

Nearer than my son whom fortune
    Beckons where the strange lands loom;
Just behind the hanging curtain,
    Serving, in another room.

Shall I doubt my Father's mercy?
    Shall I think of death as doom,
Or the stepping o'er the threshold
    To a bigger, brighter room?

Shall I blame my Father's wisdom?
    Shall I sit enswathed in gloom,
When I know my loves are happy,
    Waiting in another room?

                                    —*Robert Freeman*
[John 14: 2]

10.   NIGHTFALL

Fold up the tent!
The sun is in the West.
To-morrow my untented soul will range
Among the blest.
    And I am well content,
    For what is sent, is sent,
    And God knows best.

Fold up the tent,
And speed the parting guest!
The night draws on, though night and day are one
On this long quest.
    This house was only lent
    For my apprenticement—
    What is, is best.

Fold up the tent!
Its tenant would be gone,
To fairer skies than mortal eyes
May look upon.
    All that I loved has passed,
    And left me at the last
    Alone!—alone!

Fold up the tent!
Above the mountain's crest,
I hear a clear voice calling, calling clear,—
"To rest! To rest!"
    And I am glad to go,
    For the sweet oil is low,
    And rest is best!

                      —*John Oxenham*

[II Cor. 5: 1]

11. REST FOR THE WEARY

The camel at the close of day
  Kneels down upon the sandy plain
To have his burden lifted off
  And rest again.

My soul, thou too shouldst to thy knees
  When daylight draweth to a close,
And let thy Master lift thy load,
  And grant repose.

Else how canst thou tomorrow meet,
  With all tomorrow's work to do,
If thou thy burden all the night
  Dost carry through?

The camel kneels at break of day
  To have his guide replace his load,
Then rises up anew to take
  The desert road.

So thou shouldst kneel at morning dawn
  That God may give thee daily care,
Assured that He no load too great
  Will make thee bear.

                                        —*Anna Temple Whitney*

[Matt. 11: 28-30]

12.   "NONE OTHER LAMB"

None other Lamb, none other Name,
  None other Hope in heaven or earth or sea,
None other Hiding-place from guilt and shame,
    None beside Thee.

My faith burns low, my hope burns low
  Only my heart's desire cries out in me
By the deep thunder of its want and woe
    Cries out to Thee.

Lord, Thou art Life tho' I be dead,
  Love's Fire Thou art, however cold I be:
Nor heaven have I, nor place to lay my head,
    Nor home, but Thee.
                                    —*Christina G. Rossetti*
[Rev. 21: 23]

13.   "BABY SLEEPS"

          The baby wept;
The mother took it from the nurse's arms,
And hushed its fears, and soothed its vain alarms,
          And baby slept.

          Again it weeps,
And God doth take it from the mother's arms,
From present griefs, and future unknown harms,
          And baby sleeps.
                                    —*Samuel Hinds*
[Isa. 66: 13]

14.   THE SLEEP

Of all the thoughts of God that are
Borne inward into souls afar,
Along the Psalmist's music deep,
Now tell me if any is,
For gift or grace, surpassing this:
"He giveth his belovèd—sleep"?

.   .   .   .   .

"Sleep soft," beloved! we sometimes say,
Who have no tune to charm away
Sad dreams that through the eyelids creep:
But never doleful dream again
Shall break the happy slumber when
He giveth *his* belovèd—sleep.

.   .   .   .   .

Ay, men may wonder while they scan
A living, thinking, feeling man
Confirmed in such a rest to keep;
But Angels say, and through the word
I think their happy smile is *heard*—
"He giveth his belovèd—sleep."

.   .   .   .   .

And friends, dear friends, when it shall be
That this low breath is gone from me,
And round my bier ye come to weep,
Let One, most loving of you all,
Say, "Not a tear must o'er her fall!
He giveth his belovèd sleep."

—*Elizabeth Barrett Browning*

[Ps. 127: 2]

15. THE ANGEL OF PATIENCE

To weary hearts, to mourning homes,
God's meekest Angel gently comes:
No power has he to banish pain,
Or give us back our lost again;
And yet in tenderest love, our dear
And Heavenly Father sends him here.

There's quiet in the Angel's glance,
There's rest in his still countenance!
He mocks no grief with idle cheer,
Nor wounds with words the mourner's ear;
But ills and woes he may not cure
He kindly trains us to endure.

—John Greenleaf Whittier

[Heb. 1: 14]

16. TO A WATERFOWL

He who, from zone to zone,
Guides through the boundless sky thy certain flight,
In the long way that I must tread alone,
Will lead my steps aright.

—William Cullen Bryant

[Ps. 139: 9, 10]

17.   CLEANSING FIRES

Let thy gold be cast in the furnace,
    The red gold, precious and bright;
Do not fear the hungry fire,
    With its caverns of burning light;
And thy gold shall return more precious,
    Free from every spot and stain;
For gold must be tried by fire,
    As a heart must be tried by pain!

In the cruel fire of Sorrow
    Cast thy heart, do not faint or wail;
Let thy hand be firm and steady
    Do not let thy spirit quail:
But wait till the trial is over
    And take thy heart again;
For as gold is tried by fire,
    So a heart must be tried by pain!

I shall know by the gleam and the glitter
    Of the golden chain you wear,
By your heart's calm strength in loving,
    Of the fire they have had to bear.
Beat on, true heart, forever!
    Shine bright, strong golden chain!
And bless the cleansing fire,
    And the furnace of living pain!
                                    —*Adelaide Anne Proctor*

[Job 23: 10]

18.   THE STRUGGLE

Say not the struggle nought availeth,
    The labor and the wounds are vain,
The enemy faints not, nor faileth,
    And as things have been they remain.

If hopes were dupes, fears may be liars;
    It may be, in yon smoke concealed,
Your comrades chase e'en now the fliers,
    And, but for you, possess the field.

For while the tired waves, vainly breaking,
    Seem here no painful inch to gain,
Far back, through creeks and inlets making,
    Comes silent, flooding in, the main.

And not by eastern windows only,
    When daylight comes, comes in the light,
In front, the sun climbs slow, how slowly;
    But westward, look, the land is bright.
                                    —*Arthur Hugh Clough*
[Ps. 130: 6]

19.   THE ASSURANCE

Because in tender love He stooped for me,
And suffered on the Cross in agony,
I longed for Him to come and set me free,—
        Because He died for me.
                                    —*Betty Scott Stam*
[I Thess. 5: 10]

20.   RABBI BEN EZRA

Grow old along with me!
The best is yet to be,
The last of life, for which the first was made:
Our times are in his hand
Who saith, "A whole I planned,
Youth shows but half; trust God: see all, nor be afraid!"

.   .   .   .   .

All that is, at all,
Lasts ever, past recall;
Earth changes, but thy soul and God stand sure:
What entered into thee,
That was, is, and shall be:
Time's wheel runs back or stops: Potter and clay endure.

.   .   .   .   .

So, take and use thy work:
Amend what flaws may lurk,
What strain o' the stuff, what warpings past the aim!
My times be in thy hand!
Perfect the cup as planned!
Let age approve of youth, and death complete the same!
                                        —*Robert Browning*

[Ps. 91: 14-16]

21.

Speak to Him, thou, for He hears, and Spirit with Spirit can meet—
Closer is He than breathing, and nearer than hands and feet.
                                        —*Alfred Tennyson*

[Heb. 4: 15, 16]

22. THE ETERNAL GOODNESS

I see the wrong that round me lies,
    I feel the guilt within;
I hear, with groan and travail-cries,
    The world confess its sin.

Yet, in the maddening maze of things,
    And tossed by storm and flood,
To one fixed trust my spirit clings;
    I know that God is good!

.   .   ,   .   .

I long for household voices gone,
    For vanished smiles I long,
But God hath led my dear ones on,
    And He can do no wrong.

I know not what the future hath
    Of marvel or surprise,
Assured alone that life and death
    His mercy underlies.

.   .   .   .   .

And so beside the Silent Sea
    I wait the muffled oar;
No harm from Him can come to me
    On ocean or on shore.

I know not where His islands lift
    Their fronded palms in air;
I only know I cannot drift
    Beyond His love and care.
                —*John Greenleaf Whittier*
[Rev. 22: 2]

23.   RESIGNATION

There is no flock, however watched and tended,
    But one dead lamb is there!
There is no fireside, howsoe'er defended,
    But has one vacant chair!

The air is full of farewells to the dying,
    And mournings for the dead;
The heart of Rachel, for her children crying,
    Will not be comforted!

Let us be patient! These severe afflictions
    Not from the ground arise,
But oftentimes celestial benedictions
    Assume this dark disguise.

We see but dimly through the mists and vapors;
    Amid these earthly damps
What seem to us but sad, funereal tapers
    May be heaven's distant lamps.

There is no Death! What seems so is transition;
    This life of mortal breath
Is but a suburb of the life elysian,
    Whose portal we call Death.
                        —*Henry Wadsworth Longfellow*
[Rom. 8: 28]

24. A MOTHER'S FAREWELL

Dear Lord, receive my son, whose winning love
To me was like a friendship, far above
The course of nature or his tender age,
Whose looks could all my bitter griefs assuage;
Let his pure soul ordained sev'n years to be
In that frail body, which was part of me,
Remain my pledge in Heav'n, as sent to show
How to this port with ev'ry step I go.
—*John Beaumont*
[Luke 2: 40]

25. A FATHER'S LOVE

I walked with one whose child had lately died.
We passed the little folk in the street at play,
When suddenly a clear voice "Father!" cried.
The man turned quick and glad; sighed; moved away.

I spoke not, but 'twas given me to discern
The love that watches through eternal years.
God surely must so start and quickly turn
Whene'er the cry of "Father!" strikes His ears.
—*William Canton*

[Ps. 103: 13]

26.

He lives, he wakes,—'tis Death is dead, not he.
—*Percy Bysshe Shelley*
[John 3: 36a]

27.   THE OPEN DOOR

You, my son,
Have shown me God,
Your kiss upon my cheek
Has made me feel the gentle touch
Of him who leads us on.
The memory of your smile, when young,
Reveals his face,
As mellowing years come on apace.
And when you went before,
You left the gates of heaven ajar
That I might glimpse,
Approaching from afar,
The glories of his grace.
Hold, son, my hand,
Guide me along the path,
That, coming,
I may stumble not
Nor roam,
Nor fail to show the way
Which leads us—home.

> —*Grace Coolidge, written in memory*
> *of Calvin Coolidge, Jr., on the fifth*
> *anniversary of his death*

[Luke 2: 52]

28.

"A soul released from prison
Is risen, is risen,—
Is risen to the glory of the Lord."

> —*John Oxenham*

[II Tim. 4: 6]

29. A SONG OF THANKSGIVING

Saints are God's flowers, fragrant souls
  That His own hand hath planted,
Not in some far-off heavenly place,
  Or solitude enchanted,
But here and there and everywhere,—
  In lonely field, or crowded town,
  God sees a flower when He looks down.

.   .   .   .   .

One such I knew,—and had the grace
  To thank my God for knowing:
The beauty of her quiet life
  Was like a rose in blowing,
So fair and sweet, so all-complete
  And all unconscious, as a flower,
  That light and fragrance were her dower.

.   .   .   .   .

A vow to keep her life alive
  In deeds of pure affection,
So that her love shall find in them
  A daily resurrection;
A constant prayer that they may wear
  Some touch of that supernal light
  With which she blossoms in God's sight.

—Henry van Dyke

[Prov. 31: 29-31]

30. FAREWELL IN AUTUMN

Not in winter, not in storm,
Nor when spring's buds are calling,
But in autumn's quiet charm,
While russet leaves are falling.

The good earth turns herself to rest,
After her time of growing,
Drawing her children to her breast,
To wait a richer sowing.

So in his autumn's golden day,
His earthly life forsaking,
In quiet peace he passed away,
To meet the last awaking.

—Will C. Osborn

[Job 5: 26]

31. GOD'S HANDWRITING

He writes in characters too grand
For our short sight to understand;
We catch but broken strokes, and try
To fathom all the mystery
Of withered hopes, of death, of life,
The endless war, the useless strife,—
But there, with larger, clearer sight,
We shall see this—His way was right.

—John Oxenham

[I Cor. 13: 12]

32. A MISSIONARY MARTYR

(A favorite poem of Betty Scott Stam)

Afraid? Of what?
To feel the spirit's glad release?
To pass from pain to perfect peace?
The strife and strain of life to cease?
Afraid—of that?

Afraid? Of what?
Afraid to see the Saviour's face?
To hear His welcome, and to trace
The glory gleam from wounds of grace?
Afraid—of that?

Afraid? Of what?
A flash—a crash—a piercèd heart!
Darkness—light—O heaven's art!
Each wound of His a counterpart!
Afraid—of that?

Afraid? Of what?
To do by death what life could not?
Baptize with blood a stony plot
Till souls shall blossom from the spot?
Afraid—of that?

—*E. H. Hamilton*

[Ps. 23: 4]

33.   THE MEANING OF DEATH

We are so stupid about death. We will not learn
How it is wages paid to those who earn,
How it is gift for which on earth we yearn,
To be set free from bondage to the flesh;
How it is turning seed-corn into grain,
How it is winning heaven's eternal gain,
How it means freedom ever more from pain.
   How it untangles every mortal mesh.

We are so selfish about death, we count our grief
Far more than we consider their relief
Whom the great Reaper gathers in the sheaf
No more to know the season's constant change:
And we forget that it means only life.
        —*William C. Doane*

[Rev. 14: 15]

34.   THE DOOR OF DEATH

The door of Death is made of gold,
That mortal eyes cannot behold;
But when the mortal eyes are closed,
And cold and pale the limbs reposed,
The soul awakes, and, wond'ring, sees
In her mild hand the golden keys.
The grave is heaven's golden gate,
And rich and poor around it wait.
        —*William Blake*

[Rev. 22: 14]

35. **PROSPICE**

Fear death?—to feel the fog in my throat,
    The mist in my face,
When the snows begin, and the blasts denote
    I am nearing the place,
The power of the night, the press of the storm,
    The post of the foe;
Where he stands, the Arch Fear in a visible form,
    Yet the strong man must go:
For the journey is done and the summit attained,
    And the barriers fall,
Though a battle's to fight ere the guerdon be gained,
    The reward of it all.
I was ever a fighter, so—one fight more,
    The best and the last!
I would hate that death bandaged my eyes, and forbore,
    And bade me creep past.
No! let me taste the whole of it, fare like my peers
    The heroes of old,
Bear the brunt, in a minute pay glad life's arrears
    Of pain, darkness and cold.
For sudden the worst turns the best to the brave,
    The black minute's at end,
And the elements' rage, the fiend-voices that rave,
    Shall dwindle, shall blend,
Shall change, shall become first a peace out of pain,
    Then a light, then thy breast,
O thou soul of my soul! I shall clasp thee again,
    And with God be the rest!

—*Robert Browning*

[Rev. 2: 10]

36.   GOING TO HEAVEN

Going to heaven!
I don't know when,
Pray do not ask me how,—
Indeed, I'm too astonished
To think of answering you!
Going to heaven!—
How dim it sounds!
And yet it will be done
As sure as flocks go home at night
Unto the shepherd's arm!

                                        —*Emily Dickinson*

[Ps. 23: 6]

37.   THE UPPER ROOMS

Father, in joy our knees we bow.
This earth is not a place of tombs.
We are but in the nursery now;
        They in the upper rooms.

For are we not at home in Thee,
And all this world a visioned show?
For, knowing what Abroad is, we
        What Home is too shall know.

                                        —*George MacDonald*

[John 14: 2]

38.

They call it death, when lo! it is my birth.

                                        —*Robert Freeman*

[John 11: 25]

39.   EMANCIPATION

Why be afraid of death
As though your life were breath?
            Death but anoints your eyes
            With clay, O glad surprise!
Why should you be forlorn?
Death only husks the corn.
            Why should you fear to meet
            The Thresher of the wheat?
Is sleep a thing to dread?
Yet, sleeping you are dead
            Till you awake and rise,
            Here, or beyond the skies.
Why should it be a wrench
To leave your wooden bench?
            Why not, with happy shout,
            Run home when school is out?
The dear ones left behind?
O foolish one and blind,
            A day, and you will meet;
            A night, and you will greet.
This is the death of death:
To breathe away a breath,
            And know the end of strife,
            And taste the deathless life,
And joy without a fear,
And smile without a tear,
            And work, nor care nor rest,
            And find the last the best.
                    —*Maltbie D. Babcock*
[Heb. 2: 15]

40.

Here in the body pent,
    Absent from Him I roam,
Yet nightly pitch my moving tent
    A day's march nearer home.
                    —*James Montgomery*
[II Peter 1: 13, 14]

41.   WITH US NO MORE

It singeth low in every heart,
   We hear it each and all—
A song of those who answer not,
   However we may call;
They throng the silence of the breast,
   We see them as of yore—
The kind, the brave, the sweet,
   Who walk with us no more.

'Tis hard to take the burden up
   When these have laid it down;
They brightened all the joy of life,
   They softened every frown;
But, Oh, 'tis good to think of them
   When we are troubled sore!
Thanks be to God that such have been,
   Although they are no more.

More homelike seems the vast unknown
   Since they have entered there;
To follow them were not so hard,
   Wherever they may fare;
They cannot be where God is not,
   On any sea or shore;
Whate'er betides, thy love abides,
   Our God, forever more.

—John White Chadwick

[Heb. 12: 1]

42.   IN MEMORIAM

Strong Son of God, immortal Love,
  Whom we, that have not seen thy face,
  By faith, and faith alone, embrace,
Believing where we cannot prove;

.   .   .   .   .

Thou wilt not leave us in the dust:
  Thou madest man, he knows not why,
  He thinks he was not made to die;
And thou hast made him: thou art just.

Thou seemest human and divine,
  The highest, holiest manhood, thou.
  Our wills are ours, we know not how;
Our wills are ours, to make them thine.

.   .   .   .   .

We have but faith: we cannot know,
  For knowledge is of things we see;
  And yet we trust it comes from thee,
A beam in darkness: let it grow.

.   .   .   .   .

Forgive my grief for one removed,
  Thy creature, whom I found so fair.
  I trust he lives in thee, and there
I find him worthier to be loved.

Forgive these wild and wandering cries,
  Confusions of a wasted youth;
  Forgive them where they fail in truth,
And in thy wisdom make me wise.
                              —*Alfred Tennyson*

[John 14: 6]

43. A BETTER RESURRECTION

I have no wit, no words, no tears;
  My heart within me like a stone
Is numbed too much for hopes or fears;
  Look right, look left, I dwell alone;
I lift mine eyes, but dimmed with grief
  No everlasting hills I see;
My life is in the falling leaf:
  O Jesus, quicken me.

My life is like a faded leaf,
  My harvest dwindled to a husk;
Truly my life is void and brief
  And tedious in the barren dusk;
My life is like a frozen thing,
  No bud nor greenness can I see:
Yet rise it shall—the sap of Spring;
  O Jesus, rise in me.

My life is like a broken bowl,
  A broken bowl that cannot hold
One drop of water for my soul
  Or cordial in the searching cold;
Cast in the fire the perished thing,
  Melt and remould it, till it be
A royal cup for Him my King:
  O Jesus, drink of me.

                                    —*Christina G. Rossetti*
[Eccl. 12: 6]

44. TRIUMPH OVER DEATH

Vital spark of heavenly flame!
Quit, oh quit this mortal frame:
   Trembling, hoping, lingering, flying,
   Oh the pain, the bliss of dying!
Cease, fond Nature, cease thy strife,
And let me languish into life.

Hark! they whisper; Angels say,
Sister Spirit, come away.
   What is this absorbs me quite?
   Steals my senses, shuts my sight,
Drowns my spirit, draws my breath?
Tell me, my Soul, can this be Death?

The world recedes; it disappears!
Heaven opens on my eyes! my ears
   With sounds seraphic ring:
   Lend, lend your wings! I mount! I fly!
O Grave! where is thy victory?
   O Death! where is thy sting?

                 —*Alexander Pope*

[I Cor. 15: 55]

45.

I will not faint, but trust in God
   Who this my lot hath given:
He leads me by the thorny road
   Which is the road to heaven.
Though sad my day that lasts so long,
At evening I shall have a song:
Though dim my day until the night,
At evening-time there shall be light.

           —*Christina G. Rossetti*

[Zech. 14: 7]

46.   RESURGENCE

Though he that, ever kind and true,
Kept stoutly step by step with you,
Your whole long, gusty lifetime through,
    Be gone a while before—
Be now a moment gone before—
Yet doubt not; soon the season shall restore
    Your friend to you.

He has but turned the corner—still
He pushes on with right good will
Through mire and marsh, by dale and hill
    The selfsame arduous way—
That selfsame, upland, hopeful way,
That you and he, through many a doubtful day
    Attempted still.

He is not dead—this friend—not dead,
But in the path we mortals tread
Got some few trifling steps ahead,
    And nearer to the end;
So that you, too, once past the bend,
Shall meet again, as face to face, this friend
    You fancy dead.

Push gaily on, brave heart, the while
You travel forward mile by mile,
He loiters, with a backward smile,
    Till you can overtake;
And strains his eyes to search his wake,
Or, whistling as he sees you through the brake,
    Waits on a stile.

                                          —*Robert Louis Stevenson*

[Heb. 11: 4c]

47. GOD OF THE LIVING

God of the living, in whose eyes
Unveiled the whole creation lies!
All souls are thine; we must not say
That those are dead who pass away;
From this our world of flesh set free;
We know them living unto thee.

Released from earthly toil and strife,
With thee is hidden still their life;
Thine are their thoughts, their words, their powers,
All thine, and yet most truly ours:
For well we know, where'er they be,
Our dead are living unto thee.

Not spilt like water on the ground,
Not wrapt in dreamless sleep profound,
Not wandering in unknown despair
Beyond thy voice, thine arm, thy care;
Not left to lie like fallen tree;
Not dead, but living unto thee.

O Breather into man of breath!
O Holder of the keys of death!
O Giver of the life within!
Save us from death, the death of sin;
That body, soul, and spirit be
Forever living unto thee!

—*John Ellerton*

[II Sam. 14: 14b]

48.   THE RIVER OF LIFE

We know not a voice of that River,
  If vocal or silent it be,
Where for ever and ever and ever
    It flows to no sea.

.   .   .   .   .

Oh goodly the banks of that River,
  Oh goodly the fruits that they bear,
Where for ever and ever and ever
    It flows and is fair.

For lo on each bank of that River
  The Tree of Life life-giving grows,
Where for ever and ever and ever
    The Pure River flows.
                                              —*Christina G. Rossetti*

[Rev. 22: 2]

49.   ALL'S WELL!

Is the burden past your bearing?
  God's in His heaven!
Hopeless?—Friendless?—No one caring?
  God's in His heaven!
Burdens shared are light to carry,
Love shall come though long He tarry.
    All's well! All's well!
                                              —*John Oxenham*

[Ps. 55: 22]

50. A RAINBOW O'ER A GRAVE

The record of a faith sublime,
  And hope, through clouds far-off discerned;
  The incense of a love that burned
Through pain and doubt defying Time:

The story of a soul at strife
  That learned at last to kiss the rod,
  And passed through sorrow up to God,
From living to a higher life:

A light that gleams across the wave
  Of darkness, down the rolling years,
  Piercing the heavy mist of tears—
A rainbow shining o'er a grave.
                                —*Henry van Dyke*

[Heb. 11:5]

51. A RAINBOW O'ER THE CROSS

O Joy that seekest me through pain,
  I cannot close my heart to thee;
I trace the rainbow through the rain,
And feel the promise is not vain
  That morn shall tearless be.
                                —*George Matheson*

[Gen. 9: 13]

52.   AT THE BURIAL

Lord of all Light and Darkness,
   Lord of all Life and Death,
Behold, we lay in earth today
   The flesh that perisheth.

Take to Thyself whatever may
   Be not as dust and breath,—
Lord of all Light and Darkness,
   Lord of all Life and Death.

                  —*William Watson*

[Ps. 103: 14]

53. THE REDEEMED IN GLORY

From North and South, and East and West,
      They come!
The sorely tried, the much oppressed,
Their Faith and Love to manifest,
      They come!
They come to tell of work well done,
They come to tell of kingdoms won,
To worship at the Great White Throne,
      They come!
In a noble consecration,
With a sound of jubilation,
      They come! They come!

                  —*John Oxenham*

[Rev. 5: 9, 10]

54. No little child has ever come from God and stayed a brief while, returning again to the Father, without making glad the home, and leaving behind some trace of heaven. The family would count themselves poorer without those quaint sayings, those cunning caresses, that soft touch, that sudden smile. This short visit was not an incident; it was a benediction.—*John Watson.*
[Matt. 19: 14]

55. This life is but the cradle of the other. Of what importance, then, are illness and time, old age and death? They are but stages in the transformation that has its beginnings here below. . . . The evening of life bears its own lamp.—*Joseph Joubert.*
[Rom. 8: 38, 39]

56. I have lived. I have labored. I have loved. To love and labor is the sum of living. Now the day is far spent, and the night is at hand. The time draweth nigh when man shall rest from his labors. But still he shall love, and he shall enter into rest through Him who is Light, and Life, and Love.—*Sir Thomas More.*
[Luke 24: 29]

57. We do not believe in immortality because we have proved it, but, we forever try to prove it because we believe it.—*James Martineau.*
[Acts 26: 8]

58. First learn to love one living man;
Then mayst thou think upon the dead.
[I John 3: 14a]

Index of Scripture Passages

Index of Subjects